Challenges to Inerrancy

A Theological Response

Edited by Gordon Lewis
and Bruce Demarest

CHALLENGES TO INERRANCY
A Theological Response

Challenges to Inerrancy

A Theological Response

Edited by

Gordon R. Lewis
and
Bruce Demarest

MOODY PRESS

CHICAGO

Library of Congress Cataloging in Publication Data

Main entry under title:

Challenges to inerrancy.

Includes index.
1. Bible—Evidences, authority, etc.—Addresses, essays, lectures. 2. Bible—Criticism, interpretation, etc.—History—20th century—Addresses, essays, lectures. I. Lewis, Gordon Russell, 1926-
II. Demarest, Bruce A.
BS480.C42   1984   220.1'3   83-22007
ISBN: 0-8024-0237-2

1 2 3 4 5 6 7 Printing/BC/Year 88 87 86 85 84

Printed in the United States of America

Contents

Series Editor's Introduction

This book is part of a series of scholarly works sponsored by the International Council on Biblical Inerrancy (ICBI). They include the following areas:

GENERAL—*Inerrancy* (Zondervan, 1979), Norman L. Geisler, ed.

PHILOSOPHICAL—*Biblical Errancy: Its Philosophical Roots* (Zondervan, 1981), Norman L. Geisler, ed.

THEOLOGICAL—*Challenges to Inerrancy* (Moody, 1984), Gordon Lewis and Bruce Demarest, eds.

HISTORICAL—*Inerrancy and the Church* (Moody, 1984), John Hannah, ed.

HERMENEUTICS—*Hermeneutics, Inerrancy, and the Bible* (Zondervan, 1984), Earl Radmacher and Robert Preus, eds.

The ICBI is a coalition of Christian scholars who believe that the reaffirmation and defense of biblical inerrancy is crucial to the life and vitality of the Christian church. In addition to these scholarly books, the council has produced two landmark statements: "The Chicago Statement on Inerrancy" (1978) and "The Chicago Statement on Hermeneutics" (1982). These two documents represent a consensus of evangelical scholarship on these fundamental topics.

The ICBI does not endorse every point made by the authors of this book, although all the writers are in agreement with the ICBI stand on inerrancy. Freedom of expression of this commitment was exercised throughout the various books. All wrote with the

hope that believers in Christ will become increasingly assured of
the firm foundation for our faith in God's inerrant Word.

NORMAN L. GEISLER
General Editor, ICBI

Preface

Contemporary discussions of biblical inerrancy have roots in theological work from the eighteenth century to the present. Those who deny the truth of all that the Bible affirms do so from assumptions that need to be clearly understood and evaluated in their theological contexts.

This book purposes to disclose some of the most influential of modern theological presuppositions leading to belief in an errant Bible and to assess them in their contexts by standard criteria of truth. In various respects the assumptions undermining normative scriptural authority are found to be logically inconsistent, factually inadequate, or existentially irrelevant to the purposes for which God gave the Scriptures.

After the exposition and evaluation of the theological schools of thought in generally chronological order in chapters 1-11, chapter 12 expounds the case for biblical inerrancy developed classically by the Old Princeton scholars.

The epilogue presents some important observations on the contemporary debate in historical perspective. A committed inerrantist suggests ways in which thinkers in the Christian church may be warned and challenged by this study.

May the Lord be pleased to use this book to honor His faithful Word.

1. The Bible in the Enlightenment Era

Bruce Demarest

INTRODUCTION TO THE ENLIGHTENMENT

The Enlightenment period in Europe—*Aufklärung* in German, *Siecle des lumieres* in French—was a movement in the intellectual history of Western man in which traditional perspectives and loyalties were abandoned in favor of man-centered alternatives. Because he was persuaded that he had come of age intellectually, modern man threw off many of the beliefs bequeathed to him by classical Christendom and began believing in his own ability to secure truth and forge his eternal destiny. The Age of Reason, as the Enlightenment is otherwise denoted, thus marked Western man's transition from an ecclesiastically oriented culture to a modern secularized one. As Anchor in a recent definitive study observes, the Enlightenment "offered the first program in the history of mankind for the construction of a human community out of natural materials alone."[1]

The Enlightenment movement in theology has been variously dated. Anchor views the Enlightenment as extending from the

1. Robert Anchor, *The Enlightenment Tradition* (Berkeley, Calif.: U. of California, 1967), p. ix.

BRUCE DEMAREST, B.S., Wheaton College; M.S., Adelphi University; M.A., Trinity Evangelical Divinity School; Ph.D., University of Manchester, England, is professor of systematic theology at Denver Conservative Baptist Seminary, Denver, Colorado. He has written the following books: *Priest After the Order of Melchizedik: A History of Interpretation of Hebrews 7:1-10* (1976), *Jesus Christ the God-Man* (1978), and *General Revelation: Historical Views and Contemporary Issues* (1982).

English Revolution of 1688 to the French Revolution of 1789.[2] That delineation needs to be modified, however, because the Enlightenment spirit persisted on German soil well into the first few decades of the nineteenth century. When the Enlightenment was well spent, Kant looked back to define the movement as follows:

> The Enlightenment is the advance of man beyond the state of voluntary immaturity. Immaturity means the inability to use one's own understanding except under the guidance of another. . . . *Sapere aude!* Have the courage to use your own understanding. This is the slogan of the Enlightenment. If the question be asked, "Do we live in a free-thinking age?" the answer is "No; but we live in an age of free-thought."[3]

HISTORICAL ANTECEDENTS

Far from arising *de novo* on the stage of history, the theological Enlightenment should be viewed as the precipitate of a variety of earlier influences. The Enlightenment, first of all, represents an outgrowth of fourteenth- through sixteenth-century Renaissance humanism. The Enlightenment picked up the thread of thought that had been boldly interrupted by the bibliocentric focus of the Protestant Reformation. The Renassiance was stimulated by the study of classical culture and values, and it developed not only a secular world view but also a representation of man as eminently a creature of reason.

The Enlightenment likewise bears an affinity to the sixteenth-century Socinian movement. The Socinians were Italian rationalists who staunchly opposed both Roman Catholic and reformational theology. Although conceding the importance of Scripture, the Socinians insisted upon a rationalistic interpretation of the Word. Because they held to a high view of human ability, the Socinians were reluctant to accept scriptural teachings that appeared to contravene hard reason and common sense. Hence the Italian humanists rejected such doctrines as the Trinity, the atoning work of Christ, and the need of spiritual regeneration. The Socinians, like later Enlightenment theologians, subscribed to an ethical religion purged of all so-called irrational mysteries.

Descartes (d. 1650) likewise had an impact on theologians in the Enlightenment tradition. The father of modern philosophy

---

2. Ibid.
3. Immanuel Kant, "Beantwortung der Frage: Was ist Aufklärung?" *Sämmtliche Werke*, 11 vols. (Berlin: n.p., 1900), 4:169.

rejected the authoritarianism of medieval thought and introduced the method of systematic doubting as the basis of philosophy and science. Descartes both reaffirmed a high view of man's natural abilities and strove to bring all claims to truth under the purview of deductive reason.

The Cambridge Platonists in the third quarter of the seventeenth century had a direct bearing on the emergence of the Enlightenment spirit in England. That group of Cambridge University philosophers extolled reason as the divinely implanted interpreter and ruler of life. At the hands of the Cambridge Platonists the distinction between rational and revealed religion gradually dissolved. Natural religion usurped the primacy that had been traditionally given to biblical religion.

Perhaps the leading factor in the emergence of the Enlightenment was the seventeenth- and eighteenth-century scientific revolution. The astronomical discoveries of Copernicus (d. 1543), Kepler (d. 1630), and Galileo (d. 1642) led many to view nature as a vast uniform system governed by precise laws. As the self-regulating character of the universe was laid bare by the newly invented telescope, the areas of mystery in the universe shrank considerably. Then came Sir Isaac Newton (d. 1727), the renowned scientist and Christian, whose discovery of the law of universal gravitation led to the precise mathematical description of the motion of heavenly bodies. In due course a mechanical interpretation of the universe began to prevail; men viewed the universe as explicable strictly according to natural law. The upshot of the new scientism was a marked shift of emphasis away from the data of special revelation toward the data of natural and physical science. Newtonian physics gave man the confidence to offer immanent explanations of the world without recourse to the "prescientific" teachings of Scripture. In short, the modern scientific revolution precipitated the formation of a new religion of nature and reason. In the words of an anonymous poet:

> Nature and Nature's law lay hid in night
> God said, Let Newton be! and all was light.[4]

LEADING TENETS

The Newtonian discovery that nature was orderly and rational prompted eighteenth-century philosophers and theologians to draw the conclusion that the natural is the reasonable and the

4. Cited in Isaiah Berlin, *The Age of Enlightenment* (New York: Books for Libraries, 1956), p. 15.

reasonable is the natural. Nature and nature's laws reveal to men everything needed to realize the highest good. The structure of the universe displayed in bold strokes the essentials of the divine purpose. The light afforded by nature was sufficient to lead men to God and to the performance of moral duty. Eighteenth-century man readily confessed that God had spoken. But His communication was said to be embedded less in Scripture and more in the structure of the universe.

Linked with that confidence in nature was a high estimate of man's natural powers and achievements. Enlightenment thinkers upheld the ideal of the natural and postulated that man is inherently good. The traditional Christian belief in the fall of Adam and the depravity of the human race was denied. Hence the "age of free thought" stressed natural man's latent intellectual and moral ability. Human resources alone were judged adequate to lead man on the path of temporal and eternal felicity. With such views the Enlightenment sanctioned what Barth would later describe as "absolute man."

The Enlightenment attributed particular power to autonomous human reason. The kind of reason envisaged was the experimental reason of Francis Bacon and John Locke that draws conclusions from the data of experience. According to Enlightenment thinkers the rational working of the mind was the standard by which all things were measured. No belief not justified at the bar of reason could be accepted as true. In the Age of Reason even "God Himself will be asked to show credentials satisfactory to reason."[5] Reason therefore gradually usurped the traditional rule of revelation during the Enlightenment. Many, in fact, define revelation as "exalted reason" and argued that those who live by the light of reason are Christians.

The Enlightenment thus involved the overthrow of revealed religion based on the Bible in favor of a natural religion disclosed in the created order and made known to all by reason. Independently of special revelation man could formulate a religion of nature and reason agreeable to the human community and acceptable to God Himself. Consequently the natural religion of the Enlightenment was a religion shorn of the supernatural. Since nature was viewed as a system operating according to fixed laws, all interruptions of the natural order were in principle disallowed.

The Age of Reason, finally, could be characterized as an era in

5. Roland N. Stromberg, *Religious Liberalism in Eighteenth Century England* (London: Oxford U., 1954), p. 12.

revolt against authority. Old forms of authority, such as Bible, church, and creed, were challenged and discredited. Having broken out of the dark night of superstition and having come into the bright light of the scientific age, Enlightenment man felt uncompelled to follow the old guides, and he no longer felt bound by any external authority.

The outcome of those several forces was that supernatural revelation was uniformly denied. The doctrine of the special inspiration of the Scriptures was judged too bizarre to be seriously entertained by persons of sound mind. At the hands of Enlightenment critics Scripture was viewed as a strictly human document. And finally, traditional dogmas such as the Trinity, the atonement, and the resurrection were viewed not only as relics of a superstitious age but also as enemies of virtue and morality.

The Enlightenment era is far from being a matter of mere antiquarian interest for the Christian scholar. Rather, the Enlightenment was a watershed period in the history of Western Christianity when the Christian consensus was broken by a radical, secular spirit. It was a time in which the supernatural theological edifice was shaken by the forces of thoroughgoing unbelief. The Enlightenment emphases cited above—the primacy of nature, low view of sin, absolutism of reason, ascendency of natural religion, antisupernatural bias, and revolt against authority—represent the building blocks of nineteenth- and twentieth-century liberal theology. In terms of theology in general and Scripture in particular it is entirely true that "the period of the Enlightenment specifically so-called is long since over, but the world is still living under the control of some of its ideals."[6] The modern assault on the authority and integrity of the Bible proves to be but a refinement of the old Enlightenment attack on the same inspired Word of God. We direct attention now to two leading expressions of the Enlightenment spirit.

THE BIBLE AND ENGLISH DEISM

The beginnings of the reductionist theology of the Enlightenment occurred on English soil. Of the English Deists one authority writes: "In history they will always be known as the group which took the first steps to inaugurate radicalism into Christian theology."[7] The destructive school of German rationalists and the

6. A. C. McGiffert, *The Rise of Modern Religious Ideas* (New York: Macmillan, 1915), p. 13.
7. Otto W. Heick, *A History of Christian Thought*, 2 vols. (Philadelphia: Muhlenberg, 1946), 2:53.

less theologically inclined French naturalists were properly the intellectual and religious heirs of the English Deists.

The Deists subscribed to the general ethos of the Enlightenment, which has been outlined in the preceding section. They professed belief in an absentee God who created the universe and subsequently ordered its operations in accordance with preestablished laws. Their presuppositions led them to propound a natural religion without providential history, without miracles, and without special inspiration of sacred books. Many later Deists were resolute in their hostility to supernatural Christianity, which they alleged was founded on irrational superstitions. They spared no effort to abolish England's Christian culture. Daniel Defoe wrote in 1722 before the Deist movement had reached its peak: "No age since the founding and forming of the Christian Church, was ever like, in open avowed atheism, blasphemies, and heresies, to the age we now live in."[8]

An issue that occupied the attention of the Deists for a century or more was the relationship between reason and revelation. Was reason an all-sufficient source of truth? Or does revelation play some part in man's quest for religious knowledge? The reason-revelation problem passed through three identifiable stages before Deism had spent itself as a movement. First, the early Deists tended to mediate between supernaturalism and naturalism by arguing that some religious truths lie above reason and are communicated by revelation. Second, certain later Deists insisted that the Christian religion contains nothing above reason; that is, all purported revelations must accord with the judgments of human reason. And third, the full-blooded Deists in the name of autonomous reason denied revelation altogether. A special revelation to prophets and apostles was said to invalidate God's original revelation of Himself in the creation.

DEISTIC THINKERS

The beginnings of the Deist movement reach back into the seventeenth century. Lord Herbert of Cherbury (d. 1648), the English historian and religious philosopher who came to be known as the "father of Deism," set forth in *De Veritate* (1624) the famous "five articles of Deism" dealing with the existence of God, man's duty toward Him, and the future life. In that essay, labeled by posterity as the "Bible of Deism," Lord Herbert argued that the five articles were "common notions" implanted by God in the

8. Cited in Stromberg, *Religious Liberalism*, p. 2.

human mind. Those commonly held ideas, formed by subjective reason and implicitly acknowledged by persons of all times, constituted the universal religion of nature and reason, according to Lord Herbert.

Furthermore, because a primordial revelation sufficient to satisfy man's spiritual requirements has impressed itself upon the minds of all, no special disclosures from God are needed. Supernatural revelations, such as those claimed by the Bible, represent preferential treatment to a particular people. Such instances of partiality contradict the character of the Supreme Being. Hence, according to Lord Herbert, special revelation is improbable and, practically speaking, superfluous. Alleged revelations in the Bible from which dogmas have arisen should be viewed as inventions of a priestly class that desire to gain control of the common people. By virtue of the extraneous accretions in the Scripture it should in no way be regarded as the very word of God. Ironically Lord Herbert, who argued that no mysterious revelation can possess the right of rational acceptance, himself claimed to have heard a voice from heaven that prompted the writing of the book *De Veritate*.[9]

John Locke (d. 1704), the English physician and philosopher, is hailed by many as the intellectual ruler of the eighteenth century. Although not strictly a Deist, Locke reached many of the same conclusions about reason, revelation, and the Bible. Many later Deists acknowledged their substantial indebtedness to Locke's ideas. Locke, as is well known, propounded a system of knowledge grounded in reflection upon the data of experience in which all knowledge begins but does not necessarily end with sense data.

With respect to the reason-revelation tension, Locke insisted that alleged truths of revelation must accord with the judgments of reason. "Reason must be our last judge and guide in everything."[10] Again, "if anything shall be thought revelation which is contrary to the plain principles of reason and the evident knowledge the mind has of its own clear and distinct ideas, there reason must be hearkened to as a matter within its provence."[11] In sum, "revelation must be judged by reason."[12] In Locke's scheme supposedly-revealed doctrines were subjected to natural judgments.

9. Cf. John M. Robertson, *A Short History of Free Thought* (New York: Arno, 1972), pp. 296-97.
10. John Locke, *An Essay Concerning Human Understanding* (New York: New American Library, 1974), p. 432. Cf. *The Reasonableness of Christianity* (Chicago: Henry Regnery, 1965), sect. 14.
11. Locke, *Essay Concerning Human Understanding*, p. 426.
12. Ibid., p. 432.

Reason rather than biblical or ecclesiastical authority came to represent the basis of religion.

Locke did not reject outright special revelation. For him, Christian revelation clarified the content of natural revelation so that the latter's truth could be presented more directly to the understanding. The resurrection of the dead, for example, is taught more clearly by special revelation than by nature. Nevertheless revelation for Locke fulfilled no more than a subsidiary function. "Whatsoever truth we come to a clearer discovery of from the knowledge and contemplation of our own ideas, will always be certainer to us than those which are conveyed to us by *traditional revelation*."[13]

In the name of reason Locke polemicized against miracles and fulfilled prophecy. From there it was but a short step to the discarding of verbal, plenary inspiration. In Locke's own words, "inspiration barely in itself cannot be a ground to receive any doctrines not conformable to reason."[14] On that basis Locke subjected the Bible to intensive scrutiny. Because he was persuaded that the essence of Christianity is belief in Jesus as the Jewish Messiah and the practice of ethical rectitude, Locke paid little attention to the New Testament except for the gospels and Acts. The simple Christianity of the gospels accords with the ethical principles of natural religion. The epistles, on the other hand, contain "accommodations to the apprehension of those they were written to, the better to make them imbibe the Christian doctrine."[15]

Locke then boldly rationalized away the theological content of Scripture. Doctrine after doctrine he dismissed as repugnant to reason. The Trinity, original sin, the atoning work of Christ, and the eternal punishment of the wicked in hell Locke excised from the Bible as irrational. Thus he could add, "A great many of the truths revealed in the gospel everyone . . . must confess a man may be ignorant of—nay, disbelieve—without danger to his salvation."[16] Locke's insistence on the autonomy of reason provided a model for later Deists as they applied the scalpel of criticism more radically to the Word of God.

John Tolland (d. 1722) expanded the views of Locke. One gains insight into his position by weighing the title of his principal work: *Christianity Not Mysterious: A Treatise Showing that there is*

13. Ibid., p. 425.
14. Cited in Herbert McLachlan, *The Religious Opinions of Milton, Locke and Newton* (New York: Russell and Russell, 1972), pp. 96-97.
15. Locke, *Reasonableness of Christianity*, p. 189.
16. Ibid., p. 191.

Nothing in the Gospel Contrary to Reason, but also Nothing Above Reason (1696). Tolland, who coined the term *freethinking*, insisted that reason, the rational element in the *imago Dei*, abides in man unimpaired. Tolland believed that God would never reveal anything that reason was incapable of explicating. Hence he concluded that religious faith is built entirely upon ratiocination.

Tolland made the bold move of revising the traditional ordering of revelation and reason. Against the Christian view that reason is the servant of revelation, Tolland insisted that reason is the primary source of religious truth. Whatever appears to the interpreter against the judgments of experimental reason is untrue, and whatever purports to lie beyond reason is inconceivable and hence invalid. All the teachings of the Bible, then, that are not corroborated by the judgments of experimental reason must be discarded. Indeed, Tolland maintains that the claim that there are revealed truths that lie above the province of reason "is the undoubted source of all the absurdities that ever were seriously vented among Christians."[17]

The Bible, under Tolland's approach, was of dubious or uncertain significance. In his own words, "all the doctrines and precepts of the New Testament must agree with natural reason and our own ordinary ideas."[18] The original system of natural religion in its enscripturation was transferred under Jewish and pagan influences into a system of esoteric mysteries. Specious doctrines were introduced into the Bible by misguided Jewish and Gentile converts. On that basis Tolland refused to accept such biblical teachings as the Trinity, the imputed righteousness of Christ, and the eternal punishment of the wicked.

Anthony Collins (d. 1729) was a devoted disciple of Locke. Collins dealt with revelation and the Bible in three treatises: *An Essay Concerning the Use of Reason in Theology* (1707), *Discourse on Freethinking* (1713), and *Discourse on the Grounds and Reasons of the Christian Religion* (1724).

Collins believed that right belief must be based on free inquiry. "If the surest and best means of arriving at truth lies in free-thinking, then the whole duty of man lies only in free-thinking. He who thinks freely does his best toward being in the right, and consequently does all that God, who can require nothing more of any man than that he should do his best, can require of him."[19] Collins regarded Jesus and the apostles as enlightened free-think-

---

17. Cited in Edward G. Waring, *Deism and Natural Religion: A Source Book* (New York: F. Ungar, 1967), p. 8.
18. Ibid., p. 12.
19. Ibid., p. 19.

ers who appealed to reason but never revelation to buttress their views. Indeed he made the bold claim that revelation should be defined as truth sanctioned by reason.

Collins expended considerable energy in attacking a leading support of supernatural revelation, namely, fulfilled prophecy. The authority of the New Testment is predicated on the divine authority of the Old Testament; but the authority of the Old Testament is predicated on specific prophecies that have totally come to pass. But according to Collins not a single Old Testament prediction has ever been fulfilled in an exact sense. The New Testament is in error when it claims a literal fulfillment of the prophecies. Collins viewed Old Testament prophecy as a kind of mystical allegorizing peculiar to the Jewish mind. In fact the Jews did not conceive of the idea of the Messiah until shortly before the birth of Jesus. In other words, "the Jews had never really expected a Messiah, and strictly speaking there were no prophecies which could be fulfilled."[20] Collins anticipated modern criticism by claiming that the book of Daniel was composed during the Maccabean period.

In sum, Collins was zealous in his attempts to prove the Bible and historic Christianity false. The orthodox churchman Philip Doddridge said that Collins the Deist was "one of those unhappy people who have made it their interest to disbelieve Christianity, and who are therefore searching for any shadow of argument to support their consistency."[21]

Matthew Tindal (d. 1733), fellow of All Souls College, Oxford, represents the zenith of the Deistic controversy. Tindal's chief work, *Christianity as Old as the Creation, or the Gospel a Republication of the Religious Nature* (1730), is recognized as the standard textbook of Deism. Tindal postulates that a God who is eternally unchangeable, good, and wise must have disclosed Himself initially in a revelation that was fully adequate for the needs of the entire human race. Indeed, at the creation God gave to mankind a rule *(lex naturae)* sufficient to communicate what should be believed and practiced. That primal natural religion, being perfect and complete, required no additions. "The religion of nature was so perfect that nothing could be added to it; and that the truth of all revelation was to be judged by its agreement with it."[22] Asked

20. Gerald Cragg, *Reason and Authority in the Eighteenth Century* (Cambridge: Cambridge U. 1964), p. 85.
21. Philip Doddridge, *The Correspondence and Diary of Philip Doddridge*, 5 vols. (London: H. Colburn and R. Bentley, 1829-31), 1:457.
22. Matthew Tindal, cited in John Redwood, *Reason, Ridicule and Religion* (Cambridge, Mass.: Harvard U., 1976), p. 145.

Tindal, "Can revelation . . . add anything to a religion thus absolutely perfect, universal, and immutable?"[23]

A special revelation such as Christendom posits in the Bible is, according to Tindal, but a republication of the original revelation written on the hearts of all men. Hence special revelation adds nothing to the perfect religion of nature and reason. For all practical purposes, then, special revelation is superfluous. And it is not only superfluous but dangerous because it has given birth to manifold superstitions and abuses and has engendered incalculable ill will and strife.

Every teaching in the Bible not in agreement with reason must be dismissed as untrue. Said Tindal, "I cannot have any faith which will not bear the test of reason."[24] But in Tindal's judgment many things in the Bible *cannot* be squared with the eternal reason of things. The Old Testament, for example, contains many immoral prescriptions. But reason judges that when criminal matters are commanded or approved the record must be false. Moreover, he observed that the Bible contains numerous supernatural occurrences that, because they fail the test of clear reason, must be regarded as superstitions. Such biblical teachings that reason rejects include the fall of the race in Adam, Christ's atoning death, and eternal punishment. "Happy is the man who is . . . directed by the laws of reason and the religion of nature as to suffer no mysteries, or unintelligible propositions, no allegories, no hyperboles, no metaphors, no types, parables, or phrases of uncertain significance to confound his understanding."[25]

Tindal outlined one other reason the Bible cannot be the authoritative Word of God. Jesus and the apostles erroneously made salvation dependent upon beliefs that most people never heard of. Tindal found it inconceivable that God could have left the whole of mankind without a revelation for more than four thousand years. "What equally concerns all must be equally knowable by all."[26] For Tindal the Bible is true only insofar as it is a republication of natural religion. If Scripture teaches anything beyond that, such additions must be viewed as extraneous superstitions and corruptions. But in Tindal's opinion the Bible *has* perverted the original natural religion by spurious accretions, hence Scripture constitutes a lie.

Another Deist who had much to say about the integrity of the Bible was Cambridge don Thomas Woolston (d. 1733). In *Dis-*

23. Tindal, cited in Waring, *Deism*, p. 109.
24. Ibid., p. 150.
25. Ibid., p. 152.
26. Ibid., p. 149.

courses on the Miracles of our Savior (1727-29), Woolston applied
to the New Testament miracles the same method that Collins
earlier had applied to the Old Testament prophecies. When
viewed in a literal, historical sense, the miracles of Jesus are
foolish and absurd. Woolston blasphemed that some of Jesus'
miracles may even have been performed under Satanic influence.
But in the main the miracle accounts are instances of outright
deception and fraud. Woolston's denial of the validity of our
Lord's miracles undercut the force of their support for the supernatural authority of the Bible. But even though the miracles lack
historical reality, Woolston argued, when interpreted allegorically
they do convey spiritual meaning. Woolston was so committed to
his method that he declared that anyone who denies the allegorical method of interpreting Scripture is guilty of blasphemy
against the Holy Ghost. A brief mention of Woolston's method of
allegorizing (fictionalizing) follows.

Woolston deals with the three miracles of Jesus' raising the
dead: Jairus's daughter (Mark 5:35-42), the widow of Nain's son
(Luke 7:11-15), and Lazarus (John 11:17-44). In Woolston's own
words, "the literal stories consist of absurdities, improbabilities,
and incredibilities."[27] Jairus's daughter was merely asleep; the
widow's son was mistakenly buried alive; and in the case of Lazarus, the napkin over his face concealed his animate condition.
Although the miracle accounts are forgeries, he says, the first
story symbolizes the eventual conversion of the Jews; the second,
the conversion of the Gentiles; and the third, the resurrection of
mankind at the end of the age.

The alleged miracle of Jesus' resurrection Woolston describes
as "the most barefaced imposture ever put upon the world."[28] The
resurrection scenario was a clear plot engineered by Jesus' followers. The chief priests and the disciples secretly agreed to seal the
grave, to cause Jesus' body to disappear, and to bear false witness
to His resurrection. When the record is allegorized, however, it
signifies the liberation of Christianity from the bondage of the
Jewish letter and its emergence into the freedom of the Spirit.

Woolston the Deist thus launched an attack on Scripture at one
of its most vital parts. He ruthlessly emasculated the miracles of
our Lord, thereby discrediting the Bible and the Christian faith
as a hoax and a fraud. It comes as no surprise to learn that
Woolston was dismissed from Cambridge University on the

27. Ibid., p. 74.
28. Thomas Woolston, cited in Cragg, *Reason and Authority,* p. 86.

grounds of insanity. Woolston was imprisoned by the English government on a charge of blasphemy against Christianity, and while in prison he died.

So as to facilitate comparison with contemporary theological reflection on the Bible, a brief summation of the Deistic attitude toward revelation and Scripture is in order. Underlying the Deistic position was the postulate of the primacy of reason as the source of all truth. Untouched by sin, unaided human reason is fully competent to unfold the fundamental tenets of religion. According to the Deists, by the process of observation and analysis of the data of the universe all men can discover the necessary truths of religion. The universal natural religion thus derived is sufficient to lead people to a life of practical morality and happiness. Moreover, being perfect and perspicuous, the religion of nature and reason requires no supernatural additions.

Given the sufficiency of natural religion, the Deists insisted first of all that special revelation was unnecessary. And given their assumption that there can be no deviations from the fixed course of nature, the Deists argued, second, that revelation was impossible. Moreover, because a loving God would not deliberately exclude the majority of mankind from the knowledge of the truth, the Christian revelation could not possibly be the mystery hidden from many generations but in these last days disclosed to a select few.

In addition, Holy Spirit inspiration was said to contravene the order of nature. The Deists insisted that the biblical writers were inspired only to the extent that any artist finds his literary talents elevated in moments of special creativity. The truthfulness and divine authority of the Bible were denied, first, on the a priori ground that the validating evidences of fulfilled prophecy and miracles were unsubstantiable. And the divine origin of Scripture was rejected, second, on the basis of various critical considerations. In this regard the Deists appealed to alleged contradictions in the text of the Bible, to the unbecoming character of its ethical teachings, and to the supposedly antithetical religious systems propounded by Jesus and Paul. The doctrinal affirmations of the Bible—the Trinity, incarnation, atonement, resurrection of Christ, and eternal punishment—were regarded as a mass of superstitions. The Deists' assault sought to strip the Bible of its central role in the church and shear it of any particular significance. "After the Deists it was far more difficult to treat Holy Writ as a simple, clear, and unequivocal doctrinal authority."[29]

Whereas Deism as a historical movement came to an end, a number of its critical assumptions regarding the Bible have endured even to the present time. Many of its objections to the integrity and truthfulness of the Bible are still being raised in our day, albeit in slightly different guise. Thus it can indeed be said of Deism, "Though dead, it yet speaketh."

THE BIBLE AND GERMAN RATIONALISM

In the speculative intellectual climate of Germany the Enlightenment is known as the *Aufklärung*, or the clearing away of traditional loyalties. As early as the latter decades of the seventeenth century a handful of German philosophers challenged the regnant Lutheran orthodoxy by adopting the basic principles of English Deism. More than the Deists, the German rationalists worked within the context of the established Protestant church. Within the broad Christian framework the rationalists sought to purify Bible and church from what they regarded as improper accommodations to superstitious beliefs and practices.

The German rationalists believed that human reason was the primary source of religious knowledge. Increasingly they affirmed the innate goodness and moral ability of natural man. And in due course the rationalists disputed the necessity of supernatural revelation. If revelation has any function it is merely to confirm the judgments of reason. In the words of Gotthold Lessing, "all revealed religion is nothing but a reconfirmation of the religion of reason. Either it has no mysteries, or, if it does, it is indifferent whether the Christian combines them with one idea or another, or with none at all."[30] It follows that the traditional church doctrine of inspired Scripture was overturned. The idea of special inspiration of holy books was redundant, for God directly impresses spiritual truths upon the hearts of men. As the typical rationalist would have put it: "Grant inspiration and you bind us down to the belief that all the contents of Scripture are true. You force us to believe what our reason does not comprehend."[31]

29. Hubert Cunliffe-Jones and Benjamin Drewery, eds., *A History of Christian Doctrine* (Philadelphia: Fortress, 1980), p. 466.
30. Cited in Peter Gay, *The Enlightenment: An Interpretation* (New York: Alfred A. Knopf, 1967), p. 330.
31. John F. Hurst, *History of Rationalism* (New York: Eaton and Mains, 1865), p. 200.

The rationalist movement in eighteenth- and early nineteenth-century Germany thus gradually undermined traditional confidence in the Bible. In the discussion to follow the several strands of the rationalists' argument will be explored in greater detail. Suffice it to say that the German rationalists "repaid with interest the debt that their eighteenth century forebears had too recklessly incurred. What had already been made in England (and discredited there) become so popular as an imported article that it changed the whole course of mental taste in Germany for generations."[32]

RATIONALIST THEOLOGIANS

The philosophy of G. W. Leibnitz (d. 1716) and his disciple Christian Wolff (d. 1754)—not Lockean empiricism—laid the foundation for the eighteenth-century German *Aufklärung*. The two German thinkers emphasized the need for vigorous mathematical demonstration of all religious beliefs. By application of the mathematical method they judged that all men could be convinced of the validity of Christianity's truths. They believed that guided by the light of reason men could rise to the eternal realm and establish a metaphysical basis for faith. As expressed by Leibnitz, "our reason illumined by the spirit of God reveals the law of nature."[33] According to Wolff, if an atheist faithfully followed the law of nature he would live as a Christian lives.

Leibnitz and Wolff did not intend that the rule of reason should usurp the prerogatives of revelation. Revelation, in principle, augments the truth-content of natural religion. As Wolff put it: "Scripture serves as an aid to natural theology. It furnishes natural theology with propositions which ought to be demonstrated. Consequently, the philosopher is bound not to invent but to demonstrate."[34] In other words, Scripture sets forth truths that reason cannot discover. Yet in order that such truths be perceived as true they must be approved by rational demonstration. The implication is that what cannot be demonstrated ought not be accepted as true. In sum, Leibnitz and Wolff assigned to reason the task of passing judgment on revelation—an agenda that more thorough-

32. Andrew L. Drummond, *German Protestantism Since Luther* (London: Epworth, 1951), p. 81.
33. Cited in Gerald Cragg, *The Church and the Age of Reason* (Grand Rapids: Eerdmans, 1960), p. 44.
34. Christian Wolff, *Theologia naturalis*, 2 parts (Frankfurt and Leipzig, 1736-37), pt. 1, p. 22.

going rationalists would carry to greater lengths.

H. S. Reimarus (d. 1768), the Hamburg Orientalist, stood solidly within the rationalist tradition in theology. His chief work was the 4,000-page essay "An Apology for the Reasonable Worshippers of God." So extreme was Reimarus's views in the "Apology" that the essay was not published during his lifetime. Gotthold Lessing claimed to have discovered the essay on the shelves of the Wolfenbüttel library where he was employed. Given the radical nature of the "Apology," Lessing published only seven sections of the essay under the title *Fragments of an Anonymous Author* (1774-78). The so-called *Wolfenbüttel Fragments* argues that true religion rests on the basis of unaided human reason. The religion commended in the *Fragments* is a strictly natural one, universal and accessible to all. With the passing of time that primal, natural religion became overlaid with extraneous accretions, and so were born the historic "revealed" religions. Reimarus's goal was to return to the original natural religion, which alone leads to human progress and fulfillment.

In the *Wolfenbüttel Fragments* Reimarus launched a frontal attack against revealed religion. According to Reimarus, biblical claims of supernatural revelation are totally fraudulent. Moreover, the biblical doctrine of inspiration is so beset with special pleading that it cannot be maintained by reasonable people.

From those radical premises Reimarus could only adopt a skeptical view of the Bible itself. He argued that many Old Testament "saints" were proud and immoral persons. The Old Testament history was a string of legends and myths. For example, the account of the Israelite passage through the Red Sea is totally preposterous. He assumed a column of people ten abreast, which would have made it a column nearly two hundred miles long and would have necessitated a passage of at least nine days. His attitude toward the New Testament was no less critical. Reimarus observed that because the four gospels differ from one another in times, places, and particulars, their material must have been falsified. Special attention was directed to variations in the resurrection narratives. Reimarus argued that either Jesus had not died or the disciples were hallucinating. The resurrection scenario was viewed as a literary cover-up for Jesus' failure to establish Himself as an earthly king.

Gotthold Lessing (d. 1781), librarian of the Duke of Brunswick's library at Wolfenbüttel, is generally regarded as the leading figure of the German Enlightenment. In the words of one authority, "he profoundly affected German theology and through it much of the thought of modern Protestantism."[35] As noted above, Lessing edited and published the *Fragments* of Reimarus and in the process appropriated many of the latter's theological views.

Lessing maintained that man's primary duty is to practice the universal religion of reason. Revelation is not a thing that is past and completed but a progressive and never-ending event. Lessing, in fact, likened revelation to the process of education. "That which education is to the individual, revelation is to the race. Education is revelation coming to the individual man; and revelation is education which has come, and is yet coming, to the human race."[36] Revelation, like education, gives man what he could have acquired on his own, only more quickly and easily. As Lessing put it: "Education gives man nothing which he might not educe out of himself: it gives him that which he might educe out of himself, only quicker and more easily. In the same way too, revelation gives nothing to the human species, which the human reason left to itself might not attain; only it has given, and still gives to it, the most important of these things earlier."[37] From a metaphysical point of view revelation is man's intuitive insight into ultimate moral truths. It is given immanently in the history of religion as a synthesis of the human and divine activity. Through the religious systems of the world, from animism to Hinduism to Christianity, God has been working out His educative program for the spiritual enrichment of the race. Lessing's concept of revelation stimulated the thinking of later liberals and modernists.

Lessing also wrestled with the problem of how the Bible's historical testimony relates to religious faith. In his work *Concerning the Demonstration of the Spirit and Power* (1777), Lessing highlighted the hopelessness of attempts to arrive at demonstrative certainty from the probabilities of historical data. Thus he argued that metaphysical and moral truths cannot be established by appeal to the contingent facts of history. In this sense Lessing spoke of the "broad and ugly ditch" between incidental historical data and eternal spiritual truths. And so, in what has become a famous line, he asserted, "the accidental truths of history can never become the proof of necessary truths of revelation."[38] The

---

35. Cragg, *Church and the Age of Reason*, p. 249.
36. G. E. Lessing, cited in J. M. Creed and J. S. Boys-Smith, *Religious Thought in the Eighteenth Century* (Cambridge: Cambridge U., 1934), p. 174.
37. Ibid., p. 175.
38. Lessing, cited in Cunliffe-Jones and Drewery, eds., *History of Christian Doctrine*, p. 7.

biblical accounts of fulfilled prophecies, miracles, and resurrection are all judgments based on historical data. Reports of these phenomena reproduced in the Bible are as reliable as historical matters can be. But by virtue of their very historical nature these accounts fall short of proved truthfulness.

Lessing concluded that religious truths cannot be addressed by simple appeal to Scripture. The only reliable source of religious truth lies in the individual's own mind and experience. If a yawning chasm exists between historical data and spiritual truths, religious certainty can be gained as one personally experiences truth for himself. By that line of argument Lessing completely undercut the authority of the Bible as a historical document. For the neologist the focus of religious truth is man himself rather than an inspired and authoritative book.

J. S. Semler (d. 1791), professor of theology at Halle, was raised in the surroundings of devout German pietism. He sought to retain a connection with the old Lutheranism, but his critical conjectures in theology earned him the title "the father of German rationalism."[39] Semler's chief interest lay in the application of the historical-critical method to the Bible. He drew a line of demarcation between personal religion and scientific theology. Although on critical grounds he was skeptical of the validity of many biblical teachings, he sought to practice private religion. One could be a Christian in heart, he argued, without accepting with the mind the precepts of the Bible. Semler thus was instrumental in creating a divorce between objectively held beliefs and subjectively lived faith.

Semler held that revelation discloses nothing that man cannot learn of God by himself. Rightly understood, revelation amounts to little more than a confirmation of the judgments of reason. Semler's teachings, moreover, did much to unsettle the Reformation view of the Bible's inspiration. No evidence for the theory of verbal inspiration, he argued, can be found in the New Testament. The idea of verbal inspiration can be traced back to the legend of the seventy translators of the Septuagint, who claimed to be led by the Holy Spirit in the selection of the exact words they used. The church appealed to the doctrine of inspiration only when it perceived the need to guarantee the contents of the Bible. Semler charged that conservatives worship the Bible rather than God Himself and thus are guilty of bibliolatry, when in fact the Bible is not the veritable Word of God. Rather, the Bible merely *con-*

tains the Word of God. Semler thus did much to loose theology from its traditional dependence upon the Scriptures.

Semler was also responsible for developing the theory of cultural relativism, according to which many biblical teachings were said to be applicable only to the culture and times addressed. He maintained that the Old Testament was a Jewish national document with no relevance for people of later times. As for the New Testament he argued that Jesus and the apostles deliberately accommodated their teachings to the prejudices of the Jews. Almost everything beyond the simple moral precepts of the New Testament—for example, teaching about angels, resurrection of the dead, and the Spirit inspiration of Scripture—was viewed as so many conscious accommodations to Jewish ideas. Whatever proved unacceptable to Semler's critical sensibilities was set aside as of only local and temporal relevance.

Semler employed the scalpel of the historical-critical method and rejected the genuineness of many books of the Bible. The Pentateuch, especially Genesis, he judged to be a collection of legends and fables. Joshua, Judges, the books of Samuel, Kings, and Chronicles together with Ezra and Nehemiah he held to be of minimal historical value. Esther and the Song of Solomon were fanciful Jewish tales. The New Testament was considered of somewhat greater value, but parts of it were seen as positively harmful to one who seeks religious edification. The gospels were suspect because of their far-fetched "miracle" stories. The general epistles were penned for the sole purpose of unifying the opposing parties into which the early church had split. And the Apocalypse Semler judged to be the work of a Judaizing fanatic. Plainly Semler rejected the genuineness of the received Scripture canon.

Semler's pointed attack upon special revelation, Holy Spirit inspiration, and the genuineness of the biblical canon would be carried to further lengths by neologists of even more reckless bent. But it is true that at the hands of Semler "the Scriptures became the carcass around which the vultures of Germany gathered to satisfy the cravings of their wanton hunger."[40]

H. E. G. Paulus, who taught Oriental languages and theology at Jena and Heidelberg, has been acclaimed "the true patriarch of rationalism."[41] The young Paulus's minister father claimed to have seen apparitions following the death of his wife. Such a claim led to his being deposed from the ministry. His father's

40. Hurst, *History of Rationalism*, p. 145.
41. F. Lichtenberger, *A History of German Theology in the Nineteenth Century* (Edinburgh: T. & T. Clark, 1889), p. 21.

visions led the younger Paulus to a complete distrust of all religious claims antithetical to reason and logic. Thus before accepting any theological belief Paulus demanded rigorous mathematical proof of its validity.

According to Paulus, mere men never predicted the outcome of events hundreds of years in advance. To prophesy *(weissagen)* was merely to say something wise *(weisses sagen)*. Likewise, because science has ruled out so-called supernatural interruptions of nature, the modern reader of the Bible must reinterpret the miracle narratives to get at the natural facts of the case. We illustrate Paulus's naturalistic interpretation of the Bible with the following examples.

Mary's supposed condition of pregnancy through the agency of the Holy Spirit was a pious hallucination. The angels who supposedly announced Christ's birth to the shepherds were merely phosphorescent natural phenomena. Jesus' miracles of healing were done by His skillful application of natural herbal remedies. The miracle of the loaves and fishes could be explained by Jesus' unselfish spirit in sharing His lunch, which was also done by the disciples. Then everyone replenished his supply from a passing caravan of camels laden with food.

Paulus explained the transfiguration as the confused recollection of three disciples who saw their master standing in the bright glow of the sunrise. Paulus further observed that Jesus did not actually die on the cross but rather suffered a fainting fit brought on by tetanus. After recovering somewhat He walked out of the tomb under His own power. Finally, Paulus explained the ascension in terms of Jesus' retirement in sickness to a high mountain, at which time a thick mist concealed Him from the sight of His followers.

Paulus thus viewed the Scriptures as a collection of Jewish mythology, that is as a heap of exaggerations, errors, and fables. The Bible was strictly a fallible human document; God had no hand whatsoever in its production.

SUMMARY OF GERMAN RATIONALISM ON THE BIBLE

Initially the German rationalists sought only to modify traditional views on biblical revelation and inspiration. A disclosure of God in the Bible was not denied, although the early rationalists insisted that the teachings of the Bible must be demonstrable by reason. Gradually the orthodox view that Scripture *is* the very Word of God gave way to the opinion that one must separate from the larger whole of Bible words those actual words of God (the

Scripture only *contains* God's Word). The rationalists concluded that those parts of Scripture that do not foster religion must be of human origin. Even in the early stages of the German Enlightenment the church doctrine of verbal inspiration was singled out as the object of special negative criticism.

In the second phase of the Enlightenment, revelation was increasingly suppressed by the claims of reason. The later rationalist typically inveighed, "Let man seek God by way of pure reason and he will find Him." Ostensibly seeking to safeguard the core truths of revelation, the rationalist postulated the theory of cultural relativism by which many Bible teachings were said to possess only a temporary relevance. Some authorities questioned whether or not historical documents such as the Scriptures could serve as vehicles for the timeless truths of divine revelation. Others affirmed the theory of degrees of inspiration: some documents were written without any divine inspiration (historical books, Acts), others by virtue of the strengthening of the writer's mind (Genesis, the prophets), and still others on the basis of some kind of heavenly enduement (Romans, Revelation). The traditional corroborative arguments of fulfilled prophecy and miracles were increasingly questioned, which placed even greater strain on the time-honored belief in the Bible's divine inspiration. The rationalists boldly ventured into the area of biblical exegesis and explained away by devious means the supernatural teachings of Scripture.

In the full flower of its development, rationalism dismissed altogether the possibility of special revelation. God may permit men to fathom certain higher secrets and mysteries, but the perception of hidden truths is accomplished by the natural powers of the mind. Scripture consequently ceased to be viewed as a body of truths published by God. The committed rationalist typically asserted: "Grant inspiration and you bind us down to the belief that all the contents of Scripture are true. You force us to believe what our reason does not comprehend. The doctrine of inspiration opens the floodgate for the belief of a mass of mythical stuff which we will no more grant to be historically true than . . . the legends of early Rome."[42] Thus at the hands of the German rationalists the supernatural inspiration of Scriptures was totally given up; the Bible was viewed as a human book.

After they measured the Bible by the yardstick of autonomous reason, the German rationalists inevitably surrendered its con-

42. Hurst, *History of Rationalism*, pp. 200-201.

tents. Reports of angels, demons, divine healings, resurrections, and so forth were viewed as preposterous Jewish legends. Bible doctrines such as the Trinity, the deity of Christ, and atonement through the cross were dismissed as ancient superstitions. By representing the Bible as a fallible human document in whose composition God had little or no part, the German rationalists were highly instrumental in the overthrow of the authority of the Word of God. In terms of its nakedly destructive attitude towards Scripture, it is true that "rationalism takes rank as one of the most corrupt tendencies of infidelity which appears anywhere upon the pages of ecclesiastical history."[43]

IMPACT ON MODERN THEOLOGY AND A CRITIQUE

The Enlightenment era in England and on the Continent ran its course and came to an end. Yet Enlightenment presuppositions regarding Scripture continue to exercise a substantial impact on the contemporary situation. Today's critical religious thinkers insist that if man would be truly modern he must be guided by the foundation premises of the eighteenth-century Enlightenment. Although space will not allow a discussion of every point of correspondence between the Enlightenment and the present situation, several of the most important features follow.

ASSERTION OF THE AUTONOMY OF REASON

Contemporary critical theologians, like their Enlightenment forebears, commonly postulate the autonomy of unaided reason. Likewise in the contemporary situation the debilitating effects of sin upon the human intellect are widely denied. According to many modern scholars reason serves as the dominant criterion of truth. L. H. DeWolf, for example, argues that truth is not attained simply by reading it off the pages of Scripture. Rather, religious truth is secured as the critical mind exercises discriminating judgments over the total range of human experience. The primacy of unaided reason is also stated by Gordon Kaufman of Harvard: "We are in a new historical situation with a new awareness of our own autonomy and responsibility to think through what we should do and by what means we should guide our thoughts and lives."[44] The Bible is viewed as a secondary resource in the process of constructing a personal understanding of God.

43. Ibid., pp. 33-34.
44. Gordon Kaufman, "What Shall We Do with the Bible?" *Interpretation* 25 (January 1971): 96.

Certainly he is no friend of God and truth who decries *any* right use of reason. Man was designed by the Creator to function as a rational being in His image. One of the noble features of the Christian religion is its powerful appeal to the rationality and coherence of propositional revelation. Reason is the indispensible tool by which man recognizes a revelation, interprets the revelation, and applies the truths thereof to life. No man can live Christianity apart from the judicious exercise of his God-given faculty of reason.

The problem resides not with the responsible use of reason but with rational*ism*, the system that claims for unaided reason supremacy and autonomy. Reason becomes perverted when it organizes into a system in which it arrogates to itself the power of originating and judging religious beliefs. As Brunner rightly insists, "Jesus Christ is not the enemy of reason, but only of the irrational arrogance of those who pride themselves on their intellect, and of the irrational self-sufficiency of reason."[45] Experience proves that there are upper limits to what can be known about God from nature and reason. Natural reason cannot fathom the hidden character or secret councils of God. It cannot inform man what God demands to render the sinner acceptable to Himself. And reason can never break the dominion of indwelling sin. Arrogant reason, which falsely usurps the function of faith, Luther described as "blind and poor" and as the "arch-prostitute and Devil's bride." Contemporary critical scholars irresponsibly follow the lead of Enlightenment theologians when they assert that the natural light of reason is adequate to establish true religion.

COLLAPSE OF SUPERNATURAL REVELATION

The Enlightenment subscribed to the view that nature is a regular system governed by fixed laws. The predictability of nature's working led many eighteenth-century thinkers to conclude that there is no supernatural power that intrudes in the realm of nature and history. In particular, the idea of supernatural communication of information fell into more and more disfavor until special revelation was denied altogether.

A contemporary scholar such as James Barr stands within the Enlightenment tradition when he argues that the modern view of the world necessitates the abandonment of a special, direct com-

45. Emil Brunner, *Revelation and Reason* (Philadelphia: Westminster, 1946), pp. 16-17.

munication from God to prophets and apostles.[46] The monolithic scientific world view allows no differentiation between revealed and natural theology. If the voice of God is heard it will come from within the depths of man's own life and experience. F. Gerald Downing in his monograph *Has Christianity a Revelation?* maintains that if God intended to make Himself plain by supernatural communication He patently failed. Downing argues that to say "God has revealed Himself" involves such heavy qualification of the word *reveal* that the assertion is radically misleading. Downing claims to find no instance of God's revealing Himself in the Bible. "It is surely nonsense, even pernicious nonsense, to pretend that it (i.e., revelation) is a present fact."[47] Thus Barr and Downing follow the Enlightenment judgment that supernatural revelation ought to be abandoned altogether. DeWolf and Beegle, on the other hand, perpetuate Lessing's thesis that revelation, viewed as the propaedeutic enlightenment of the race, shall continue as long as mankind endures. In the same manner C. H. Dodd expressly contemplates revelation as a progressive and ongoing process of educating the human family.[48]

Scripture and experience, however, amply confirm that behind the flux of temporal existence there dwells an infinite, external, and all-powerful mind. The Creator should not be confounded with His creation in a scheme of monistic pantheism. If God truly be God, He is free and capable of communicating to man both Himself and knowledge about Himself. Denial of the possibility of revelation, based on a monistic world view that merges the supernatural into the natural, flies in the face of facts. Likewise, rejection of the reality of revelation hopelessly conflicts with the testimony down through the ages of men who, by miraculous signs, were certified to be bearers of a unique message from God. Scripture, viewed as a reasonably reliable historical document, discloses that individuals such as Adam, Noah, Abraham, Moses, and David were recipients of immediate supernatural communications from God. Those men believed they had received information from God and wrote it down. The resultant writings, described as "the word of the Lord," "the testimony of God," "the commandment of the Lord," and so forth, are more cogently viewed as divinely given revelation than are the excogitations of human reason. The historic Christian response to the Enlighten-

46. James Barr, *The Bible in the Modern World* (London: SCM, 1973), p. 17.
47. F. Gerald Downing, *Has Christianity a Revelation?* (Philadelphia: Westminster, 1964), p. 238.
48. C. H. Dodd, *The Bible Today* (Cambridge: Cambridge U., 1947), p. 98.

ment denial of special revelation is that sinful man stands in dire need of direct disclosure of God's nature and saving purposes. Only by knowing who God is and what He has accomplished for the sinner can human guilt and estrangement be overcome. In sum, supernatural, propositional revelation is neither inconsistent with the nature of God nor derogatory to human reason. Quite to the contrary, it satisfied people's deepest spiritual needs.

LOSS OF DIVINE INSPIRATION

Attending the Enlightenment collapse of special revelation was the loss of the verbal inspiration of Scripture. In the Age of Reason inspiration was either rejected altogether or attributed to the creativity of the human writer. The penmen of the Bible were said to be inspired in the same way any artist or poet might be inspired.

Many recent theologians similarly compromise the verbal inspiration of the Bible. Raymond Abba insists that "inspiration is something attributed primarily to men rather than to a book."[49] By inspiration the biblical writers' mental powers were elevated to the point of genius. DeWolf likewise denies the concept of verbal inspiration. The Bible was not "produced by any method through which God insured the unfailing truth and usefulness of every word." Inspiration means only "an extraordinary stimulation and elevation of the powers of men who devoutly guided themselves to God's will."[50] Barr argues that the word *inspired* appears only once in the Bible, and that occurrence is in a late marginal document (2 Tim. 3:16). "It is an open question which books or documents are included within 'scripture' by the writer of II Timothy, and an open question also what was implied in his mind by 'inspired,' what it involved and what it excluded."[51] The inspiration pertains only to the excitation of the writer's natural powers. Thus Barr concludes that "this conception would suggest not so much historical or theological accuracy, inerrancy, and infallibility, but rather sublimity, profundity of insight, and existential power of communication."[52] Beegle, who claims to be an evangelical, adopts the same Enlightenment conclusion. Neither the phenomena of Scripture nor the claims of the biblical writers

---

49. Raymond Abba, *The Nature and Authority of the Bible* (London: James Clarke, 1958), p. 102.
50. L. H. DeWolf, *A Theology of the Living Church* (New York: Harper and Brothers, 1953), p. 76.
51. Barr, *Bible in the Modern World*, p. 14.
52. Ibid., p. 17.

warrant the doctrine of verbal inspiration. But lest one throw out the baby with the bathwater, Beegle concludes: "We can speak of the Bible as being inspired from cover to cover, human mistakes and all."[53] Moreover has the Reformed scholar G. C. Berkouwer brought in the critical spirit of the Enlightenment when in *Holy Scripture* he postulates a theory of partial inspiration, namely, an inspiration limited to the purpose of the biblical writer and not inclusive of all the particulars of his writing?[54]

Reply to the dilution of the classical postulate of divine inspiration of the Scripture must be brief. Jesus and those certified to speak on the authority of God made five assertions about the character of Holy Scripture: (1) The focus of God's inspiration activity is the writing itself, not the human writer. What is inspired by divine power Paul asserts to be "all Scripture" (2 Tim. 3:16). (2) Scripture has its origin not in man (however elevated his intellectual powers) but in God Himself. Thus Paul speaks about Scripture as being "God-breathed" *(theopneustos)*, a judgment with which the apostle Peter concurs (2 Pet. 1:21). (3) Divine inspiration pertains to the totality of the sacred writings (Rom. 3:2; 2 Tim. 3:16). The Bible knows nothing about "partial inspiration." (4) The divine origin of Scripture ensures its complete and unqualified truthfulness (John 17:17). The Word that originates from the mouth of God is as true and blameless as God Himself. And (5) Scripture is inspired not because of its sublimity and existential relevance. Rather, the Bible is glorious and life transforming precisely because it is inspired of God. Finally, because critics both old and new consistently speak of inspiration in terms of the elevation of man's poetic powers, a further observation is in order. If inspiration is no more than an inherent superiority called "religious genius," on what basis should one ascribe greater authority to the Bible than to other writings that display signs of religious genius, for example, *Paradise Lost* or *Screwtape Letters?* If the critics value consistency they would be compelled to order teaching and worship around a plethora of religious classics that are on an equal basis with the Bible. The critics, in other words, provide no rationale for the unique role of the Bible in the life of the church.

53. Dewey Beegle, *Scripture, Tradition and Infallibility* (Grand Rapids: Eerdmans, 1973), p. 208.
54. G. C. Berkouwer, *Holy Scripture* (Grand Rapids: Eerdmans, 1975), pp. 141, 166-67.

REJECTION OF BIBLICAL MIRACLES

Enlightenment thinkers and modern critics alike reject the reality of reported miracles in the Bible. Deists and rationalists were persuaded that modern scientific discoveries rule out disruptions of the processes of nature; therefore they viewed the Bible's miracle accounts as deceptions and fraud. Denial of the miracle accounts by Enlightenment skeptics not only decimated the biblical text but also undermined an important evidential argument for the integrity of Scripture.

Many contemporary critics reiterate the old Enlightenment claim that no alteration of nature's fixed order is possible. Old Testament scholars such as H. H. Rowley and Wheeler Robinson insist that accounts of the sun standing still at Gibeon (Josh. 10:12-14), Balaam's ass speaking (Num. 22:22-35), or Elisha causing an ax head to float in a stream (2 Kings 6:5-7) are not miracles but fantastic dreams. Theologians such as DeWolf openly confess that "we live in an age in which miracle stories are a stumbling block rather than an evidence of truth."[55] And Bultmann argues that in order to commend Christianity to modern man the miracles must be eliminated. According to him, the modern scientific view of the world rules out every instance of the miraculous in Scripture. "It is impossible to make use of electric light and the radio, and, in the case of illness, to claim the help of modern medical and clinical methods and at the same time to believe in the New Testament's world of spirits and miracles."[56] Of course when the miracle accounts are rejected as spurious the integrity of the Bible is seriously compromised.

The postulate of the general regularity of nature does not rule out extraordinary acts of God in it. The sovereign and omnipotent God who created and governs the world is fully capable of interposing in its affairs to execute His redemptive purposes. Augustine long ago argued that miracles do not constitute arbitrary and irrational interferences in nature. "How can that be against Nature which is effected by the will of God, the Lord and Maker of all nature?"[57] God is not bound by the working in the created order, but is Lord even of it. The miracles, in truth, are signs of the inbreaking of God's rule over fallen men and history. Moreover, the incarnation of God in Christ is the supreme miracle to

55. DeWolf, *A Case for Theology in a Liberal Perspective* (Philadelphia: Westminster, 1959), p. 43.
56. Rudolf Bultmann, *Kerygma and Myth* (New York: Abingdon, 1962), p. 18.
57. Augustine *De civitate Dei* 21:8.

which all others point. He who rejects the Bible's miracles repudiates not only the biblical view of God (who is the source of all power), but also the fact that the kingdom of God has invaded the present world order. In short, to believe in the living God is to believe in miracles. To disbelieve miracles is to disbelieve the God of the Judeo-Christian tradition.

DENIAL OF THE HISTORICAL BASIS OF REVELATION

We recall Lessing's insistence that no accidental data of history, not even that recorded in the Bible, can function as the necessary truths of revelation or provide a basis for spiritual truth. Not historical events but man's own reason and experience serve as the only means of sustaining religious truth.

That Enlightenment depreciation of history's role in mediating revelation is especially evident in neo-orthodox theology. Barth, for example, condemned all attempts to go behind the biblical text to piece together the historical details of Jesus' life.[58] Brunner insisted that revelation never breaks through and invades history. Rather, revelation lies behind time and history, at most tangentially touching it. Beliefs such as the atoning work of Christ, His resurrection, and His bodily ascension to heaven lie outside the relativities of history *(Historie)* in the realm of certainty, or primal history *(Urgeschichte)*. Bultmann likewise claims that revelation lies entirely beyond the scope of ordinary history. *Geschichte*, the event that possesses existential meaning for the individual, can exist quite apart from *Historie* or ordinary history. Jesus' resurrection, for example, possesses significance for faith even though its reality as an historical event cannot be vouchsafed. All Bultmann claims to know about the historical Jesus is that He was executed by the Romans as a political criminal. But that lack of historicity is no loss because for Bultmann faith is unconcerned with the events of ordinary space-time history. Therefore, Lessing's seed thought has caused neo-orthodoxy to set aside the historicity of the Bible as a matter of little spiritual moment.

Depreciation of the historical as outlined above flows from a refusal to concede the objective truth content of revelation and from the corresponding postulate that revelation is subjective. Yet the historical features of the Christian faith are not incidental but intrinsic to its reality. The most basic Christian assertion,

58. Karl Barth, *Church Dogmatics*, ed. G. W. Bromiley and T. F. Torrence, 13 vols. (Edinburgh: T. & T. Clark, 1936-69), vol. 1, pt. 2, pp. 492-95.

"Christ died for our sins" (1 Cor. 15:3), involves a synthesis of both history and theology. The Christian gospel focuses on the good news of God's space-time intervention in man's history (Emmanuel="God with us"). Refusal to identify God's revelation with specific events of history constitutes a distortion of the plan of God. If God did not actually become man in Jesus of Nazareth, did not die a cruel death on the cross, and did not come alive from the tomb, the plan of salvation would be an irrelevant phantasm. Christ had to immerse Himself in man's history in order to save man as a historical being. We conclude, then, that if the events of the Bible are not solidly historical, all that remains of special revelation is historical relativism.

CULTURALLY BOUND CHARACTER OF THE BIBLE'S TEACHING

Various Enlightenment critics argued that Scripture is applicable only to the time and culture in which it was written. Some maintained that the Old Testament was strictly a Jewish national document and the New Testament a literature meaningful only to a first-century Mediterranean mind. The point raised by many Enlightenment thinkers was that the Bible is of only marginal relevance to later generations of people living in other cultural contexts.

James Smart raises the same issue two hundred years later when he insists that the modern knowledge explosion has pointed up the vast gap that exists between the language and concepts of modern man. Thus he concludes that "everything in Scripture is a time-condition expression of faith from which no eternal essence can be extracted."[59] Another critic who has dealt extensively with the problem of cultural relativism is James Barr. He argues that deep differences in outlook exist between biblical people and those who live in the twentieth-century industrialized world. Hence, "a work like the Bible, which is the product of one particular cultural situation . . . cannot therefore be authoritative in any decisive sense for other cultures; the idea is so absurd as not to be worth discussing."[60] Continues Barr, "The idea that the Bible, of all things, can serve as the dominant criterion for Christian faith and ethics in the modern situation is a towering irrationality. What else can one say of a situation where scholars meticulously search through St. Paul's writings in order to decide whether

59. James D. Smart, *The Strange Silence of the Bible in the Church* (Philadelphia: Westminster, 1970), p. 123.
60. Barr, *Bible in the Modern World*, p. 41.

women can come to church without hats?"[61] Barr's own position on the matter is clear: "If . . . by some stretch of the imagination one can see that these Pauline passages were right for their own time, should we not admit that when applied to our modern situation they are simply a lot of nonsense?"[62] Berkouwer, fearful of attributing to the Bible timeless or eternal truths, draws less radical but still illegitimate distinction between the intent and scope of Scripture applicable to all ages and the culturally bound shape of the Bible's commands and prohibitions that do not speak immediately to the contemporary situation. For Berkouwer, Scripture as a time bound document was not written for us but for people of other times and places.[63] Charles Kraft, in a recent cross-cultural study, similarly argues that the Bible is a culturally skewed document.[64] Biblical doctrinal assertions and ethical precepts are sufficently cultural as not to be directly transferable to later contexts. Therefore Old and New Testaments contain few if any propositional teachings immediately meaningful to people of all ages.

It certainly is true that the Bible reflects the customs, styles, and perspectives of the times in which it was written. In that limited sense Scripture is definitely culturally related. On the other hand, Scripture was communicated from God's absolute mind to man's rational being, which was created in God's image. Prophets and apostles moved by the Spirit recorded truths that have since been translated into the conceptual and linguistic forms of many other cultural groups. Given the transcendent origin of the Bible and a common human nature with similar needs for forgiveness, acceptance, and love, we should expect that God-breathed Scripture would contain universal truths meaningful to persons of all times and places. Foreign missionaries offer ample testimony that the Bible speaks relevantly and powerfully to the spiritual needs of persons of the most diverse cultures. Whereas Scripture may in certain respects be *conditioned* by culture, all that the Bible affirms is never *bound* by culture.

THE MYTHOLOGICAL CHARACTER OF SCRIPTURE

The Enlightenment assertion that the biblical world view is scientifically inaccurate and that the regular order of nature is

61. Ibid., p. 42.
62. Ibid.
63. Berkouwer, *Holy Scripture*, pp. 183-91.
64. Charles H. Kraft, *Christianity in Culture* (Maryknoll, N.Y.: Orbis, 1979). See also the critical review of Carl F. H. Henry, "The Cultural Relativising of Revelation," *Trinity Journal* 1 NS (Fall 1980): 153-64.

never perforated by supernatural events led many eighteenth-century scholars to assert that much of the Bible's teaching is mythological. Myth is a story or an event that expresses suprahistorical truths in symbolic form. The task of the Enlightenment exegete is to reinterpret the biblical myths in order to unlock their hidden spiritual meaning.

The rubric of myth looms large in contemporary attitudes to Scripture. A wide range of scholars such as Brunner, Abba, Robinson, and Barr claim that the entire Bible history, from creation and the Fall to the second coming and the last judgment, is mythological in character. Those suprahistorical and suprascientific stories, never enacted on the stage of history, nevertheless encapsulate timeless truths for man's spiritual edification. No one, however, has made more of the notion of myth in Scripture than Rudolf Bultmann. The Marburg scholar claimed that the biblical account of creation, the Bible's picture of a three-story universe (heaven, earth, and hell), and its representation of a world infested with demons are all pure myths. Equally mythological are the Bible's discussion of the triunity of God, the incarnation of the Logos, Christ's atoning death, bodily resurrection and ascension to heaven, and a future life of rewards or punishment. Just as Enlightenment scholars gave an allegorical interpretation to the miracle stories and myths to get at their timeless message, so Bultmann in more sophisticated fashion demythologizes the biblical record to extract its existential meaning for man. On the Roman Catholic side, Hans Küng adopts the same mythological understanding of the Bible with the consequent need to demythologize its contents. With respect to the Bible's Christology he asserts:

> All statements about divine sonship, pre-existence, creation, mediatorship and incarnation—often clothed in the mythological or semi-mythological forms of the time—are meant in the last resort to do no more than substantiate the *uniqueness, underivability and unsurpassability* of the *call, offer and claim* made known in and with Jesus, ultimately not of human but of divine origin and therefore absolutely reliable, requiring man's unconditional involvement.[65]

The earlier critique concerning denials of the Bible's historicity applies equally to the assertion that the biblical narratives are mythological. If, for example, God is merely a myth or symbol of the transcendent dimension in man, then Christianity becomes no

65. Hans Küng, *On Being a Christian* (Garden City, N.Y.: Doubleday, 1976), p. 449.

more than an analysis of human existence or a system of wisdom centered on the creature. If, moreover, the enfleshment of God in Christ, the Savior's atoning sacrifice on the cross, His mighty resurrection from the dead, and His return to claim His people are no more than myths, then such things are no more relevant or ultimate than the fairy tales of the Greeks and Romans. Reymond is surely correct in asserting that "a gospel whose Christ is a phantom, whose cross is merely a symbol, and whose resurrection occurs only in primal history but not in our history simply has no salvation in it."[66] If the biblical record is pervaded with myth then the Christian faith is hopelessly illusory.

THE BIBLE AN ERRONEOUS BOOK

On the basis of the foregoing considerations Enlightenment critics drew the conclusions that the Bible is a strictly human and error-ridden book. Old and New Testaments are not pure purveyors of truth but literary compositions that partake of the shortcomings of their human authors.

Many contemporary scholars concur with the Enlightenment judgment that the Scripture seriously errs. Brunner alleges numerous legendary accretions and contradictions and claims that "the Bible is the human, and therefore not the infallible, witness to the divine revelation."[67] Barr agrees that the biblical record cannot be accepted at face value. "There are 'events' which are not events at all. . . . There was no flood that covered the world and wiped out all living things; there was no ark; there was no Jonah who fell into the sea and was swallowed by a fish. . . . No one who is a serious participant in the discussion supposes that there were real 'events' behind these stories."[68] Commenting on the accuracy of the biblical text, Kaufman maintains that "the central theological question for any modern is not whether God did this or that as claimed by the Yahwist of Isaiah or Paul—no one believes *that* any longer."[69] And Beegle views the Bible as a collection of competing and conflicting traditions (Mosaic, Davidic, priestly, etc.): "All of these cannot be fitted into one scheme and so in the New Testament, as in the Old, there are various traditions, some more authentic than others."[70]

66. Robert L. Reymond, *Brunner's Dialectical Encounter* (Philadelphia: Presbyterian and Reformed, 1967), p. 24.
67. Brunner, *Revelation and Reason*, p. 276.
68. Barr, *Bible in the Modern World*, p. 82.
69. Kaufman, "What Shall We Do with the Bible?" p. 101.
70. Beegle, *Scripture, Tradition and Infallibility*, p. 85.

The allegation of errors in the Bible is far more easily made than firmly proved. Differences of perspective, emphasis, or incidental detail are not sufficient basis for claiming actual errors in the text. Many rejections of the truthfulness of the Bible are rooted in an a priori bias against miracles, predictive prophecy, and other manifestations of supernatural power (which we have judged to be perfectly consistent with the nature of God). Moreover, the liberal emphasis on the human origin and character of the Bible has greatly obscured its divine side. It cannot immediately be assumed that whatever partakes of the human must be fallible and error-ridden. Mary's conception of Jesus proves that the holy power of God may preserve a natural human act from sin. If, however, the Bible were a collection of legends, fables, and fictions as charged by critics old and new, the Holy Book would rank lower as literature than many religious classics. But such a low ranking would contradict the high view of the Bible held by the church through the ages.

DENIAL THAT THE BIBLE IS THE WORD OF GOD

As an immediate consequence of all the critical arguments Enlightenment scholars denied that the Bible is the Word of God. It was claimed that the Bible may *contain* the Word of God, but it was denied that it could *be* the pure Word of God. Some Enlightenment spokesmen insisted that he who regards the Bible to be the very Word of God is guilty of bibliolatry.

The conviction that the Bible is not the Word of God is a familiar theme in modern theology. Neo-orthodox spokesmen commonly speak of Scripture not as being but as *becoming* the Word of God. The Bible, but not its propositional assertions, is said to become the Word of God in that moment when Christ is disclosed to the individual who responds in faith. Comments Barth, "The Bible is God's Word so far as God lets it be His Word, so far as God speaks through it."[71] Similarly, Brunner claims that the Bible is not formally the Word of God, but only instrumentally. The Word of God "is not identical with the Word of Scripture, although it is only given to one through the Scriptures, and as the Word of the Scriptures."[72] Indeed, Brunner claims that to equate the words of the Bible with the Word of God is "a breach of the Second Commandment: it is the deification of a creature, bibliola-

71. Barth, *Church Dogmatics*, vol. 1, pt. 1, p. 123.
72. Brunner, *Dogmatics*, 3 vols. (Philadelphia: Westminster, 1950-62), 1:111.

try."[73] Likewise Kaufman makes the claim that the Bible "contains glorious literature, important historical documents, exalted ethical teachings, but it is no longer the Word of God (if there is a God) to man."[74] Smart insists that the church must desist from the practice of calling the Bible the Word of God. "There is so much in Scripture in which men can hear no word of God, or which seems to contradict the gospel as we hear it from Jesus Christ."[75] In sum, then, neo-orthodoxy affirms that the Bible contains, presents, or conveys the living Word of God (canon within canon), whereas liberalism tends to deny any connection between the Bible and the Word of God (no canon at all).

By definition, any communication that has its origin in God properly may be denoted the "Word of God." But Paul plainly declares that Scripture—indeed "all Scripture"—is "God-breathed," that is, has come into existence through the creative power of God (2 Tim. 3:16). Elsewhere (Rom. 9:6) the apostle regarded the Old Testament *en toto* as the "Word of God," as did Jesus Himself (implied in Matt. 5:17 and elsewhere). Our Lord viewed the Old Testament uniformly as the "truth" (John 17:17). Thus the title *Word of God* legitimately may be applied to God's self-communication in the Scripture, with no gradations of the validity of that Word. Indeed, the opinion that a biblical text becomes the Word of God as God chooses to speak through it betrays a preference for an existential understanding of truth as opposed to a legitimate objective understanding. The position that only parts of the Bible are rightly the Word of God involves the interpreter in a hopelessly subjective and privatistic enterprise. Moreover, if the title *Word of God* in no sense can be applied to scriptural teaching, the Bible ought to be retired from active service in the churches. All of those defective views of the Bible, each in its own way, have contributed to what Smart has called "the strange silence of the bible in the churches."

LOSS OF BIBLICAL AUTHORITY

The essence of the Enlightenment development was that as a human, fallible document the Bible possesses little or no divine authority. Scholars in the Age of Reason concluded that Scripture is not the church's authoritative rule of faith and practice. Religious authority was posited not in the teachings of a book but in

73. Brunner, *Revelation and Reason*, p. 120.
74. Kaufman, "What Shall We Do with the Bible?" p. 96.
75. Smart, *Strange Silence*, p. 149.

the independent judgments of the rational human agent.

Contemporary critical theology follows the Enlightenment in modifying or overthrowing altogether the concept of biblical authority. Kaufman, for example, argues that "only in rare and isolated pockets—and surely these are rapidly disappearing forever—has the Bible anything like the kind of existential authority and significance which it once enjoyed throughout Western culture."[76] Precisely because Scripture is no longer regarded as God's authoritative revelation Kaufman concludes, "We are not concerned to recover simply 'what the Bible says.'"[77] Barr likewise has much to say on the subject of biblical authority. Barr comments concerning his own position: "In English speaking theology one hears the more radical question: why should we affirm at all anything so strange as 'biblical authority'? Why should this collection of old books have any more influence over us than another lot of books, and why should it have more importance than all sorts of preceptions which we gain from the sources, both ancient and modern, written and unwritten?"[78] Barr judges that the conservative wing of the church suffers from "an authority neurosis"[79] that seeks to find a definitive pronouncement on every doubtful question. For scholars such as Nineham, Hodgson, and Barr the job of the church today is to affirm what *it* believes, rather than merely parrot the sayings of a fallible ancient document.

The collapse of biblical authority today plainly represents the inevitable consequence of the prior rejection of special objective revelation and the divine inspiration of Old and New Testaments. If one postulates the human origination of the Scriptues, he is left with but a relative human authority. But if, as prophets, apostles, and church through the ages have testified, the Bible is composed of the very oracles of God, then Scripture possesses authority over every facet of human life and thought on which it speaks. The cumulative evidence clearly rests on the side of this assertion.

THE EROSION OF CHRISTIAN DOCTRINE

As in the Enlightenment era so in the modern period: rejection of special revelation and the divine inspiration has precipitated

76. Kaufman, "What Shall We Do with the Bible?" p. 96.
77. Ibid., p. 105.
78. Barr, *Bible in the Modern World*, p. 9.
79. Ibid., p. 113.

the collapse of the edifice of Christian doctrine. If revelation is merely God giving *Himself* to the exclusion of truths *about* Himself, and if by inspiration one means only humanly formed judgments about existential interests, then the idea of a body of timelessly revealed truths evaporates as mist. Bultmann speaks for the modern critical mind when he asks the question "What, then, has been revealed? Nothing at all, so far as the question about revelation asks for doctrines—doctrines, say, that no man could have discovered for himself—or for mysteries that become known once and for all as soon as they are communicated."[80]

A recitation, even brief, of the modern denial of classical Christian doctrines is discouraging. Tillich, Altizer, and Robinson dismiss the idea of a personal, transcendent God; Pike, Pittenger, Cobb, Küng, and H. Berkhof the idea of a divine triunity. DeWolf, Niebuhr, Bultmann, and Hick deny the Fall of the race in Adam; Bultmann, Tillich, Hick, and Küng the incarnation of God in Christ. DeWolf, Robinson, Schillebeeckx, and Schoonenberg repudiate the deity of our Lord; Aulen, Brunner, and Bultmann the reality of the virgin birth. Altizer, Küng, and Hick reject the atoning death of Christ; Bultmann, Altizer, and Marxen His bodily resurrection from the tomb. Brunner, Bultmann, and Robinson disown the literal second coming of the Lord; and most all modern critics disclaim the reality of eternal rewards in heaven and eternal punishment in hell. The lesson one learns from both the Enlightenment and the modern scene is obvious. Compromise or deny propositional revelation and verbal inspiration and one inevitably dissolves the entire body of Christian truth. Theology (discourse about God) unerringly reduces to anthropology (discourse about man).

NOBLE INTENTIONS NOTWITHSTANDING

Enlightenment critics frequently professed respect and admiration for the Bible. The Deists and rationalists perceived their task as that of purifying true religion, not destroying it. They believed that their calling was to deliver the Bible from misconceptions and superstitions that had grown up around it. The sum of their critical labors was directed towards deepening man's understanding of and appreciation for the Scriptures. Yet Enlightenment theology ended up in thoroughgoing unbelief and irreligion.

Likewise in the modern situation the Bultmannian school seeks

80. Bultmann, *Existence and Faith* (New York: Meridian, 1960), p. 85.

to strip away the prescientific mindset of the Bible and restore faith to its primordial purity. Hosts of contemporary scholars apply the scalpel of criticism with the intention of rendering the Bible believable to technological people. What one clearly learns from these developments is that high ideals and noble intentions are not enough. Unless Scripture is valued as the divinely inspired and authoritative Word of God, modern man forfeits the possibility of hearing the voice of the living Lord. It is the most tragic kind of delusion to believe that one can tread the Word of God under foot with impunity and yet hope to hear good news of divine forgiveness and healing. By virtue of modern man's scornful attitude toward the Bible inherited from the Enlightenment, one must agree with the judgment that today "the church is threatened with a disaster that can only be likened to a man going blind."[81]

81. Smart, *Strange Silence*, p. 32.

2. Romanticism and the Bible

Harold O. J. Brown

Romanticism, then, and this is the best definition I can give of it, is spilt religion.

—T. E. Hulme, "Romanticism and Classicism"

WHAT IS ROMANTICISM?

T. E. Hulme's classic definition of Romanticism suggests two things about it: (1) that parts of it, at least, were deeply religious; (2) if we may preserve the fluid metaphor, that its religion was sloppy. The literary-cultural movement that immediately preceded Romanticism, that is, *classicism*, may be characterized by an architectural metaphor—clarity, visibility, balance were all-important. Romanticism was fluid, formless, capable of spilling and seeping. The movement may be dated roughly from 1780 to 1840, although it had anticipations and late echoes. It began just before the French Revolution (1789) and had died out by the time of the revolutions of 1848. But something like Romanticism has reappeared from time to time since 1848. Friedrich Nietzsche (1844-1900) was not a Romantic, but he developed and transformed a

HAROLD O. J. BROWN, A.B., Harvard University; S.T.B., S.T.M., Harvard Divinity School; Ph.D., Harvard Graduate School of Arts and Sciences, is professor of theology at Trinity Evangelical Divinity School, Deerfield, Illinois. Among his publications are *The Protest of a Troubled Protestant* (1969), *Christianity and the Class Struggle* (1970), *The Reconstruction of the Republic* (1977), and *Death Before Birth* (1977).

number of Romantic ideas. Modern evangelicalism, as it has become more open to literature and art, is showing a certain affinity for Romanticism, or at least for themes that we may call Romantic.

As a literary term within our definition, *Romantic* means something quite different from its common reference to the attraction between the sexes, and it has little in common with the term *romance*. *Romanticism*, in our sense, represents a second way of appreciating the past, a way of appreciating its great men and its heroic moments rather than its ideas and institutions. Rome organized the ancient world, gave it centralized government, codified laws, and built good roads. That aspect of the heritage of antiquity is honored in letters, particularly philosophy, and in law. But in the Enlightenment of the eighteenth century there was a tendency to treat the classical heritage as the natural product of men's minds working in an orderly fashion. Classicism extolled antiquity not as rational and normal, but as great and unparalled. The Christianity that superseded it was regarded as a decline.

Renaissance, Reformation, and Beginnings of Romanticism

The humanistic Renaissance extolled pagan antiquity as the ideal or norm for the humane and denigrated Israel and the Christian faith as narrow and petty. By contrast, both the Protestant Reformation and the Catholic Counter-Reformation again stressed the unique, incomparable truth of Christianity and its spiritual values. But that stress did not last. By the middle of the eighteenth century, the rationalism of the Enlightenment had triumphed in the intellectual world and classical antiquity was once again extolled as the most glorious period of human history (prior to the eighteenth century, of course). Christianity, the church, and the concept of a Christian civilization, were widely regarded as aberrations and roadblocks on man's upward path of progress. Such religious concepts were necessary for primitive man, but not, however, for the enlightened.

Gotthold Ephraim Lessing (1729-1781) is known to biblical scholars as the man who contributed to launching biblical higher criticism by publishing, as the anonymous *Wolfenbüttel Fragments*, the works of Hermann Samuel Reimarus (1694-1768). But Lessing did much more. He represented a high point of human self-confidence, not to say conceit, in his belief that modern man (in the late eighteenth century) had "come of age" and no longer needed any guidance from God or revelation. His *Education of the Human Race* appeared in 1780. Immanuel Kant (1724-1804), in *Religion Within the Limits of Reason Alone* (1793), presented all religion, including Christianity, as the logically necessary development of human reflection on duty and morals. He rehabilitated religion as valuable, but only as a guide and incentive to duty. The rationalism of the Enlightenment with its emphasis on the universality of all philosophical principles contrasts somewhat with the specifically literary and artistic movement called classicism, represented for example by the Germans Johann Wolfgang Goethe (1749-1832) and Friedrich Schiller (1759-1805). Both of those thinkers considered humanity the highest value and venerated pagan antiquity above Christianity, but they thought humanity needed to be perfected not by moral but rather by aesthetic and artistic education. Rather than the metaphysics and ethics of Greece, it was its art that inspired them. But both the Enlightenment and classicism had in common a high veneration for pagan antiquity and the confidence that the human race could raise itself by its own efforts. Both Goethe and Schiller passed from classicism into Romanticism and each wrote works in both styles.

When Romanticism began, particularly in Germany, it at first appeared to be a purely artistic and aesthetic movement with no interest in religion. Rather abruptly it underwent a dramatic transformation and became permeated with religious enthusiasm. German and British Romanticism began in Protestant circles, but soon spread to Roman Catholic ones and developed a tendency to idealize Catholicism; in addition, there were similar Romantic movements in the Catholic countries of Europe. As a literary movement, Romanticism was a phenomenon, not a philosophy. There were two distinct currents in the Romantic movement; as A.S.P. Woodhouse describes them, "One is radical, and . . . still traces its inheritance in considerable degree to the eighteenth century. The other is conservative, and reacts against that inheritance in two ways: first, by an appeal to history, not forgetting the Middle Ages. . . ; and, secondly, by the demands for a new philosophical approach to the questions of evaluation and belief."[1] Romanticism is not a school, and as such it does not have doctrines or a statement of faith. It is both a milieu and an attitude; where the influence of the milieu is pervasive, it even

---

1. A.S.P. Woodhouse, *The Poet and His Faith. Religion and Poetry in England from Spenser to Eliot and Anden* (Chicago and London: U. of Chicago, 1965), p. 168.

affects those who do not share any fundamental Romantic attitudes. Particularly in Germany, some of the outstanding Romantic figures, such as Friedrich Schiller and Friedrich Hölderlin, began (like the great philosophers Fichte, Hegel, and Schelling) as students of theology. The most noted Romantic among the theological students who actually went on to become a theologian was, of course, Friedrich Daniel Ernst Schleiermacher (1768-1834). He will receive particular attention from us. If Hulme calls Romanticism spilt religion, we may say that Schleiermacher is spilt theology. The fact that Schleiermacher is the great Romantic theologian should make evangelicals approach the whole Romantic movement with some caution.

The German Romantics were more flamboyant than the English—perhaps because in their day the English had the British Empire on which to expend their creative energy, whereas the Germans had only the realm of the spirit. The German Romantics appear to us more religious than the English, but their religion is even less frequently identifiable as Christian.

A DESCRIPTION OF ROMANTICISM

Romanticism is such a complex and elusive movement that we hesitate to define it and shall limit ourselves to trying to describe it. Romanticism interests us because of the new interest it brought to religion, to the church, to biblical and Christian history, and ultimately to the Bible. However, we must approach it carefully, for it was less a friend to true religion than merely a foe of some of the things that were and are hostile to religion. Although Romanticism was a Continent-wide movement and many of its best-known figures wrote in English, we shall look most closely at some of the German Romantics, particularly because it was German Romanticism through Schleiermacher that influenced later Protestant theology. As we have noted, although Romanticism was not religious when it began, it quickly became so. Friedrich Schlegel (1772-1829) wrote, "You are amazed by our age, by its gigantic ferment, and know not what new birth to expect? The resurrection of Religion!"

Romanticism was less a movement in favor of religion than an artistic-literary movement that became religious. Why did it do so? Because its leaders perceived religion as an invaluable asset in their worship of art. In a relatively old but valuable study, Hoxie N. Fairchild indicates that much of the sympathy Romanticism appeared to display for religion was at heart nothing but an attack on something else, namely on reason, which it perceived as the common enemy of beauty and of art. The fact that in attacking reason they expressed approval for religion was secondary:

> The desire to restore the warmth and mystery of religion took several forms, of which the common element is hostility to analytical reason. Logic had left its proper domain of science to invade the dim land ruled by intuition. The time for revelation had come: faith must not only defend its own boundaries but must wage aggressive warfare against the hairsplitting dialectic which dares to oppose the alliance of the natural with the supernatural.[2]

As Fairchild indicates, the Romantic concern was not with religion as an expression of truth, but with its warmth and mystery. There may well be both warmth and mystery in Christian truth, but these are not its most precious and important characteristics.

Although it began with that negative motive—hostility to barren rationalism and mechanism—there was also a positive interest in things that are in themselves an important part of biblical religion. There was an interest in the importance of the individual, particularly of the heroic individual, and an interest in history, particularly (but not only) in the grand design of biblical history.

> A conspicuous Romantic tendency, after the rationalism and decorum of the Enlightenment, was a reversion to the stark drama and suprarational mysteries of the Christian story and doctrines and to the violent conflicts and abrupt reversals of the Christian inner life, turning on the extremes of destruction and creation, hell and heaven, exile and reunion, death and rebirth, dejection and joy, paradise lost and paradise regained.[3]

All that is undeniable, easily verifiable from countless works of the period, and frequently asserted by scholars and critics. But what bearing does it have on the specific problems of sin and salvation, the knowledge of God, and, more particularly, of the inspiration and authority of Scripture, which is our special concern in these pages? Christ is the noblest of human figures, but He is not a hero in the Romantic sense. It is necessary to acknowl-

2. Hoxie Neale Fairchild, *The Noble Savage. A Study in Romantic Naturalism* (New York: Columbia U., 1928), pp. 413-14.
3. M. H. Abrams, *Natural Supernaturalism. Tradition and Revolution in Romantic Literature* (London: Oxford U., 1971), p. 66.

edge that Romanticism is a literary and cultural current that is indeed related to the great spiritual movements of its day, but we must also see that it is only tangential to them and is neither their cause nor their consequence; certainly it is not their equivalent.

Even a superficial acquaintance with the literature of Romanticism will make it apparent to us that the movement is both an asset and a liability in the struggle of biblical faith with scepticism. It is an asset in that it wakens and fosters a degree of emotional sensitivity and personal engagement that is highly compatible with the life of faith, and in that it affirms the significance of spiritual values, personal commitment, beauty, and love. But it is also a liability in that it considers those things largely as categories and as vehicles for artistic expression, rather than as concrete, objective realities related to objective and unique truths.

We are familiar with the slogan *l'art pour l'art.* Art is the highest value, it is its own purpose. Even as we acknowledge the religious impulse in Romanticism, we have to say that for most Romantic poets and writers, it was there for the sake of something else—*la réligion pour l'art.* Of what use to true religion is a defense of religion that accepts it, even exalts it, not for the sake of its content or its possible truthfulness, but because it enhances an artistic effect? It is rather like joining a church with a particularly eloquent pastor because one desires to have a nice funeral; it is not that funerals should not be nice, but that the effect that will be made by the sermon at one's funeral is of trivial significance compared to what true religion is meant to secure for the departed—eternal life. In short, we must say that even as we are moved by the religious fervor of so many Romantics, we must acknowledge that for all too many, all they seek in religion is to be *moved*, not to be *saved*.

RELIGIOUS ELEMENTS

One literary scholar, H. G. Schenk, entitles a major chapter in his book *The Mind of the European Romantics* "Christian Revival: Promise and Unfulfilment."[4] He speaks of "the Romantic attempt

4. H. G. Schenk, *The Mind of the European Romantics* (London: Constable, 1966), part 3.

to revive Christianity" and offers as an example the youthful Saxon Protestant and engineer Friedrich von Hardenberg, better known as Novalis (1772-1801). But the "return" of Novalis to Christianity is at best ambiguous. Like many other Romantics, he was influenced by the writings of Jakob Boehme (1575-1624), a mystic with strong pantheistic tendencies. Novalis rejected the Enlightenment as sterile and spoke, glowingly, of "a new history, a new humanity, the sweetest embrace of a young, astonished church and a loving God, the inner conception of a new Messiah in her thousand members at once. The Newborn will be the image of his Father, a new, golden age with dark, endless eyes . . . taken up into the inmost parts of the tempestuous love."[5]

Is he speaking of revival? The language of Novalis is certainly not that of the Enlightenment or of rationalism, but although its mood may be closer to that at a sermon by John Wesley than that at a lecture by Immanuel Kant, one cannot claim he is thinking of the Great Awakening. Friedrich Schlegel, too, wanted to found a new religion. A typical Romantic, he saw himself as the new religion's hero and none too modestly claimed to be capable of preaching like Luther, conquering like Mohammed, and dying like Christ.[6] Novalis, less pretentious, appealed to the Bible and its history, rather than to himself. But it is not clear that he thought Scripture any more than a symbolic representation of man's quest for freedom, of the tragedy of his rebellion and subsequent alienation. For Novalis, religion and Christianity were identical; that is to say, he was not interested in the dogmatic content of Christianity, which distinguishes it from the other religions, but in its effects. The remarkable Boehme, whose works were very much in vogue with the Romantics, had called paganism "undeveloped Christianity," and for Novalis only the consistent atheist or materialist could be called a non-Christian. The Romantic among the theologians, Schleiermacher, also extolled Christianity as the universal or highest religion, within which every other possible religion could and should be accommodated. Schleiermacher's views were greeted with indignation by the orthodox, but it is Schleiermacher and not his orthodox opponents who have marked subsequent theology.

The Christ of the Romantics was a noble friend, a transfigured brother.[7] They could speak of the mystery of the unity of the two

5. Novalis, "Die Christenheit oder Europa," in *Gesammelte Werke* (Herrliberg-Zürich: Bühle, 1945), 5:28.
6. Richarda Huch, *Blütezeit der Romantik* (Leipzig: Haeffel, 1901), pp. 183-84.
7. Ibid., p. 194.

natures, divine and human; Caroline Schlegel (later married to Schelling), wife of Friedrich's brother August Wilhelm, saw Jesus as the symbol of androgyny, the unity of the two sexes. His mediatorial role was acknowledged, exalted, and sung, but it was one far different from that of Paul's "one Mediator between God and man" (1 Tim. 2:5). All things mediate: bread and wine, stones, flowers, man. That view is more neo-Platonic than biblical. Monotheistic Christianity, seen through the eye of the Romantic artist, becomes indistinguishable from pagan pantheism. Schenk speaks of Novalis as having been genuinely converted, and it is true that his posthumously published *Spiritual Songs* do sound a very evangelical note:

> Of the thousand happy hours
> That in life my lot become,
> May but one to me be faithful,
> One, when in a thousand pains,
> I discovered in my heart,
> Who it is who died for us.

Of Christ, Novalis writes, "With Him I first became human." Novalis was raised in a pietistic home and ought to have known what personal conversion is, but so it was with Schleiermacher, who admits explicitly pantheistic ideas into his major dogmatic text, *The Christian Faith* (1821).[8] A pietistic background certainly does not exclude a turn to pantheism. Contemporary Christians, such as Schenk, who admire the Romantics and think they rendered Christianity a helpful service, are willing to overlook pantheistic elements in Novalis's writings. On the basis of comments like those cited, Romantic admirers are willing to claim that Novalis came to a personal knowledge of Jesus Christ. That is certainly possible, but we must remember that Novalis was the most explicitly Christian of the early Romantics and also that one can interpret his Christian statements just as well as his pantheistic ones as poetic license.

If the Romantics were interested in the religious exaltation that Christianity could bring, they were also interested in other kinds of emotional experiences, and many turned to the occult, to horror, and to a world view like that of Gnosticism, which described the God of the Bible as evil. Among those Romantics, William Blake (1757-1827) is probably the most striking example, with his *Marriage of Heaven and Hell* (1793). Although the

8. Friedrich Schleiermacher, *Der Christliche Glaube*, ed. Martin Redeker (Berlin: De Gruyter, 1961), section 8, zusatz 2a, 1:57-58.

strange beauty of Blake's lyrics causes him to be listed among religious poets, and excerpts from his *Jerusalem* are often quoted in sermons and sung in churches, he is more a forerunner of Nietzsche and the "Christian atheism" of Thomas J. J. Altizer than of T. S. Eliot or Christian revival.

There also was a strong romantic interest in the devil, who was extolled as a hero, as well as in the demonic and sin; Lord Byron's *Don Juan* is a well-known case in point (George Gordon Byron, 1788-1824). The wife of Percy Bysshe Shelly (1792-1822), Mary Wollstonecraft Shelley (1797-1851), gave us the first modern horror story in *Frankenstein* (1818); she describes her hero as "the modern Prometheus," that is, as man against the gods.

ROMANTICISM'S IMPACT ON SCRIPTURE

The Romantic revival of interest in religion in general and in Christianity in particular contributed to breaking the momentary dominance that rationalism and scepticism had exercised over European culture; it may have made it easier for people to listen to the Christian message. But to the extent that it was equally as enthusiastic about myth and romance as it was about the history of Israel and the life of Christ, it did nothing at all to strengthen faith in the reliability of Scripture as the Word of God. The interest in the symbolism and mythology of all ancient peoples tended to reduce the Bible to the level of other religious writings.

Traditionally, the rise of Covenant, or Federal, Theology from the time of Johannes Cocceius (1603-1669) onward is given credit for having awakened interest in the history of the Old Testament as the working out of God's plan for His people in their history. Prior to that, the Old Testament was regarded more as a manual of religion. We must acknowledge that another powerful influence toward viewing the Bible as history and not merely as doctrine was the Romantic movement. One of the forerunners of Romanticism, Johann Gottfried Herder (1744-1803), a Lutheran pastor and general superintendent (bishop), extolled the beauty of the Bible and the religious and poetic genius of the Hebrew people in *On the Spirit of Hebrew Poetry* (1782). But the acclaim Herder sought to win for the Bible was hardly different from the enthusiasm the Romantics brought to the works of and about the legendary Irish hero Ossian.[9] In addition to the legendary Ossian, Ro-

9. During the 1760s the Scottish poet James Macpherson (1736-1796) published three volumes purporting to be translations of original works by the third-century Irish hero, but in large measure they were apparently his own composition.

mantic heroes were chosen from other ancient epics, genuine and fraudulent, and often enough they were not real heroes in the classical or medieval sense, but savages.[10]

THE BIBLE AS LITERATURE

The Romantic movement created great interest in the Bible as literature and consequently reduced it to one among many documents to be studied by scholars in comparative literature and religion. There can be little doubt that the influence of the Romantics, who were enthusiastic about the beauty and passion of Scripture and its "heroes" but indifferent to its truth claims, contributed substantially to the loss of a high view of Scripture in the nineteenth century. It was easier for Christians to oppose the outright scepticism of biblical critics who denigrated the Bible to a scissors-and-paste fabrication of some of the less cultivated representatives of ancient Near Eastern culture than it was to deal effectively with the destructive enthusiasm of the Romantics who admired it and glorified it, but for all the wrong reasons. Their glorification of the Bible was rather like that of Christ in the Old Saxon epic *Der Heiland* (*The Savior*, c. 830), which sought to make Christ acceptable to the Germanic tribes by presenting Him as a warrior chief with the apostles as His trusty blades. If the Bible could be damaged by placing it alongside other supposedly early documents, some genuine, some less so, and suggesting that it has no more authority than they do, it could also be reduced in influence by placing other documents alongside the Bible and implying that they have an authority similar to the Bible's.

LITERATURE AS THE BIBLE

Contemporary evangelicals are generally far more prudent than Herder and the Romantics and are not in danger of lowering the Bible to the level of mythical and legendary literature. On the other hand, there is a certain similar tendency among evangelicals today again to give religious value to mythology. Somewhat like the Romantics, who exalted literature that they thought emanated from the heroic, beautiful, savage dawn of mankind, many modern evangelicals exalt similar literature although they are perfectly aware that it is the product of one man's literary cre-

10. Lilian R. Furst on "The Romantic Hero," chapter 3 of her monograph *The Contours of European Romanticism* (London: Macmillan, 1979), pp. 40-41.

ativity. The most prominent examples are the Narnia and Perelandra cycles of C. S. Lewis (1896-1963) and the *Lord of the Rings*
trilogy of J. R. R. Tolkien (1892-1973).

If there was a Romantic tendency to adopt religion because it
was thought beautiful, there is the beginning of a modern evangelical tendency to adopt beauty and call it religion. The Narnia
and Perelandra cycles were acknowledged, but not intended, by
Lewis to be allegorical restatements of what he believed to be the
real events of the Fall and redemption of man. The danger in
exalting them as though they were somehow better than straightforward biblical exposition or doctrinal teaching lies in the implication that the truth alone, unless it is beautified by an appropriate literary or artistic embellishment, may not be enough. Inasmuch as the corpus of Lewis's religious fantasy is not large, there
is a tendency to bring in the Hobbit and the Rings cycle of Tolkien
as well. Tolkien's work is vastly more complicated than that of
Lewis, and it is really more on the scale of Ossian, as created or
recreated by Macpherson, than are Lewis's transparent allegories.
At the same time Tolkien, although a believing Roman Catholic,
carefully kept both explicit and symbolic Christian elements out
of his work. To use Lewis's fantasy to communicate Christianity,
as many evangelicals now do, may well be defensible because
Lewis himself acknowledged their distinctly Christian content
and meaning (although he denied that it was originally his intention to write Christian allegories). But to go on to use the works
of Tolkien and others, after the mine of Lewis's identifiably Christian material has been worked out, may be akin to the Romantic
substitution of literary imagination for biblical inspiration. To
oppose the Christian use of art and fantasy may be too pietistic or
puritanical, but a measure of caution is indicated, as the enthusiastic excesses of the religious spirits among the Romantics show.

An example of the way in which even the most Christian of the
Romantics could develop his religious emotions without reference
to what Scripture actually says is given by one of Novalis's *geist-
liche Lieder* (spiritual songs), written shortly before his premature death. In "Wenn all untreu werden" he writes,

> When all others become faithless
> To Thee I'll faithfull stay,
> That gratitude on earth,
> Not fully pass away.

Novalis was almost certainly aware that his hymn echoes Peter's
boast in Matthew 26:33, and of course he knew that immediately
after making it Peter was overcome by terror and denied Jesus.

Novalis's song has a worthy purpose, but it needs to reckon with the Bible's realistic understanding of human nature and human psychology.

SCHLEIERMACHER'S BIOLOGY AND HERMENEUTICS

The Romantics were attracted to religion, to the sweep of biblical history, to the drama, passion, and sentimentality of the story of Jesus; they could readily identify with the language of the Roman Catholic mystics or the Protestant pietists in speaking of the "tender Jesus" and of his "sweet wounds." They were not attracted to the Scripture as such, and certainly not to Protestant orthodoxy. (As we have already noted, the Romantics were also attracted to the occult, to evil, and even to Satan; they were interested in what excited the emotions and stimulated the imagination of the artist, not in what one must do to be saved.) In contrast to their comparative disdain for Protestantism with its dry dogmatism—which was particularly dry before and during the Enlightenment—many Romantics, even the Protestants such as Novalis, were drawn to the veneration of Mary, to the Middle Ages, and to the image of the monastic life (there was, of course, no tendency to practice the monastic virtues of chastity or obedience, although many of the Romantics, willingly or not, had the opportunity to practice poverty). Nevertheless, there was hardly any more genuine interest in orthodox Roman Catholicism and its doctrines than in orthodox Protestantism.

Most of the Romantics we can consult were literary figures; several began as students of theology, but most ended as poets or philosophers. What about the towering figure who did continue as a professional theologian—the passionate preacher, university professor, and friend of the "converted" Novalis, Friedrich Schleiermacher? Was he more faithful to Scripture? How did he deal with it?

Those questions have more than a merely literary interest, for Schleiermacher accomplished three things of great, if baleful, significance for Christianity and for theological education: (1) in his spectacularly successful early work *Lectures on Religion to Its Cultured Despisers* (1799) he succeeded in making religion attractive, or at least socially acceptable, among people who no longer took the Bible and its doctrines seriously, by showing how it could appeal to and fulfill man's aesthetic sensitivities; (2) by so doing he attracted to the study of theology countless young men who were interested in religion primarily as an expression of man's imaginative spirit, and who without Schleiermacher's stimulus might have studied comparative literature or art instead, areas of study in which they would have caused the church less harm; (3) perhaps most significant of Schleiermacher's accomplishments was to change, at least for some time, biblical criticism from the historical analysis with which it had begun to a literary analysis similar to that which one would apply to Shakespeare or Goethe's *Faust*. In studying *Hamlet*, one is not interested in the extent to which Shakespeare has accurately portrayed a real incident from Danish history, nor in *Faust* in whether Faust's agreement with Mephistopheles is historically verifiable. Schleiermacher deliberately introduced psychology—the attempt to understand the minds of the putative authors, as well as psychological reflection on the subjective impression the authors make on the reader.

In the light of that fundamental shift of perspective in hermeneutics from the attempt to interpret the message to an attempt to understand and empathize with the messengers, Schleiermacher's actual treatment of the Bible is of less importance. By accepting subjective factors such as taste and religious sense as valid sources of religious knowledge and as the appropriate means of authenticating religious teachings, Schleiermacher effectively destroyed the Reformation principle of *sola Scriptura*. In an important way Schleiermacher's attack on *sola Scriptura* was worse than the familiar Roman Catholic practice of placing "holy tradition" alongside the Bible (or even above it, as the Reformers charged). Christian tradition, despite its vagaries, was mostly the product of Christian minds and of Christians attempting to construct their lives in obedience to Christ. Taste, by contrast, did not originate with Scripture or the church; in fact, the arbiters of taste through the centuries have generally tended to look down upon the pious as uncultivated and boorish. Suddenly to accept the canons of taste and sensitivity, as defined for the most part by unbelieving Romantic poets and artists, was to introduce a factor potentially far less compatible with Christianity than was the bulk of church tradition.

In his actual treatment of the text of Scripture, Schleiermacher was relatively conservative. That is to say, he did not approach the Bible with the radically sceptical attitude that had been pioneered by Reimarus and was coming into vogue in his own era. For example, Schleiermacher defended the apostolic authorship of several disputed biblical books, such as the gospel of John and 1 John, as well as 1 Peter, although he denied it to 2 and 3 John, to Revelation, and to 2 Peter.[11] On the other hand, he did not show the restraint of some of his theological colleagues about propagating sceptical ideas among the Christian public. Learned theological books were still frequently written in Latin, and at least some sceptical theologians, whether hypocritically or out of a genuine concern not to upset simple Christians, presented their destructive theories in forms that were hardly accessible to the general public. When Schleiermacher attacked the apostolic authorship of 1 Timothy, he created the first real breach in the integrity of the New Testament and, despite the criticism of a colleague, published his attack in German, to make it more available to the laity.[12]

Schleiermacher seemed to have been rather oblivious to the kind of havoc that undermining the authority of the New Testament text could wreak among the general public, and that insouciance was probably natural in the light of his own conviction that the value of religion lies in its aesthetic quality, not in the historical reliability of its documents. Because he was interested in creativity and the imagination, he could be as enthusiastic about the imagination of the interpreter as about the imagination of the biblical authors—the latter usually being harder to evaluate, because of the nature of Scripture. Perhaps Schleiermacher's approach helps to explain how the wild flights of imaginative fancy in interpreting texts became more common and acceptible in biblical studies—and to some extent still are —than in the secular study of contemporaneous historical and literary documents. Schleiermacher imported "creativity" as a canon into biblical studies. As a result a scholar today can still get away with uncontrolled speculation in the religious area that would be ridiculed as absurd or pitiable even in so free-wheeling an area as comparative literature. It would be an exaggeration to attribute the development of biblical studies since Schleiermacher's day solely or even primarily to his influence, but it seems fair to note that in introducing the new criterion of creativity he did more to transform the nature of biblical studies than did any of his predecessors.

The modern readers of Schleiermacher's *Introduction to the New Testament* will discover that his position resembles that of many moderately conservative scholars today. There is no radical

11. Friedrich Schleiermacher, *Einleitung in das Neue Testament*, in *Werke*, vol. 3 (Berlin: Reimer, 1845), sections 84, 91-97, 109.
12. Friedrich Schleiermacher, *Über den ersten Brief Pauli an Timotheus*, (Braunschweig, Reuter, 1898), pp. iii-iv, 124-25.

questioning of early church traditions, no blanket denial of the authenticity of the New Testament texts, no a priori assertion that the texts cannot be considered reliable history. Principles of criticism are admitted as the necessary expression of intellectual honesty in a critical age. He makes moderate concessions to rationalism and historical scepticism, while recognizing, on the whole, the bulk of the historical record as authentic. But Schleiermacher has put the whole Bible slightly out of focus; one can no longer rely on individual details. (The old Reformation practice of establishing doctrines on the basis of individual *sedes doctrinae* (prooftexts) is entirely reasonable if one believes in plenary inspiration and inerrancy, respects the context, and uses sound principles of hermeneutics, as orthodox Protestants sought to do. It would have been compatible with the rationalistic analysis of the Enlightenment era, *if* the leading minds of the period had been willing to accept the presupposition that the Bible is inerrant propositional revelation, which they were not.)

Of course Schleiermacher did not accept the Bible as literally true, propositional revelation, but it was not so much that he contested that view as that he substituted another as more plausible, more appealing, and in much better taste. As the Latin proverb has it, *De gustibus non disputandum est*—"there's no disputing tastes." It is extremely difficult to argue with Schleiermacher's position or to refute it with rational arguments. That is not because rational arguments, such as those used by old Protestant orthodoxy, the nineteenth-century Princeton school, or modern defenders of inerrancy such as Francis Schaeffer, John W. Montgomery, and Norman Geisler are not valid, but because they are simply dismissed out of hand as "too rationalistic" and hence entirely uninteresting. Indeed, that aesthetic disdain for the rationalism of the orthodox is shared by a number of relatively conservative evangelicals in our own day, and it may be the door through which a Schleiermacherian approach will enter evangelicalism.

Schleiermacher makes his disdain for rational analysis clear when he defines hermeneutics as "the art of understanding, not the presentation of that which is understood."[13] Although traditional Protestant hermeneutics, as Schleiermacher notes, relied on sound common sense (as well as on the Holy Spirit, which he neglects to mention), he contends that one can also rely on

13. Friedrich Daniel Ernst Schleiermacher, *Hermenentic und Kritik. Mit einem Anhang sprachphilosophischer Texte Schleiermachers*, ed. Manfred Frank (Frankfurt: Suhrkamp, 1977), p. 75.

"healthy feeling"—we might even say on "good taste." He stress-es the psychological and artistic elements of interpretation: one must be able to feel what the author felt and to apply a like or new creativity to the topic. The historical-grammatical is almost incidental. With such an approach to interpretation, Schleier-macher's relative conservativism about accepting the authenticity of the bulk of the New Testament text is of little value.[14]

Schleiermacher's approach to biblical criticism is basically that of literary criticism. By this we do not mean source criticism per se, but rather treatment of the Bible as literature and interac-tion with it as a Romantic critic would interact with Shakespeare in an effort to produce a fresh triumph of the artistic imagina-tion. In Schleiermacher's approach we see the full implications of "studying the Bible as literature." The Bible *is* literature in the descriptive sense, but it is not solely the product of human artistic creativity, and to interact with it as though it were such is com-pletely to misunderstand it and to falsify its message. In his approach to Scripture, Schleiermacher really never went beyond aesthetics.

Although Schleiermacher wrote major volumes on both dog-matics and ethics, it is important to note that neither the doctrine of inspiration nor the specific doctrinal and moral teachings of Scripture play an important role in the volumes. One can say that Schleiermacher simply develops, in a systematic way, not what the Scripture says but rather what his feelings and sense of taste tell him is best in Christianity, the best of religions. His impor-tance to the history of Protestant theology and to the way in which theologians deal with Scripture has more to do with the mood he created and with the method—or non-method—of his approach to Scripture than with any specific doctrine he advocat-ed. A great American conservative theologian, A. H. Strong, speaks approvingly of Schleiermacher as having "freed theology from the toils of rationalistic criticism." Unfortunately Strong did not fully recognize the degree to which Schleiermacher "freed" theology from rationalism only to banish it onto the misty marshes and soggy swamps of Romantic sentimentality and emo-tionalism.

14. A major European library with an extensive Schleiermacher collection, the Basel Universitäts—und Kantonalbibliothek, lists many monographs and ar-ticles on his aesthetics, his pedagogy, his psychology, and his preaching, but none on his use of Scripture.

CONCLUSION: ROMANTICISM'S IRRATIONALISM

The topic "Romanticism and the Bible" now appears almost as elusive as the famous "blue flower" to which Novalis's hero Heinrich von Ofterdingen devoted a life-long but fruitless search. Unlike Heinrich, we shall not pursue it for the rest of our lives, but we shall attempt an evaluation of Romanticism on the basis of what we have ascertained. Romanticism was defined as "spilt religion," and we have taken the liberty of calling Schleiermacher's work "spilt theology." In conclusion, we may observe that to have something and spill it may be more dangerous than not to have it at all. Whatever positive things the Romantic movement may have contributed to Protestant theology are certainly undermined if not totally demolished by its legacy of irrationalism. Christianity is not rationalistic; it is and must remain rational, and to attack rationality because it can threaten faith is to give Christianity only a very temporary relief from the assaults of scepticism.

Romanticism, as we have seen, represented a rebellion against what it considered a sterile rationalism. The reaction struck out not merely at the sterility of self-confident rationalism, but against the analytical use of reason itself. Though not a Romantic poet, Archibald MacLeish expressed this sentiment with his oft-quoted line "A poem does not mean, a poem is." For the Romantic, the Bible, even when he exalts it, does not *mean* at all, not in the sense that it can be rationally analyzed and broken down into a series of doctrinal and moral teachings; it merely *is*. It *is*—to be experienced, felt, inspired by, mused over, and sung (not, of course, to be *believed* in the traditional Christian sense). The Romantic revival may have rehabilitated the concept of religion and brought it back into the literary salons of the day, but it was no more congenial to a rational understanding and application of Scripture than it was to the humanistic rationalism of the Enlightenment. To the extent that European Romanticism helped create the intellectual atmosphere within which nineteenth-century German theology arose, we can say that its contribution is outweighed by the confusion it fostered. Religion, even Christianity, may in some sense be Romantic, but Romanticism is a far cry from biblical religion.

3. Liberalism: The Challenge of Progress

D. Clair Davis

Background

Study of the Protestant "liberal" approach to Scripture must begin with some consideration of the phenomenon of liberalism itself. Although frequently the term has been applied to any Protestant religious movement that calls into question the basic doctrines of evangelical Christianity (from the Enlightenment down to the present day), more specifically it refers to the attempt, which prevailed in Europe and America from the mid-nineteenth century until World War I, to harmonize the Christian faith with all of human culture. That movement was a reaction to the alleged "monastic" or pietistic, introspective Romanticism of the philosopher Immanuel Kant and the theologian Friedrich Schleiermacher. It included a host of literary and artistic leaders who hoped to utilize an aesthetic appreciation of Christianity as a means to escape the near-elimination of religion and morality that the sterile mathematical rationalism of the eighteenth century had brought about. Romanticism had "saved Christianity" at the terrible cost of depriving it of its relevance to civilization. In particular the relegation of Christianity to the realm of aesthetic feeling and personal morality effectively removed it from the

D. Clair Davis, B.A., M.A., Wheaton College; B.D., Westminster Theological Seminary; Th.D., Georg-August Universität, Göttingen, West Germany, is professor of church history at Westminster Theological Seminary, Philadelphia, Pennsylvania. He has served as editor of the *Westminster Theological Journal.*

realm of history, where nineteenth-century man was convinced middle class progress could be seen in all its glory.

Liberalism then was virtually the same thing as what has come to be more popularly known as "civil religion" *(Kulturprotestantismus)*, the casual blending of the Kingdom of God with human aspirations toward peace and progress. From this broader point of view it is apparent that the German and the American phenomena of the same period were strikingly similar. How easy it also was for Americans to identify the causes of slavery abolition and alcoholic beverage temperance with the Kingdom—and to be absolutely sure, even when Scripture remained silent, about "what Jesus would have done."

REJECTION OF ROMANTICISM

Liberalism resisted the easy answer of Romanticism, the compartmentalization of religion and the culture of modern science, and took up anew the head-on challenge of the Enlightenment, which demanded that the new way of looking at the world (that truth after all was one) necessitated a new religion to correspond to that way. Although his influence was diverse, in many ways the philosopher of liberalism was Georg W. F. Hegel (1770-1831). His commitment to unity in thought through the identity of the rational and the historical did much to explode the old dichotomy of the rational/mathematical/static on the one hand and the romantic/dynamic/progressive on the other.

Although the entire post-Reformation era was identified with the belief in historical movement, it could hardly be called a belief in progress. The spirit of Romanticism was after all one of return to the kernel of the unspoiled primitive by the removal of later institutional accretions. Therefore Romanticism's historical movement was actually not one of progress, but of retrogression. That is perhaps seen most clearly in Romanticist biblical criticism: the primitive faith of J and E was clearly to be preferred to the later D and P; Jesus versus Paul was hardly a contest; and the syncretism of Luke-Acts in turn was clearly inferior to the forthrightness of either Peter or Paul.

IDEALISM AND CULTURE

But the liberal spirit wished to move forward, not backward. Here Hegel used the tool of the dialectic, by which the accomplished synthesis became at once the new thesis, in which no static institutionalism could be possible in a universe of constantly arising new challenges. The essence of history, of civilization, and of Christianity was to be the process itself, which for vulgar consumption was the most up-to-date expression of the Prussian spirit. That philosophical Babbittry was ideally suited to the purposes of the great founder of theological liberalism, Albrecht Ritschl (1822-1889). He was convinced that Christianity could not be equated with any narrow mystical or pietistic vision but had to be seen from the perspective of the interaction of the two foci of the Christian ellipse, the concerns of society and civilization as well as those of personal salvation. A proper usage of the Bible, then, could not be confined to just the question of how it brings me personal salvation but must also correlate with larger concerns.

IMPLICATIONS FOR SCRIPTURE

How did that theological setting influence the practical approach to Scripture, in particular the question of its inspiration? It must first be observed that for liberalism the question was no longer one of whether or not there are errors in the Bible, that is, whether or not the teaching of Scripture and the newly discovered truths of modern thought could be harmonized. Such questions and their negative answers were considered long settled. The doctrine of verbal inspiration was simply regarded as a seventeenth-century viewpoint, understandable in its day but long since untenable. Just as Kant had introduced his Copernican revolution by rejecting the question of *if* knowledge is possible and replacing by one of *how* knowledge is possible, so also liberalism did not even entertain the question of the historical or scientific reliability of the Bible, but only how the Bible in its assumed inaccuracy could be utilized.

Romanticism in its exaltation of the primitive could attempt to get back to prescientific faith and accept it as it was, for religious validity had little to do with scientific validity. But liberalism was concerned with the historical process in its unity, not merely in evaluating its specific stages. Consequently liberalism was concerned not merely with scientific progress, but most important of all with cultural progress, and hence with the progress of religion, of Christianity itself. Liberalism then sought not to penetrate *behind* the editorial accretions of the Bible but rather to discover how the church had gone *beyond* the religion of its founders. First it asked how the church had gone beyond within the New Testament itself. In this regard the movement beyond Jesus to Paul was viewed as a necessary and helpful one. Second, liberalism considered with the same appreciation and respect what it saw as a similar development within the postcanonical church. As Barth has spoken of Hegel—that in his method there can be no pause for breath for science, since there never are assured results—so also is that true for theology, as it ever presses on to an interaction with the march of culture and science.[1]

GERMAN LIBERALISM

ALBRECHT RITSCHL

Ritschl's methodology is most simply and instructively presented in his greatest work, *The Christian Doctrine of Justification and Reconciliation*, in a transition section between his study of the history of church doctrine and his exegetical work. There he discusses the questions of the authority of Scripture in theology and the nature of a biblical theology. He first analyzes the value of a doctrine of inspiration from the Protestant hermeneutical perspective of Scripture interpreting itself. He states that first of all the question of canonicity must be determined. (This may be one of the first descriptions in theology of the now well-known "hermeneutical circle.") He then states that the criterion of apostolicity is of little value, for not only did most apostles not write, but several New Testament books are not by apostles, and some apostolic books, James and Hebrews, are not of that much value to the church anyway.

Even more significant, though, is that the Bible can be employed only for theology and basic morality, but not in the details of life because of the change in the position of Christianity in society.[2]

At any rate, the question of what are the earliest writings was not the primary criterion for determining the theological usability of the Scripture. In the Old Testament it is clear, says Ritschl, that the prophets represent a unique development, of a higher level than the earliest writings. Conceivably the early writings in the New Testament could be unduly influenced by Gnosticism, as Ritschl argued in his *Rise of the Old Catholic Church*. Such elements would not present the religion based upon the heart of the

---

1. Karl Barth, *Protestant Theology in the Nineteenth Century* (London: SCM, 1972), p. 413.
2. Albrecht Ritschl, *Die christliche Lehre von der Rechtfertigung und Versöehnung* (Bonn: Adolph Marcus, 1882), 2:12.

Old Testament and would not need to be utilized theologically.[3]

If the binding elements of the Bible can be recognized by their content, then the doctrine of verbal inspiration is no longer of any value or necessity. Ritschl then seeks to show how such an approach has always been true of Lutheranism, in distinction from Calvinism. Calvin held to the doctrine of double predestination because he found it in Paul, even though he himself regarded it as an impractical doctrine. Calvin accepted church discipline and the parity of elders simply because he found it in biblical descriptions of early Christianity. Pietism has held that the New Testament social relationships are still binding on the church. The Bengel emphasis in Pietism has even made the Millennium and the early Christian emphasis on the imminent return of Christ the conclusion of theology, just because those doctrines are found in the last book of the Bible. Ritschl tells us that we need only to observe the collapse of Calvinism and Pietism's lack of direction in order to know that the Lutheran way is the proper one.[4]

Ritschl turns in conclusion to the relation of this approach to the doctrine of justification, the main subject of his major book. He notes that the doctrine of justification by faith alone is the heart of Protestantism but that there have always been those in the church whose faith has been based upon James or John, who will always remain behind the ideal of Lutheranism. So the church and her theology will always have a certain view of history determined for them in advance. But what Christians now understand as the background for justification is their own moral imperfection—not the same as Paul's doctrine, which was formulated against the background of Pharisaic legalism.[5]

For Ritschl that now makes clear the relation of theology to the Bible. One cannot determine in advance if the Bible does support this foundational element of Protestantism. One cannot determine what aspects of New Testament teaching are useful for theology. Rather there must be an "experimental comparison" of New Testament doctrines to which the Protestant and also Pietist understanding of justification must be added. A simple reproduction of scriptural teaching, if it goes against all of church history, is an insufficient substitute for a dogmatic theology. At least in the area of the application of redemption the Christian life has outgrown the perspective of the New Testament writers. A valid

3. Ibid., 2:16.
4. Ibid., 2:19.
5. Wilhelm Herrmann, *The Communion of the Christian with God*, trans. J. Sandys Stanton (Philadelphia: Fortress, 1971), p. 24.

approach to theology must recognize its own limitations as it seeks results useful to the church.

As we leave the description of Ritschl's theological approach in relation to the use of the Bible, some preliminary evaluation is in order. It is clear that Ritschl makes every effort to dissociate himself from the notion that the way to understand a movement is to grasp the original intentions of its founders. Whereas it is the orthodox position on canonicity that he has primarily opposed, he also rejects Calvinistic, Anabaptist, Pietist, and eschatological overemphasis upon the details of the early church. Is it going too far to speculate that he may also have in mind the primitivism of all nineteenth-century Romantics? Although he certainly does endorse a normative role for the New Testament emphases that incorporate the most developed ideals of the Old Testament, the most striking of his emphases is that there is religious development within the Christian church also, going *beyond* the New Testament. That development must be taken account of, and not simply regarded as going against the Bible. Apparently the supremacy of Lutheranism over Calvinism, for example, can be seen in its comparative success in history.

According to Ritschl, evangelicals ought to examine their practical hermeneutics concerning how they *use* the Bible in their lives. To the extent that one emphasizes certain aspects or writers over others, to that extent one does not utilize the Bible as being completely inspired. It is apparent that with liberalism we have received a new challenge; no longer is it just a question of responding to this or that rationalist listing of scientific or historical problems in Scripture that bear upon a theory of inspiration, but from now on it is a question of how the church, evangelicals included, actually uses that Bible.

Is it sufficient to reply that Calvinism and Puritanism with their far-reaching attempts to make use of the entire Bible, are not such failures as Ritschl believes? Is it even true that it is possible to have a theology that does justice to Johannine elements as well as to Pauline justification?

It would appear that with Ritschl the answers to those questions are much too obvious and that his viewpoint betrays its provinciality throughout. It is certainly true, as he insists most vigorously, that the apostles are themselves members of the believing community, and that their letters have other purposes in addition to instructional. But the conclusion that, because this is so, their writings do not possess doctrinal authority, simply does not follow. Perhaps it is worth saying that there may well have been theologies that had as their ideal the avoiding of the practical and the devotional; but for Ritschl to assume that a theology has to be that way, and then to disqualify aspects of Scripture because of that, is extremely strange—especially because he wanted to call that process biblical theology.

WILHELM HERRMANN

Nevertheless, there is no question that Ritschlianism was an incredibly powerful movement, emphasizing as it did the dynamic and the historical movement of God and His Kingdom throughout human history. Certainly a meaningful faith must have relevance to the great concerns of the world in which we live. Christianity must again and again be appropriated as personal conviction, not merely as repetition of what was once significant but is now only unintelligible. Here was the continuing strength of the movement, seen in its greatest personal appeal in the writings of Wilhelm Herrmann (1846-1922), professor of theology at Marburg. Herrmann was the great teacher of both Barth and Bultmann—not to mention of J. Gresham Machen, the intellectual leader of American evangelicalism in the early twentieth century.

For his distinctive development within the liberal school, one can do no better than to work through his most influential work, *The Communion of the Christian with God.* Early in this book he addresses one of the most complex of all theological issues, the manner of salvation. Herrmann did not wish to get entangled in a psychological analysis of conversion, with its "undesirable emphasis on human activity." How can a man appropriate doctrines "when these doctrines were the expression of a life that he lacked."[6] There is no question but that Herrmann has correctly identified a very real problem, as any student of the controversies over "preparation for grace" (particularly in the New England theology) must be aware. Herrmann's solution was not to have anything to do with the problem as usually described (how can a sinner come to know something which is not his own?). Instead he affirmed, "The thoughts of others who are redeemed cannot redeem me. If I am to be saved, everything depends on my being transplanted into the inner condition of mind in which such thoughts begin to be generated in myself, and this happens only when God lifts me into communion with Himself."[7]

Herrmann then goes on to state that one does not become a

6. Ibid., pp. 41-42.
7. Ibid., p. 42.

Christian by submitting to some doctrines but by recognizing the great fact of Jesus. Faith in the doctrines about Him cannot be demanded as the prerequisite for salvation by Jesus, but rather as the result of that salvation. Only that which transforms a person can constitute a saving fact. The only objective ground for the truth of Christianity is one's moral transformation, when doing right ceases to be a problem for him and becomes the atmosphere in which he lives. One does not become a Christian when he tries to think thoughts not his own, for this is a form of legalism that denies the whole Reformation principle of justification by faith alone. The results of modern biblical criticism are therefore helpful because they show clearly how foreign certain biblical teaching is to our world, and thereby enable us to focus on that relation to Jesus that alone is needful.[8]

By way of preliminary summary and evaluation, we may say Herrmann believes that knowledge of one's inability to accept scriptural teaching frees the person from the impossible task of securing salvation through the works-righteousness of attempting to believe things that are at best incomprehensible to him. Perhaps that may be paraphrased by saying one is not required to become a supranaturalist in general as a prior commitment to his trust in the glorified Christ; one is not required first to change his world view before trusting in Christ. Gullibility is not the foundation of faith. In response, we may say there has been a variety of Christian apologetic that Herrmann is portraying fairly accurately. It gave great weight to the supernatural events recorded in Scripture as the attestation for the credibility of Christ's teaching, including that teaching concerning Himself. It was hardly mentioned that the reason for those supernatural events was the salvation of sinners, and that the events' extraordinary character was necessary to respond adequately to the radical effect that sin had had upon mankind. It could fairly be said that there is an element of truth in Herrmann's response to such an apologetic. Certainly he was correct in seeing that it may undermine the very message it intends to support.

However, Herrmann's solution hardly seems any better. It is not really clear if he believes that doctrinal affirmations about Christ are really necessary, or, strictly speaking, even correct. If he has been right methodologically in rejecting the old "common sense" apologetic, it does not at all mean that he has provided anything approaching a recognizable biblical Christ. Has he not

8. Ibid., pp. 52-53, 72, 76, 223-37.

thrown the baby out with the bathwater, the historical content of the faith along with a pseudohistorical methodology?

Herrmann was interested in more than personal faith, however. In harmony with the Ritschlian tradition, he was just as much concerned with the aims of a Christian society and was one of the moving spirits in the Christian socialist movement. As one would anticipate, his view of the Bible is even more easily seen as he sets out to relate its teaching to the demands of a rapidly changing world.

That is particularly true when modern man, with his hope for progress, encounters Jesus with his eschatological pessimism. We are forced to admit, says Herrmann, that we do not share His standpoint, that "we are not greatly affected by the idea of an approaching end of the world." Further, Jesus anticipated only ruin ahead, and therefore "in Him there was nothing of the zeal of the political and economic reformer." But Herrmann sees this realization not as a great loss for us, but instead a great gain.

> Endeavours to imitate Jesus in points inseparable from His especial mission in the world, and His position—which is not ours,—towards that world—efforts like these lacking the sincerity of really necessary tasks, have so long injured the name of Jesus, that our joy will be unalloyed when scientific study at last reveals to every one the impossibility of all such attempts.[9]

He sought to distance himself from those who conclude that Jesus' teaching is irrelevant for modern life, and who find that fact painful. For Herrmann:

> As a result of that frame of mind whereby we are united with him, we desire the existence of a national State, with a character and with duties with which Jesus was not yet acquainted; we will not let ourselves be led astray, even if in this form of human nature various features are as sharply opposed to the mode of life and standpoint of Jesus as is the dauntless use of arms.[10]

No doubt all Christians, with the exception of Anabaptist pacifists, have their difficulties with the harmonization of the Sermon on the Mount and long-range goals of reform, especially when it seems necessary to pursue those goals with military means. But it remained for Herrmann to make out of that apparent difficult

9. Adolph Harnack and Wilhelm Herrmann, *Essays on the Social Gospel*, trans. G. M. Craik (New York: Putnam, 1907), pp. 179-81.
10. Ibid., p. 217.

necessity a positive virtue. For him it is precisely through the inability of Scripture to supply answers to modern questions that we capture something of the mind of Christ and His freedom. Again, for liberalism it is not a matter of this or that particular Scripture difficulty that makes belief in verbal inspiration no longer possible, but rather modern man's whole situation of living in a totally different world from the world of Jesus and the Bible.

ADOLF VON HARNACK

Before leaving the arena of German liberalism we can best conclude with at least a passing glance at one whose influence lived on well into our own century, the great church historian of Berlin, Adolf von Harnack (1851-1930). His *What Is Christianity* certainly is the best known and most popular expression of the whole liberal movement. It presents in positive form the conclusions of his monumental *History of Doctrine*, which sought to demonstrate the great changes brought into Christianity through the utilization of Greek thought forms. Christianity is not a matter of correct doctrines (that idea is from the Greek influence) but of a total life involvement, Harnack says. Specifically, in his popular book he addresses himself to the question of the resurrection and the empty tomb. Because there is no way of constructing a clear account of the postresurrection appearances and no tradition that is quite trustworthy, either our faith rests upon a "foundation always exposed to fresh doubts" or we must seek another foundation for our faith. That foundation, says Harnack, does not come through one's speculative philosophical ideas but by the "feeling of his imperishable union with God." This is not demonstrable by logic, but is rather "the *act* of the freedom which is born of God."[11]

The same procedure is also true of the doctrine of the Person of Christ. Although Christ exhibits God's power and love, "to demand assent to a series of propositions about Christ's person is a different thing altogether."[12] Even more striking is Harnack's understanding of the proper treatment of the very teachings of Christ. With Paul, we must broaden the horizons of the faith "without being able to appeal to a single word of his master's . . . by the help of the spirit and with the letter against him." Christ's disciples broke through the husk of the Jewish limitations attach-

---

11. Adolf Harnack, *What Is Christianity?* trans. Thomas Bailey Saunders (New York: Putnam, 1923), p. 140.
12. Ibid., p. 159.

ing to Jesus' message, including His words "I am not sent but unto the lost sheep of the house of Israel."[13] But even Paul proclaimed certain Old Testament laws as still authoritative, and even when such laws are "inoffensive in substance, it was a menace to Christian freedom" that he did so both to freedom from within and also to the freedom of the community.[14]

The liberal pattern becomes familiar to us. What Harnack adds is his Hellenistic thesis and the more striking, clear statement that even in the apostolic age, out of Christian freedom it was necessary for the closest followers of Christ to contradict His specific teaching. Harnack intends this to be the example for the present day, when our knowledge of Christ's spirit demands that we contradict His words!

AMERICAN LIBERALISM

Nineteenth-century America presented strong social and political challenges to evangelicals and their Bibles, in particular to those who demanded the abolition of slavery and beverage alcohol. In both those cases, clear biblical teaching did not appear to be available, but at least one could appeal to "the spirit of Christ" to support one's convictions. That spirit seemed to vary, even for American evangelicals, according to one's increasing perception of what needed to be done. The question was not just the alcoholic content of biblical wine; rather it was how Christians should respond to the manifest evils arising from the consumption of alcohol. Perhaps the biblical teaching on slavery was equally ambiguous and even in favor of that institution; but nineteenth-century American Christians were capable of perceiving its obvious evil. The enormous popularity of Charles Sheldon's *In His Steps*, with its repeated question "What would Jesus have done?" is hardly different at all from German Romantic and liberal "psychologizing of Jesus." The cultural needs of the day, and the desire for Christians to have something specific to say in answer to those needs, could lead very easily to the same tendencies found in liberalism. That resulted in convictions on what Christianity *should* say serving as a means of avoiding what the Bible really did, or did not, say. Perhaps evangelical abolitionists accepted too uncritically the leadership of New England Unitarians and too easily rejected the exegesis of the Southern evangelical slaveholders.

13. Ibid., p. 155.
14. Ibid., p. 161.

Certainly if evangelicals were susceptible to such "psychologizing," it is not surprising to discover that American liberals (the proponents of "the social gospel") were even more adept at it. Just as German liberals had done, they hardly bothered to argue the nature of biblical authority; it was sufficient to observe that Christians as a matter of fact utilized Scripture as if it did not possess literal, ultimate authority. That a posteriori approach could then justify further, more radical applications of the now time-honored procedure.

WASHINGTON GLADDEN

Generally regarded as the "father of the social gospel" was Washington Gladden (1836-1918), Congregationalist pastor in Columbus, Ohio. With reference to the slavery question, he affirms that although there was no biblical legislation against it, "What Christianity did was to create a moral atmosphere in which slavery could not exist. Men have always been quoting the Bible on the side of slavery; but, while pettifogging theologians have been searching its pages for texts with which to prop their system, the spirit of the book has been steadily undermining the system."[15]

Gladden develops his position in a chapter entitled "How Much Is the Bible Worth?" There he dismisses the infallibility of the Scripture by referring to the history of the canon and the various readings in the differing manuscripts. Not only is the Bible fallible historically (there are "mistakes in dates and numbers and the order of events"), scientifically (because of the discrepancies with geology), but most to the point, it is fallible morally.

> The standards of the earlier time are therefore inadequate and misleading in these later times; and that any man who accepts the Bible as a code of moral rules, all of which are equally binding, will be led into the gravest errors. It is no more true that the ceremonial legislation of the Old Testament is obsolete than that large portions of the moral legislation are obsolete. The notions of the writers of these books concerning their duties to God were dim and imperfect; so were their notions concerning their duties to man. All the truth that they could receive was given to them; but there were many truths which they could not receive, which to us are as plain as daylight. Not to recognize the partialness and imperfection of this record in all these respects is to be guilty of a grave disloyalty to the kingdom of the truth.[16]

15. Washington Gladden, "Labor and Capital," in *The Social Gospel in America*, ed. Robert T. Handy (New York: Oxford, 1966), p. 39.
16. Gladden, "How Much Is the Bible Worth?" in *The Social Gospel*, p. 85.

Gladden continues by affirming that "laws which conformed to our moral ideal would have been powerless to control such a semibarbarous people as the Hebrews were when they came out of Egypt. The higher morality must be imparted little by little." In short, we are to follow the example of Christ in His approach to the Old Testament found in the Sermon on the Mount. "When we refuse to apply his method and go on to declare every portion of those old records authoritative, we are not honoring him."[17]

In replying to the dichotomy of the orthodox apologists, who claim that if the Bible is not accepted as absolutely inerrant, the only alternative is to treat it as if it were any other book, Gladden states that one cannot treat the Bible that way, but must come to it "with the expectation of finding in it wisdom and light and life. He must not stultify his reason and stifle his moral sense when he reads it; he must keep his mind awake and his conscience active; but there is treasure there if he will search for it." We are "to use the book rationally, but reverently; to refrain from worshipping the letter, but to rejoice in the gifts of the Spirit which it proffers."[18]

It is hardly necessary to attempt an exposition of such a popular work. It is worth noting, however, that Gladden will not go the final step with the German liberals. At least he does not explicitly contemplate the necessity of going beyond the teaching of Jesus, though perhaps an "awake mind" and "unstifled moral sense" could be extremely "creative" indeed. While he has some passing interest in the scientific and historical problems surrounding the Bible, clearly it is the moral issues that command his closest attention, reflecting the same concerns that aroused German liberalism in the same period.

WALTER RAUSCHENBUSCH

Final investigation of the liberal movement will concentrate on the Baptist church historian at Rochester (N.Y.) Theological Seminary, Walter Rauschenbusch (1861-1918). His approach is clear even in his earliest work, *The Righteousness of the Kingdom.* In responding to the argument that the apostles did not interfere in political or social questions, he takes up Paul's failure to tell Philemon that slavery was wrong.

> But, Paul notwithstanding, we have abolished slavery and hold it to be wrong. The same thing is going to be done with the social

17. Ibid., pp. 91, 95.
18. Ibid., p. 100.

questions now before us, and those who hide behind Paul's non-interference are again going to bring shame upon Christianity. Their guilt lies in making of Christianity a set of rules instead of a living spirit. The question is not what Paul did then, but what he would do now . . . He that adheres most strictly to Paul's rules of conduct will most fatally deny Paul's principles and spirit. His decisions on what was lawful and prudent to do are buoys which he anchored at the farthest points to which in his day the channel of the future had been explored. We shall use them best by keeping to the direction he marked out and passing beyond them, and not by padlocking our boat to his buoys.[19]

As the argument develops, it is important to note that Rauschenbusch is referring to Christians' responsibility in a democratic society, which responsibility they did not have under Nero's dictatorship. He protests that he also is committed to the "old gospel," but not that "we must express those eternal verities in the terminology of past ages and limit their application to those circumstances of life to which men in the past were by their historical condition compelled to limit them . . . We refuse to imprison the living Spirit even in its own words."[20]

As one examines Rauschenbusch's practical application of his principles to the goal of a more Christian society, particularly from the point of view of the late twentieth century, it is difficult to detect anything particularly startling. It is regrettable that he found it necessary to use the language customary in the Ritschlian movement.

POST-LIBERAL THOUGHT

Before any evaluation of the whole liberal movement can properly be attempted, some attention must be given to the subsequent development of theology. That is, an evangelical appraisal must take into account how nonevangelical theology responded to the liberal orientation. Generally liberalism was followed by a complex of theological directions to which these labels can be attached: neo-Kantian, eschatological, neo-orthodox. Subsequent development was neo-Kantian in that idealism was rapidly succeeded by a movement so similar to that which had gone before it that in retrospect it appeared to be merely a transitory parenthesis. Hegelianism and Ritschlianism seemed to be attempting too

19. Walter Rauschenbusch, *The Righteousness of the Kingdom* (Nashville: Abingdon, 1968), p. 167.
20. Ibid., p. 177.

much for modern man; in the unraveling of culture at the turn of the century it seemed unreasonable even to attempt such a tremendous synthesis of modern culture and Christianity. Not only was it intellectually too great a task, but it was also a denial of man's sinfulness to expect his proud culture to make peace with the gospel.

ALBERT SCHWEITZER

More specifically, New Testament scholarship, as led by William Wrede (1859-1900) and Albert Schweitzer (1875-1965), insisted that the eschatological elements in the teaching and expectations of Jesus were not being taken seriously. Jesus did not expect, they said, that society would find its answers in the march of human progress; rather He was convinced that that society was going to come completely to an end and then be replaced by the eschatological Kingdom of God. From the point of view of the consistent or radical eschatology, the whole liberal movement had had practically nothing to do with the Jesus of the Bible; instead, all it had done was to baptize conventional secular interests of the nineteenth century and assume that Jesus' spirit (not His words) was identical with one's own aspirations. From a truly biblical, eschatological perspective, there was very little difference between the old Romantic, "pietist," individualistic "psychologizing" of Jesus (reading His mind) and the liberal, culturally orientated "sociologizing" of Him. To be sure, Schweitzer had nothing positive to put in the place of the liberal Jesus but rather an unknown phantom striding through history—for obviously the Kingdom anticipated by Jesus did not come; but at least the dishonesty of liberalism had been made transparent. The positive replacement was to be neo-orthodoxy, which accepted the challenge of eschatology but saw in it the opportunity to reaffirm that Christian faith is *not* to be identified with human expectations, but is indeed God Himself breaking into and disrupting human history. Particularly when Nazi theologians attempted a synthesis of their views and the Bible, Barth and his followers emphasized even more vigorously that such endeavors were simply blasphemy.

DISPENSATIONALISM

There are many striking, though infrequently stressed, parallels between the nonevangelical repudiation of the liberal theology of cultural progress and the American/British evangelical repudiation of nineteenth-century evangelical postmillenialism.

Virtually all American evangelicals were at least implicitly post-millenial until the Civil War. (How many Congregationalist colleges pepper the Mid-Western landscape, all with some reference to Christ's Kingdom in their mottos!) But somehow Union victory did not lead to even a comparatively golden age, but rather to Mark Twain's gilded age, as political corruption, industrial robber barons, and new waves of not-easily-evangelized Catholic and Jewish immigrants gave rise to a different kind of America.

Against that background the theological orientation known as dispensationalism emerged. Although of course there are many roots of that theology, not the least of them new exegetical insights, there is no denying the timeliness of the movement. Although dispensationalists continued participation in the older reform movements of their predecessors (temperance, for example), it was clear that such activities were not to be identified with the Kingdom yet to come. Instead, the eschatological significance of this age was seen to be evangelism and missions (prophetic conferences had a definite missions orientation). Concretely, the ethical difficulties of the radical ethic of the Sermon on the Mount were resolved by referring its application to the age yet to come. In addition, the ethical demands of the New Testament that appeared to blur the "simple gospel" could readily be referred to a Jewish audience. Whatever one thinks today of the details of the dispensationalist program, there is no denying that it recognized that the great compelling need of the church in a changing age was a new understanding of the proper, specific hermeneutical principles. It was no longer enough just to say that Scripture interprets Scripture.

EVANGELICAL RESPONSE

With a basic historical orientation of the "Bible and culture" phenomenon in mind, how can the evangelical evaluate that movement? What will be the implications for his view of inerrancy of the Bible? First of all, he should be challenged by the dimensions of the issues. The evangelical world has been coming to see that "secular humanism" is a total challenge to the Christian faith, not a series of sniping operations on the periphery. The history of liberalism makes clear that an all-embracing doctrine of Scripture is needed. It must include not only an adequate statement of inspiration but also of the canon and hermeneutics. Such a doctrine should facilitate the appreciation of revelation in the differing epochs of redemptive history—in short, a biblical theology. Finally, some progress in the formulation of a Christian social ethic must be made; otherwise that unpaid debt will continue to haunt the church, in her doctrine as well as in her life.

CONSISTENT OBEDIENCE

The challenge for evangelicals will demand a response from all the theological disciplines, for liberalism did not just confront a *doctrine* of the Bible but was much more concerned with the *use* of the Bible. As the evangelical cause looks to its resources today, it should discover that it is precisely in the area needed that it has one of its greatest strengths, both theoretically and practically. That is the area of the communication of the gospel from one culture into another—missions. It is in missions that the evangelical church has been learning its lessons well, at least since the days of Hudson Taylor with his insistence that missionaries adapt as much as possible to their new culture, in order that the force of the gospel might not be blunted with Western ways. Whatever translators of the Bible have learned in the overseas field, whatever scholars of contextualism have learned in the study, needs to be put to work at home. That becomes easier to appreciate as our own society becomes more deliberately and obviously pagan, and it is a task that requires not only reevaluation of our thoughts but also of our style of living.

Humility, modesty, and painful reassessment of what in our lives is biblical and what is conventional is the price for a proper response to modern theology. Whereas in the past conventionalism was conservativism, today it may be the counterculture that is the stumbling block. In the past there was too easy an identification of Christianity with the values of middle-class self-sufficiency, with the corresponding difficulty of taking seriously the biblical teaching concerning the rich and the poor. Today concern over sex discrimination makes it difficult to take seriously the biblical directions concerning male leadership in family and church. Frequently evangelicals have been guilty of the Phariseeism that liberalism so vigorously denounced. How often have evangelical churches deliberately refused to follow biblical teaching on legitimate divorce and remarriage? How frequently have churches been so fond of their independency that they have refused cooperation with other churches in matters of church discipline? The list could be substantially longer. Clearly the only effective response to liberalism's charges of using the Bible hypocritically is to be more alert and willing to obey—sanctification!

Obviously even genuine sanctification will not stop all mouths. Ritschl was certainly cavalier in his rejection of those in his experience who were trying to take the Bible seriously, which ranged from those who were attempting to come to grips with biblical teaching on the Millennium to those who were trying to implement the biblical view of the equality of all elders. Those today who are committed to the biblical "holy kiss" are not always understood! At least it should be possible to show consistency in Christian living, to point out the inconsistency in the approach of someone who still refuses to believe that the Bible can have contemporary relevance.

RETHINKING HERMENEUTICS

Obeying God's Word can hardly be improved upon, but questions of interpretation still remain. Dispensationalism was of use for many evangelicals in resolving the puzzling questions of the present applicability of the moral law of the Old Testament, or even of the Sermon on the Mount. Covenant theology has functioned in the same way, though with different conclusions, for other evangelicals. Perhaps it is even possible to contemplate a true evangelical consensus, as both movements are coming to understand each other better, and as some hermeneutical crudities are quietly being dropped. No doubt such a consensus will be of value, but the two interpretive movements have hardly distinguished themselves in providing clear statements of Christian social ethics, whatever they may have accomplished in areas of personal ethics.

To be sure, there are many evangelicals today who are doing a great deal of hard work as they seek for biblical guidelines on questions of war, poverty, capital punishment, and the like. However, it seems that most of that effort is hardly related at all to evangelical hermeneutical or exegetical work, or else it is being carried on by the "new Anabaptism," with its conscious rejection of the hermeneutical traditions of other evangelical groups. At the very least, dialogue between evangelical pacifists and advocates of national defense, between those who wish to fight poverty through resource redistribution and those who wish to do it through revitalizing the traditional economy, is urgently required. That dialogue dare not be along the lines of questioning motives or of informal excommunication of the other side. It should not even be carried on with an uncritical desire to follow the "spirit of

Christ," but it should be done solely on the basis of exegetical and hermeneutical considerations.

It is particularly important that stages in human civilization not be confused with redemptive-historical epochs. The discovery of the laser cannot be compared with Pentecost. The confusion of technical progress with God's program of redemption has been the greatest single error of the liberals. That is just to say that the great events of the life and ministry of Jesus Christ are still ones that determine our world today, and no scientific, cultural, or spiritual advance is worthy to be considered in the same breath with Easter. It is simply incredible that liberalism made such an elementary error as to conclude that human accomplishments (what men *think* are accomplishments) are of significance for our lives comparable with redemptive history.

Only when the preceding analysis is clearly grasped can meaningful work be done in the area of differing applications of the principles God has ordained for this age. There is a great deal of truth in Rauschenbusch's observation that one's responsibilities as a citizen in a democracy are substantially different from those of a subject in a dictatorship. Surely under our circumstances Christians have the obligation to advise government according to Christian principles. Although it will be easier to derive those from the Old Testament, because there godly rulers are found, surely it just will not do to impose theocratic principles in this age. Rather, the more difficult task must be attempted, that of determining how the transtheocratic principles of Scripture should have application in society. Similar applications must be possible for the whole cultural world. However, this must always be done with humility. John Calvin's observation that there are several possible forms of the state that correspond to biblical norms must be remembered; it is likely there will be many possible options for practical application of biblical principles.

The most theoretical and intellectually difficult challenge of liberalism still remains the question of the meaning of history. Liberalism simultaneously recognized that its strength was in its desire to relate the meaning of the Christian faith to the entire unfolding of human history, and that its weakness was in thus subjecting the validity of Christianity to the judgment of the professional historian, who after all is able to deal only with probabilities. How can the Christian faith be seen to be more than romantic sentiment or pious wish, precisely because of its firm roots in the reality of history, without its becoming in turn caught up in the subjective relativism of historical change, a relativism that affects the historian himself? How can such a history serve as the basis of Christian faith?

Liberalism thus minimized the value of the historical base of Christianity and preferred to see evidence for the Christian faith within the *ongoing* historical process itself. Accordingly, the evidence for the faith depended a great deal upon the impact it was having upon culture. It seemed inconceivable that a faith that did not speak to, and was not accepted by, the intellectual leadership of the day could really be true Christianity. No doubt much of Ritschl's antipathy for Pietism came from its acceptance of the "withdrawn" condition of Christianity. This modernized form of the *consensus gentium* ("universal consent") argument did not take seriously the clear biblical teaching of the antithesis between the church and the world, and hence made the credibility of the faith depend upon its acceptability. Although the position of Abraham Kuyper in the Netherlands may not be flawless, his careful balance between that antithesis and common grace is surely more true to both the Bible and the modern situation. It is possible to see the kind hand of God behind the gifts we receive through modern culture, without for one minute conceding to the world the right to sit in judgment on the Christian faith.

Here also is a note of warning to contemporary evangelicalism. Our uneasy or downright bad conscience over our past lack of involvement in securing justice for all races, for example, may have tended to produce an unduly uncritical attitude toward those non-Christian movements that proclaim their desire for social progress. It simply must be possible to be "co-belligerents," to use Francis Schaeffer's phrase, without being religious allies. Not all evangelical abolitionists in the past century became blind, deaf, and dumb toward the anti-Christian stance of the Unitarian abolitionists. Evangelicals can cooperate in supporting anti-poverty movements today without identifying with their predominantly humanistic stance.

RETHINKING APOLOGETICS

A satisfactory evangelical alternative to the liberal attack on the inerrancy of the Bible involves not only a complete reappraisal of the relation of Christianity and culture, but also a reevaluation of evangelical apologetics throughout, in particular the branch involving scientific probability arguments (evidences).

The older Princeton approach of B. B. Warfield may still be the most influential in evangelical circles. Warfield's method for making the transition from the world of historical probability to the world of Christian certainty was to begin with arguments claiming a high probability for the general truth of the Bible, then to find in them evidence attesting the deity of Christ and His consequent teaching authority. Finally Warfield went from there to His authoritative teaching on the inerrancy of the whole Bible.

That older approach may still have usefulness among those whose experience of life's probabilities is basically positive. But for many, nineteenth-century optimism on the probable course of human history appears increasingly dated. Perhaps a life based upon a few probabilities is the best a non-Christian can hope for, but it is hardly an attractive option. Because of this, the presuppositional approach may be of more value in apologetics today. That method, expressed in different forms by Cornelius Van Til, Gordon Clark, E. J. Carnell, and perhaps Francis Schaeffer, states at the outset that without accepting inerrant Scripture one cannot arrive at the truth. No criteria can or should stand in judgment upon God and His Word, although criteria of truth distinguish the Bible from other books claiming to be from God. Any refusal to accept God's Word is simply blasphemous rebellion. Here is certainly an attempt at a truly comprehensive apologetic, which should be fitted to counter a comprehensive challenge to the faith. Perhaps the foundation of an apologetic better suited for the radical attacks of liberalism should be found in this approach.

It is one thing to affirm that with a reliance upon the Word of God meaning for life is possible, both in society and in individual living; but evangelical scholarship must build upon that affirmation concretely. In smaller and greater ways it must be shown *how* that inerrant Word relates to society and culture. All that, however, must also be done within the context of the clear affirmation that this world is under judgment and that striving toward a Christianized society can never be permitted to replace justification by faith.

That is to say that an imbalanced answer, one that simply responds to the old liberal challenge, will not do. Only comprehensive Christian teaching and obedience will serve. Only individual and group commitment to Christian thinking and living can ever refute the idea that Christianity must be changed to meet the needs of modern man.

LOOKING AHEAD

Is such an evangelical response worth making? Is liberalism only of interest to theological antiquarians? Has not neo-orthodoxy, with its demands to resist *Kulturprotestantismus*, long since carried the day? Temporarily, perhaps. However, even Barth found it necessary to resist *new* forms of civil religion, in particular that of Nazism. Certainly today it is taken for granted that the Christian religion must have *some* implications for the pressing social problems of the nation and the world. Perhaps a few years ago it was considered un-American to interject "ideological" or religious questions into political affairs, but hardly now. Precisely within the delicate but necessary definition of evangelicalism's relationship to the generally moral is a fresh evaluation of all those issues absolutely and urgently needed.

Surely the hermeneutical questions are the most pressing of all before the evangelical world. A doctrine of inerrancy with no perceptible use, which in practice makes no difference, is hardly worth exerting the energies of the church for. But today's evangelicals have been putting their doctrine to use. Perhaps the most prominent example is the great movement in consistent biblical counseling, which has already radically altered the face of the evangelical church. Small group involvement, again on a solidly biblical foundation, is doing much to produce a New Testament style of mutual encouragement. There is the hope, the confidence of the Lord's blessing, as we go ahead to be comprehensively biblical in bringing the gospel to bear on the cultures of Uganda and Illinois. That is the answer to old or new liberalism, and, more important, it is our calling as Christians.

4. The Bible in Twentieth-Century British Theology

H. D. McDonald

Apart from what J. A. T. Robinson has called "the conservatism of the committed," which he mischieviously castigates as no less "a seriously reactionary force" than "the fundamentalism of the fearful,"[1] British theology in the twentieth century, yielding to the incessant clamour to "update," has been generally expressed in relation to the prevailing philosophical *Zeitgeist*. The dominant idea of the time has been identified and then theologized. So can the theology of the period be branded according to the specific interest, from the category of historicism through the supremacy of evolutionism, the mood of relativism, the subjectivity of psychologism, the thesis of existentialism, the linguistics of empiricism, the declarations of secularism, to the justification of revolutionism. More than one name has gained notoriety as the advocate of one or other of those views by meshing into it Christian phraseology and so giving it other than its biblical and historical connotation.

It is not, however, our business in this chapter to give account of the several systems reared on such ephemeral principles that were generally successive but that sometimes overlapped. Our

1. J. A. T. Robinson, *Can We Trust the New Testament?* (London: Mobrays, 1967), pp. 9, 27; cf. p. 16.

H. D. McDonald, B.A., B.D., Ph.D., University of London, is former professor and vice-principal at London Bible College, London, England. Among his many publications are: *Ideas of Revelation 1700-1860, Theories of Revelation 1860-1960, Jesus—Human and Divine, Living Doctrine of the New Testament*, and *What the Bible Says About the Bible*.

purpose is rather to unfold how the Bible fared in the shaping and statement of those designated ideas that characterize twentieth-century British theology. For it must be clear that any theology, in the final analysis, deserves the ascription *Christian* only insofar as it derives directly from the biblical revelation. It is in proportion to its faithfulness to the historical valuation of the church's Scriptures that every theological system claiming to set forth Christian doctrine has its ultimate justification. The measure in which it is related to and grounded in its revelatory original is the measure in which it will have its validity and permanency.

Yet, although we have eschewed the task of detailing the several distinctive theologies advanced, which derive their basic premise from the prevailing climate of opinion, we consider it necessary to allude to at least one such as paradigmatic of how heavily reliance is placed on extrabiblical notions for the formulation of theological concepts. As a consequence we shall indicate the unsure position accorded to the Bible in the scheme.

John MacQuarrie, in *Principles of Christian Theology*, declares at the outset his intention of presenting his theology in the context of the phenomonology of Edmund Husserl (1859-1938) and the existentialism of Martin Heidegger (1889-1976). The former we conceive to condition his theological methodology,[2] and the latter his theological terminology.[3] Consonant with Husserl's phenomenology, MacQuarrie contends that theology is a description of the content of the religious consciousness. The application of that principle means that an appeal to an objective normative revelation is ruled out from the start and distinction between general and special revelation is consequently eroded. Identifying God, then, with Heidegger's category of "being" as set forth in the latter's *Sein und Zeit*, the essence of which is precisely the characteristic of dynamic "letting-be,"[4] MacQuarrie affirms "that the confrontation of man with being cannot be regarded as a personal subject-to-subject encounter."[5] Evidently then the reality with which man is concerned is conceived of as ultimately nonpersonal. It is only when one is "seized" by that "being" that "it" can be credited with those personal attributes required for the satisfaction of individual religious needs and so be written

2. John MacQuarrie, *Principles of Christian Theology* (London: SCM, 1966), p. 30.
3. Ibid., pp. 94-99.
4. Ibid., p. 99.
5. Ibid., p. 96.

with a capital B—"Being." Such a conclusion is, of course, inevitable when revelation is understood in such subpersonal terms as the "letting-be" of "being," instead of the self-disclosure of God as ultimate personhood. It is, indeed, this failure to give effective emphasis to the indispensible role of personal agency that necessitates the forthright rejection of MacQuarrie's basic unbiblical presuppositions.

MacQuarrie justifies his speculative thoughts and terms as Christian on the premise that the theologian is no longer bound by the Bible as his objective norm. He therefore declares that "Scripture is not itself revelation," but "one important way (not the only way) by which the community of faith keeps open its access to the primordial revelation on which the community is founded."[6] Scripture is nothing more or less than "the sacred writings of the community of faith,"[7] and as such must not be "absolutized as a formative factor in theology."[8] The Christian revelation is not located in the Bible, which is not only not in itself infallible, it "is not even an infallible record or witness to this revelation."[9] In line with that valuation of Scripture, it will be no surprise to find how little MacQuarrie alludes to the actual biblical text except by way of devaluing its plain meaning and rejecting its traditional exegesis.

It is a well accredited fact that prior to about the middle of the nineteenth century there was virtual unanimity in the church that the Scriptures were to be taken as the divinely inspired documentation of God's own self-disclosure and consequently the one authoritative source and only absolute norm for the totality of Christian faith and doctrine. About the year 1860, due mainly to the influence of the Enlightenment, the impact of Deism, and the imperialism of evolutionism, this historic valuation of the Bible was called in question. Therefore, when the twentieth century began, the division between those who continued to emphasize the divinity of Scripture and those who came to regard it as at most a spiritually inspiring production of religiously-minded authors had widened.

Two factors coalesced in our period to bring about the change from the historic view of the Bible to that which presented it as the story of the religious development of a special people in which

God's revelation was "affected to a large extent by the action of ordinary forces, developed in ways we should call natural rather than supernatural."[10]

THE AFTERMATH OF EVOLUTIONISM

By the beginning of the twentieth century, on the premise of natural development, was reared the view of Scripture that has dominated its theology to the present day among those referred to by J. A. T. Robinson, in an egoistic phrase of self-contradiction, as "the scepticism of the wise."[11] To be sure, this original premise has been modified and in some cases even abandoned, but others have been advanced to sustain the same conclusion. It is accordingly proclaimed that the history of the Old Testament is to be read as a gradual process in which the prophets stand out as key figures marking advances in religious and theological understanding. Certain occasions of apparent purposeful interventions in the historical succession were perceived by those men of spiritual insight and declared to be signal acts of God. Revelation is consequently to be conceived, not as a divinely communicated message of which God Himself is both the source and object, but subjectively, as the numinous awareness of the divine presence. Not primarily is revelation a matter of God's own disclosure, but essentially that of man's own discovery.

It follows, therefore, that revelation can in no way be identified with the words of Scripture. Rather the Bible is to be acceepted as the account of man's religious development written by men who, however divinely illuminated they may claim themselves to have been, betray their humanness in the several verbal and historical errors in their records. Nonetheless, the worth of such men's records remains as in some way a witness and a pointer to a transcendental reality beyond themselves with which they had identified and would have others make the same discovery.

S. R. Driver declared in 1891 that "none of the historians of the Bible claim supernatural enlightenment for the *materials* of their narrative,"[12] while three years after its commencement J. Eslin Carpenter affirmed that "the Old Testament as now interpreted tells the story of the rise and growth of a religion."[13] At a later

10. S. R. Driver and A. F. Kirkpatrick, eds., *The Higher Criticism* (London: Hodder & Stoughton, 1911), p. 11.
11. J. A. T. Robinson, *Can We Trust the New Testament?* p. 20.
12. S. R. Driver, *Introduction to the Literature of the Old Testament* (Edinburgh: T. & T. Clark, 1898), p. x.
13. J. Eslin Carpenter, *The Bible in the Nineteenth Century* (London: Longmans and Green, 1903), p. 463.

date S. A. Cook maintained that "in the Old Testament some fundamental religious ideas not unique in themselves were uniquely shaped by Israel."[14]

H. Wheeler Robinson sought to soften that stark naturalistic explanation of the rise and growth of the religion of Israel. He granted that the new view of the Bible does "seem to many to exclude the reality of revelation by surrendering the history to purely naturalistic or, at any rate, purely human factors."[15] Robinson, however, disallowed there to be any fundamental opposition between the natural and the supernatural. The issue, he declared, "is not to the presence here and there of a "supernatural" element amid "natural" conditions. The distinction, so used, is a legacy from the eighteenth century. We gain a much deeper insight into the divine activity, when we conceive the evolution of the nation's life as both natural and supernatural throughout, and not a mosaic of both."[16]

At the present time James Barr seems to come to the same view. He contends that "the Word-of-God type of language" in reference to the Bible is unjustified because he can give an account "of the formation of the biblical tradition" as "a *human* work." The "proper term," he then avers, for the Old Testament is "Word of Israel," and for the New, "Word of some leading Christians."[17] Underlying Barr's contention is his disapproval of the concept of the supernatural as a reality above and beyond the natural. He inveighs against conservative scholars on the basis that their belief in the supernatural is a priori "theological," deriving from "their belief that there is, not only a God, but also angels, devils, heaven, hell and so on," which "form part of a supernatural world."[18]

Barr evidently wants to break down a clean-cut distinction between the natural and the supernatural by charging that it is such that conservative scholars and commentators cannot well maintain in their exegesis. The upshot of Barr's position is, then, virtually so to wed the supernatural and the natural as to rob the term *revelation* of any distinctive meaning. As in the case of Wheeler Robinson, Barr leaves the impression that the supernatural and the natural are but reverse sides of the same coin: the

14. S. A. Cook, *The Place of the Old Testament in Modern Research* (Cambridge: Cambridge U., 1932), p. 28.

15. H. Wheeler Robinson, *The Religious Ideas of the Old Testament* (London: Duckworth, 1947), p. 216.

16. Ibid., p. 25.

17. James Barr, *The Bible in the Modern World* (London: SCM, 1973), p. 120.

18. James Barr, *Fundamentalism* (London, SCM, 1977), p. 278.

supernatural appears as the natural read religiously, and the natural as the supernatural read historically. So can Leonard Hodgson declare that "Christian theology should be thought of as a special form of natural theology."[19]

It is that blurring of the distinction between the natural and the supernatural that has led some contemporary writers to deny the uniqueness of the biblical revelation altogether. Christianity is consequently being presented—in the interests, it appears, of a general religious ecumenicity—as one of several expressions of a native instinct in human beings to relate to the ultimate. Thus has there developed a sort of panentheistic interpretation of Christianity in which revelation as historically understood, as an actual and personal disclosure of God of His being, nature, and purposes, has been lost, because the total historical process, natural phenomena, and human existence are regarded as alike the unfolding of the one "divine" life. J. A. T. Robinson has given enthusiastic exposition of this view. With the premise that "the attachment of Christianity to the supernaturalist projection is becoming less and less obvious,"[20] he bids us press beyond theism and see all included in God as " 'the Centre of centres' in an interlocking web of free spiritual relationships in which the All and the personal are no longer exclusive."[21]

Against that background, a criticism of the supernatural character of Christianity as God's self-disclosure became inevitable. John McIntyre, Gerald Downing, and A. O. Dyson, for example, agree to denigrate this historic doctrine. Dyson considers Downing's book *Has Christianity a Revelation?* to have made clear "the dangers inherent in an overdependence on the notion of revelation,"[22] while McIntyre sees revelation as an uncertain source for the several doctrines of the Christian faith.[23] Downing doubts that Christianity has a revelation; and he considers that the paucity of words in the Bible itself for "to reveal" is a sufficient justification for that denial. Yet this numerical calculation of a term cannot sustain his conclusion, for it overlooks the fact, as we have stated elsewhere, that "so omnipresent is the thought of God making himself known, of disclosing his presence, of making manifest truths about Himself previously concealed and other-

---

19. Leonard Hodgson, "The Bible," in *For Faith and Freedom* (Oxford: Blackwell, 1957), 2:3.
20. J. A. T. Robinson, *Exploration into God* (London: SCM, 1967), p. 37.
21. Ibid., p. 145.
22. A. O. Dyson, *Who Is Jesus Christ?* (London: SCM, 1969), p. 22.
23. John McIntyre, *The Shape of Christology* (London: SCM, 1966), p. 168.

wise undiscoverable, that the conviction is inescapable that God cannot be known at all unless and until he makes Himself known."[24] The truth is that "the idea of God *making himself known* in acts of redemption and judgment and in prophetic, interpretive utterances, pervade the Bible. It is not so much *a* biblical idea, as it is *the* biblical idea."[25]

In revelation God communicates with men, names His own name to them, and shows Himself as the God He is. This disclosure of God is distinct from any general awareness of a necessary "Something Other" that man may possess or gain. In this revelation God speaks and acts. This verbalization and actualization of God's self-disclosure makes Christianity a supernatural revelation not tied to

> some native God-consciousness or ideal on man's side; as if there were some sure and supreme knowledge of God prior and permissive to the self-revelation of God. A lower revelation may prepare for a higher, and provide psychology for it, but it cannot measure and therefore cannot test or vouch for it. There is no final and innate revelation of God in human nature, nothing so much deeper than the Gospel that can lend it a licence—there are only points of attachment or modes of action, an economy for action when it comes.[26]

THE ASSEVERATIONS OF CRITICISM

As the twentieth century opened, what had come to be known as "the higher criticism"—a designation first introduced by J. G. Eichhorn (1752-1827)—was in full tide. Cradled in the scepticism of English Deism and the rationalism of the German *Aufklärung*, the new school of biblical scholars set themselves to negate what they believed to be a magical view of the Bible—a book divinely communicated without a history and without roots in the successive cultures of its origin. The Bible, it was proclaimed, must be read and treated as any other volume of ancient religious literature. Approached in that way, it was held to reflect the theological ideas of eras past and of peoples unsophisticated. Excessive emphasis was consequently given to the supposed differences in

24. H. D. McDonald, *I Want to Know What the Bible Says About the Bible* (Eastbourne: Kingsway, 1979; Wheaton, Ill.: Tyndale House, 1980), p. 11.
25. H. D. McDonald, "Revelation," in *The New International Dictionary of the Bible*, ed. J. D. Douglas (Grand Rapids: Zondervan, 1974), p. 843.
26. P. T. Forsyth, *The Principle of Authority* (London: Independent Press, 1952), pp. 121-22.

religious outlook and linguistic forms of the several biblical books.

The historical method was first applied to the Old Testament in an attempt "to reconstruct the history from the conflicting material at our disposal" and so to unfold "the process by which Israel developed its higher religious truth."[27] But the method so rigorously applied to the Old Testament could not, as James Orr early saw, be thus restricted. Orr can quote N. Schmidt, who in 1905 boldly affirmed that "the movement could not stop at the Old Testament."[28] Critics had at the beginning thought to keep the two Testaments apart and treat the former as essentially the document of ancient Hebrew religion. But, as the early church by a right instinct clearly saw, the two belong together as basis for the Christian faith. The culmination of the progressive revelation of the Old Testament is the Christ of the New. It is He who clasps the two Testaments into one; and in His light the earlier word to Israel has its final meaning.

The "delusion," as Orr called it, that the sceptical criticism of the Old Testament would leave the New Testament intact soon passed so that the principles and methods of the radical criticism that had been applied to the Old Testament had "only to be applied with like thoroughness to the New Testament to work like havoc. The fundamental ideas of God and His revelation which underlay that criticism could not, as we set out by affirming, lead up to a doctrine of the Incarnation, but only to a negation of it."[29] The application of the "historical-religious" canons of criticism to the New Testament certainly has had disasterous results in all areas of Christian theology and especially in that of Christology. The volume *The Myth of God Incarnate*,[30] the basic principle of which is that the gospel history is not "real" history, and that the exalted statements about Christ in the epistles are little more than the overenthusiastic verbalizations of regard for Jesus of Nazareth by the early church, is a sufficient illustration of this verdict.

The twentieth century, according to David Edwards, has witnessed a wider dissemination and a more thorough application of the critical methodology that "has been bold to assess the early

27. T. H. Robinson, "The Methods of the Higher Criticism," in *The People and the Book*, ed. A. S. Peake (Oxford: Clarendon, 1925), pp. 154-56.
28. James Orr, *The Bible Under Trial* (London: Marshall Brothers, 1907), p. 150; cf. N. Schmidt, *The Prophet of Nazareth* (New York: Macmillan, 1905), p. 29.
29. James Orr, *The Problem of the Old Testament* (London: Nisbet, 1909), p. 477.
30. John Hick, ed., *The Myth of God Incarnate* (London: SCM, 1977).

books of the Bible as folk-tales, to discriminate between the Old Testament prophets for their religious and ethical values, to reject miracles including the resurrection of Jesus, to assert that neither of the two spiritual giants of the primitive church, Paul and John, correctly interpreted Jesus, and even to question freely the authority of the teaching ascribed to Jesus in the synoptic (the first three) gospels."[31]

New and often conflicting theories have been advanced by critics from time to time regarding the composition, the content, and the character of the biblical writings, so that in 1925 J. E. McFadyen could declare "there is at the moment practically no unanimity anywhere."[32] Twenty-six years later, emanating from the same association of Old Testament critics, there came the declaration that "many of the conclusions that seemed more sure, have been challenged, and there is now a greater variety of views on many questions than there has been for a long time."[33]

But what has remained constant throughout is the critical presupposition that there is no essential tie between the record and God's self-disclosure, with the consequent rejection of the Bible's own claim to be itself the supernaturally inspired Word of God. By that divorce between the record and the revelation, clearance has been given to the right to treat the record in the most sceptical manner. The thesis of H. Wheeler Robinson's volume *Record and Revelation* (1938) is that a clear distinction must be drawn between them both and that the two cannot be held to overlap or dovetail in any respect. That insistence could be paralleled from a host of works that reiterate the same view that "the Bible is not revelation, but the record of it."[34]

Two results of momentous significance for the place of the Bible in the church follow from this disjunction. It has induced a growing uncertainty among preachers regarding the validity of the Bible's message. Such lack of faith in Scripture must be attributed directly to a century of critical appraisement of the biblical record in which the Bible has been torn apart, split up, and separated out to such an extent that the critic has left the preacher with little authentic material to treat and expound. Herbert Danby has declared that as a result "a defensive, almost a diffi-

---

31. David L. Edwards, *Religion and Change* (London: Hodder & Stoughton, 1969), p. 161.
32. J. E. McFadyen, "The Present Position of Old Testament Criticism," in *The People and the Book*, p. 183.
33. H. H. Rowley, *The Old Testament and Modern Study* (Oxford: Clarendon, 1951), p. xvi.
34. C. B. Moss, *The Christian Faith* (London: SPCK, n.d.), p. 211.

dent, attitude is considered fitting to him who today would put forward the Old Testament's claim to be a usable and even a useful item in the Christian's spiritual armoury."[35] D. E. Nineham is irked by "the attempt to lay down 'biblical norms' " for ecumenical unity because gone is the "understanding of the Bible as a source-book from which Christians derive their characteristic beliefs and ways of behaving."[36] If what we have in the Bible, according to most critics of the present time, are tales "told around the camp fires or when the day's farming was done or over tables in Jerusalem or in meetings for worship in the early Christians' homes,"[37] then indeed will "a whole new art of preaching and a whole new practice and literature of devotion need to be developed in order to bring out the significance of the Bible in these terms."[38]

The aforementioned critical approach to the Bible accords it, at its highest, a mere functional use in the church. Yet such a view has no meaningful account to give of the Bible's place in worship, doctrine, and life of the church to those for whom it does not function, or where, by the nature of its contents, it cannot. The Bible is not in the church merely to give us a historical account of the series of "symbols," or "myths," in which it is contended the first Christians sought to express their religious insights; it is there rather as the vehicle in which God's revelation is given durability, immediacy, and catholicity. To know God for who and what He is in His self-disclosure is, then, to be shut up to Scripture, where those manifestations of God are preserved and perpetuated. It thus is a matter of fact that "the line between revelation and its record is becoming very thin, and that, in another true sense, *the record*, in the fulness of its contents, *is itself for us the revelation.*"[39] The Bible, therefore, "is indispensible if we are to know God and if we are to be in truth the body of the risen Lord, because through it alone we are able to listen with Israel and with the apostolic church for the unique word out of the unseen which for them, and can be for us, the power of God bringing our human life to its fulness."[40]

35. Herbert Danby, "The Old Testament," in *The Study of Theology*, ed. K. E. Kirk (London: Hodder & Stoughton, 1939), p. 189.
36. D. E. Nineham, *The Church's Use of the Bible* (London: SPCK, 1963), pp. 147-48.
37. Edwards, *Religion and Change*, p. 16.
38. Ibid., p. 193.
39. James Orr, *Revelation and Inspiration* (London: Duckworth, 1910), p. 159.
40. James D. Smart, *The Strange Silence of the Bible in the Church* (London: SCM, 1971), p. 98.

The other result of seeing the Bible as a mere record uncon-
nected with divine revelation is the call to surrender it to the
critics as alone the sure judges of what it is all about. Thus for
example, Christopher Evans, following Ernst Käsemann, contends that when it comes to giving the Bible its true valuation, it
is the decision of the scholar rather than "the piety of the pious"
that must have the last word."[41] The same view finds expression
in James Barr's *Fundamentalism*, where the contention is
throughout defended that the critical approach to Scripture is
alone valid and able to provide the key to the true understanding
of its meaning. Barr insists that it is only the biblical scholar who
comes to his task unfettered by any prior belief in the Bible's
authority as the Word of God who can use it aright in setting
forth an acceptable contemporary Christian theology.

But such a dictum would most surely rule out as genuinely
Christian the work of the great theologians of the church before
the admission of the critical reorigination of the biblical literature—while the contention itself has little merit or credibility. It
would be equally fatuous, for example, for a scientific researcher
into the problems of darkness to be castigated for retaining his
previous knowledge and experience of light as the more fundamental reality. It is after all only in relation to the light that his
researches can be carried out with any expectation of success. In
that regard, a remark of Athanasius might well be pondered:
"Behold, we speak confidently on the basis of the divine Scriptures concerning the religious faith and set it up as a light on a
candlestick, saying . . . He is the very stamp of the nature of the
Father and Light from Light and the true image of the essence of
the Father."[42] It is those very "divine Scriptures" that are in
themselves a light to our feet and a lamp to our path.

Barr is strong in his condemnation of those who contend for an
inerrant Bible; but he has the surest belief in his own and other
critics' infallibility. He resents the little credence given to the
theologizing of some academics by the evangelically devout in the
churches. But the irritation he expresses is born out of a failure to
appreciate that the soul's last need is not for a rationalized Christianity, but for a redemptive. And that is an absolute fact "not to
be obscured by extenuations which plead that the function of
ideas is redemptive, or that redemption is the profoundest rationality in the world, the 'passion which is highest reason in the

---

41. C. F. Evans, *Is "Holy Scripture" Christian?* (London: SCM, 1971), p. 38.
42. Athanasius *Orationis contra Arianos* i. 9.

soul divine.' That was the line that nearly lost Christianity to the pagan public of the old apologists, whose chief object was to make their religion stand well with the Universities and the State—a perilous attempt for Christianity."[43]

Certain ideas of our period relative to the status of the Bible have arisen out of the Darwinian influence, which has weakened the sense of the supernatural, and out of the advance of criticism, which has undermined the Scriptures as divine revelation.

THE DISQUALIFICATION OF A WITNESS

Right from its beginning the leaders of criticism were bothered by the claim that the testimony of Jesus prohibited acceptance of their radical views of the Old Testament. The acknowledgement in Christian faith of the lordship of Christ was held to carry with it His regard for the Old Testament as the document of God's revelation. Again and again, with it in context, Jesus had rung out the challenge "It is written" and "Have you not read?" He quoted from all its parts as being divinely authoritative; and His meditation on that earlier Testament showed that He had "penetrated the Scriptures as a *unity* rather than a compilation."[44] To its pages He turned constantly for the vindication of His Person and the validation of His mission; and He declared all the Scriptures to testify of Him. In giving it that status in relation to Himself,

> the testimony of our Lord to the Old Testament and his claim to divinity are, it would seem, more closely associated than many in our day are prepared to acknowledge." Those who had found Christ in those Old Testament Scriptures consequently found themselves "bound to look at that unique literature primarily through the eyes of him who claimed to be the light of the world, our Lord and Savior Jesus Christ.[45]

That estimate of the Old Testament as God's Word written passed over to include the New Testament. In calling its accepted writings "Scripture," the primitive church was fully aware of the connotation of that term. Thus did both Testaments, of which Jesus is Himself the theme, become for Christian faith and life absolute, because they are stamped with Christ's own authority.

43. P. T. Forsyth, *The Person and Place of Jesus Christ* (London: Independent Press, 1946), p. 96.
44. Maisie Spens, *Concerning Himself* (London: Hodder & Stoughton, 1937), p. 6.
45. R. V. G. Tasker *The Old Testament in the New Testament* (London: Hodder & Stoughton, 1962), p. 23.

In the saving experience of Christ, the gospel enshrined in the New Testament was again and again demonstrated as authentic. And it is only because the term *Christ* has its meaning surely fixed in reference to the New Testament that such an experience of God's salvation in Him is contemporaneously possible.

If the critics' new approach were to make any headway, biblical reference to the final authority of Christ had in some way to be waived or weakened. The program thus to nullify that testimony to the divinity of Scripture has been carried through in the following three main ways and advocated according to individual preference.

By lessening the interest of Christ's concern. Charles Gore and S. R. Driver had set the "accommodationist" theory going: Gore in his Bampton Lectures on *The Incarnation of the Son of God* of 1891 and Driver in his *Introduction to the Literature of the Old Testament* of the same year. The former had vigorously contended that it was no part of our Lord's purpose to bind us "to the acceptance of the Jewish tradition in regard to the Old Testament."[46] The latter, conscious of the objection "that some of the conclusions respecting the Old Testament are incompatable with the authority of our blessed Lord, and that in loyalty to Him we are precluded from accepting them,"[47] nevertheless declared that Christ accepted without question Jewish tradition regarding His ancient Scripture. "In no single instance," he then affirmed, "so far as we are aware, did He anticipate the results of scientific inquiry or historical research."[48] On the authority of those scholars, the "accommodationist" view of Christ's relation to the Old Testament was widely accepted. Accordingly, it was proclaimed that Christ did not concern Himself with such peripheral matters as the Mosaic authorship of the Pentateuch or the Davidic authorship of Psalm 110.

It is precisely here, however, that the question must be asked, Can it seriously be maintained that if Jesus were aware of the wrongness of the Jewish views of the origin and history of their Scriptures, which were also His, He could have "adapted" Himself to their ignorance and prejudices regarding them? It was, after all, part of His mission to dispel error; and in that regard He condemned the tradition of the elders. It is, therefore, unacceptable "to credit him, who came as the truth, with unreadiness, on

46. Charles Gore, *The Incarnation of the Son of God* (London: John Murray, 1891), p. 195.
47. Driver, *Introduction to Old Testament*, p. xii.
48. Ibid.

any pretext, to correct a known falsehood."[49] For if

> as some "accommodationists" urge, it is a harmless thing to allow that he accepted uncritically the Mosaic authorship of the Pentateuch or the Davidic authorship of Psalm 110, then the question must be posed, Why consequently all the fuss about the results of criticism? For it is a presupposition of the critical analysis of Scripture that the key to its interpretation lies in giving the correct dating, authoring, and sectionalizing of its contents. How, then, can it be supposed that Christ interpreted them aright if he did not openly set them in the context demanded by the new analysis and the historical method?[50]

By reducing the area of Christ's knowledge. R. L. Ottley's Bampton Lectures of 1896 gave vogue to the "kenotic" view of Christ's Person, in which it was declared that our Lord, in the days of His flesh, either voluntarily or of necessity, was limited in knowledge of what lay within the immediate sphere of His messianic mission. A. F. Kirkpatrick made use of the doctrine of our Lord's self-emptying to put critical questions regarding the Old Testament beyond the range of His knowability.[51] In spite of the critical rejection of kenoticism (but it is true for other reasons than to admit Christ's testimony to the divinity of Scripture) by William Temple[52] and Donald Baillie,[53] the idea of the self-emptying of the Son of God of His divine attributes during His earthly life was generally accepted by critics. Vincent Taylor's declaration that Christology is "incurably kenotic,"[54] only confirmed the acceptance of this escape route from allowing Christ as a witness on biblical issues. A. H. McNeile in an essay entitled "Our Lord's Use of the Old Testament" contended that as a partial result of His self-emptying Christ refused "to know, as man, anything he could learn by human methods."[55] Admitting that the knowledge so gained is not like ours clouded by sin, McNeile goes on to assert that regarding the facts relating to the literature and history of

49. McDonald, *I Want to Know*, p. 88.
50. Ibid.
51. A. F. Kirkpatrick, "The Inevitability and Legitimacy of Criticism," in *The Higher Criticism*, ed. Driver and Kirkpatrick, p. 27; cf. A. B. Davidson, *Biblical and Literary Essays* (London: Hodder & Stoughton, 1903), chap. 8.
52. William Temple, *Christus Veritas* (London: Macmillan, 1924), p. 142.
53. D. M. Baillie, *God Was in Christ* (London: Faber and Faber, 1948), pp. 94-98.
54. Vincent Taylor, *The Person of Christ in the New Testament* (London: Macmillan, 1958), p. 287.
55. A. H. McNeile, "Our Lord's Use of the Old Testament," in *Cambridge Biblical Essays*, ed. H. B. Swete (London: Macmillan, 1909), p. 249.

the Bible, *"He could not because he would not* know."[56] Jesus accepted without question traditional ideas about the Scriptures that reflected the "intellectual standpoint of his day and country" because, for the purposes of His mission, He did not need to know whether or not they were accurate.

The bold attempt to permit the legitimacy of criticism by reducing the area of Christ's knowledge, however, does less than justice to the facts of the situation. The Bible thus subjected to critical reconstruction is no less His Bible. It can consequently be unacceptable to allow that He would want to remain in ignorance and uncertainty regarding Scripture's origin. He most surely would want assurance that the word of the Father concerning Himself given to this prophet and that was indeed from God. It must follow, therefore, that any kenotic doctrine that denies to Christ infallibility as a teacher of divine truth cannot stand. To contend on the basis of Philippians 2:1-10 that our Lord was so emptied of all knowledge that He was altogether ignorant about the shaping of His own sacred literature and the true religious history of His own people would make an end of all certainty. For His assertion that Moses wrote of Him and that Jonah was for three days entombed in the belly of a fish, Jesus deduced doctrines of eternal moment. He made special reference to David, who spoke of Him as the One to sit at God's right hand. But what if Moses did not write and if Jonah did not reside in the fish? And what if David, to whom is referred the great declaration of the Messiah's triumph, did not so speak? Jesus looked to the Old Testament as assuring the warrant and credentials of His mission, but momentous consequences for faith follow if the certainty of such warrant and credentials is in doubt. Of a book concerned with His own life and work, "here, if anywhere, we should expect our Lord to speak with divine authority and absolute truth."[57]

The kenotic principle, interpreted so as to denude Jesus of the knowledge of the truth regarding His own Scriptures, becomes all the more disconcerting when applied to His own declarations of an intimate union with the Father guaranteed on the authority of those very Scriptures. Must such stupendous claims, too, be written off as pious guesses? There is nothing "docetic" about the figure of Christ in the gospels. At the same time He was, even on the plane of the human, what none of us is—a perfect man,

56. Ibid., p. 250.
57. Tasker, *Old Testament in the New Testament*, p. 37.

supremely endowed by the Holy Spirit. Even on that basis we cannot possibly attribute to Him such ignorance concerning the origin of these Scriptures, which He could not but be aware would be perpetuated in the church of His followers. His words, He affirmed, were not His but the Father's. Such claims are not the tentative speculations of pseudoknowledge or the musings of one hedged in by the notions of his time and place. The words He spoke, He knew to be true. It must, then, be merely in the interests of a theory that His verdicts on the contents and contexts of Scripture are set aside.

By humanizing the account of Christ's Person. Some theologians do indeed appear to approach their valuation of Scripture by way of their Christology. But their Christology, in its turn, has been formulated on speculative principles to present a Christ whose Person cannot be validated by reference to the biblical account. He is consequently conceived of in many such statements as one who hardly oversteps the limits of a special sort of human.[58] Only a few of those declarations concerning Christ can be given here, but enough to illustrate our contention that they are of such a nature that His testimony to the biblical records would carry little weight.

S. G. F. Bradon sees Jesus chiefly as an associate of a group of revolutionary Zealots whose own vision of the kingdom of God "necessarily involved the elimination of the Roman government of Judaea."[59] W. R. Matthews considered Jesus to be a type of the truly spiritual man who, in contrast with the general run of that class, experienced a continuous flow of divine inspiration. The fact, however, that He was supremely inspired does not put Him outside the category of the altogether human: "On the contrary, it makes him fully human, the representative man, the human person after God's image."[60] James Dunn speaks of Jesus as "a Spirit-inspired exorcist and healer" who "saw himself as a charismatic worker of miracles."[61] J. A. T. Robinson raises the question, "How can Christ *be* God for us without ceasing to be man?" Robinson's answer is that He never was or could be other than man. For if He were ever more than man in Himself—the God-

---

58. Cf. H. D. McDonald, "The Person of Christ in Contemporary Speculation and Biblical Faith" (the Sir John Laing Lecture, 1978), in *Vox Evangelica*, ed. Donald Guthrie, 1979.

59. S. G. V. Brandon, *Jesus and the Zealots: A Study in the Political Factors of Primitive Christianity* (Manchester: Manchester U., 1967), p. 344.

60. W. R. Matthews, *The Problem of Christ in the Twentieth Century* (London: Oxford U., 1950), pp. 79-81.

61. James Dunn, *Jesus and the Spirit* (London: SCM, 1975), p. 71; cf. pp. 88-89.

man—He would have ceased to be man. So he concludes that the Father-Son language of the gospels is symbolic, designed to express a unique relationship of the man Jesus with God.[62] That view of Christ's Person permits Robinson to state elsewhere that His specific reference to the Davidic origin of Psalm 110 "simply shows Jesus to be a true Jew." He asserts, consequently, that "it is entirely compatible with Christian belief that he could (by our standards) have been mistaken on that and other matters and still be the Word of God to that generation—and to ours."[63] James Barr declares that only by postulating a "superhuman and inhuman" Jesus can evangelicals maintain that He taught "eternally correct information." For his own part, he regards Jesus' teaching as "time-bound and situation bound," so that "what he taught was not eternal truth valid for all times and situations, but personal address concerned with the situation of Jesus and his hearers at that time."[64]

It does not belong to this chapter to discuss the inadequacies of those Christologies. The only observations we need to make here are these: It is not easy to comprehend—à la Robinson—how Christ, the incarnation of divine truth, could be both "mistaken" regarding the origin of His own Scriptures and on "other matters" and at the same time be the Word of God for our day. As for Barr, the Bible seems to have ultimately a past functional use only, while the teaching of Jesus is apparently relative merely to an age long gone.

THE FOCUSING OF AN AUTHORITY

A number of writers, more sensitive to the biblical and historical account of the Person and place of Jesus Christ in Christian faith, have made their appeal for relinquishing belief in the infallibility of the Bible by focusing on Christ as the ultimate seat of authority. We thus, for example, find two New Testament scholars, who otherwise have much to teach us toward an understanding of the gospels, argue that the acceptance of Christ as Lord turns us away from the falsity of regarding the Bible as authoritative. William Barclay contends that there is no such external and final authority for man. For the Christian, he affirms, "there is only one authority, and that authority is Jesus Christ interpret-

62. J. A. T. Robinson, *The Human Face of God* (London: SCM, 1973), p. 186.
63. J. A. T. Robinson, *Can We Trust the New Testament?* pp. 18-19.
64. James Barr, *Fundamentalism*, p. 171.

ed by the Holy Spirit."[65] A. M. Hunter, focusing on Christ as the Word of God, sees the Bible as the vehicle of that Word. Yet he declares that very understanding of the relationship of Christ to the Scripture delivers us "from the mistaken view, held by some people, that every word of the Bible is the inerrant word of God, written down in divine dictation."[66]

Apart from the false characterization of the doctrine of verbal inspiration in A. M. Hunter's concluding remark, all Christians will warm to the sentiment and statement that Jesus Christ is the Christian's last word both for faith and living. Writing on "the Authority of Christ," James Denney declared that "in the work of revelation, and especially in the revelation of Himself as Father, God has no organ but Christ, and in Christ, He has an adequate organ."[67] D. Martyn Lloyd-Jones, with equal emphasis, observes that "the really big claim which is made in the whole New Testament, is for the supreme authority of the Lord Jesus Christ."[68] But instead of such declarations making void the authority of Scripture, both those writers see that authority as established through Christ's authority. It is, in fact, the authority of Christ that finally settles and vindicates the divinity of Scripture; for the tie between Christ and the Scriptures is truly a vital and necessary one. P. T. Forsyth warns that "to say vaguely that the revelation is Christ, or that Christ is its centre, is the source of all our confusion."[69] The question that has to be asked is, What Christ is thus authoritative? The only Christ we know as Lord and Savior is the biblical Christ; for it "is the whole biblical Christ who is truly and deeply historical Christ."[70] Such is the Christ

> in the Old Testament prefigured, and in the New presented. It is impossible to speak of an authoritative Christ apart from the Bible in which he is set forth. The historical presentation and the apostolic interpretation are essential to a full estimate of the Saviour who alone is absolute. The Old Testament preparation for the revelation in Christ is not a mere ornamental prefix to it, nor is the apostolic understanding of God's revealed will in Christ a mere addition to it. They are part of it. In the one revelation is figured,

65. Denis Duncan, ed., *Through the Year with William Barclay* (London: Hodder & Stoughton, 1972), p. 209.

66. A. M. Hunter, *Jesus, Lord and Saviour* (London: SCM, 1976), p. 5.

67. James Denney, "The Authority of Christ," in *Hastings' Dictionary of Christ and the Gospels* (Edinburgh: T. & T. Clark, 1906), 1:146.

68. D. Martyn Lloyd-Jones, *Authority* (London: Inter-Varsity, 1958), p. 15.

69. Forsyth, *Person and Place of Jesus Christ*, p. 151.

70. Ibid., p. 169.

in the other it is finalized. When, therefore, it is said that Christ is
authoritative it must be understood that this is the Christ who is
so.[71]

Neither the prophetic indications nor the apostolic interpretations are the result of human musings on the divine. They are
part and parcel of the revealing act. It is consequently impossible
to speak of an authoritative Christ apart from the Scriptures in
which He is set forth; for we cannot know Christ at all if we do
not know the Scriptures, and we do not know the Scriptures at all
if we fail to find Christ. The authority of Christ is, then, one and
the same with the authority of Scripture. So does it come about
that "the most important argument of all is that we should believe in the authority of the Scriptures because the Scriptures
themselves claim that authority."[72] For in claiming their own authority they are asserting Christ's, and vice versa.

William Temple's Gifford Lectures gave a more studied statement of the prevalent view that authority cannot be allowed to
what is external. Authority must operate, according to Temple,
within the area of the "fully spiritual," for "revelation itself came
in a living experience; that in it which is of permanent authority
is not capable of being stated in formulae; it is the living apprehension of the divine will in living intercourse of the human with
the divine."[73] Therefore he argues, "If Christ designed to evoke a
response spiritual in every part, He must write no book, but leave
the general impact of His person and work to reach mankind in
general through the account of him which his disciples would
give. . . . His faithful but not infallible disciples."[74]

Such views as those found wide advocacy and were given appealing statement by theologians like H. H. Farmer, who maintained God's specific revelation to be actualized in the I-Thou
encounter. The result has been to shift the locus of authority from
the external to the internal and to deny to Scripture the position
of objective norm. That tune thus hummed by individual writers
came to full chorus in the general rejection of the Bible as an
infallible word. For, the chorus went, "if the infallibilities have
been overthrown by inquiry and reason, they cannot be raised
again by affirmation or even the strongest conviction of their

71. H. D. McDonald, *Theories of Revelation* (London: Allen & Unwin, 1963),
p. 360.
72. Lloyd-Jones, *Authority,* p. 50.
73. William Temple, *Nature, Man and God* (London: Macmillan, 1947), p. 343.
74. Ibid., p. 351.

utility." And any such effort made to reestablish them can only be undertaken by "persons encased in a jointless armour of obscurantism hard enough to turn the edge of any fact."[75]

Two presuppositions that underlie the position here presented are commonplaces of twentieth-century theologizing. First, that there is no such thing as revealed truths; and second, that the Bible is not to be read as embodying an authoritative divine revelation but at most as a stammering witness or a signpost that can be but unsurely deciphered, which merely points toward something.

In spite of the concern in the first of those presuppositions to emphasize that in revelation there is a direct confrontation between God through Christ and the human person, it is unjust and unnecessary to the facts of the case to deny that revelation is consequently devoid of any truth content. Temple is emphatic—and he puts his words in italics to give them stress—that *what is offered to man's apprehension in any specific revelation is not truth concerning God but the living God Himself.*[76] This disavowal of the truth content of revelation has resulted in a fatal subjectivization of God's self-disclosure, which robs faith of its objective authority. Thus C. H. Dodd contends that "nowhere is the truth given in such purely 'objective' form that we can find a self subsistent external authority." He therefore reduces the value of the Bible to that of "inducing in us a religious attitude and outlook."[77]

The chief reason for the refusal to take seriously the propositional aspect of revelation is found in the modern view of locating revelation in deeds and acts rather than words and declarations. Leonard Hodgson's statement may be taken as typical. Revelation, he declares, "is given primarily not in words but in deeds, in events which become revelatory to us as the Holy Spirit opens our eyes to see their significance as acts of God."[78] Such a pronouncement may indeed sound appealing until its real intent is examined; and that intention is to get rid of the historic view of the Bible as the written speech of God. The upshot, then, of Hodgson's position is to unite sheer subjectivity with the call to surrender the Bible to the critic. As Hodgson develops his thesis it appears the Holy Spirit's enlightenment is to be equated with his own critical expertise. When the question How do we come to perceive

---

75. John Oman, *Grace and Personality* (Cambridge: Cambridge U., 1919), p. 9.
76. Temple, *Nature, Man and God*, p. 322.
77. C. H. Dodd, *The Authority of the Bible* (London: Nisbet, 1928), pp. 289, 297.
78. Leonard Hodgson, "God and the Bible," in *On the Authority of the Bible, Theological Collections* (London: SPCK, 1960), 1:4.

the events as revelatory? is asked, Hodson answers, "By the way we see them." And that comes about "as a result of scholars putting alongside of one another their various readings of the evidence, each saying to the rest, 'This is how I see it. Cannot you see it too?' "[79] Apparently, then, an event is revelatory when we come to see it as such; or, rather, as we are persuaded by the critic that it should be seen his way.

A. M. Ramsey gives his archepiscopal encouragement to that misplaced academic egoism by his remark that "God is the giver of the scholar's search for truth as he sets out for it, as one now knowing whither he goes."[80] The last part of his comment is, alas, too true; too many do set out unsure of where they are going, and arrive nowhere.

It is, however, this restriction of revelation to bare acts that is at fault. No single event in itself is revelatory. It is not true that the seers and prophets of the Old Testament, or the apostolic preachers of the New, looked at certain real or alleged events and "read God" into them. For their interpretation of actual historical events is itself divinely communicated and put into a form of sound words congruous with the disclosure. It is, therefore, in the union of event and word that the very essence of revelation consists. That being so, the propositional nature of revelation cannot be evaded. In revelation God reveals *that* He is, and *what* He is; but His "thatness" and His "whatness" can only be expressed in direct speech.

We may have sympathy with those who would emphasize the personal, face-to-face aspect of revelation in which God comes to be known intimately and directly. But the fact is that we could not be sure it is God we are meeting unless He declares Himself. The God of the Bible is not simply the sovereign God who performs a series of acts; He is, in addition, the speaking God who declares in understandable linguistic form the significance of His acts. He tells us what He is about. So we read in the very first chapter of the Bible these recurrent phrases: "God created" and "God said"—that is, His acts and His words.

James Barr disapproves of J. I. Packer's contention that revelation is in its essence propositional—that "the Word of God consists of *revealed truths*"[81]—on the score that such a contention

79. Ibid., p. 10.
80. A. M. Ramsey, "The Authority of the Bible," *Peake's Bible*, ed. Matthew Black and H. H. Rowley (London: Nelson, 1962), p. 11.
81. Cf. J. I. Packer, *"Fundamentalism" and the Word of God* (London: Inter-Varsity, 1958), p. 91.

permits the conception of faith as assent to "real information."[82] But Barr's attack is open to the same charge that he brings against "some conservative apologists" as "surely rather foolish."[83] Packer is perfectly right in declaring that "Scripture is in its nature revealed truth in writing and an authoritative norm for human thought about God."[84] It is Barr who is wrong to draw the conclusion that faith must therefore be defined as mere *assensus*. Packer would not grant a final dichotomy between the propositional and the personal. For although Christian faith is certainly not mere assent to a set of propositions, yet it is not, nor can it ever be, belief apart from propositions. Donald MacKinnon, therefore, is right to insist that "there is more in faith than assent to propositions, but to allow that there is more is not to disallow that assent to propositions has a place in it."[85] On the truth of God's revelation is saving faith finally grounded. Packer is, in fact, careful to state the element of personal dealing and involvement in the relationship with God as central to such knowledge.[86] When dealing with the subject of revelation, Packer correctly stresses its propositional nature; and when dealing with the subject of knowing God he truly underscores the personal aspect.

Those two emphases do not stand in opposition; they belong together. There is no ultimate conflict between the idea of revelation as propositional and as personal. If Christian knowledge of God is not belief in a set of propositions, nor yet is it belief apart from propositions. It is, as we have argued elsewhere, a knowledge of God mediated *through* propositions.

> To deny the mediate in the interests of the immediate, or vice versa, appears to ignore the experience of multitudes of believing people who attest the fact that a revelation which is mediated does not become immediately direct and creatively real in the living experience of Christian faith. In the truths revealed, as, for example, God as active, as incarnate, as revealing, and, so forth, there is somehow found an experience of God Himself.[87]

It is faith's certainty that "in Scripture—in the very words and

82. Barr, *Fundamentalism*, p. 226.
83. Ibid.
84. J. I. Packer, "Contemporary Views of Revelation," in *Revelation and the Bible*, (London: Tyndale, 1959), p. 103.
85. Donald MacKinnon, *Borderlands of Theology* (London: Lutterworth, 1968), p. 82.
86. J. I. Packer, *Knowing God* (London: Hodder & Stoughton, 1973), pp. 37-41.
87. H. D. McDonald, *Ideas of Revelation, 1700-1860* (London: Macmillan, 1959), p. 82.

propositions of Scripture—God reveals Himself."[88]

Throughout our period a number of views have come into the open, each with its own descriptive phrase, but all agreeing to a divorce or, at most, a nebulous connection between the Bible and the Word of God. A. S. Peake, following the lead of the earlier F. W. Farrar,[89] contended that to speak of the Bible as "the Word of God" is to be committed to a "high sounding" and "impossible" theory of its divine inspiration.[90] C. H. Dodd insists that "in the expression 'the Word of God' there lurks an equivocation."[91] He then declares that in reference to the Bible it must be given a "symbolic" sense, for the Bible cannot be regarded as "the utterance of God in the same sense in which it is the utterance of men." To grant that, he argues, would give validity to the argument that "it must possess God's own infallibility."[92] Should the designation still be allowed, it must be with the sense that it is "not as the 'last word' on religious questions, but as the 'seminal word' out of which new apprehension of truth springs to the mind."[93]

In Alan Richardson's judgment, the Scriptures are not even distinctive on account of the ideas they contain, for similar views are to be found in other books. To be sure, the Bible is unique as "the authoritative historical witness to Christ," although Richardson immediately adds that those who were called to be witnesses were "subject to all the limitations of their historical situation" and being thus "historically conditioned" were necessarily "fallible."[94] For A. G. Hebert, the very confession of the Bible as "the word of God" is declared to be a grave menace to the church.[95] To think of Scripture as itself the Word of God would, according to J. K. S. Reid—although for some reason not clearly stated—compromise the divine sovereignty and bring about the result of God's Word being "petrified in a dead letter."[96]

88. H. D. McDonald, "Revelation," in *New International Dictionary of Christian Church*, ed. J. D. Douglas, p. 843.
89. F. W. Farrar, *The Bible: Its Meaning and Supremacy* (London: Longmans and Green, 1897), p. 130.
90. A. S. Peake, *The Bible: Its Origin, Its Significance, and Its Abiding Worth* (London: Hodder & Stoughton, 1914), pp. 398-99.
91. Dodd, *Authority of the Bible*, p. 16.
92. Ibid.
93. Ibid., p. 300.
94. Alan Richardson, "Authority of Scripture," in *The Interpreter's Dictionary of the Bible*, ed. George A. Buttrick (New York: Abingdon, 1962), pp. 250-51.
95. A. G. Hebert, *Fundamentalism and the Church of God* (London: SCM, 1957), p. 307; *The Authority of the Old Testament* (London: Faber & Faber, 1947), pp.10-11.
96. J. K. S. Reid, *The Authority of Scripture* (London: Methuen, 1957), p. 279.

H. Wheeler Robinson contends that the Bible can only be referred to as the Word of God because of its "moral appeal" as testimony to the divine nature. "It is," he writes, "the nature of God which is the only final authority in all truth, and the Word of God is authoritative because it testifies to that nature and convinces of the truth of Christ through the power of His present Spirit, who is Himself."[97] H. H. Farmer felt compelled to add a footnote to one of his chapters in *The World and God* to state his view of the relation between revelation and the Bible. His statement is reproduced here in full because it has the merit of putting more sensitively than most, and in short compass, the prevailing critical understanding of that relationship.

> A word may be added concerning the Bible considered as the revelation of God. In the light of the principles set forth in this chapter it is clear that the Bible *per se*, i.e. considered simply as a written text is not, and never can be, a revelation of God. It becomes revelation only as God speaks through it relevantly to my situation, and it becomes unique revelation only as He speaks through it relevantly to something unique in my situation. It is as mediating Christ the Reconciler to my basic need of reconciliation in my present historical circumstances that the Bible becomes a unique source of God's revealing word to the soul. But I, or someone, has to bring it into my present situation, make it part of it, before God can speak livingly through it. Thus if we use the term "the Word" in the sense of God's living speech with the soul, it is true to say that the Bible is not the Word of God, but the Word of God is in the Bible, or—in the categories of this chapter—the Bible is not the Revelation of God, but the Revelation of God is in the Bible.[98]

But however crudely or cautiously the relationship between Scripture and the Word of God is stated, the basic divorce first introduced to allow the critic freedom to reconstitute the biblical literature according to his own canons has been maintained. And one result of setting up such an antithesis has been that "the Christian Church is uncertain at the present time, how to treat the Bible as the Word of God."[99]

By rejecting the historical declaration of Scripture as per se

97. H. Wheeler Robinson, *Redemption and Revelation* (London: Nisbet, 1942), p. 193.
98. H. H. Farmer, *The World and God* (London: Nisbet, 1936), p. 91n.
99. H. Cunliffe-Jones, *The Authority of the Biblical Revelation* (London: James Clarke, 1945), p. 132.

the divine Word, theologians found themselves compelled to redefine the relationship in terms that upheld the disjunction between the two. There thus emerged a number of views, each focusing on its own key term, but all agreeing in the refusal to declare the Bible as in itself God's Word. It became the fashion to refer to the Bible as "containing" or as "witnessing to" or as "becoming" the Word of God in certain ways and at certain times. It is not, however, made clear actually why or precisely when any one of those abilities credited to the Bible work in that fashion, or how adequately.

It is true, as those writers are fond of pointing out, that in the New Testament Christ is referred to as "Word of God," or "the Word" absolutely. But it does not detract from His position as the unique, incarnate, utterance of God to speak of the Bible in the same way.[100] It is indeed significant that among the disciples of the New Testament the title "Word of God" for Christ was not in general vogue. That may have been because when He ascended they regarded Him as present and speaking as the Word of God in the inspired Scriptures, in which His revelation was made complete. At any rate, it is worthy of note that in the New Testament there is a significant overlapping of the term in such a way as to relate the efficacy of the gospel indifferently to Christ and to the biblical Word. In other words, a number of passages focus on the saving adequacy of God's revelation in either Christ or the scriptural message as alike "the Word of God." Thus are the incarnate Word and the written Word so identified that we are not always sure to which one reference is being made. The fundamental resemblance is that both are the tangible expression of the living God; and thus, for the purpose of grace, the embodiment of His otherwise invisible and inaccessible thought.

We must, therefore, assert emphatically with J. K. Mozley that "in the Christian view of the Bible, it is finally true that it is the Word of God, just as it is finally true about Christ that He is the Word of God."[101] Such is certainly the historical Christian understanding of the Bible and is one that evangelical faith must unequivocally maintain. Read in the light of its own claims, the Bible presents itself as emphatically "the Word of God." When, then, "we call the Bible the Word of God, we mean, or should

100. Cf. William Nichols, *Revelation in Christ* (London: SCM, 1958), pp. 33-39.
101. J. K. Mozley, "The Bible: Its Unity, Inspiration and Authority," in *The Christian Faith in Explanation and Defense*, ed. W. R. Matthews (London: Eyre and Spottiswoode, 1944), p. 55.

mean, that its message constitutes a single utterance of which God is the author."[102]

THE REPUDIATION OF A VERDICT

Two statements by recent theologians will show how radical is the contemporary repudiation of the divine origin and absolute trustworthiness of Scripture. According to Alan Richardson, "the rise of biblical scholarship made necessary a new doctrine of the inspiration of Holy Scripture."[103] In addition John Baillie would himself apparently accept the proposition, which at any rate he allows to be generally advanced by others, that "most Protestant theologians have now surrendered the doctrine that Holy Scripture is inerrant."[104] The words *new* and *now* in those assertions are significant. They amount to the admission, on the one hand, that the contemporary understanding of the inspiration of the Bible is not that of the church throughout the centuries; and, on the other hand, that the idea of an errant Scripture is out of harmony with the church's traditional verdict.

Regarding the first of those issues, that of inspiration, the general view has been to shift the locus of inspiration from the actual words of Scripture to that of the men behind the records or to the ideas the words express. But in either statement, occasion is taken to castigate the historic doctrine of verbal inspiration as "automatic" or "mechanical."

Thus C. H. Dodd says regarding the recorders of God's acts in history, "it is not their *words* that are inspired—as one might say perhaps of 'automatic writing'—it is the *men* who are inspired."[105] A. S. Peake contended that "the inspiration we find in the Bible is that of supreme religious genius, often combined, it is true, with a superb gift of expression, but still having its value rather in the fact that it is religious, than that it is great literature."[106] Other quotations with similar intent could be given to show how widely entertained among academic scholars is the rejection of verbal inspiration.

That rejection has not, however, been total. For contrary to what W. R. Nicoll had to say in a letter to James Denney as far

102. Packer, *"Fundamentalism" and the Word of God*, p. 89.
103. Alan Richardson, *A Preface to Bible Study* (London: SCM, 1943), p. 33.
104. John Baillie, *The Sense of the Presence of God*, Gifford Lectures, 1961-62, (London: Oxford U., 1962), p. 70.
105. Dodd, *Authority of the Bible*, p. 30.
106. Peake, *The Bible*, p. 258.

back as August 7, 1894, that "the only *respectable* defenders of verbal inspiration" were in "the Princeton school of Green and Warfield,"[107] there were those who saw the profound sense in the traditional doctrine. Whereas most of those who stood out against the popularized subjectivist theory of inspiration were careful to repudiate a mechanical process, they were equally emphatic that God did not relinquish concern for the language in which the biblical writers clothed their thoughts and ideas. To admit inspiration at all, they argued, must surely allow it to reach the words of Scripture. Words are an essential expression of thought and the only effective medium of communication and mutual intercourse. Therefore the Cambridge scholar Fredrick Watson declared in an essay published after his death in 1906, "The Bible differs from all other books in the character and degree of its inspiration. It is the supreme manifestation of Divine inspiration embodied in human words."[108] Later, that protagonist of historic orthodoxy T. C. Hammond was to insist that although inspiration certainly affected the subjective nature of the human medium of revelation, it is not enough to conclude that "the men indeed were inspired but not their utterances."[109] Hammond consequently argued for the verbal character of biblical inspiration.

The true referenda is, then, not simply its specific agents. Inspiration cannot be limited to anything done on man, or even yet *in* man. Its focus is on the writings as such. The Scriptures are consequently inspired because, although produced by man for man, they are nevertheless so decisively the result of the action of the Holy Spirit that they are truly and rightly designated "the Word of God." Therefore, when "we speak of the *Scriptures*, we use a word that etymologically denotes the writings and not the material"; without writing, there would be no Bible at all "for the Bible is God's word *written*."[110] Therefore does the historic doctrine hold that "Biblical inspiration is thus verbal by its very nature; for it is of God-given words that God-breathed Scripture consists."[111]

The question of inerrancy raised by the quotation from John

107. T. H. Darlow, *William Robertson Nicoll: Life and Letters* (London: Hodder & Stoughton, 1925), p. 341.
108. Fredrick Watson, *Inspiration* (London: SPCK, 1906), p. 2.
109. T. C. Hammond, *Inspiration and Authority* (London: Inver-Varsity, 1935), p. 23.
110. F. F. Bruce, *The Books and the Parchments* (London: Pickering & Inglis, 1950), p. 150.
111. J. I. Packer, "Inspiration," in *New Bible Dictionary*, ed. J. D. Douglas (London: Inter-Varsity, 1962), p. 565.

Baillie has become in recent days a major issue of debate on both sides of the Atlantic. Prior to the advance of criticism, the idea of the Bible's inerrancy was a certain belief in the church; even if the word was not in general vogue, it was implicit in the church's confessions of the divine inspiration, infallibility, and authority of the Scriptures. It would have been unthinkable that there should be errors and mistakes in the Bible. It was only fair to the dictates of historical factuality for John Burnaby to acknowledge that the biblical idea of inspiration that relates it to the action of the Holy Spirit "makes it incompatible with any error in the writings so inspired" and makes it "the traditional belief of Christendom."[112]

But the general acceptance of the Darwinian evolutionary hypothesis brought about a change of opinion regarding the absolute trustworthiness of the biblical account. The outline of events in the Old Testament records could not be squared with the new thesis, and the palm for accuracy was consequently accorded to Darwin. The unity of Scripture was disrupted to fit into an evolutionary context. The vigorous application of the historical method, wedded as it was to an increasing uncertainty regarding the miraculous elements in the record, led many to declare openly that the Bible could no longer be considered an unerring, divinely inspired volume. Into that atmosphere of uncertainty higher criticism was born, and it readily set itself to disclose the existence of the many mistakes alleged in the biblical text.

So it was that Marcus Dods could declare at the beginning of our period that "until criticism made it impossible for us any longer to identify infallibility with literal inerrancy, it was a delusive and non-existent infallibility that we ascribed to the Bible."[113] And A. S. Peake with equal assurance declared that the new criticism destroyed "the theory of the infallibility and inerrancy of Scripture."[114]

It almost seems that throughout our period critical writers vied with each other in their effort to discover errors in the biblical record, as if the greater the number of errors found, the better the scholarship. Charles Gore was goaded to protest in 1924 against belief in an infallible book and against the evidence he saw of "a revival today of the position that faith in Christianity, as really the divinely-given gospel for the world, is bound up

112. John Burnaby, *Is the Bible Inspired?* (London: Duckworth, 1949), p. 111.
113. Marcus Dods, *The Bible: Its Origin and Nature* (Edinburgh: T. & T. Clark, 1905), pp. 138-39.
114. Peake, *The Bible*, p. 310.

with the old-fashioned belief in the infallible book."[115] A. G. Hebert, branding the idea of "factual inerrancy" as "rigid" and "too narrow," went on to affirm the existence of mistakes in the Scriptures of the Old Testament, not only "in small matters of literal fact, but in matters of faith and morals."[116]

By a combination of ridicule and reason, James Barr seeks to dispose of the doctrine of inerrancy as irrelevant, impossible to sustain, and involving a circular argument.[117]

Supporters of inerrancy can sufficiently reply to each of those objections. To say, as Hebert does, that it is irrelevant to Christian faith that the Bible is erroneous in several particulars must surely undermine the fundamental basis of the gospel. For whose judgment is to be accepted as to what is fact and what is not? The critics? Then the question arises, Which one? For there is little agreement among them on many matters. Experience? But that would subject Christian faith to a dangerous subjectivism in which every man would be disposed to accept only what appealed to him. God's revelation is not made authoritative by experience, however much its truthfulness is confirmed by experience. For, as P. T. Forsyth says, "a real authority is indeed *within* experience, but it is not the authority *of* experience, it is an authority for experience, it is an authority experienced."[118]

To say that Scripture is inerrant is one with saying that it is infallible concerning its truth and dependable concerning its facts. It is, of course, to be granted that neither *inerrant* nor *infallible* are in themselves biblical terms. Both terms are, however, clearly necessary to express in our contemporary era what was accepted in former days as a crucial aspect of the Bible's inspiration—namely, that it is wholly trustworthy and wholly true. Those twin facts about God's revelation cannot be surrendered. What the human recorders have given us of the divine self-disclosure is neither spawned of human guesses nor of mere human genius. The biblical record focuses on Christ, the Word of Truth, and is itself the result of the action of the Spirit of Truth. We can hardly acclaim the Bible as divine truth if it is mixed with error.

Barr's contention that inerrancy is impossible to sustain really begs the question, since many of the alleged errors adduced over the past decades have, in the light of archaeological research, been shown to be ill-founded. That observation should warn

115. Charles Gore, *The Doctrine of the Infallible Book* (London: SCM, 1924), p. 7.
116. A. G. Hebert, *Fundamentalism and the Church of God*, pp. 48, 55; cf. p. 148.
117. Cf. Barr, *Fundamentalism*, pp. 72-84; cf. pp. 51-56.
118. Forsyth, *Principle of Authority*, p. 75.

against too hastily demoting Scripture's factualness, even where the issue is regarded as a minor matter.[119] We are not, of course, unaware that in the process of transmission and translation "errors" have crept into the various manuscripts and texts. But that admission in no way affects the issue that the Scriptures are truly divine and consequently trustworthy.

Neither is the appeal to the Bible to vindicate its own divine authority vitiated by the charge of circularity. It is accepted that Christ's own testimony provides true and basic data for the Christian understanding of His Person. Equally, therefore, should Scripture be allowed to speak for itself; and its claim to be the "out-breathed" Word of God should be accepted.

Logicians argue among themselves whether all forms of syllogistic argument are not finally circular because the conclusion seems to be already contained in the major premise. In fact, many logicians claim that all types of argument are circular. As far as systematic theology is concerned its circular character cannot be avoided, so that even Paul Tillich was obliged to declare it as a fact that "theologians should not be afraid to admit," since "it is not a shortcoming."[120]

The history of the critical analysis of Scripture gives abundant evidence that as soon as errors are allowed in "small matters" they are inevitably seen in the more decisive areas of faith, doctrine, and morals. However, it simply does not seem reasonable to hold God's truth to be revealed through statements that are in themselves erroneous. Of course, there are things in the Bible hard to understand. But the easy solution that dubs as error what cannot be easily explained must be given no credence by the serious biblical student. For the Christian approach to Scripture must surely be with the presupposition that the Book of God's self-disclosure must be true to Him. In fact, so constant throughout the Bible are the references to truth and so numerous the declaration "Thus says the Lord," that the conclusion is all but inescapable that the whole is surely covered by that all-comprehensive phrase.

The conclusion, therefore, stands unweakened that the biblical doctrine of inerrancy derives ultimately from the attitude of the

---

119. Cf. McDonald, *I Want to Know*, pp. 79-83.
120. Paul Tillich, *Systematic Theology* (London: Nisbet, 1950), 1:135. For a comparison of a circular way, with five noncircular ways of reasoning in defense of the God revealed in the historical Jesus and the teaching of Scripture, see Gordon R. Lewis, *Testing Christianity's Truth Claims* (Chicago: Moody, 1976).

Bible to itself, as that is confirmed by Christ's own verdict. Without that certainty in an absolute Word of God:

> Things fall apart; the center
> Cannot hold[121]

121. W. B. Yeats, "The Second Coming," in *Selected Poetry* (London: Macmillan, 1967), p. 97.

5. The Neo-orthodox Reduction

Roger Nicole

The neo-orthodox movement originated after the First World War and exercised its major influence between 1919 and 1955. Characterized by a renewed emphasis on divine transcendence and the importance of the Scripture as a fundamental basis for Christian theology (in contrast to liberalism), it precipitated a renewal of interest in what is still called "biblical theology." Of continued importance, therefore, is the neo-orthodox doctrine of Scripture.[1] This chapter confines itself to a modest presentation and appraisal of the foremost neo-orthodox leader, Karl Barth, and one very influential follower, Emil Brunner.

1. My esteemed colleague, professor David Wells, in a manuscript note addressed to me, suggests the following three elements as characteristic of neo-orthodoxy: "(a) It is true that the importance of Scripture was recognized, but all neo-orthodox thinkers accepted critical presuppositions by which the content of Scripture was analyzed. (b) Also, all shared the Kantian presupposition that revelation is opposed to reason, so God is essentially beyond the reach of the mind. (c) All shared a theological method by which the substance of theology was crystalized out of those perceptions and insights given by the Spirit with or without the biblical Word. It was not grounded either upon human endeavor, rational proofs, logical reflection, or even exegesis, although most of them were not loath to use logic or to quote Scripture when it seemed to suit their purpose."

ROGER NICOLE, A.B., Gymnase Classique, Lausanne, Switzerland; M.A., Sorbonne; B.D., S.T.M., Th.D., Gordon Divinity School; Ph.D., Harvard University, is Andrew Mutch Professor of Theology at Gordon-Conwell Theological Seminary, South Hamilton, Massachusetts, where he has served since 1945. He has written *Moyse Amyraut: A Bibliography;* he also has been a joint editor for *B. B. Warfield: A Bibliography* and *Inerrancy and Common Sense.*

KARL BARTH

When one undertakes to present Karl Barth's view of the Scripture, it is appropriate to recognize certain difficulties that inevitably arise.

First of all, there is a monumental amount of material to be considered, for Barth's output was immense. His major presentation in his *Church Dogmatics*, Part 1, may be safely considered as a fundamental guide to his thought on Scripture. However, he has a number of lesser treatments that deserve to be examined also— brief monographs or articles appearing in *Zwischen den Zeiten* and *Theologische Studien*, and other general presentations of Christian truth in a more compact form. Furthermore, Barth's attitude toward the Scripture is reflected in the totality of his *Church Dogmatics*, in his commentaries, in his sermons, and in his letters.

A second difficulty arises from the paradoxical nature of Karl Barth's theology. For him transcendental truth cannot be expressed in rational categories, but it needs to be made manifest by the clash of opposites. It is therefore very difficult to ascertain the precise meaning he gives to statements and the precise place that his statements must obtain in the total structure of his thought. By quoting actual statements of Barth, one is not assured of having properly expressed his view, for there may be balancing statements that appear in opposition and that need to be taken into consideration for a full view. This problem is somewhat alleviated because in *Church Dogmatics* Barth himself has not permitted this ambiguity to prevail. Thus, a number of his interpreters have felt confident they had a means of assessing what Barth held.

Third, it is not at once evident that Barth remained throughout his career firmly committed to one exclusive position on Scripture. In some other respects people have detected certain shifts in his stance, especially between 1915 and 1935. Some have gone so far as to distinguish rather sharply five different phases in his approach. It is not claimed here, however, that his position on the Holy Scripture really changed very much during the course of his theological career.

Fourth, some statements of Barth may yet be ambiguous because of the variety of meanings the term *Word of God* can receive in his writings. In his *Church Dogmatics* Barth makes plain that the Word (Logos) of God manifests Himself in three forms: the incarnate Word; the inscripturated Word heard in connection with the Bible; and the proclaimed (preached) Word. In any given context of Barth's writings we need to ascertain in which of these senses the term is used. Here again the difficulty is alleviated by the fact that in his *Church Dogmatics* Karl Barth deals with these usages in distinct categories.

Finally, it must be noted that careful distinction must be maintained between Barth and Barthianism. Even those who claim to follow Barth's leadership cannot always be viewed as appropriate expositors or interpreters of his position. The very fact that they are disciples may prompt them to "annex" the master, to assimilate unwarrantably his views to theirs. In this chapter we will rely primarily on Barth's own statements.

EXPOSITION

Karl Barth emphasizes first of all the three forms in which the Word of God manifests Himself.[2] At the ultimate level is the revealed Word, identical with the Logos, the second Person of the Trinity. Revelation therefore is God Himself speaking (present tense). Every other form of the Word must relate to Him and is effective only insofar as God in His free grace is condescending to use it for revelational encounters.[3] What is revealed, Barth maintains, is not information about God, but God Himself. Revelation "happens" to a person; it is not reliable statements in human language about God.

The inscripturated Word, comprising the whole canon of Scripture, is a witness to revelation.[4] It embodies the record of the prophets and apostles who communicated with God by a supernatural encounter. The written Word is not in itself revelation: to view it like that, Barth thinks, is bibliolatry. It is written by men

2. Karl Barth, *The Doctrine of the Word of God (Prolegomena)*, vol. 1, pt. 1, 2d ed., of *Church Dogmatics*, trans. G. W. Bromiley and T. R. Torrance (Edinburgh: T. & T. Clark, 1975), pp. 88-111 (1st ed., pp. 98-135).
3. Ibid., vol. 1, pt. 2 of *Church Dogmatics*, trans. G. T. Thompson and Harold Knight (Edinburgh: T. & T. Clark, 1956), pp. 1-25.
4. Ibid., 1, 2, 456-527 *(Bezeugung, Hinweis)*.
"The Bible is not in itself and as such God's past revelation. As it is God's Word it bears witness to God's past revelation, and it is God's past revelation in the form of attestation," ibid., 1, 1, p. 111 (125).
"We have to call the Bible a witness of divine revelation. We have here an undoubted limitation: we distinguish the Bible as such from revelation," ibid., 1, 2, p. 463.
"We believe in and with the Church that Holy Scripture has this priority over all other writings and authorities, even those of the Church. We believe in and with the Church that Holy Scripture as the original and legitimate witness of divine revelation is itself the Word of God," ibid., 1, 2, p. 502.

in the words of men and is in itself fallible at every point.[5] Yet, as
a witness to revelation it may be used by God if and when it
pleases Him to encounter individuals (who are therefore confronted by the living Word of God). In God's own appointment
this written word in its entirety may be called the Word of God
because in it and through it God is still encountering human
beings according to His own sovereign freedom.[6]

The proclaimed Word depends upon the written Word because
it is based upon this witness to revelation. Whereas the Bible
looks back to the revelation of God in Jesus Christ, the proclamation looks forward to the continued implementation of the sovereign purpose today and in the future. Needless to say, the proclamation also is couched in fallible human words and must therefore not be identified with revelation itself. It functions as the
Word of God under God's sovereign appointment but is subject to
all the frailties characteristic of humanity.[7]

One perceives therefore in the structure of Karl Barth's
thought a close relation between the three forms of the Word, but
only the first form (revealed Word) has an absolute character.[8]
The other two are relative and can be properly labeled the Word
of God only to the extent that God freely chooses to use them to
address individual men and women. The impact of this outlook on
Barth's doctrine of Scripture is very far-reaching. Here are some
of the consequences drawn by Barth and articulated in Part 1 of
his *Church Dogmatics*.

(1) The authority of the Bible and its divine character are not
subject to any human demonstration whatsoever. It is only when
God, by the Holy Spirit, speaks through the Bible that a person
hears the Word of God. This activity of the Holy Spirit is self-
evident and not subject to any demonstration. The authority of
the Bible is therefore not a proper subject for apologetics. "We
will not ask: why the Bible? and look for external or internal
grounds and reasons. We will leave it to the Bible itself, if we are
to be obedient to it, to vindicate itself by what takes place, i.e., to
vindicate the witness to divine revelation which we have heard in
it."[9]

(2) The human authors of Scripture were men and women who

5. Ibid., 1, 2, pp. 462-69.
6. Ibid., 1, 2, pp. 472-76.
7. Ibid., 1, 2, pp. 743-58.
8. Ibid., 1, 1, pp. 120-24 (135-40).
9. Ibid., 1, 2, pp. 458, 506, 536-37.

witnessed a revelatory encounter with God. There is therefore an authentic experience that is at the root of their activity as divine spokesmen.[10] Prophets and apostles, therefore, do have an essential relation to the perception of divine truth, but that relation is not of itself sufficient to convey the truth to others or to mediate for others an encounter with God. Only God can speak for God, even when such speaking is initiated by reading the written word.[11]

(3) The Bible consists of the sixty-six canonical books recognized in the church, not because the church confers on them a special authority but because they embody the record of those who witnessed to revelation in its original form.[12] The canon strictly speaking is not closed because God is always free to do what He pleases. For practical purposes, however, it is inappropriate to reopen the question because within the church community God has been pleased to bear witness through the existing collection.[13]

(4) Since God uses the very language of Scripture as the witness to revelation, Barth considers it appropriate to speak of "verbal inspiration." However, he does not imply verbal inspiredness, an outlook that he thinks attempts to lock God's revelation in the words of Scripture.

> If God speaks to man, He really speaks the language of this concrete human word of man. That is the right and necessary truth in the concept of verbal inspiration. If the word is not to be separated from the matter, if there is no such thing as verbal inspiredness, the matter is not to be separated from the word, and there is real inspiration, the hearing of the Word of God, only in the form of verbal inspiration, the hearing of the Word of God only in the concrete form of the biblical word. Verbal inspiration does not mean the infallibility of the biblical word in its linguistic, historical and theological character as a human word. It means that the fallible and faulty human word is as such used by God and has to be received and heard in spite of its human fallibility.[14]

(5) The Bible written by fallible men and women in human language is fallible in every respect and contains errors and contra-

10. Ibid., 1, 1, pp. 102-4 (114-16); 1, 2, pp. 502-6.
11. Ibid., 1, 2, pp. 512-17.
12. Ibid., 1, 1, pp. 107-9 (120-22); 1, 2, pp. 473-75.
13. Ibid., 1, 2, pp. 476-81; pp. 599-603.
14. Ibid., 1, 2, pp. 532-33 *(Vervalinspiration* versus *Verbalinspiriertheit).*

dictions not only in peripheral matters like history, geography, natural science, and so forth, but also in theology and ethics. Yet this human witness, in spite of its erroneousness, may be used by God as the vehicle through which He speaks and confronts individuals.

> There are obvious overlappings and contradictions—e.g., between the Law and the prophets, between John and the Synoptics, between Paul and James. But nowhere are we given a single rule by which to make a common order, perhaps an order of precedence, but at any rate of synthesis, of what is in itself such a varied whole. Nowhere do we find a rule which enables us to grasp it in such a way that we can make organic parts of the distinctions and evade the contradictions as such. . . .
>
> If the prophets and apostles are not real and therefore fallible men, even in their office, even when they speak and write of God's revelation, then it is not a miracle that they speak the Word of God.[15]

According to Barth, there is no way in which a person can segregate in the Bible what is erroneous from what is true and then insist that it is only through the true passages that God speaks to human beings. God may, and indeed does, speak through the whole canon of Holy Scripture. It is, therefore, appropriate to say that the whole Bible from Genesis to Revelation *is* the Word of God, but it is very harmful to confuse this form of the Word of God with revelation itself, which is Jesus Christ—the Logos incarnate.[16] Barth rejects the formulation "The Bible contains the Word of God" because for him this suggests the possibility of a sorting out of the genuine from the spurious.

> We are absolved from differentiating the Word of God in the Bible from other contents, infallible portions and expressions from the erroneous ones, the infallible from the fallible, and from imagining that by means of such discoveries we can create for ourselves encounters with the genuine Word of God in the Bible.[17]

15. Ibid., 1, 2, pp. 509-29.
16. Ibid., 1, 2, pp. 512-14.
"Precisely in His Word God is person. But this then means concretely that He is Lord of the wording of His Word. He is not bound to it but it to Him. He has free control over the wording of Holy Scripture. He can use it or not use it. He can use it in this way or in that way. He can choose a new wording beyond that of Holy Scripture," ibid., 1, 1, pp. 137 (157).
17. Ibid., 1, 2, p. 531.

(6) The task of the church is to search diligently the written text in order to ascertain its meaning and to proclaim its teaching. When Christian people perform this task in faithfulness, God is pleased to speak and confront men and women.[18]

(7) Because the necessity of an immediacy of God's speech to individuals is emphasized, it may be said that the Bible *becomes* the Word of God if and when God is pleased to speak through it. Thus, great stress is placed on the dynamic significance of Scripture, and Barth evinces a strong reluctance to view the Bible as intrinsically and statically the Word of God.

> The Bible is God's Word to the extent that God causes it to be His Word, to the extent that He speaks through it. . . .
> The statement that the Bible is God's Word is a confession of faith, a statement of the faith which hears God Himself speak through the biblical word of man. . . . The Bible . . . becomes God's Word in this event, and in the statement that the Bible is God's Word the little word "is" refers to its being in this becoming. It does not become God's Word because we accord it faith but in the fact that it becomes revelation to us. . . .
> The direct identification between revelation and the Bible which is in fact at issue is not one that we can presuppose or anticipate. It takes place as an event when and where the biblical word becomes God's Word. . . .
> Without wanting to deny or even limit their character as God's Word we must bear in mind that the Word of God is mediated here, first through the human persons of the prophets and apostles who receive it and pass it on, and then through the human persons of its expositors and preachers, so that Holy Scripture and proclamation must always become God's Word in order to be it. If the Word of God is God Himself even in Holy Scripture and Church proclamation, it is because this is so in the revelation to which they bear witness.[19]

(8) The relationship between the divine and the human in Holy Scripture remains a mystery,[20] analogous in some respects to the mystery of the union of divine and human natures in the one Person of Jesus Christ.[21]

18. Ibid., 1, 2, pp. 468-71, 538-41, 712-15.
19. See also ibid., 1, 2, p. 530.
20. Ibid., 1, 1, pp. 162-86 (184-212); 1, 2, p. 518.
21. Ibid., 1, 2, pp. 499-501.

(9) Karl Barth claims that his position is in line with the view of Scripture itself,[22] with the teaching of some of the early church Fathers, and with the position of the Reformers, notably Luther and Calvin.[23] He holds that the developments in Lutheran and Reformed orthodoxy in the seventeenth century represent a hardening in the doctrine of Scripture—a sclerosis that has transferred the authority of the Bible from the living God, who speaks, to the written page, which may be a "dead letter."[24] In this objectivization of Scripture the sovereign freedom of God's grace has been impugned, in Barth's view, to the great detriment of the life of the church.

APPRAISAL

Commendation. Certain laudable elements in Karl Barth's view of Scripture, in contrast to liberal views, deserve emphasis.

(1) *Church Dogmatics* is clearly a monumental work in which the place of Scripture in the church and in theology receives most careful attention from Barth. In his own characteristic manner he has structured the topic in unprecedented ways, replete with interesting insights on particular passages of Scripture, historical perspectives on the development of doctrine, and vigorous challenges to those who differ from him, notably the Roman Catholic church and liberal thinkers of various schools. Anyone who reads this material is bound to be enriched.

(2) Barth, in contrast to the prevailing liberal theology of the late nineteenth and early twentieth centuries, vigorously calls us back to the recognition of Scripture as testimony to the Word of God.

(3) In his strong emphasis on God's freedom to speak or not to speak through the Bible, Barth does call attention, although not without some excess, to the importance of the illumination of the Holy Spirit, whereby alone the Scripture can be read with true spiritual benefits. The problem lies in the blindness of the readers, however, not in some sporadic or intermittent character of the light issuing from the Scripture (1 Cor. 2:6-16; 2 Cor. 3:4-18).

(4) Barth does acknowledge (sometimes to excess) the true hu-

---

22. See ibid., 1, 2, pp. 504-6.
23. Ibid., 1, 2, pp. 520-22.
24. Ibid., 1, 2, pp. 523-26.

manity of the biblical authors. This indeed is one of the components of a proper doctrine of Scripture, for in truth the Bible was written by human beings in human words that can convey a message to humans.

(5) Barth emphasizes the auto-pistic character of Scripture so that its authority is not made dependent upon some rational demonstration that would subordinate the Word of God to our reasoning process. However, he fails to explain the scriptural mandate to test the spirits and distinguish true from false prophetic and apostolic spokesmen.

(6) Barth recognizes that the locus of God's speaking to us is the canonical Holy Scripture, and he therefore asserts, and often exemplifies, the centrality of Scripture for the faith.

(7) In his treatment of Scripture, Barth frequently functions as a careful exegete and does not attempt to dismiss the statements of Scripture on the ground that they embody fallible human ideas. Furthermore, he rightly perceives that every text must be understood in the light of the whole Bible and that no text can be properly considered in isolation.

(8) Barth rightly emphasizes that the Bible is not simply a collection of true propositions designed to enlarge our knowledge in a number of areas. Rather he asserts the Bible has a focus or center that gives meaning to every part. This he designates as Jesus-Christ, the Word. One may entertain differences of opinion as to how this works out and what specifically is meant by this language. The "Christomonism" of Karl Barth has aroused considerable criticism, but the insight that there is a fundamental unity in the revelation of Scripture and that this unity focuses on the redemptive purpose of God appears to us worthy of commendation. This is what Pascal had stated: "Jesus Christ, whom the two Testament regard, the Old as its hope, the New as its model, and both as their centre" (*Thoughts* 740).

(9) Barth is right in asserting that our faith is not ultimately directed to a book, the Bible, but to the triune God, made known supremely through the incarnation. We should not, therefore, worship the Bible but reserve our adoration for God Himself. The Bible is the instrument by which our attention is directed to the true God, the vehicle by which our faith, prompted by the Holy

Spirit, focuses on the proper object. How this instrumentality of the Bible works, however, is an area in which we would sharply differ with Barth.

Criticism. The following might be mentioned as serious weaknesses in Karl Barth's position.

(1) In attempting to safeguard the freedom of God to speak or not to speak through Scripture, Barth has undermined the essential character of Scripture, which is to be in itself the authoritative Word of God. This is a most grievous distortion that could annihilate the true authority of Scripture if logic is permitted to have its course. By a happy inconsistency Barth has not drifted as far away from scriptural moorings as his position would permit, but this does not appear to be because of his doctrine of Scripture, but rather because of an inconsistent adherence to what Scripture says when fairly interpreted. On Barth's terms, however, what Scripture says is simply the fallible word of men and therefore there cannot be any obligation to adhere to it unless God in His free grace invigorates it by His Spirit. Even if Barth had experienced this invigorating, it would still not necessarily apply to his readers. If the Bible is to have authority anywhere, it must be by virtue of some intrinsic character.

(2) That intrinsic authority of the Bible is precisely what Scripture itself affirms. The Bible is not merely a witness to revelation, it is revelation. When Moses came down from Mount Sinai, he did not present the Ten Commandments as a "witness to God's revelation," but he said, "These words the Lord spoke. . . . And He [God] wrote them on two tablets of stone and gave them to me" (Deut. 5:22). The prophets similarly, hundreds of times, introduced their message with the words "Thus says the Lord." And our Lord in making use of the Scripture never adduces any quotation with a conditional clause such as "if indeed God is speaking through this passage." Rather, He emphasizes even with respect to minor details that "the Scripture cannot be broken" (John 10:35) or "not the smallest letter or stroke shall pass away" (Matt. 5:18). It is true, of course, that because of the blindness of sinful humanity we as humans are impervious to the truth of Scripture unless God illumines us by His Spirit to understand it in a saving manner. But that does not affect the fact that in itself the Scripture is light (Ps. 119:105, 130) and truth (Ps. 119:160; John 17:17).

Specifically our Lord and His apostles viewed the Old Testament in the aforementioned way. There was in their form of quoting the Scripture an underlying assumption of the full equivalency of the phrase "Scripture says" with "God says." This was beautifully expressed by Augustine in his *Confessions* (XIII, 29), where he represents God as saying to him, "That which my Scripture says, I say." This thought was developed with great fullness on exegetical grounds by B. B. Warfield in his article " 'It says:,' 'Scripture says:,' 'God says:' ".[25] Also, word studies of *revelation* and *word* show that revelation was both personal and propositional, not merely personal (relational or functional).

The objective nature of the Scripture's authority is exemplified in a notable way in the account of Christ's temptation in the desert (Matt. 4 and Luke 4). Here our Lord makes no reference to any encounter that either He or Satan would have had with certain passages so that they would have "become the Word of God"! Rather the Word of God Incarnate three times pointed to a text in Deuteronomy with the simple introduction "It is written." And each time Satan desisted, without further argument. Surely that makes plain that Christ did not operate with a Barthian concept of Scripture, and that, in the presence of our Lord, Satan knew better than to attempt a Barthian kind of evasion from the impregnable authority of the written Word.

(3) The previous stricture shows that, in my judgment, Karl Barth's claim to have given us a faithful representation of the biblical doctrine of Holy Scripture[26] cannot be sustained. Some aspects of Barth's position are indeed in harmony with scriptural teaching, but that which is distinctive—specifically the view that the written word is only a "witness to revelation" and that it has to "become the Word of God" if it is to transcend human fallibility—does not find any valid support in the Bible. The two texts on which Barth relies (1 Cor. 2:6-16 and 2 Cor. 3:4-18) do not substantiate his point but relate to the blindness of sinful men and women rather than to any inadequacy in the text or even in preaching (cf. also 2 Cor. 4:3-4). Even Christ, whose words Barth

25. " 'It says:,' 'Scripture says:,' 'God says:' " *Presbyterian and Reformed Review* 10 (July 1899): 472-510. Reprinted in *Revelation and Inspiration* (New York: Oxford, 1927; and Grand Rapids: Baker, 1981), pp. 283-332. Reprinted also in *The Inspiration and Authority of the Bible* (Philadelphia: Presbyterian and Reformed, 1948), pp. 299-348.

26. "The right doctrine of Holy Scripture cannot claim abstract validity, but its confirmation must always be sought and found in exegesis and therefore in Holy Scripture itself," Barth, *Church Dogmatics*, 1, 2, p. 462. Cf. also ibid., 1, 2, pp. 485-86.

(we hope) would not characterize as "capable of error and guilty of error" encountered that blindness in His ministry (Matt. 13:13-17; Mark 4:11-12; Luke 8:10; John 3:19-20; 5:39-40; 9:39-41; 10:26; 12:37-40). Unfortunately, Barth has confused revelation with salvation and inspiration with illumination.

(4) Barth's claim to have recaptured the doctrine of the Reformers, particularly Luther and Calvin, is open to very serious question. In the case of Luther, he has some fairly impressive quotations, which could, however, be matched by an even greater number of passages in which Luther affirms that the text *is* the Word of God, that the Bible cannot contradict itself, and that difficulties or discrepancies are only apparent. Luther's vacillation on the question of the canon, whereby he considered excluding certain books like Ecclesiastes, Song of Solomon, and James, is obviously the result of a conviction that in the canon there could not be any theological error. On Barthian terms those books would not cause any difficulty.

In the case of Calvin, with whom I am much more intimately acquainted, the claim appears simply preposterous. None of the numerous Calvin quotations advanced by Barth even remotely supports Barthian distinctives, and one remains puzzled that Barth could ever have thought that he could claim support from Calvin.[27]

There is also in Barth undue harshness toward the theologians of the seventeenth century and toward apologetics. Indeed some of them may have been carried away by the evidential strength that the indicia of Scripture's supernatural character exhibited. In turn they may have grounded on a rational argument their

---

27. We are, of course, aware that the precise nature of Calvin's doctrine of Holy Scripture is the subject of considerable scholarly discussion. A number of writers, including E. Doumergue, W. Niesel, H. Noltensmeier, R. S. Wallace, J. T. McNeill, J. K. S. Reid, R. C. Prust, F. L. Battles, R. Stauffer, and J. Rogers have vigorously contended that Calvin accepted the infallible authority of Scripture only insofar as it relates to religious matters. But on "secular" subjects they contend he would have allowed for errors in the Bible. On the other hand, B. B. Warfield, R. Seeberg, R. E. Davies, E. Dowey, D. J. de Groot, J. Murray, J. I. Packer, K. Kantzer, P. E. Hughes, and H. J. Forstmann, have vigorously contended that Calvin held to a very strict doctrine of Bible inspiration, such that every word was seen as controlled by the Holy Spirit and therefore inerrant. A valuable listing of much literature on this subject may be found in Richard Stauffer, *Dieu, la Création et la Providence dans la Prédication de Calvin* (Bern, Switzerland: Peter Lang, 1978), p. 72. My own position is articulated in a review of J. Rogers and D. McKim, *The Authority and Interpretation of the Bible*, found in *Christian Scholar's Review* 10/2 (1981): 163-64.

conviction, which conviction ultimately only the testimony of the Holy Spirit can really establish. But in their way of looking at the Scripture as the embodiment of the Word of God those theologians did not differ materially from the Reformers and theologians of the sixteenth century. The Spirit of truth attests the reality and significance of verbal and enacted "signs" and employs consistency of doctrine to help the people of God distinguish true from false spokesmen for God (Deut. 13:1-5; 18:20-22; 1 John 4:1-3), true Scripture from counterfeit.

The same undue harshness toward the whole evangelical (conservative, fundamentalist) tradition's attitude to the Scripture is also a weakness in Barth's approach.

(5) According to Barth, there is an inadequate basis for the canon of Scripture. Indeed he affirms that the sixty-six books *are* the canon, but he leaves the door open to extensions and is not very decisive in his attitude to reductions. Barth's subjectivistic inadequacy at this point may be an index to the questionable nature of his presentation. It illustrates also his lack of responsibility to objective evidence.

(6) Barth asserts that Holy Scripture contains errors of various kinds, that it knows "nothing of the distinction of fact and value which is so important to us, between history on the one hand, and saga and legend on the other,"[28] and that the Bible may be subjected like any other book to historical criticism.[29] Concerning "historical criticism," Barth leaves the door wide open, although he himself makes little use of critical notions such as the documentary hypothesis for the origin of the Pentateuch, multiple authorship of Isaiah, or pseudonymous authorship of certain New Testament books.[30] The use of the concepts "saga" and "legend" appears mischievous; they damage the historicity of the narratives to which they are applied, even as does the concept of "myth," which Barth emphatically rejects.[31]

When it comes to errors, Barth does not give a list of them or even some significant sampling. He is content to affirm that the Bible contains errors and is actually "simply quite unconcerned" in this respect.[32]

28. Barth, *Chruch Dogmatics*, 1, 2, pp. 509; cf. ibid., 1, 1, pp. 326-27 (375-76).
29. Ibid., 1, 2, p. 494.
30. In ibid., 1, 2, p. 504 he ascribes 2 Timothy to Paul.
31. E.g., ibid., 1, 1, pp. 327-29 (376-78).
32. Ibid., 1, 1, p. 326 (374).

Karl Barth goes so far as to affirm that "there are obvious overlappings *[Überschneidungen]* and contradictions *[Widersprüche]*, e.g. between the Law the the prophets, between John and the Synoptists, between Paul and James."[33] But that ruins the true authority of the Bible! Apparently in naming Paul and James, Barth refers to their presentation on justification. But precisely here, if they are construed to be divergent, we have an area where they themselves are not tolerant of divergences but denounce roundly those who differ from them. The solution, obviously, will be to assume and hopefully to manifest an underlying harmony between those two apostles. If we do not, we probably would be constrained to follow Luther's example and rule either Paul or James out of the canon. Yet the conflict is not so deep if we recognize that Paul contends against those who sought justification by dead works, and James against those who advocated justification by a dead faith. Both of those contentions are in harmony with a doctrine of justification on the ground of Christ's work alone, appropriated through faith alone, and evidenced by an obedient spirit and good works.

(7) Barth very stoutly affirms that the Scripture alone with the proclamation based on it is the channel through which God now speaks. However, he barely gives us any evidence that he believes this affirmation. It would appear that the sovereign freedom of God would be better preserved if no limitation were indicated here,[34] which is a point Emil Brunner clearly perceives. Thus Brunner assumes that God speaks in other ways than through Scripture and the Christian message alone, although He does so somewhat less clearly. This manifests a dilution of the Christian message in the wake of neo-orthodoxy.

By a happy inconsistency Barth has strenuously resisted Brunner's inclination, but there appears to be no sufficient ground for doing so on his own terms. In fact, Barth's outlook is characterized by a kind of creeping universalism that has an eroding effect in all areas where the Christian faith lays claim to a uniqueness that includes revelation and salvation. Barth functions with a kind of uneasy tension here, with a tendency to accentuate increasingly the universalistic theme in his own theological development.

33. Ibid., 1, 2, p. 509.
34. Barth appears to have strengthened his position in this area with the passage of time. Perhaps his controversy with Rudolf Bultmann led him to assert increasingly the exclusivity of Scripture as the channel of divine revelation.

(8) The principle of divine transcendence by which Barth intends to safeguard God's freedom and majesty, so that humans could not hold Him as a prisoner "at their disposal," is probably at the root of his doctrine of Scripture as a witness to revelation rather than the embodiment of revelation. But this view of transcendence, even though it rightly counteracts human pride, is not itself a balanced, scriptural representation of God. It leads Barth to an inordinate denunciation of natural revelation. It could lead to very serious distortions of the concept of the incarnation, as illustrated in the following diagram:

The Bible	Jesus Christ
being fallible as a human word	being fallible and capable of sinning as a man
must be taken up by God in His freedom in order to become God's words.	must be taken up by God in His freedom in order to become God's Word.
Barth's view of Scripture	*Adoptionism in Christology*

We are not here accusing Barth of holding to an adoptionist Christology; we only suggest that to hold his intermittent adoptionism in bibliology may logically lead to an erosion of one's Christology as well. In fact Barth is playing with fire in this area when he says in relation to John 1:14 that "flesh is the concrete form of human nature marked by Adam's fall,"[35] or again that "the New Testament certainly did not present Jesus Christ as the moral ideal,"[36] even though in those contexts he also asserts the sinlessness of Christ. Those statements surely are most unfortunate, and they give us a measure of the dangers implicit in Barth's position.

On balance, it would appear from the appraisal just conducted that in spite of very signal merits in the work of Karl Barth, there are also very serious flaws in his outlook on revelation and the Scriptures. It is a melancholy fact that relatively few people have accepted completely the approach of Barth and that his followers have in most cases tended to veer considerably to the left of him.

35. Barth, *Church Dogmatics*, 1, 2, p. 151.
36. Ibid., 1, 2, p. 156.

Rudolf Bultmann notably, who was one of the early followers, turned out to be a very radical critic whose influence in the theological world from an evangelical point of view must be adjudged largely nefarious. Particularly in Barth's own handling of Scripture, he has not had an important following. Neo-orthodoxy by and large has taken much more liberty with the authority of the Bible than Barth ever did, but it is difficult to acquit him altogether from responsibility in this development.

EMIL BRUNNER

In view of the extent of our comments on Karl Barth, a much briefer treatment of Emil Brunner will suffice, even though his views differ at some important points from those of Barth.

EXPOSITION

Emil Brunner's approach to Scripture is perhaps expressed most fully in his book *Revelation and Reason* (German edition, 1941); but a very convenient summary with some developments due to the passing of the years may be found in *The Christian Doctrine of God* (German edition, 1946). Brunner's approach is dominated primarily by the basic outlook that revelation, and indeed truth in the religious realm, is personal in nature. It cannot, therefore, be expressed through propositions but has to find expression in an "I-Thou" encounter of persons. An encounter by the reader is necessary as much as, and perhaps even more than, in the original disclosure. This outlook, steeped in the personalism of Martin Buber, tends to reduce the importance of a verbal formulation of any religious concepts.

> It is therefore no accident that the Johannine Gospel in particular, which begins with the concept of the Logos, and thus describes Jesus directly as the Word of God, *only* uses this term in the Prologue, and nowhere else in the Gospel. The use of the idea of the Logos, therefore, does not mean that *Jesus is the Word*, but that *the "Word" is Jesus*. All that was called the "Word" in the Old Testament, all that was indicated in the Old Testament narrative of the Creation by the words "and God said," all that had to be said in words in the Old Testament, is now here Himself in Person, no longer merely in speech about Him. It is for this reason that the One whom men describe as the Logos, may also be described in other terms: Light, Life, and above all: Son of God.
>
> In order to make it clear that this change has taken place,

henceforth the expression "Logos, Word of God" will no longer be used.[37]

Specifically, Brunner is prepared to affirm that the Bible in relation to earthly matters such as history, geography, natural science, and others is in no way protected from considerable error. Those matters are entirely subsidiary to its main purpose, which is to precipitate an encounter with the living God. Therefore Brunner, in a much more sweeping manner than Karl Barth, is ready to discount the biblical teaching at many points.

In the matter of history[38] he does view the early chapters of Genesis as primal history *(Urgeschichte)*, which is a kind of history that does not have to recount events but which explains a modern situation in view of some primal development that eludes investigation on our scientific terms.[39] In the New Testament he rejects the virgin birth of Jesus Christ in spite of its clear attestation in Matthew and Luke.[40] He also rejects the empty tomb of Christ as an evidence for the resurrection.[41] In view of his stance Emil Brunner would not be embarrassed by any historical inadequacies or even contradictions within the Holy Scripture.

> That God can speak to us His single, never contradictory Word through the priestly writings of the Old Testament as well as through the prophetic or the New Testament writings, even though these several writings are very various and in part contradictory, just as He can speak His single, never contradictory Word through the contradictory accounts of Luke and Matthew in regard to this or that incident in the life of Jesus—this correct proposition was converted into the following false one: There are no contradictions in the Bible, either in statements or in doctrine; all such contradictions are only apparent, and can be resolved by means of the harmonizing or allegorizing interpretation.[42]

37. Emil Brunner, *The Christian Doctrine of God*, trans. Olive Wyon (Philadelphia: Westminster, 1980), p. 26; cf. Brunner, *The Divine-Human Encounter*, trans. W. Amandus Loos (1943; reprint, Westport, Conn.: Greenwood, 1980), pp. 20-21, 30-32; Brunner, *Revelation and Reason* (1941; reprint, Philadelphia: Westminster, 1956), pp. 362-74.

38. Brunner, *The Philosophy of Religion* (Naperville, Ill.: Allenson, 1958), pp. 156-71.

39. Brunner, *Revelation and Reason*, p. 286.

40. Brunner, *The Christian Doctrine of Creation and Redemption*, vol. 2 of *Dogmatics* (Philadelphia: Westminster, 1952), pp. 352-56.

41. Ibid., pp. 368-70.

42. Brunner, *The Divine-Human Encounter*, pp. 173-74.

With respect to the connection between natural science and the Bible,[43] Brunner holds that the Scripture does reflect a primitive and on that account inadequate understanding of cosmology, of the nature of the created world, and even of the place of humanity within it.

> The Old Testament story of creation gives us the story of God's creation in connexion with a definite picture of space, of time, and still more definitely, of the beginning of all forms of life which have ever been and are unalterable. At all three points the position of modern knowledge forces us to abandon this view and to replace it by other ideas. . . .
>
> In whatever way this question will be answered—one thing can no longer be conceived as a mere hypothesis, but must be regarded as a proved scientific truth: that man has evolved out of the more primitive forms of animal life.[44]

His discarding of scriptural data in those areas is therefore much more sweeping than that of Karl Barth. It is interesting to note that whereas Barth almost invariably speaks of "Holy Scripture," Brunner appears to be generally satisfied with the formulation "Scripture." The Bible is useful, however, because it is a channel whereby a witness to revelation is presented so that the believer may be led to encounter God as He addresses us.

APPRAISAL

We need not repeat what has already been stated with reference to Karl Barth and thus applies equally to the position of Emil Brunner. Our interest is to call attention here to certain points of commendation and criticism, which are markedly distinctive.

Commendation. Emil Brunner has managed to express his approach in a much more compact and understandable form than Karl Barth. Although his thought is sometimes subtle and nuanced, his formulations are generally quite lucid and fairly clearly related to one fundamental structure of thinking, which did not greatly vary throughout the time of his teaching ministry.

(1) In emphasizing the personal nature of religious truth, Brunner has pointed to an important aspect of our religious experience. It is surely true that there is more to faith than mere

43. Cf. Brunner, *The Philosophy of Religion*, pp. 171-78.
44. Brunner, *Doctrine of Creation and Redemption*, pp. 31, 79.

intellectual conveyance and perception. The personal dimension of true faith needs therefore to be acknowledged, even though many would be greatly disinclined to do so in Brunner's terms.

(2) Brunner is notably concerned to recognize elements of truth even in the positions he criticizes. This is manifest, for instance, in the major divisions of the second part of his work *The Philosophy of Religion*, all of which begin with the words "The Element of Truth in." Then he deals with rationalism, subjectivism, historicism, and orthodoxy, all of which he rejects as one-sided. This spirit of generosity is surely to be commended and does not inevitably entail damaging concessions.

(3) Brunner is concerned to reflect the insights in science, history, psychology, philosophy, and so on, available in the modern world. At times this concern may have led him, however, to accept too readily theories that remain open to question and that appear to be in conflict with biblical revelation. As examples, one could cite Brunner's endorsement of the Wellhausen view of Israel's development,[45] or again his ready acceptance of an evolutionary origin of mankind.[46]

Criticism. It is obvious that very serious criticisms arise in connection with Emil Brunner's position, especially as it is contrasted with an evangelical point of view.

(1) Brunner's approach to history simply does not seem to be that of the Scripture, specifically in relation to the resurrection of Christ. Paul (1 Cor. 15) strongly insists on the historicity of the event, and to allow this to become negotiable is in intolerable conflict with the biblical outlook. A large portion of the biblical writings *are* history, and it *does* matter whether or not the events described there have taken place. If they have not, not even the dialectic skill of Emil Brunner can relieve the Scripture of the devastating charge that it is a fable or a myth that twentieth-century thinking people can no longer accept.

45. Cf. Brunner, *Revelation and Reason*, p. 287, "A great part of the Old Testament which used to be almost inaccessible has now become magnificently alive. The labors of scientific historical critics . . . have given us the Prophets of Israel anew."
46. Cf. Brunner, *Doctrine of Creation and Redemption*, p. 79, "One thing can no longer be conceived as mere hypothesis, but must be regarded as a proved scientific truth [*gesicherte wissenschaftliche Erkenntnis*]: that man has evolved out of the more primitive forms of animal life."

(2) The notion of the canon in Brunner is very fluid. One can easily perceive why it should be so, for the freedom of God should not be abridged by limitations to a certain book for the conveyance of truth. Brunner holds that the Bible represents the most adequate channel for God's speaking because it includes the witness of people who surely were recipients of revelation in a personal encounter. But he would assert that the Bible is not the exclusive channel for God's words. In some other ways as well God can and does mediate encounter with Himself. This leads to a creeping universalism even more accentuated than in Karl Barth's system. Because of its striking clarity we quote in full Brunner's famous illustration drawn from phonograph records.

> Every one has seen the trade slogan "His Master's Voice." If you buy a phonograph record you are told that you will hear the Master Caruso. Is that true! Of course! But really his voice? Certainly! And yet—there are some noises made by the machine which are not the Master's voice, but the scratching of the steel needle upon the hard disk. But do not become impatient with the hard disk! For only by means of the record can you hear "the master's voice." So, too, is it with the Bible. It makes the real Master's voice audible,—really his voice, his words, what he wants to say. But there are incidental noises accompanying, just because God speaks His Word through the voice of man. Paul, Peter, Isaiah, and Moses are such men. But through them God speaks His Word. God has also come into the world as man, really God, but really *man* too. Therefore the Bible is all His voice, notwithstanding all the disturbing things, which, being human are unavoidable. Only a fool listens to the incidental noises when he might listen to the sound of his Master's voice! The importance of the Bible is that God speaks to us through it.
>
> How then, are we to regard those other books which claim to be God's word also? There are two things to be said: first, are you a Mohammedan or a Hindu? If not, then these books do not apply to you. Second, if you still want to know how we are to regard those other books, I can tell you only one thing: a different voice is to be heard in them than that which we hear in the Bible. It is not the same God, not the Good Shepherd who comes to His sheep. It is the voice of a stranger. It may be that somehow it is God's voice, too. But if so, a scarcely recognizable voice, just as a poor photograph may resemble you, but not at all look as you are.
>
> Now are there any other questions? It is my opinion that if this is the way it stands, there is only one conclusion to be drawn: Go now, and begin at last to listen attentively to the Master's voice.[47]

47. Brunner, *Our Faith* (New York: Scribner's, 1936), pp. 10-11.

In that illustration obviously an effort is made to provide a unique place of significance for the Scripture, but a dilution is manifestly present, which is more in line with universalism than with biblical particularism: "Somehow it is God's voice, too, in the Koran, or the Vedas."

(3) Brunner asserts a profound difference between revelation in the Old Testament and revelation in the New Testament, in which the former was couched in words, whereas "the latter is here and now, in Person, no longer in speech about Him."[48] But the Scripture itself never makes that distinction,[49] and Jesus Christ and His apostles are precisely the ones who refer to the written Scripture as the embodiment of divine revelation. In a note concerning 2 Timothy 3:16,[50] Brunner acknowledges that an identification between the written text and the Word of God, far from being merely a distortion of the biblical view resulting from a misunderstanding by later generations of Christians, actually surfaces within the New Testament itself. He may take comfort in thinking that the 2 Timothy text was not penned by the apostle Paul,[51] but it is a matter of plain record that this text is not isolated and that the New Testament as a whole, "and our Lord in His recorded teaching in particular, do give ample support to the propriety of this identification."[52]

(4) In spite of his strong insistence upon the personal nature of religious truth, Emil Brunner has great difficulty in showing that there is an epistemological difference between the propositions "Thou art the Christ" and "He is the Christ." As Paul Jewett very aptly put it, "If God can infallibly inspire a man to say, 'Thou art the Christ,' there is no reason why He could not inspire him to say, 'He is the Christ.' The Holy Ghost is certainly able to conjugate the verb 'to be.'"[53]

48. Brunner, *The Christian Doctrine of God*, vol. 1 of *Dogmatics* (Philadelphia: Westminster, 1950), p. 26.
49. Specifically Hebrews 1:1 does not so much contrast two modes of revelation but the intrinsic dignity of God's spokesmen, Christ being far above the prophets of old.
50. Brunner, *Revelation and Reason*, p. 9, n. 13.
51. "This letter is a writing of the second century," Brunner, *The Christian Doctrine of the Church, Faith, and the Consummation*, vol. 3 of *Dogmatics* (Philadelphia: Westminster, 1962), p. 190.
52. Cf. on this point Paul K. Jewett, *Emil Brunner's Concept of Revelation (London: J. Clarke, 1954)*, pp. 159-60.
53. Ibid., p. 163. See Jewett's whole development of this point in pp. 161-64.

(5) Brunner's claim to be in line with the Reformers' doctrine of Scripture, even as Karl Barth's claim to the same effect, must be recognized as flawed. In his earlier writings (notably *The Philosophy of Religion*, pp. 26-29) this claim was presented in a very sweeping and categorical form. In *Revelation and Reason* he distinguishes between the various Reformers of the first generation, Luther and Zwingli, and Melanchthon, and Calvin and Bullinger, who are favorable to the doctrine of verbal inspiration.[54] In *The Christian Doctrine of God* we read that "Calvin is already moving away from Luther towards the doctrine of Verbal Inspiration. His *doctrine* of the Bible is entirely the traditional, formally authoritative view."[55] Thus we have a more realistic account of Calvin's view than is given by Barth, but this may undermine the Reformers' support, which Brunner was surely eager to claim for himself.

The recognition that Melanchthon, Calvin, and Bullinger, all solidly anchored in the first part of the sixteenth century, are favorable to the doctrine of verbal inspiration and inerrancy should certainly have tempered Brunner's criticism of the orthodoxy of the seventeenth century and later. This, however, is not the case, and we are confronted with accusations of paper popes,[56] of Roman Catholic principle,[57] of bibliolatry,[58] of making the Bible a fetish,[59] not to speak about recriminations concerning the inspiration of vowel points.[60] All of these may be labeled "emotional outbursts"[61] rather than sober-minded criticisms. They document the depth of the cleavage between the neo-orthodox movement and the historic doctrine of the plenary inspiration of Scripture.

(6) One can also note the very brash way in which Brunner designates the alleged flaws in Scripture:

> It [the Bible] is full of errors, contradictions, and misleading views of various circumstances relating to man, nature, and history. (*The Philosophy of Religion*, p. 155)
> With all its contradictions. (*Revelation and Reason*, p. 130)
> Various contradictions in the book of Acts . . . and various in-

54. Brunner, *Revelation and Reason*, pp. 127-28, 275. The evolution in Brunner's claims in this area is documented well in Jewett, p. 159.
55. Brunner, *Doctrine of God*, p. 111. Similar statements appear in *Doctrine of the Church, Faith and the Consummation*, p. 248.
56. Brunner, *The Divine-Human Encounter*, pp. 32, 172; *Revelation and Reason*, p. 11; *Doctrine of the Church, Faith and the Consummation*, p. 239.
57. Brunner, *Revelation and Reason*, pp. 11, 276.
58. Brunner, *The Philosophy of Religion*, p. 155; *Revelation and Reason*, pp. 181.
59. Brunner, *The Philosophy of Reason*, pp. 35, 155.
60. Ibid., p. 35; *Revelation and Reason*, p. 274; *Doctrine of God*, p. 111.
61. Carl F. H. Henry, *God, Revelation and Authority* (Waco, Tex.: Word, 1979), 4:381.

consistencies in the assignment of certain definite writings to well-known Apostles as their authors. (*Revelation and Reason*, p. 285)

This whole "primal history" in the historical sense, that is, in the sense of a credible record of events, has been completely lost. (*Revelation and Reason*, p. 286)

In spite of all the dislocations in the text, of all the gaps that have appeared, and of others that have been filled. (*Revelation and Reason*, p. 287)

There is a synoptic, a Pauline, and a Johannine type of doctrine; each differs considerably from the other, and no theological art reduces them to the same common denominator. (*Revelation and Reason*, p. 129)

At some points the variety of Apostolic doctrine, regarded purely from the theological and intellectual point of view, is an irreconcilable contradiction. (*Revelation and Reason*, p. 290)

One could multiply the examples, for that kind of statement abounds in the writings of Emil Brunner. It is noteworthy, however, that in spite of such phenomena, Brunner does not despair of finding a fundamental principle of unity in the Bible, a principle that transcends these trivial differences: it is "the unity of the Word of God in the Holy Scriptures of the Old and New Testaments."[62] Yet he does not provide us a norm by which this can be tested, and even the norm ascribed to Luther, "Christ is Lord and King of the Scripture,"[63] still requires that we use the Scriptures to know who this Christ is.

If Brunner is confronted by biblical difficulties, he appears to enjoy the luxury of choice between three lines of explanation (or evasion).

• He can say the problem lies in the failure to recognize that Truth is personal and cannot be reduced to a purely matter-of-fact, objective level.

• He can say the difficulty arises because of the paradoxical nature of Truth, which is made manifest in the clash of opposites.

• He can say the difficulty arises from the human frailties of the biblical authors and that it can be disregarded because it is peripheral. God is concerned only with what is central!

Although recognizing that God is personal, that full comprehension of God is impossible, and that human writers were not omniscient, Brunner's use of the three points listed are inappropriate and destructive of the nature of truth and of Scripture's authority.

62. Brunner, *Revelation and Reason*, p. 293.
63. E.g. Brunner, *Revelation and Reason*, p. 276 and elsewhere.

(7) The Christology implications of Emil Brunner's formulation of the doctrine of Scripture parallel closely what has been said concerning Karl Barth on this point. (See the discussion of this on pages 135-36 above.) The importance of this objection is so great that I must mention it again, even at the risk of repeating myself.

CONCLUSION

The neo-orthodox movement, although attempting to recapture the doctrine of the transcendence of God and calling attention to the importance of the biblical revelation, has not succeeded in providing us with a biblical view of Scripture itself. In spite of some favorable developments in the vanguard of the movement, such as the renewal of interest in biblical theology and in biblical preaching, we are compelled to the conclusion that the failure to recognize the Holy Scripture as intrinsically the Word of God has weakened the whole attitude toward Holy Writ. In opening the door to biblical errancy, it has also weakened the fabric of biblical authority and precluded the Scripture from functioning as the norm. This normative place of Scripture is the truth that the Reformers clearly recaptured in the sixteenth century, that the orthodoxy of the seventeenth century more formally defined (although at times not without a tinge of rationalism), and that is still proclaimed by evangelicals today. The fact that both Karl Barth and Emil Brunner could function as caricatures of the evangelical position provides a warning that should lead evangelicals to articulate their view of Scripture, its biblical moorings, and its connection with the whole history of God's people in such a way that misconceptions about Barth's and Brunner's positions might be safely laid to rest.

A comparison of neo-orthodox views of revelation with those of G. C. Berkouwer (see chapter 10 in this volume), Bruce Larsen, Helmut Thielicke, and John Bright in Gordon Lewis's "Categories in Collision," in *Perspectives on Evangelical Theology*, ed. Kenneth Kantzer and Stanley Gundry (Grand Rapids: Baker, 1979), pp. 251-64, will indicate something of the impact Barth and Brunner still have upon some evangelical thinking about the Scripture.

6. The Niebuhrs' Relativism, Relationalism, Contextualization, and Revelation

Gordon R. Lewis

Were the human writers of Scripture culturally determined to the point of teaching falsehoods, or merely culturally related in their teaching of truth? Did their writings convey a "truth" only for their times and cultures or did they also convey *the truth* for all times and cultures?

Those questions are, as Richard Coleman shows in *Issues of Theological Conflict*, at "the heart of the matter" between contemporary evangelical and nonevangelical thinking about relativism and revelation.

> In essence the evangelical argues that revealed truth, because it is supernaturally revealed, escapes the timebound character of man's progressive knowledge. The liberal argues that revealed truth, even though it has its origin in God, cannot escape historical relativity and therefore is not different in form from human insight.[1]

Does the Bible teach God's changeless thought on the subject addressed, or does it merely reflect human thinking about reli-

1. Richard J. Coleman, *Issues of Theological Conflict*, rev. ed. (Grand Rapids: Eerdmans, 1980), p. 114.

GORDON R. LEWIS, B.A., Gordon College; M. Div., Faith Theological Seminary; M.A., Ph.D., Syracuse University, is professor of theology and philosophy at Denver Conservative Baptist Seminary, Denver, Colorado. His books include: *Confronting the Cults* (1966), *Decide for Yourself: A Theological Workbook* (1970), *Judge for Yourself* (1974), *What Everyone Should Know About Transcendental Meditation* (1975), and *Testing Christianity's Truth Claims* (1976).

gious matters at the historical periods it represents? Is the Bible revelation from God as it stands written, or is it merely a human pointer to a noninformational, nonverbal kind of revelation in uninterpreted experience of a God who does not speak?

Among the multitude of nonevangelical writers who have excluded sound information from divine revelation were the highly influential Niebuhr brothers, Reinhold and Richard. They fathered recent trends in understanding scriptural revelation relativistically, relationally, and contextually.

Evangelicals generally defend three absolutes related to space and time but not determined by human culture in history: (1) the triune God, who created humanity in His personal and intellectual likeness, revealed in (2) the incarnate Jesus of history, and (3) the Spirit-taught teachings of general and special revelation. In contrast, the Niebuhrs and their followers defend only one absolute, which transcends timebound human history: a God totally unlike human persons and disclosed only *symbolically* in the human Jesus of history and the human teachings of the Bible.

Few issues are more crucial to the contemporary debate on the authority of Scripture than whether its true humanity means its relativity and errancy like all else merely human, or whether it may, like Jesus, be both human (without teaching error) and at the same time truly divine. Although some with Reinhold Niebuhr at one point seek to defend (quite inconsistently) the absoluteness of Christ's Person but not His teachings, there remains a consistent denial of culture-transcending truth in inscripturated revelation. Evangelicals today must understand and respond to the considerations leading Richard and Reinhold Niebuhr to those conclusions if they are to defend the divinely revealed inerrancy of the Bible's teachings against contemporary denials of that doctrine.

H. RICHARD NIEBUHR

H. Richard Niebuhr (1894-1962) graduated from Elmhurst College, Elmhurst, Illinois; Eden Theological Seminary, St. Louis; Washington University, St. Louis; and Yale Divinity School and Graduate School. An ordained minister of the Evangelical and Reformed Church (United Church of Christ), he pastored for two years, taught at Eden Seminary, and served as Yale Divinity School's Sterling Professor of Theology and Christian Ethics.

His earliest publication, *The Social Sources of Denominationalism,* attacked the great evil of absolutizing the relative in ecclesiastical politics. Nationalism came to birth with humanism and the denial of transcendent reality and ideals. For the church of Christ to become nationalized, he argued, was sinful. "When Christianity of the first three centuries entered into alliance with the Roman Empire to become the religion of the world-state, its leaders could scarcely have been aware of the extent to which they were surrendering the supra-national ideals of Jesus and Paul."[2] The evils of denominationalism that Niebuhr saw included confusing the temporal means with the eternal end. Those evils developed with "the failure of the churches to transcend the social conditions which fashion them into caste-organizations, . . . to resist the temptation of making their own self-preservation and extension the primary object of their endeavor."[3] In the course of time, Niebuhr observed, denominationalism and nationalism became more powerful than the common religious ideas and ideals. His warnings about an enculturated message are as relevant in today's shrinking world as in 1929.

All, whether evangelical or not, can profitably listen to Richard Niebuhr's development of the dangers inherent in claiming absolute authority for relative notions. *The Kingdom of God in America* argued that no human plan or organization could be identified with God's universal kingdom, for "every such plan was a product of a relative, self-interested and therefore corrupted reason."[4] Prophetically he condemned "the evil habit of men in all times to criticize their predecessors for having seen only half of the truth," for it "hides them from their own partiality and incompleteness. Thought and faith remain fragmentary; only the object is one."[5] Similarly he later argued, "Not the conscience but the reality which conscience apprehended was absolute."[6]

Proponents of liberalism developed that confusion of themselves with their cause, of God's ideas with their latest ideas, and so deserved Niebuhr's frequently quoted dictum "A God without wrath brought men without sin into a kingdom without judgment through the ministrations of a Christ without a cross."[7] Furthermore, "Since no reconciliation to the divine sovereign was necessary the reign of Christ, in the new interpretation, involved no

2. H. Richard Niebuhr, *The Social Sources of Denominationalism* (New York: Living Age Books, 1929), p. 111.
3. Ibid., p. 21.
4. H. Richard Niebuhr, *The Kingdom of God in America* (New York: Harper and Brothers, 1937), p. 23.
5. Ibid., p. xv.
6. Ibid., p. 84.
7. Ibid., p. 193.

revolutionary events in history of the life of individuals."[8]

It remains questionable, however, whether Niebuhr's corrective for that plight of liberalism is sufficient or successful. Parallel to the last sentence I suggest, in criticism of Richard Niebuhr, "Since no understanding of the Sovereign's changeless plans and purposes for history was necessary, relationship to Christ involved no changeless information in biblical revelation and no assent to a changeless gospel in faith!" H. Richard Niebuhr may have a transcendent God, but he has an inadequate basis for the transcendent end for human service in history that he calls the kingdom of God.

In *The Meaning of Revelation* (1941) Niebuhr argued that "no other influence has affected twentieth century thought more deeply than the discovery of spatial and temporal relativity."[9] From that descriptively true observation, Niebuhr infers that the spatio-temporal point of view of an observer enters into his knowledge of reality, so that "no universal knowledge of things as they are in themselves is possible," and "all knowledge is conditioned by the standpoint of the knower. . . ."[10] With Schleiermacher and many others after Kant, Niebuhr argues that we have no knowledge of God as He is in Himself, but only in changing human experience.[11] Truth about God, then, even in inspired Scripture, is impossible. The best that Bible students can attain is truth about people's thinking about God at their respective times and places.

Neither we nor biblical authors could know truth about God or the world, Niebuhr added, because "our concepts are something less than the categories of universal reason."[12] Who can deny the changing perspectives evident in metaphysics, logic, ethics, theology, as well as economics, politics, and rhetoric.

> The patterns and models we employ to understand the historical world may have had a heavenly origin, but as we know and use them, they are, like ourselves, creatures of history and time; though we direct our thought to eternal and transcendent beings, it is not eternal and transcendent; though we regard the universal the image of the universal in our mind is not a universal image.[13]

8. Ibid., p. 192.
9. H. Richard Niebuhr, *The Meaning of Revelation* (New York: Macmillan, 1941), p. 5.
10. Ibid.
11. Ibid., p. 6.
12. Ibid., p. 7.
13. Ibid.

We may seek objectivity and our language about objective relations may appear useful, but in all such formulations we observe elements "which are thoroughly relative to historical background, to a will to believe, and to the specific interests of certain social groups.[14] Kant may have discovered universal meaning in his categorical imperatives, but his formulations of it are historically relative. People cannot describe the universal, according to Niebuhr, except from a relative point of view.

In any field, to understand what others are trying to communicate, we must first occupy the same standpoint, look in the same direction, and use the same instruments under the same conditions. Niebuhr explains:

> Our historical relativism affirms the historicity of the subject even more than that of the object; man, it points out, is not only in time but time is in man. Moreover and more significantly, the time that is in man is not abstract but particular, and concrete . . . of a definite society with distinct language, economic and political relations, religious faith and social organization.[15]

Biblical theologians have discovered that the Bible was historically and socially "conditioned" as were the words of Jesus. "To think with Jesus was to think also as historically conditioned beings with Rabbinic, prophetic and apocalyptic ideas in mind."[16] Each community is a particular thing, the product of its own past and the possessor of a limited culture. No observer, Niebuhr also assumes, can get out of history into a realm beyond time and space; if reason is to work at all, it must be content to work as historically conditioned reason.

Hence Niebuhr's theology can attempt to state the grammar, not of a universal religious language, but of a particular language. Theology, then, cannot be an enterprise, either offensive or defensive, that attempts to prove the superiority of Christianity to all other faiths. Only a confessional theology can carry on the work of self-criticism and self-knowledge in the church.[17]

What then keeps Niebuhr from total subjectivism and skepticism? Faith in a critical realism. "It is not evident that the man who is forced to confess that his view of things is conditioned by the standpoint he occupies must doubt the reality of what he sees." Again, "It is not apparent that one who knows that his

14. Ibid., p. 8.
15. Ibid., p. 10.
16. Ibid., p. 11.
17. Ibid., p. 13.

concepts are not universal must also doubt that they are concepts of the universal, or that one who understands how all his experience is historically mediated must believe that nothing is mediated through history."[18] Admittedly,

> The acceptance of the reality of what we see in psychological and historically conditioned experience is always something of an act of faith; but such faith is inevitable and justifies itself or is justified by its fruits. A critical idealism is always accompanied, openly or disguisedly, by a critical realism which accepts on faith the independent reality of what is mediated through sense, though it discriminates between uninterpreted and unintelligible impressions and verifiable, constant, intelligible content.[19]

The inconsistency of Niebuhr's appeal to a critical realism with his relativistic confessionalism has been observed by James C. Livingston.

> But if we are willing to acknowledge that what we see from our relative point of view is also true beyond the limits of our community, then we have moved beyond the circle of confessional theology into philosophical or apologetical theology. This raises the question of whether such a Christian theology can finally avoid engaging in the metaphysical discussion. The alternative would appear to be a theological positivism which Niebuhr would disavow.[20]

If Niebuhr has no evidence that his relative confessions support the existence of the one Lord of all, his faith, whatever pragmatic "fruit" he seeks, may be as much wishful thinking as that of cultic confessions that wish to assume their universal validity.

Why not begin with divine revelation? Niebuhr thinks he has! Revelation, for him, is the historic faith of the Christian community. As he says, "Theology, then, must begin in Christian history and with Christian history because it has no other choice; in this sense it is forced to begin with revelation, meaning by that word simply historic Christian faith. But such a limited beginning is a true beginning and not the end of the inquiry."[21] What does revelation mean? Niebuhr adds that "to the limited point of view of historic Christian faith a reality discloses itself which invites all

18. Ibid.
19. Ibid., p. 15.
20. James C. Livingston, *Modern Christian Thought* (New York: Macmillan, 1971), p. 455.
21. H. Richard Niebuhr, *The Meaning of Revelation*, p. 16.

the trust and devotion of finite, temporal men." Niebuhr has reduced revelation from the Lord of history to the faith of its recipients in history.

What sort of theology results from Niebuhr's view of "revelation"? "Such a theology of revelation is objectively relativistic, proceeding with confidence in the independent reality of what is seen, though recognizing that its assertions about that reality are meaningful only to those who look upon it from the same standpoint."[22] Christian affirmations about God, sin, Christ, salvation, and so forth, "are meaningful only in a Christian context" or where "there has been a response of the whole feeling, willing, desiring person."[23] Believers cannot speak of God, the good, the beginning, the end, but only of "my God," "our good," "our beginning," and "our end."[24] No disinterested, neutral standpoint or faithless starting point can be made to Christianity, apart from faith. The great sin for relativists becomes defense of the faith as objectively true for all people of all times and all places. Every effort to deal with the subject must be resolutely confessional. Revelation cannot be possessed in a static book, creed, or set of doctrines.

Endeavoring to free the sovereign, living God from such static things, Niebuhr insists that revelation cannot be a thing of the past, but is "a contemporary event" and "solely a function of this teaching group."[25] He makes revelation to be the faith of people who call themselves Christians in the present. While freeing revelation from human control in the propositions of inspired Scripture given once-for-all in the past, he has enslaved all to the changing and conflicting claims of alleged Christians in the present. He seeks the emotive power of the historic concept revelation but denies the "faithful words" through which the Spirit generates that power.

What is the sum of the matter? Niebuhr declares,

> Christian theology must begin today with revelation because it knows that men cannot think about God save as historic, communal beings and save as believers. It must ask what revelation means for Christians rather than what it ought to mean for all men, everywhere and at all times. And it can pursue its inquiry only by

22. Ibid.
23. Ibid., p. 18.
24. Ibid., pp. 18-19.
25. Ibid., p. 30.

recalling the story of Christian life and by analyzing what Christians see from their limited point of view in history and faith.[26]

However, there are many denominations, sects, cults, and subcultures within Christendom. Shall we analyze what each has said from its limited point of view? How shall we regard the confession of the church when some say a transcendent Lord in control of history has died, and others say the living Lord of all rules history?

How shall we understand the confession of the church when some who call themselves Christians affirm the Trinity and deity of Jesus Christ, whereas many others in the name of Christianity deny the Trinity and the deity of Christ? In what shall faith repose when the confessions of some church leaders affirm that the Bible's assertions are true logically and factually, whereas others confess that in those respects the assertions may be in error and are "true" only functionally? Contradictory "confessions" cannot both be trusted, and Niebuhr seems to have given us little basis for deciding in which to place our confidence.

Niebuhr neatly sets aside the central affirmations of biblical teaching by failing to distinguish revelation as originally *given* from revelation as *taken* in the history of the church. He writes, "When the church speaks of revelation it never means simply the Scriptures, but only Scriptures read from the point of view and in the context of church history."[27] So it turns out to be his or another's contemporary interpretation of church history that identifies revelation.

Like nature, he claims, "the Bible can be read in many different contexts and will *mean* different things accordingly."[28] Indeed biblical teaching has multiple applications and relationships, but its *meaning as given* by the authors inspired by the Holy Spirit can hardly be just anything any allegedly Christian group assigns it. Contrary to the gospel, Niebuhr proposes that "faith was not belief in the actuality of historical events but confidence in an abiding, ruling will of love."[29] Yet on the same page he concedes that "the church has always thought in historical terms."

Niebuhr then argues at length that the sphere in which revelation occurs is that of the believing and worshiping persons' internal history, in contrast to external history, which is impersonal.

26. Ibid., pp. 30-31.
27. Ibid., p. 37.
28. Ibid., p. 38.
29. Ibid., p. 42.

Revelation occurs to Niebuhr, not in a way that can be seen from without by pure reason, but only from within by practical reason.[30] From the standpoint of practical reason, a self with values and a destiny has a god and so a history connecting events in meaningful patterns.[31] The church hears external histories of itself by non-Christians and knows that such stories are not *the* truth about it, but recognizes *a* truth about it in each one. Strangely enough, the church could not continue without the Bible and the rites of the institutional church.[32]

Yet revelation is not simply the inner history of believers as a whole, nor is it any arbitrarily chosen part of that inner history. Revelation means for Niebuhr that part of our inner history which illuminates the rest of it and which is itself intelligible.[33] Revelation designates the intelligible event that makes all other events intelligible. In the Christian church that event is Jesus Christ, to believers the righteousness, wisdom, and power of God.[34] However inconsistently, he seeks to affirm the Christ as Lord of all, not Lord of some people or a part of life.

Faith in Christ illuminates our past, present, and future potentialities, enabling Christians to speak of original sin, forgiveness of sins, reconciliation, obedience, and a new self. "Concepts and doctrines derived from the unique historical moment are important but less illuminating than the occasion itself. For what is revealed is not so much the mode of divine behavior as the divine self."[35]

Although Niebuhr realizes that assurance grows out of both immediate perception and social corroboration and out of neither of those alone,[36] he imagines that in revelatory experiences we deal with selves, *not* concepts.[37] Revelation with Martin Buber is simply an I-Thou encounter. And with Herrman it is God's giving of Himself in communion, not information about Himself. Revelation is thus defined as a divine self-disclosure.[38] Revelation is not a possession (like a Bible) but an event that happens over and over again when we remember the illuminating center of our history.[39] A dumb God revolutionizes all our religious knowledge,

30. Ibid., p. 56.
31. Ibid., p. 59.
32. Ibid., p. 65.
33. Ibid., p. 68.
34. Ibid., p. 70.
35. Ibid., p. 95.
36. Ibid., p. 103.
37. Ibid., p. 105.
38. Ibid., p. 113.
39. Ibid., p. 129.

allegedly without conveying any information about Himself or His redemptive plan.

In his *Purpose of the Church and Its Ministry*, Niebuhr explains his consequent relational theology. Theology as a pure science does not have as its object God in isolation.

> What is known and knowable in theology is God in relation to self and to neighbor, and self and neighbor in relation to God. This complex of related beings is the object of theology. In the great, nearly central figure of Christianity, the God-man, this complex appears at least symbolically, though theology is distorted if it is converted into Christology. . . . True and substantial wisdom consists of three parts: the knowledge of God, of companions, and of the self; and that these three are so intimately related, that they cannot be separated.[40]

Out of a reductive historical relativism, Niebuhr has developed a relationalism between a personal God, disclosed in Christ, and fallen persons. Clyde Holbrook suggests that if Niebuhr had used "relationalism" to describe the ethical situation, possibly the taint of "relativism" could be removed from his position.[41] Are not some evangelicals attempting to disguise a relativism in terms of relationalism today? Relational theologians properly stress a personal commitment to the living Christ, but like Niebuhr they may bifurcate that faith from belief in propositional truth once-for-all revealed and inspired in biblical canon.

Holbrook himself criticizes Niebuhr for cutting off participants in Christian experience from significant discourse about the experience with those who have not passed through it. He asks, What possible grounds remain for intelligible discourse between Niebuhr and his critics? What criteria can be offered by which to test the validity of revelation?[42]

As in some relational theology today, Niebuhr regards apologetics, a Christian's *self*-defense, as "the most prevalent source of error in all thinking and perhaps especially in theology and ethics."[43] However, Lonnie Kliever claims that

> the philosophic and apological character of Niebuhr's work has often been overlooked or misconstrued. His insistence that theol-

40. H. Richard Niebuhr, *The Purpose of the Church and Its Ministry* (New York: Harper and Brothers, 1956), pp. 112-13.
41. Clyde A. Holbrook, "H. Richard Niebuhr," in Peerman and Marty, eds., *A Handbook of Christian Theologians* (New York: World, 1965), p. 394.
42. Ibid., pp. 392-93.
43. H. Richard Niebuhr, *The Meaning of Revelation*, p. 4.

ogy start with revelation and proceed confessionally has been interpreted as a categorical rejection of philosophical methods. This demand is a rejection of all philosophical or universal proofs.[44]

Kliever alleges that there are no universally applicable assumptions or evidences: "That does not preclude commending the Christian faith on the grounds of its power to make all human experience intelligible."[45] One must ask Kliever and Niebuhr, however, What are the criteria of intelligibility on which to judge *all* human experience? If Niebuhr shows that his personal faith makes "reasonable sense of human life and thought" (presumably in general), is he not appealing to some universal standards of meaning and truth given by creation in God's image? When Niebuhr presents an apologetic from the standpoint of values, as "a reasoned communication of faith rather than a rational demonstration of faith," does he not appeal to some objective, nonconfessional meaning of *reasoned* and of *value?*[46]

How can relational theologians regard their interpretation of their experience superior in value to interpretations of people in other religions and at the same time insist with Kliever that "the truth about God and man cannot be consistently maintained or intelligibly related unless the historical and religious relativism of every theological standpoint is accepted."[47] To the extent that Niebuhr manages to avoid subjectivism and skepticism he inconsistently appeals to universal principles of logic, evidence, and value originating in general revelation. To the extent that Niebuhr does not utilize criteria of common grace for responsible discernment he loses the superiority of Christ and of Christianity to other religious and cultic communities.

Kleiver himself has some serious criticisms of Niebuhr's relativism, relationalism, and we might say contextualism after trying seriously but unsuccessfully to defend his position.

> Niebuhr's relativism has its difficulties. The greatest problem has to do with how relative viewpoints are confirmed or changed, compared or synthesized. Niebuhr's epistemology sees all human understanding as language dependent and socially determinate. How then does reality break through these conditioned categories in such a way that those very categories can be critically revised or

44. Lonnie Kliever, *H. Richard Niebuhr* (Waco, Tex.: Word, 1977), pp. 182-83.
45. Ibid., p. 183.
46. Ibid., p. 184.
47. Ibid., p. 66.

validated? How are different symbol systems from different speech communities compared or synthesized with one another?[48]

Unless Niebuhr can recognize basic categories of thought and being, in the world and in persons created to know and rule the world, he lacks a basis for communication and progress in thought among different communities of people. And unless those basic categories of thought are made after God's image there is no way to grow in knowledge of God, as God exists in reality. Interpreters of Scripture must also recognize some similarities of consistent and factual criteria, or their words too will pass each other like ships in the night. On the basis of general revelation in nature and the human heart, all people, not just believing Christians, are accountable for the truth God revealed. Non-Christians know it, but suppress it in unrighteousness.

Niebuhr is properly concerned about the danger of absolutizing the relative. Since Jim Jones and the Guyana tragedy all know the great dangers along that line. But another danger must be faced. It is relativizing the absolutes of general and special revelation. In Niebuhr's zeal to do away with any finite absolutes, he has sought in vain to abolish the universal and necessary principles of thought and communication between God and mankind, and between persons of one culture and another. Those principles in turn are indispensable to the accreditation of authentic revelation and its responsible interpretation and proclamation from one culture community and context to another.

After careful treatment of Richard Niebuhr, James C. Livingston concludes that many theologians "do not limit Christian theology to a confessional role. As will become clear, what distinguishes Reinhold Niebuhr's theological method, in part, from that of his brother is his willingness to engage in the apologetic task."[49] Livingston says further of Reinhold Niebuhr, "To scorn the apologetic task is to court a prideful irrelevance."[50]

REINHOLD NIEBUHR

Reinhold Niebuhr (1892-1971), after attending Elmhurst College and Eden Theological Seminary, enrolled in Yale University. However, the needs of his family and the impractical nature of his

48. Ibid., p. 171.
49. James C. Livingston, *Modern Christian Thought*, p. 456.
50. Ibid., p. 459.

graduate studies led him to accept a pastorate of a newly established mission of the Evangelical and Reformed Church (now the United Church of Christ) in Detroit. At the Bethel Evangelical Church in 1915, with the world at war, he judged his preaching by its effects upon the growing number of automobile workers. To avoid an "ivory tower" kind of clericalism he studied firsthand the labor unions and Marxist philosophy. Contributing to the growth of his church from forty to eight hundred members in fifteen years was Niebuhr's concern for the member's everyday problems in the Ford factories.[51] In 1928 Reinhold Niebuhr became professor of applied Christianity at Union Theological Seminary, where he remained until his retirement in 1960. In addition to publishing many volumes on social and political issues, he was involved in numerous social causes. Robert Stone's book focuses on *Reinhold Niebuhr Prophet to Politicians.*[52]

Basic to Niebuhr's ethical and political as well as his religious thought was his epistemological relativism. Reinhold's pervasive relativism grew out of his view of history like his brother's, but also from broader philosophical, theological, and ethical considerations. Insufficient attention has been given to the impact of his relativistic thinking upon his theology and his views of God, Christ, and Scripture in particular. In 1965 Hans Hofmann could write, "Niebuhr quite properly can be called the 'father of contextual ethics.' His understanding of ethics has become dominant in American Protestantism."[53]

Why did Niebuhr confine human knowing to the changing, contextual and relative? Why did he frequently say that we can never know *the truth*, but only *our* truth? His reasons are brought out forcefully in his magnum opus, *The Nature and Destiny of Man.* Human knowing cannot be considered apart from the nature of human existence ontologically and morally. First, ontologically, people are creatures of two worlds, the worlds of spirit and nature. As spirit, people are free and self-transcendent; as children of nature people are limited and bound by physical necessities. Complicating matters further, on each of those levels is the duality between the form or order and vitality or energy.

The distinctive energy of the human spirit Niebuhr finds in its

---

51. On Reinhold Niebuhr's life see his "Intellectual Autobiography," in Charles W. Kegley and Robert W. Bretall, eds., *Reinhold Niebuhr* (New York: Macmillan, 1956), pp. 1-24.
52. Robert H. Stone, *Reinhold Niebuhr Prophet to Politician* (Nashville: Abingdon, 1972).
53. Hans Hofman, "Reinhold Niebuhr," in *a Handbook of Christian Theologians*, p. 371.

power of self-transcendence. As a result, a person who has discovered truth today will transcend his own research tomorrow and come up with further insights. The freedom of the human spirit opens up new and higher vantage points for judging finite perspectives in the light of more inclusive truths.[54] The very recognition of human self-transcendence confines concepts to our present limited personal viewpoints. The difference between human finiteness and freedom seemed to Niebuhr prior to human essence and paradoxical. So he found himself in the unending tension of "having and not having the truth."[55] Like Moses he must always perish outside the promised land. He could see what he could not reach.[56]

Second, Reinhold, like his brother Richard, stresses a historical and cultural relativism. "Our involvement in natural and historical flux sets final limits upon our quest for truth and insures the partial and particular character of even the highest cultural vantage point."[57] Because our minds are united with our bodies at particular times and places in history, such as East or West, our objectivity upon the whole is suspect.

Third, since the mind is an organic unity with the vital capacities of will and emotions, the play of passion and self-interest enters. "Knowledge of the truth is thus invariably slanted by an 'ideological taint' of interest, which makes our apprehension of the truth something less than knowledge of the truth and reduces it to *our* truth."[58] Reason, he argued, can never be the pure instrument of justice. "The wise men (liberals) cannot gauge the actions of the strong correctly because they do not understand the tragic facts of human nature. They do not know to what degree the impulses of life are able to defy the canons of reason and the dictates of conscience."[59] On that basis Niebuhr has less than full confidence in the morality of social planning.

A fourth factor confining human knowledge to relative rather than absolute truth appears in a pride-filled claim to a premature finality. Pride provides the major force behind an ideological taint of self-interest. "It includes not merely the effort to deny the finiteness of our perspectives but to hide and obscure the taint of

54. Reinhold Niebuhr, *The Nature and Destiny of Man* (New York: Scribner's, 1941, 1943), 2:214.
55. Reinhold Niebuhr, *The Interpretation of Christian Ethics*, 3d ed., (New York: Harper and Brothers, 1935), pp. 205, 215.
56. Ibid., p. 80.
57. Reinhold Niebuhr, *The Nature and Destiny of Man*, 2:214.
58. Ibid.
59. Ibid., 2:48.

interest and passion of our knowledge." Without that pride, Niebuhr continues, "the partial character of all human knowledge would be harmless and would encourage men to invite the supplementation and completion of their incomplete knowledge from other partial perspectives."[60]

Like all sin, the pride-filled claim to finality is a result of ignorance of one's ignorance to a certain extent, but it is also partially a result of conscious effort to obscure the limitations of one's knowledge. There is an element of ignorance, but there is also an element of perversity. It is not merely an error of judgment, but also a rebellion against the Christian revelation. That is the root of great evil in history and presents one of the most common barriers to apprehending final truth.

Now the implications of those ontological and moral reasons for relativism apply in Reinhold Niebuhr's thinking not only to interpreters of Scripture, but equally to the writers of the Bible. The biblical doctrines of God, Christ, and revelation are fallible human opinions of the times. It is important to note briefly Reinhold Niebuhr's concepts on such basic doctrines in order to appreciate that the struggle for biblical inerrancy is no mere technicality having to do with irrelevant details of inspiration's results. At stake are orthodox doctrines of Christ's person and work and the relation of God to the world.

If no human being in his highest moments of self-transcendent knowledge can achieve anything more than relative opinion, how can he know there is a God beyond the confines of space and time to reveal Himself in history? Niebuhr wants to affirm that there is a final truth beyond human reason in Christianity. Can he or any other relativist rise above the confines of reason to establish the truth for which he claims finality? How is it after a sustained polemic against absoluteness that Niebuhr himself can claim absoluteness for Christian faith?

In his effort to escape the confines of reason and establish finality for the faith, Niebuhr employs three major concepts: revelation, symbolism or myth, and faith. In seeking to transcend reason by revelation, he begins with mankind, as usual. The human environment includes both time and eternity, the changeless source of man's changing being and ability to juxtapose himself to time, nature, and being per se. So man stands beyond cultural limitations.[61] Reason's inability to cope with that complexity re-

60. Ibid., 2:214-15.
61. Ibid., 2:124-25.

quires a fulcrum in revelation beyond man for the comprehension of man. We need a principle of comprehension beyond our comprehension to understand the "thatness" beyond ourselves. The answer is not found in mysticism, for it accounts for an incomprehensible source of existence but does not explain the significance of the creaturely elements in man. The adequate answer is found in a God who is more transcendent than in mystical religions and can in no sense be identical with the depths of human consciousness, yet is intimately concerned with the world. The twofold conception of God's transcendence and immanence is the most important "ultra-rational presupposition" of the Christian faith and alone can do justice to human nature. That presuppositon is endangered when rationally explicated because it transcends the canons and antinomies of rationality.[62] In that Niebuhr sees himself aligned more with contemporary trends called biblical theology than with the early Barth.

Although God is *Deus Absconditus*, that is not identical with agnosticism. God does disclose His purposes. The disclosure takes place, not in biblical teaching, but in significant events in history, which are apprehended by faith. So apprehended they become "mighty acts" of God in which the meaning of the whole drama is made clear.[63] The modern Barthian emphasis on "the qualitative difference between time and eternity" has much more in common with Greek Platonism than with the paradoxical religion of Jesus.[64]

How can Niebuhr claim to comprehend that incomprehensible and illogical God? Through revelation, both general and special. General revelation occurs in man's consciousness, in nature and history; special revelation in Christ. Notice that scriptural teaching is not identified with revelation.

Revelation in man's consciousness discloses God's existence as a reality beyond the rim of man's consciousness, which reality impinges on consciousness. Similar to Schleiermacher's "unqualified dependence," the experience however includes a responsibility to a personal God. Once accepted, that assumption proves to be the only basis of a correct analysis of all the factors.[65]

Revelation in nature discloses God as Creator. The world is not self-explanatory, self-derived, or self-sufficing, but points to a

62. Ibid., 1:12.
63. Ibid., 1:102-6.
64. Reinhold Niebuhr, *Reflections at the End of an Era* (New York: Scribner's, 1934), p. 286.
65. Reinhold Niebuhr, *The Nature and Destiny of Man*, 1:127-29.

source of being beyond itself. Niebuhr claims no proof, but only things that point to a Creator already known in man's moral experience. "The Biblical doctrine of the Creator, and the world as His creation, is itself not a doctrine of revelation, but it is basic for the doctrine of revelation."[66] Clearly Niebuhr uses the term *biblical* in a sense very different from a propositional revelation. "It must be understood that the term 'Biblical' is meant to embrace the explication of the Biblical paradox of grace in Christian history particularly in the Reformation."[67] It is evident that Niebuhr appeals to Scripture only when it can be interpreted to illuminate the paradox between finiteness and freedom as he understands it. He finds the idea of creation incompatible with the idea of natural causation and marking the limits of rationality, "the dividing line between intelligibility and mystery."[68] He finds no rational solution for the problem and quotes with approval the statement of Whitehead that God is "the ultimate irrationality."[69]

Revelation in history discloses God as Judge. He does not mean simply the liberal's history of man's quest for God or the record of man's increasingly adequate definitions of the Person of God, but "the record of those events in history in which faith discerns the self-disclosure of God."[70] Men insist on usurping the position and prerogatives of Deity and so cause judgment to fall upon them. "Sin is thus the unwillingness of man to acknowledge his creaturely dependence upon God and his effort to make his own life independent and secure."[71] So in his philosophy of history, judgment upon sin is "the first category of interpretation."[72] It follows that "the most obvious meaning of history is that every nation, culture and civilization brings destruction upon itself by exceeding the bounds of creatureliness which God has set upon all human enterprises."[73] The prophets observed that sin in Israel and strongly denounced it. They also found it in the nations that were instrumental in the punishment of Israel. The whole of history is a clarified revelation of the personal experience of being judged from beyond ourselves.

Revelation in Christ discloses God as Redeemer. Jesus Christ

66. Ibid., 1:133.
67. Ibid., 2:216.
68. Reinhold Niebuhr, *Faith and History* (New York: Scribner's 1949), p. 48.
69. Ibid., p. 50.
70. Reinhold Niebuhr, *The Nature and Destiny of Man*, 1:136.
71. Ibid., 1:137-38.
72. Ibid., 1:140.
73. Ibid.

confronts men not only with the wrath of God but also with God's mercy and forgiveness. Christian faith sees in the cross of Christ assurance that judgment is not the final word of God to man, but does not obliterate the distinctions between good and evil in history. Surprisingly enough the good news of the gospel is that God takes the sinfulness of man into Himself, doing for man what man could never do for himself. However paradoxical, that is "*the final* revelation" of God to man. The gospel is final because the ultimate problem of man's egregious evil is solved and yet man is not given an easy conscience and a license to sin more. That claim is an "absurd claim" for "the final truth about life is always an absurdity," but he differs with Kierkegaard in saying that "it cannot be an absolute absurdity." What does that mean? "It is an absurdity insofar as it must transcend the 'system' of meaning which the human mind always prematurely constructs with itself as center. But it cannot be a complete absurdity or it could not achieve any credence."[74]

A Christ is not expected in history when history is reduced to nature, as illustrated in the classical materialism from Democritus to Lucretius. Neither is a Christ expected when history is abandoned for eternal affinities, as in classical idealism and mysticism. Both outlooks minimize or annul the significance of history. Neither expects a further fulfillment of meaning. "No Christ could validate himself as the disclosure of a hidden divine sovereignty over history or as a vindication of the meaningfulness of history, if a Christ were not expected."[75] Appreciation for both levels of man's nature is crucial for a meaning that will provide historical significance for both. Unless the profundity of man is grasped and the possibility and expectation of meaning is present, Christ will inevitably be either foolishness or a stumbling block. However, Christ could not fulfill the desires of any particular messianic claim because that would be tainted with an ideological bias of selfish interest. Thus He disappointed advocates of an egoistic-nationalistic messianism, as well as those who expected a simple combination of power and goodness in an earthly kingdom. The content of Christ's revelation is an act of reconciliation, synthesizing the ideas of Isaiah's "suffering servant" with the concept of the Son of Man, applying the former to His first coming and the latter to a "second coming, either his own or another."[76]

74. Reinhold Niebuhr, *The Nature and Destiny of Man*, 2:38n.
75. Ibid., 2:15.
76. Ibid., 2:48.

Sin is overcome in principle but not in fact, and love must continue as a suffering love rather than a triumphant love. That distinction becomes a basic category of interpreting history in all profound versions of the Christian faith.[77]

Niebuhr's four forms of revelation—in human consciousness, in nature, in history, and supremely in Christ—exclude any treatment of the Bible as revelation. Scripture turns out to be simply a human pointer to revelation in those four other ways. Without conceptual revelation and verbal inspiration, we must pause to ask whether Niebuhr's claim to final truth in Christ is justified. Has he been able to transcend his own finiteness, pride, ideological taint, and future insights to assert an absolute truth for all people of all times? In reply he resorts to paradox.

> This is the paradox of grace applied to truth. The truth, as it is contained in the Christian revelation, includes the recognition that it is neither possible for man to know the truth fully nor to avoid the error of pretending that he does. It is recognized that that "grace" always remains in partial contradiction to "nature," and is not merely its fulfillment.

Is Niebuhr then just pretending that he has attained final truth concerning Christ? He continues,

> The very apprehension of this paradox is itself an expression of the twofold aspect of grace. It is a thought beyond all human thought and can affect thinking only indirectly. For it is not possible to remain fully conscious of the egoistic corruption in the truth, while we seek to establish and advance it in our thought and action. But it is possible in moments of prayerful transcendence over the sphere of interested thought and action to be conscious of the corruption; and it is also possible to carry this insight into our interested thoughts and actions so that it creates some sense of pity and forgiveness for those who contend against our truth and oppose our action.[78]

Niebuhr's spirit is commendable, but he has not answered the question. He has simply assumed he has discovered final truth. The appeal to prayer is important but not a sufficient guarantee that one following prayerful insights is not accepting the absolutes of a Jim Jones or other impostors rather than a true prophet or apostle of the one Lord of all.

77. Ibid., 2:49.
78. Ibid., 2:217.

Again Niebuhr attempts an answer by quoting Paul Tillich:

> What is true, however, of all knowledge cannot be true of the knowledge of knowledge, otherwise it would cease to have universal significance. . . . Whatever stands in the context of knowledge is subject to the ambiguity of knowledge. Therefore such a proposition must be removed from the context of knowledge. . . . It is the judgment which constitutes truth as truth.[79]

Admirable as this attempt is to defend an absolute in the sea of relativism that Niebuhr created for himself, a question arises: By what criteria can Niebuhr determine the true knowledge of knowledge from the false knowledge of knowledge? Once the door is open for proposing absolutes, each writer will read his own out of or into the flux of history. Is that revelation?

Niebuhr has so removed human knowledge in time from God's knowledge in eternity that his attempt to state one conceptual truth, even about truth itself, has become self-contradictory. Edward John Carnell commented:

> Any principle which explains the corruption of all knowledge explains the corruption of no knowledge, for it has already corrupted itself.
>
> An absolute impasse must be admitted. If one claims that the dialectical relation between time and eternity *is* a final piece of knowledge he destroys the dialectic by admitting that finite creatures have overcome the ambiguity of existence at one point in history; and if one claims that the dialectical relation between time and eternity is *not* a final piece of knowledge, then he destroys the dialectic by leaving open the possibility that a non-dialectical view of life may serve us. In either decision a *final* Christian dialectic is destroyed.[80]

If we leave the paradox of grace and turn to the paradoxical pointers of general revelation, there always remains the possibility of another interpretation of the data regarding self-transcendence, a sense of dependence and moral obligation, the origins of the world and the downfall of individuals and nations. N. P. Jacobson, in reviewing Niebuhr's second volume, *Human Destiny,* listed eight lines of empirical evidence Niebuhr employed to sup-

---

79. Paul Tillich, *The Interpretation of History,* pp. 169-70; cited in Reinhold Niebuhr, *The Nature and Destiny of Man,* 2:217-18n.
80. Edward John Carnell, *The Theology of Reinhold Niebuhr* (Grand Rapids: Eerdmans, 1950), p. 239.

port the transcendent realm, but concluded that all of them could be interpreted within a naturalistic philosophy. Niebuhr's evidence supported man's freedom but not the all-important realm of suprahistory. "It is evident that Niebuhr's entire philosophy of history is erected upon his concept of supra-history and its role in the progress of meaning."[81] At best, however, the indications of general revelation do not support the one final truth concerning God's paradoxical forgiveness in Christ.

Without a conceptual revelation and a verbal inspiration neither Niebuhr nor any evangelical today has a solid foundation upon which to build a meaningful belief in the transcendent reality of the triune God, who declared in "faithful sayings" that Christ Jesus came into the world and died once-for-all for the salvation of sinners. Others who deny propositional revelation, in the name of relativism and a dialectical or contradictory relation between temporal man and the eternal God, will eventually find themselves unable to defend even the central affirmations of the gospel.

In response to arguments from the humanness of the Bible's writers to the time-boundness of Scripture, which leave it only functional in value (like Berkouwer's), I argued in "The Human Authorship of Inspired Scripture" that the Bible's teaching is truly divine and truly human without error, just as Jesus Christ was truly divine and truly human without sin. The inerrancy of finite fallen human authors must be understood in the context of orthodox doctrines of God, creation, providence, and miracles. The human writers were not autonomous but lived and moved and had their being in the all-wise Lord of all. Created with a capacity for self-transcendence (with Niebuhr) in God's image, they could receive changeless truths by revelation (even though they might be unable to invent them). Nebuhr, however, failed to incorporate a *mental* likeness in the image of God in man, which enables God and man to communicate (Col. 3:10).

Providentially prepared by God in their unique personalities, the biblical authors also had characteristics in common with all other human beings in all times and cultures. Their teaching originated, however, not with their own wills but God's, and it came to them through a variety of means. In all the human writing processes, they were supernaturally overshadowed by the Holy Spirit, not in a way analogous to mechanical or unworthy

81. N. P. Jacobson, "Niebuhr's Philosophy of History," *Harvard Theological Review*, 37 (October 1944): 237-68.

human relationships, but as one loving person effectually influences another. What stands written, therefore, in human language is not merely human but also divine. What the human sentences teach, God teaches. The Bible's affirmations conform to the mind of God and to the reality God created. Although time related, they are not time bound. They are objectively true for all people of all times and all cultures, whether received or not. The reason the Bible can function effectively to bring people to Christ is that its teachings are inerrant.[82]

Although the Bible, for Niebuhr, is not revelation, its *use* is important to him, as it is to many committed to the functional values of an errant Bible today. Given the impossibility of a non-paradoxical conceptual revelation because of the paradoxical relation between time and eternity, Niebuhr finds great value in myth. Mythical stories about events in time convey profound truths about eternity. "An adequate philosophy of history must, in short, be a mythology rather than a philosophy. . . . It must combine the exact data of the scientist with the vision of the artist and must add religious depth to philosophical generalizations."[83] Myths provide a vision of the whole and profound truths about the existence of man, truths of meaning in distinction from truths of fact. Mythical thought is not only prescientific, it is also, he assumes, suprascientific.[84] As such, the scientists and liberal theologians have erred in not taking myths and symbols seriously.

The other danger is that myths be taken literally, and in that direction Niebuhr says fundamentalists and orthodox Christianity have erred.

> In one sense all Orthodox Christian theology has been guilty of the sin of profanity. It has insisted on the literal and historic truth of its myths, forgetting that it is the function and character of religious myth to speak of the eternal in relation to time, and that it cannot therefore be a statement of temporal sequence.[85]

So the creation myth expresses the transcendence and immanence of God and the goodness of creation, describing a quality of existence. The story of the Fall of Adam and Eve portrays the

---

82. For support of this summation see my essay "The Human Authorship of Inspired Scripture," in Norman Geisler, ed., *Inerrancy* (Grand Rapids: Zondervan, 1979), pp. 228-64.

83. Reinhold Niebuhr, *Reflections on the End of an Era*, p. 122.

84. Reinhold Niebuhr, *Interpretation of Christian Ethics*, pp. 25-26.

85. Reinhold Niebuhr, *Christianity and Power Politics* (New York: Scribner's, 1940), pp. 220-21.

constant falling of mankind.

The most important myth for Niebuhr's final truth relates the story of Jesus Christ. Niebuhr thinks the history of the church was unnecessarily torn with attempts to define how Christ was both human and divine metaphysically. Contradictions could have been transcended by speaking about the paradoxical relation of a divine *agape*, which stoops to conquer, and the human *agape*, which rises above history in a sacrificial act.[86] The scriptural references to the incarnation, according to Niebuhr, did not mean to imply that Jesus Christ was composed of two natures, one of which was actually divine. Rather, "The Jesus of history is a perfect symbol of the absolute in history because the perfect love to which pure spirit aspires is vividly realized in the drama of his life and cross. Thus man becomes the symbol of God and the religious sense that the absolute invades the relative and the historical is adequately expressed."[87]

Niebuhr cannot accept Christ's virgin birth, and he rejects Christ's sinlessness, for no historical person can be totally free from anxiety that inevitably leads to sin.[88] Niebuhr distinguishes the Jesus of history from the Christ of faith in typical liberal fashion and fails to see that his myths do not answer his own criticism of liberalism. As he said, liberal Christianity "can give no satisfactory answer to the question why Christ, rather than some other 'good' character in history, should be revered as divine, or how we can have the assurance that an evolutionary development may not produce a higher form of 'goodness' more worthy of our highest devotion."[89] He rejects the Thomistic notion that grace must necessarily be infused through the sacraments of the church and goes so far as to deny that "even in the Christian faith is its only possible presupposition."[90] Nevertheless Christ is considered to be the *final* revelation of God to man, and the cross the "symbolic point where this story most obviously ceases to be merely a story in history and becomes revelatory of a very unique divine 'glory,' namely, the glory and majesty of a suffering God, whose love and forgiveness is the final triumph over the recalcitrance of human sin and the confusion of human history."[91]

How different is the contemporary view that dismisses onto-

86. Reinhold Niebuhr, *The Nature and Destiny of Man*, 2:71.
87. Reinhold Niebuhr, *Reflections on the End of an Era*, p. 287.
88. Reinhold Niebuhr, *The Nature and Destiny of Man*, 2:73.
89. Ibid., 2:54.
90. Reinhold Niebuhr, *The Interpretation of Christian Ethics*, p. 217.
91. Reinhold Niebuhr, *Faith and History*, p. 169.

logical categories as Greek philosophical trappings and simply concerns itself with the functional power of biblical accounts of Christ's death? At stake in the defense of the Bible's inerrant teaching is the very heart of the faith, *Christology.* Like Niebuhr, many today divorce the historical or scientific truth from truths of faith. By what criteria then may we know which myths to take seriously and what aspects of them to emphasize? The extremes of allegorical interpretation in the history of the church are notorious. Niebuhr reads biblical passages as symbols whenever it suits his purposes. Biblical and nonbiblical materials (such as alleged Mormon revelations) are not interpreted by the same standards. If a rational criterion of truth were suggested, the alleged ability of myth to go beyond meaningful criteria would be controverted; since a conceptual criterion cannot be provided, we are left with a host of conflicting myths from numerous traditions.

Niebuhr's mythical treatment of important historical events at the foundation of Christianity reminds one of Hegel's view that religion employs imagination, history, and figures to express the same truth that philosophy presents in a different form. Harald Hoffding's comment on Hegel applies with equal force to Niebuhr.

> In his speculative zeal Hegel overlooked the fact that to the believer in revelation the whole point is that dogma is more than a figure. Every positive religion must assume that at certain points, the difference between symbol and reality disappears—only under this condition can the concept of revelation possess validity.[92]

Arguing from anthropological considerations remarkably similar to those of Niebuhr for the relativism of all conceptual formulations, Charles Kraft regards the forms of the scriptural practices and teachings to be expendable if the equivalent functions are achieved in a different culture. "The Scriptures, like human beings who serve God, are to be valued for the function they perform and for the meanings they convey, rather than for the perfection of their form."[93] Like Niebuhr he has dismissed meaning as propositional truth and espouses an existentialist or pragmatist view of meaning as function or use. So "the greater the linguistic and cultural distance between the source and receptor languages, the greater the number and extent of the formal changes required to preserve the meaning."[94] The dynamic of

92. Harald Hoffding, *A History of Modern Philosophy* (New York: Humanities Press, 1900), 2:191.
93. Charles Kraft, *Christianity in Culture* (Maryknoll, N.Y.: Orbis, 1979), p. 210.
94. Ibid., pp. 273, 326.

Christianity, Kraft concludes, "is not in the sacredness of cultural forms—even those that God once used" (in the Bible as a case-book).[95]

Before following Kraft one ought to consider the effect upon Christianity when Hegel and then Niebuhr changed the form of Scripture in the name of communicating its meanings to people in today's cultures. Hoffding's words regarding Hegel come to life again in relation to contemporary debates about the Bible's inspired meaning and form.

> Hegel disregards the fact that a change of form may very possibly denote an opposition in principle. He explains the dogmas of creation and of the atonement as symbolic expressions of the interconnection between the elements of existence. . . . But even if this exegesis were right—even if it were really the case that such an experience of life had found in these dogmas symbolic expression, yet if the creation denote a supernatural act, and the atonement an historical happening in which a supernatural God suffered and died as man, we get a very different conception of life from Hegel's. The change of form which Hegel represents as quite harmless, effects, as a matter of fact, a transition from a dualistic to a naturalistic or monistic conception of the world.[96]

By changing the human form of Scripture, Niebuhr like Hegel has changed the content of his final truth from the supernatural atonement of the God-man into a time-bound natural symbol or human representation of God's forgiveness. Could not Niebuhr, if he held to a literal incarnation, strengthen his position that nature is ultimately meaningful? God's actual incarnate concern for sinful people on earth would be stronger than God's symbolic concern as pictured in a human martyr.

Niebuhr admits that his mythical use of historical accounts provisionally distorts their scientific and historical significance, but he defends himself by quoting Paul's statement that Christians were "as deceivers, and yet true."[97] Niebuhr's mythical use of scriptural narratives allegedly leads to a "higher" level of truth but fails to transcend the confines of reason he built himself. A. E. Murphy pointedly criticizes that change of the Bible's form.

> If what it teaches is true, let those who propound it tell us so plainly. . . . It is hardly helpful to tell us that it is profoundly true

95. Ibid., p. 382.
96. Harald Hoffding, *Modern Philosophy*, 2:191.
97. Reinhold Niebuhr, *Interpretation of Christian Ethics*, p. 12.

indeed, but in a fashion which negates its literal assertions and precepts, and which is in any case beyond our capacity to understand, and that we must accept its apparent incoherence with humility as the basis for a moral judgment before which all human goodness stands condemned as sinful and all human truth (save that which announces this dismal verdict) as egoistically corrupt. Surely the good news of the gospels was better and more straightforward than this.[98]

Niebuhr not only fails to establish absolute truth transcending the time-bound cultures of human writers but vigorously opposes all who accept a conceptual revelation in the verbally inspired Scripture, including the entire Reformation tradition. Calvin's attempt "to collect from various places in Scripture a rule for the reformation of life,"[99] Niebuhr thinks, was made without reference to "the historical relativities enshrined in the sacred canon." Niebuhr charges Calvin with biblicism, bibliolatry, obscurantism, and pretension.[100] "The conviction of the faithful that the Bible gave them final truth, transcending all finite perspectives and all sinful corruptions, thus contributed to individual spiritual arrogance, no less intolerable than the collective arrogance of the older (Roman) church."[101] The authority used to break the proud authority of the Roman Church became another instrument of human pride, "a paper pope."[102]

Niebuhr's charges need to be heard by defenders of the Bible's inerrancy lest they imagine that there are two inerrant sources of authority, the Bible and their own pronouncements. At the same time the subtle temptations of pride are no less for those who deny the Bible's final authority. Neither Niebuhr nor his critics have escaped an equally great danger. Henry Nelson Wieman charged that Niebuhr claims to base his faith upon the Bible and calls it a biblical faith. But a careful examination shows that he corrects the Bible according to his own convictions. For example, admitting the difficulty of interpreting myths about a paradoxical reality, Niebuhr grants that they may easily lead to illusions. "Jesus, no less than Paul, was not free of these illusions."[103] Wieman, who thinks Niebuhr is quite right in treating the Bible as

98. A. E. Murphy, "Coming to Grips with the Nature and Destiny of Man," in *Religious Liberals Reply* (Boston: Beacon, 1947), p. 19.
99. John Calvin *Institutes of the Christian Religion* 3.6.1.
100. Reinhold Niebuhr, *The Nature and Destiny of Man*, 1:202.
101. Ibid., 1:229.
102. Ibid., 1:231.
103. Reinhold Niebuhr, *An Interpretation of Christian Ethics*, p. 57.

myth, simply complains about Niebuhr's claiming to have a "biblical faith." "In sum, I demand that neither Niebuhr nor the Bible, but reason, adjudicate the truth."[104]

Those who start with the relativism of all human thought, including that of the Scriptures, like Niebuhr will eventually place their own relative notions above those of Jesus Christ and Paul. Ought they not say so as candidly as Wieman? One can appreciate G. C. Berkouwer's desire to stress the power of God's Word but yet not concur with his charge that biblical teaching is "time-bound."[105] That the Bible is "time-related" and penetrates human life in all its forms and situations is indeed true.[106] But that it is time bound as Berkouwer and Kraft[107] have written reduces it to a product of its times and leaves inspiration to apply only in a functional sense today. Building the confines of human reason as Niebuhr did results in a loss of biblical authority.

In conclusion, we express our indebtedness to H. Richard and Rinehold Niebuhr for poignant reminders of the limitations of noninspired writers. Powerfully the Niebuhrs destroy the idols of arrogant pretenders to final truth. Evangelicals ought to proclaim those devastating arguments against the countless gurus, cultists, and Christians who claim to speak for God with absoluteness when God has not spoken. May God deliver all of us from presumptuousness of "prophetic" ministries when our denunciation comes from our own hearts and not from Him!

At the same time, the Niebuhrs have dreadfully missed the mark in failing to recognize the supernatural ways in which God brought Christ into the world, kept Him from sin, enabled Him to teach eternal truth in human language to people of specific cultures, and actually provide an atonement for actually guilty people on a literal cross. Tragically, the Niebuhrs also failed to acknowledge that the same Lord of all providentially prepared and supernaturally revealed information about Himself and *His plans for history* to prophetic and apostolic men who were supernaturally inspired to convey in faithful words content that had originated not in time-bound human opinion about God but in eternity as sound information (noncontradictory, factual, and viable).

In Christ's kenosis He did not cease to be God, and in the Bible's adaptation to the human level its divinely originated con-

---

104. Henry Nelson Wieman, "A Religious Naturalist Looks at Reinhold Niebuhr," in Kegley and Bretall, eds., *Reinhold Niebuhr*, p. 339.

105. G. C. Berkouwer, *Holy Scripture* (Grand Rapids: Eerdmans, 1975), p. 185.

106. Ibid., p. 188, 190.

107. Charles Kraft, *Christianity in Culture*, p. 300.

tent was not accommodated to human error. Just as Jesus Christ was truly human and truly divine, the Bible was truly human and truly divine. No Niebuhrian dialectic between eternity and time can keep us from those central Christian realities.

By reason of man's creation in God's image intellectually, categories of human thought (principles of logic) and categories of human speech (principles of grammar) need not be assumed to be totally other than God's. God gave people power to transcend time and space to communicate with Him in mind as well as in spirit. Furthermore God made man to rule the world and the world to be ruled by man, so that there is no reason to manufacture an unbiblical total difference between the categories of human thought and reality in the world. A basis for knowledge of things as they are in themselves, under God, is laid in the doctrine of creation and the divine image in man. Because of man's fallenness, however, naïve realism is often misled by superstition, fascination with the mysterious, and so forth. Therefore, a critical realism requiring adequate verification becomes necessary to verify revelation claims made by both true and false prophets and apostles, the Christ and the many antichrists. I have defended such a critical realism and a verificational epistemology elsewhere.[108]

Furthermore, the doctrine of human creation in God's image means that there are limits to relativism's emphasis upon the differences among cultures and historical periods. All people of all times and all places have been able to communicate with God and others. The initial problems of understanding may be great indeed, but some common categories of thought enable people eventually to grasp one another's meanings. The Niebuhrs and other relativists have failed to recognize that the Scriptures may be addressing propositionally and with finality matters in one culture that are not essentially different in other cultures. All peoples were created by God. All peoples were created in the divine likeness. All people have sinned and defaced that likeness. All people need forgiveness of sins, and Jesus Christ came into the world to provide a salvation sufficient for all. Jesus literally died and rose and will come again. He commanded His disciples to make disciples of all varieties of people and baptize them in the name of the Father, the Son, and the Holy Spirit into His Body. Only by broadening our epistemology to include the reception of some revealed information conveying final, noncontradictory, factual, and viable truth can we proclaim those truths to all people.

108. Gordon R. Lewis, *Testing Christianity's Truth Claims* (Chicago: Moody, 1975).

Either biblically revealed Christianity is conceptually true for everyone or it is true for no one.

May any evangelicals enamored of relativisms, relationalisms, and contextualisms like those of the Niebuhrs see where their epistemological assumptions are leading them before it is too late. The startling thing about the nonpretentious Niebuhrs and their relativistic followers is *the absoluteness* with which they reduced everything, including the Scriptures and Christ, to another book and person not essentially different from other sacred writings and other founders of world religions. An evangelical, in contrast to total relativists, has at least three absolutes, not just (1) the transcendent God beyond time, space, and human history, but also (2) the once-for-all, supernatural incarnation of Jesus Christ, who differs from the founders of other world religions not only in degree but also in kind, and (3) the once-for-all supernatural inscripturation of sound information in the biblical canon that differs from all other sacred writings not merely in degree, but also in kind.

7. Revelation and Scripture in Existentialist Theology

Fred H. Klooster

Theologians do not generally publicize their philosophical pedigrees. Thomas Aquinas was an exception, of course; he frankly worked out a synthesis of Christianity and Aristotelian philosophy. Protestant Scholasticism was deeply indebted to Descartes and other philosophers but usually less forthright in acknowledging those influences. Karl Barth recognized the impact of Søren Kierkegaard when he wrote his *Commentary on Romans*, but he subsequently disavowed that influence and claimed to use philosophy only as a tool for expressing his thought. Nevertheless, Barth remained greatly indebted to Kierkegaard as well as to neo-Kantianism; existentialist motifs are also present in the *Church Dogmatics*.

Existentialist theologians, however, candidly admit their indebtedness to Martin Heidegger and his existentialist philosophy. That link accounts, at least in part, for the name "existentialist theology." This essay will concentrate on the revelational views of Rudolf Bultmann, Paul Tillich, and John Macquarrie. Bultmann, Tillich, and Macquarrie, in their respective writings, all acknowl-

FRED H. KLOOSTER, A.B., Calvin College; B.D., Calvin Theological Seminary; Th.M., Westminster Theological Seminary; Th.D., Free University of Amsterdam, is professor of systematic theology at Calvin Theological Seminary, Grand Rapids, Michigan. His publications include *The Incomprehensibility of God in the Orthodox Presbyterian Conflict* (1951), *The Significance of Barth's Theology: An Appraisal with Special Reference to Election and Reconciliation* (1961), *Calvin's Doctrine of Predestination* (2d ed., 1977), *Quests for the Historical Jesus* (1977), *The Heidelberg Catechism: Origin and History* (1980).

edge that Heidegger's philosophy had a great impact on their theologies. Bultmann once stated that Heidegger's philosophy and the New Testament arrived at the same destination by different routes. Because the primary emphasis of existentialism is upon the human subject, existentialists generally make their presuppositions known. That is at least more forthright than the claimed neutrality and objectivity of the positivistic era.

The existentialist theologians devote considerable attention to their views of revelation. They generally employ Heidegger's new category of knowing to describe the place and the nature of their unique view of revelation. They do not devote much attention to Scripture, however, and rarely speak of infallibility; the term *inerrancy* is conspicuous by its absence. Their brief comments on Scripture are uually quite negative as they reject any identification of Scripture and revelation. Although this volume of essays is primarily devoted to theological presuppositions concerning the inerrancy of Scripture, consideration of the existentialist theologians requires that primary attention be given to their unique views of revelation. This essay will consider what those theologians say about Scripture and infallibility, but primary attention will have to be devoted to their views of revelation if they are to be given a fair hearing. Existentialist views of revelation lead those theologians to speak pejoratively of the evangelical, Reformed view of Scripture and infallibility.

AUTHOR'S CONFESSIONAL PERSPECTIVE

The reader of this essay on the existentialist theologians may be helped if I also frankly state the confessional perspective from which I write. As a member of a Reformed church, I personally subscribe to the Heidelberg Catechism, the Belgic Confession, and the Canons of Dort. I endorse the Reformed view of revelation and Scripture as expressed in those and similar confessions. I acknowledge the Reformed creeds as a faithful echo of the authoritative Scriptures. I participated in drawing up the Chicago Statement on Biblical Inerrancy (1978)[1] and agree with it. John Calvin's views of revelation and Scripture as set forth in the early chapters of the *Institutes* have helped to shape my personal theological views on revelation, but many other theologians have contributed as well. Hence this essay is written from the perspective

---

1. Reference may also be made to "Decision of the Synod of 1961 of the Christian Reformed Church on Infallibility and Inspiration" (*Acts*, 1961), and "The Nature and Extent of Biblical Authority" (*Acts*, 1972).

of classic Reformed theology in the evangelical tradition. I recognize, of course, that that position is considered untenable by the existentialist theologians surveyed in this essay.

I also attempt to work constructively with the Christian philosophical perspectives developed within the Reformed community during the past half-century.[2] By that I mean that I regard Scripture as normative for philosophical and scientific activity also. I believe that the biblical motif of creation, fall into sin, and redemption through Jesus Christ in the fellowship of the Holy Spirit should govern our philosophical and scientific activity. I realize that Tillich, for example, does not think Christian philosophy is a legitimate option. And I must frankly acknowledge that Christian philosophy with its creation, Fall, redemption perspectives stands in sharp conflict with existentialistic philosophy, as will become evident below. Yet the above-mentioned confessional stance provides the presuppositions from which I write, and the reader is entitled to know that at the outset.

Existentialism Philosophy

The close link between existentialist theology and existentialism calls for some reference to the chief characteristics of that philosophy. Of course, only key features can be considered here. Readers unacquainted with existentialism will have to look elsewhere for more detailed orientation.

The term *existentialism* probably goes back to Søren Kierkegaard (1813-1855), whose writings were not widely known outside of Denmark until after 1918. Like the more recent Dietrich Bonhoeffer, Kierkegaard is subject to varied interpretations, partly because of the occasional nature of his writings. I am not convinced of Kierkegaard's actual link to existentialism;[3] hence I exclude him from consideration below, both from my exposition of and my critique of existentialist theologians.

Existentialism was influenced by the phenomenological movement through Edmund Husserl (1859-1938), who considered phenomenology a descriptive science that can avoid all metaphysical questions when discovering and analyzing essences and essential meanings. A student of Husserl, Martin Heidegger (1889-1976), became the leading proponent of existentialist philosophy. Heidegger discontinued his preparation for the Roman Catholic

2. See the writings of H. Dooyeweerd, H. Stoker, C. van Til, D. H. Th. Vollenhoven, and others.
3. I have considered Kierkegaard briefly in "The Adjective in 'Systematic Theology' " (Grand Rapids: Calvin Theological Seminary, 1963), pp. 12-15.

priesthood to pursue philosophical studies. In rather obscure language Heidegger vigorously opposed the entire Western tradition of Greek thought and developed his ontology of the human person.

Existentialist philosophers are actually quite diverse. Some interpreters suggest that only common themes unite them. Some existentialists are Christian, others are humanistic, and a few are openly atheistic. Christian existentialists are found within both Roman Catholic and Protestant churches. Kierkegaard, Paul Ricoeur, and Goerges Gusdorf are regarded as representative of Protestant existentialists. Gabriel Marcel and Gustav E. Mueller are Roman Catholic representatives. Karl Jaspers, although personally Roman Catholic, represented the existentialism of religious humanism. Jean Paul Sartre, Merleau-Ponty, and Jean A. Wahl were openly atheistic existentialists. Sartre, who was also a student of Husserl, was a professed Communist as well. Albert Camus and Simon de Beavoir were existentialist novelists closely associated with Sartre. Although existentialism has greatly influenced several contemporary Roman Catholic theologians, Pope Pius XII's encyclical *Humani Generis* condemned the existentialist movement in 1950.

Because existentialist philosophy focuses concretely on the human person in the daily needs and experiences of existence, there are some parallels between Continental existentialism and North American process philosophy, as well as certain links with the pragmatism of William James and the instrumentalism of John Dewey. There are also parallels between existentialism and the personalistic theology developed by Martin Buber in his famous *Ich und Du* (I and Thou). Such parallels have also contributed to confusion on central issues. Existentialism has made inroads into evangelical Christian circles, sometimes unwittingly, because existentialism has become part of the current *Zeitgeist*. Its "personalistic" and "existential" concerns appeal to many who do not seem to realize the basic perspectives involved in existentialistic modes of thought.

Existentialism is difficult to summarize because of its diversity. The following four characteristics of existentialism, although not exhaustive, are especially relevant to the present essay. First, existentialists all oppose Hegel and the Western metaphysical tradition with its supposedly abstract ideas and systems of thought. From that perspective, existentialist theologians reject the classic Roman Catholic and Protestant views of Scripture as the written Word of God. Second, the chief emphasis of existentialism is upon the existing human person in his everyday needs and concerns. Although existentialists criticize the Western tradition for its objectivity, their radical concern for the individual existing person opens them to the criticism of subjectivity and anthropocentricity, even though they generally reject such charges. From that perspective the existentialist theologians concentrate their views of revelation on the human person in the "revelatory experience." Third, existentialism is marked by such pessimistic themes as death, finitude, limitation, guilt, anxiety, and dread as forms of "inauthentic existence." The themes' aim is to promote life, "being," or "authentic existence." Existentialist theologians draw on scriptural statements for endorsement of those themes, but a radical change in meaning *(Umdeutung)* is generally involved. Fourth, existentialism emphasizes that "existence precedes essence." That is the major philosophical perspective of the movement and has become its decisive slogan. Sartre frankly admitted that the contention that "existence precedes essence" was a radical rejection of God's creation and involved a pervasive subjectivity and an anthropocentric approach. We must examine that in greater detail.

Sartre maintained that what all existentialists have in common "is simply the fact that they believe that *existence* comes before *essence*—or, if you will, that we must begin from the subjective." He explains it this way:

> We mean that man first of all exists, encounters himself, surges up in the world—and defines himself afterwards. If man as the existentialist sees him as not definable, it is because to begin with he is nothing. He will not be anything until later, and then he will be what he makes of himself. Thus, there is no human nature, because there is no God to have a conception of it. Man simply is. Not that he is simply what he conceives himself to be, but he is what he wills, and as he conceives himself after already existing—as he wills to be after that leap toward existence. Man is nothing else but that which he makes of himself. That is the first principle of existentialism.[4]

Sartre also amplified that explanation: "If, however, it is true that existence is prior to essence, [then] man is responsible for what he is," and "the first effect of existentialism is that it puts every man in possession of himself as he is, and places the entire responsibility for his existence squarely upon his own shoulders."[5]

4. J. P. Sartre, *Existentialism and Humanism*, trans. Philip Mariet (London: Methuen & Co., 1948), p. 28.
5. Ibid., p. 29.

Sartre's rejection of the charge of "subjectivism" against that explanation is characteristic of the existentialists on this score; this is not "subjectivism," Sartre insisted, because each individual person is responsible for all other humans. Yet Sartre admitted that existentialism was subjectivistic in the sense that "man cannot pass beyond human subjectivity."[6] It is apparent that the existentialistic position involves the rejection of the created essence of all things and is clearly Pelagian in its view of the human subject.

THEOLOGICAL EXISTENTIALISTS

We must now turn to the major theologians who adopt existentialism or at least work primarily within that philosophical context. We shall leave aside the question of the impact of existentialism on neo-orthodoxy and Barthian theology. Barth's initial appeal to Kierkegaard has been mentioned. Emil Brunner referred to the divine-human encounter, but he relied primarily on Martin Buber for his form of personalism. The fact that Bultmann and Tillich were initially part of the Barthian dialectical movement is itself instructive. But we shall limit the concern of this essay to those who readily acknowledge their indebtedness to existentialism.

Bultmann frankly acknowledged his debt to Martin Heidegger and existentialism. The same is true of Paul Tillich and John Macquarrie. Schubert Ogden and other Bultmannians reflect the same influence, although North Americans tend to make greater use of Alfred North Whitehead and process philosophy. Heinrich Ott has attempted a *via media* between Barth and Bultmann. The students of Bultmann who began the "new quest" of the historical Jesus continued to embrace existentialistic modes of thought. That is true of Ernst Käsemann, Günther Bornkamm, Hans Conzelmann, Erich Dinkler, and especially of Ernst Fuchs and Gerhard Ebeling as representatives of the "new hermeneutic." Ebeling's depiction of the "word event" is an example of the view of revelation common in existentialist theology. Several leading contemporary Roman Catholic theologians have also been influenced by existentialist modes of thought. That is clearly the case in Karl Rahner, who is probably the most influential, though not the most popular, of these. Hans Küng and Edward Schillebeeckx, as well as others, could be mentioned.

6. Ibid.

Because the problem of description is so complex and the diversity among the existentialist theologians considerable, this essay will concentrate on Bultmann, Tillich, and Macquarrie. Rudolf Bultmann (1884-1976) taught New Testament studies at the University of Marburg from 1921 until his retirement in 1951. He was a colleague of Martin Heidegger at Marburg from 1923 to 1928. In 1929 Bultmann published an article, "The Concept of Revelation in the New Testament."[7] By then he had embraced Heidegger's existentialism as expressed in *Sein und Zeit* (1927). Around the same time Bultmann prepared a briefer article, "Revelation in the New Testament," for the second edition of *Religion in Geschichte und Gegenwart*.[8]

Paul Tillich (1886-1965) was also a major German theologian until Hitler forced his move to the United States where he taught at Union Theological Seminary in New York, Harvard University, and the University of Chicago. Tillich was a student of Husserl and was deeply indebted to Heidegger for his philosophical theology. In addition to the relevant sections of his *Systematic Theology*, Tillich also has an article on "Revelation and the Philosophy of Religion," which he contributed to the second edition of *Religion in Geschichte und Gegenwart*.[9]

John Macquarrie came from Scotland, taught for eight years at Union Seminary in New York, and presently teaches at Oxford University in England. He also is a systematic theologian, and his *Principles of Christian Theology*, published in 1966 and revised in 1977, will be our chief source.[10] Macquarrie acknowledged the impact that Heidegger and Rahner made on his theology.

Those three theologians provide a good sample of existentialist theology with sufficient diversity. Bultmann and Tillich had Lutheran roots and came from the Evangelical Church of Germany, whereas Macquarrie is Anglican. Bultmann was a New Testament scholar, whereas Macquarrie and Tillich are and were systematic theologians, the latter especially a philosophical theologian. The primary works considered in this essay also provide an interesting chronological balance covering roughly one-half century with quarter-century intervals. Bultmann's essays comes from 1929,

7. *Existence and Faith: Shorter Writings of Rudolf Bultmann*, ed. S. M. Ogden (New York: Meridian Books, 1960), pp. 58-91.
8. "English Translation," in *Twentieth-Century Theology in the Making*, ed. J. Pelikan (New York: Harper & Row, 1971), 2:41-46.
9. Paul Tillich, *Systematic Theology* (Chicago: U. of Chicago, 1951), vol. 1, "English Translation," in *Twentieth-Century Theology in the Making*, 2:45-56.
10. John Macquarrie, *Principles of Christian Theology*, 2d ed. (New York: Scribner's, 1977).

Tillich's *Systematic Theology* from 1950, and Macquarrie's *Principles of Christian Theology* (second edition) from 1977.

Our chief interest in this essay is the existentialist view of the Bible and inerrancy as reflected in such representative theologians as Bultmann, Tillich, and Macquarrie. Because those theologians have so little to say about the Scriptures as such or about the questions of infallibility and inerrancy, we shall have to deal largely with their views of "revelation." What does "revelation" mean to those theologians? What role does "revelation" play in the movement from "existence" to "essence," from "inauthentic existence" to "authentic being"? What does "revelation" really involve? Those questions are not easily answered, but it is only in the light of these men's answers to such questions that one can understand the existentialist attitude to the Bible and inerrancy.

MACQUARRIE'S VIEW OF REVELATION

We can best begin our consideration of the existentialist theologians with John Macquarrie, who sets forth "the epistemology of revelation" to clarify the existentialist understanding of revelation. Existentialist theologians locate the "revelatory experience" in a new category of knowing and knowledge that was delineated by Heidegger.

SCRIPTURE AND INFALLIBILITY

Before summarizing Macquarrie's description of the three categories in the "epistemology of revelation," we should observe what he has to say about Scripture. Macquarrie lists six "formative factors" or sources of theology. They are experience, revelation, Scripture, tradition, culture, and reason. Revelation and Scripture are two distinct factors. Macquarrie explains: "Scripture is not itself revelation, but it is one important way (not the only one) by which the community of faith keeps open its access to the primordial revelation on which the community has been founded."[11] The Scriptures are "the sacred writings of the community of faith," but they must become revelation. "The scriptures do not indeed automatically lay this revelation before us but, in conjunction with a present experience of the holy in the community of faith, the scriptures come alive, so to speak, and renew for us the disclosure of the holy which was the content of the primordial revelation."[12] What Macquarrie means by the "inspiration of scripture" is "this power of bringing again or re-presenting the

11. Ibid., p. 9. Hereafter unnumbered quotations come from the same page as the previous note.
12. Ibid., p. 19.

disclosure of the primordial revelation so that it speaks to us in our present experience." He adds that "such inspiration does not lie in the words (it is not 'verbal inspiration'), but belongs to the scriptures only as they are set in the context of the whole life of faith in the community."[13]

Macquarrie contends that the danger of slighting the Bible is less common than the danger "that the Bible may get absolutized as a formative factor in theology." He adds that "the belief that the Bible is infallible is one that dies hard in some parts of the Christian world." He insists that "the Bible is not itself revelation. The Christian revelation comes in a person, not in a book. But the Bible is not even an infallible record or witness to this revelation."[14]

Macquarrie thinks that "textual variants" destroy "the old idea of an infallible book," but that is only the beginning of "demolishing the idea of biblical infallibility." He also mentions "divergencies and discrepancies" on such trivial matters as the number of animals entering the ark and the identity of the women at the tomb as well as on major questions of theology and ethics. He thinks that doubts about authorship and dates of composition of Bible books imply that we have only "anonymous accounts" that call "historical accuracy" into grave question.

"But enough of this," Macquarrie adds. "I am not trying to impugn the Bible (far from it!), but only that misuse of the Bible which absolutizes it. . . ." In his judgment "the critical study of the Bible . . . will in the long run do more justice to the biblical teaching" than "this exaggerated regard for the Bible" that considers it as infallible revelation. His comments were directed chiefly against "ultra-conservative biblicists," but he also rejects "the biblical theology that has so greatly flourished in recent times," that is, the neo-orthodox biblical theology.[15]

To understand those harsh negative comments about the evangelical view of Scripture, one must understand Macquarrie's view of "revelation" or "primordial revelation." His description of the "epistemology of revelation" helps to locate this "revelatory experience."

EPISTEMOLOGY OF REVELATION

Macquarrie follows Heidegger and distinguishes the following three kinds of thinking and kinds of knowledge: (1) calculative

13. Ibid., p. 9.
14. Ibid., p. 10.
15. Ibid., p. 11.

thinking and objective knowledge (the subject-object or I-it relation); (2) existential thinking and personal knowledge (the subject-subject or I-thou relation); (3) essential thinking and revealed or giftlike knowledge.[16] Macquarrie states that the outline of this scheme reflects the philosophy of Heidegger, but he worked it out in greater detail and explicitness than Heidegger had done.

We must briefly examine each of those categories to understand especially the third because that is where the existentialists locate revelation (the "revelatory experience" or "primordial revelation"). We should also observe that Macquarrie and the existentialists locate the evangelical view of Scripture in the first category. It is equally important to observe that the existentialist theologians do not locate the revelatory event in the second category; the I-thou relation of Buber and neo-orthodox theologians is often confused with the existentialist view of revelation. What adds to the confusion is the terminology; existentialist theologians reject "existential thinking" of the second category and endorse "essential thinking" of the third category when referring to "revelation." The exposition of those three categories in the "epistemology of revelation" follows Macquarrie, but observations are added for clarification.

Calculative thinking and objective knowledge. Martin Heidegger used the term "calculative thinking" to describe the classic subject-object pattern of thought. As subjects, persons think about objects that are out there, outside of them, over against them. The subject is active while the object is passive; the subject handles, uses, and manipulates the object. Calculative thinking probes; the subject observes, experiments, measures, deduces, demonstrates, and shows connections between the object and other objects. The knowing subject transcends the object to be known; "we *subject* it, in the sense of rising above it and, to some extent, mastering it."[17]

The kind of "knowledge" that results from that calculative mode of thought is "objective knowledge," that is, information, propositional knowledge. Martin Buber referred to this as the "I-it" relationship that involves cold, abstract thought and knowledge.

According to Heidegger and Macquarrie, calculative thinking and objective knowledge were prominent in Western philosophy

16. Ibid., p. 91-96.
17. Ibid., p. 91.

from the Greeks to Hegel. That mode of thinking is still common in everyday activity. All the theoretical sciences employ it, and its most sophisticated form is found in modern technology. Heidegger opposed this dominant form of Western thought so vigorously that at times he hardly allowed it to be considered a form of thinking.

From this description it is evident why existentialist theologians reject the evangelical view of Scripture and why they vehemently reject the infallibility and inerrancy of Scripture. The classic Christian view of general revelation and of Scripture as God's inscripturated special revelation is said to fall within the category of calculative thinking and objective knowledge.

Existential thinking and personal knowledge. On the "existential level of thinking," according to Macquarrie and Heidegger, "there is a subject-subject relationship." That kind of thinking is "proper to existential or personal being."[18] Such thinking does not aim at calculation and exploitation as in the subject-object relation, but at "well-being, either one's own or another's." One does not think about an object but about another subject "having the same kind of being as the person who does the thinking." Such thinking requires "participation," "thinking into the existence of the other subject," and "thinking into" is possible because both subjects have the same kind of being.

"Existential thinking" is common in everyday interpersonal relations, but it can also become "theoretical, where practical solicitude or interest has been dimmed down." Macquarrie sees "Heidegger's own existential analytic" an an illustration of that kind of thinking.

As an example of the differences between "calculative thinking" and "existential thinking," Macquarrie reflects on how each would handle the topic of "fear." Calculative thought describes fear objectively in terms of "physiological changes and overt behavior." Heidegger's "existential analysis" of fear, on the other hand, is based "on the existent's own firsthand participation in the experience of fear, and, prior to that, on his participation in a finite existence for which fear is a possibility."

In that connection Macquarrie refers to "repetitive" thinking as an important special case of such existential thinking, because of its significance for the "revelatory experience." "Repetition" then implies "going into some experience that has been handed down in such a way that it is . . . brought into the present and its

18. Ibid., p. 92.

insights and possibilities made alive again." "Repetitive" thinking can occur in connection with historical happenings or documents such as poems or sayings. "A mere mechanical" repetition is not involved; understanding requires that we "think *into* it, and so think *again* and *with* the agent or the author." Repetitive thinking is needed to understand the experiences described in Scripture, according to Macquarrie. That perspective appears to be a carry-over from the hermeneutics of the early Schleiermacher.

The kind of knowledge that results from "the existential mode of thinking" is called "personal knowledge." Martin Buber spoke of "I-thou" knowledge; the "I" and the "thou" meet and recognize each other as subjects.[19] There is activity by both knowing subjects. The other person makes himself known or lets himself be known; "we know him not only by his overt behavior but to the extent to which he opens himself to us and actively meets us in our approach to him." Knowledge results from this meeting "on a footing of mutuality and reciprocity."

Since Buber, Barth, and Brunner view revelation in terms of the "I-thou" encounter, it is important to understand that Macquarrie clearly excludes the "revelatory experience" of the existentialist theologians from this second category. Macquarrie's reasons for rejecting the "I-thou" kind of knowledge as the locus of the "revelatory experience" enables one to understand better what the existentialist theologians mean by "revelation" and how they view Scripture as the occasion for revelation.

According to Macquarrie there are many reasons for rejecting the second category of knowing as an unsatisfactory explanation of the "revelatory experience." He considers these three reasons as conclusive:[20]

(1) The first reason is striking. Macquarrie notes that the meeting of two persons involves "an actual physical meeting" in which "words are spoken and heard, looks and gestures communicated and understood." But that basic requirement for interpersonal meeting is absent from the revelatory encounter, according to Macquarrie. At best the revelatory experience could only be "remotely analogous" to the "I-thou" meetings of two persons.

(2) A second reason is that in the human "I-thou" encounter "reciprocity and give-and-take are essential." But "in the revelatory experience," according to existentialist theologians, "the person who receives the revelation is utterly transcended by the holy

19. Ibid., p. 93.
20. Ibid.

being that reveals itself; and this utter one-sidedness again implies that a personal encounter could be only a very remote analogue."

(3) Third, in the "I-thou" encounter "two particular beings know each other." But Macquarrie contends that "in revelation we do not know another being, but simply being." That is very significant for the existentialist theologians. From that perspective one can better understand why the existentialists reject the classic Christian view of Scripture as revelation from a living God to His creatures.

The main point of all this is that, according to Macquarrie and the existentialist theologians, personal language is required to describe revelation, but personal language is still inadequate for describing the "revelatory experience." Barth, Brunner, and pehaps even an evangelical may use that personalist language within the framework of his own theology; not so the existentialist theologians. "Certainly personal knowledge and the related existential thinking bring us nearer to the revelatory experience than the objective knowledge that arises from calculative thinking," Macquarrie continues, "especially because personal knowledge is made possible only by the active self-disclosure of the person known, and so we get something like a parallel to the initiative of the holy in revealed knowledge."[21] But one has not yet described the "revelatory experience" in existentialist terms. For that Macquarrie leads us to the third mode of thinking and knowing.

Essential thinking and gift-like knowledge. The third mode of thinking or knowing is a new category pointed out by Heidegger. It is not subject-object, or subject-subject; it is not the "I-it," or the "I-thou" relation. Rather, essential thinking is the mode "in which I would be subject to that which is known, one in which I am transcended, mastered, and, indeed, known myself."[22] "Essential" or "primordial" thinking has "a meditative character which contrasts with the probing activity of calculative thinking." As "meditative" one "waits and listens;" Heidegger refers to it as an " 'occurrence of being' " or as thinking that " 'answers to the demands of being.' " While "primordial thinking" is philosophical, it is a "thinking which responds to the address of being, and is explicitly compared both to the insights of religion and to those of poetry."

The knowledge that corresponds to that "primordial" or "es-

21. Ibid.
22. Ibid., p. 94.

sential" thinking has "a gift-like character"; it is "revelatory knowledge" or "revealed knowledge." Person-to-person knowledge of the second category also has a gift like character, but in essential thinking, "the gift-character is enhanced and we have become almost passive recipients."[23] Yet we are "not *entirely* passive" since there is always "an element of appropriation" and there is "a capacity *for* revelation."[24] "Appropriation is involved in the revelatory experience," yet it is an "appropriation" in which "being grasps us" and "it grasps us in such a way that we are not simply overwhelmed by it." In the religious experience of revelation, "the overwhelmingness of being is matched by its grace, the *tremendum* by the *fascinans*, for being gives itself and opens itself, so that we stand in the grace and openness of being. It reveals itself not only in otherness but also in kinship, so that even as we are grasped by it, we can to some extent grasp it in turn and hold to it."[25]

Heidegger's "primordial" or "essential" knowing with "gift-like, meditative" knowledge provides the category for the existentialist understanding of "revelation." The "revelatory experience" is compared with the insights of religion and poetry. Macquarrie concludes that "this kind of philosophical thinking, then, provides a kind of paradigm for the understanding of what is meant by 'revelation,' and shows where revelation is to be located in the range of man's cognitive experience."[26] That "epistemology of revelation" already "reveals" a great deal about the existentialist view of revelation. For futher clarification we now turn to the 1929 essay of Rudolf Bultmann, "Revelation According to the New Testament."

BULTMANN'S VIEW OF REVELATION

Rudolf Bultmann was a New Testament scholar who began teaching at Marburg in 1912 and, after brief periods at Breslau and Berlin, returned to Marburg in 1921 where he taught until his retirement in 1951. He died in 1976 at the age of 92. He was a radical critic of the New Testament, who employed the method of form-criticism and introduced a program of demythologizing. Bultmann's approach to the New Testament was governed by the conviction that modern science made it impossible to accept the

23. Ibid., p. 95.
24. Ibid. (italics added).
25. Ibid. Macquarrie here uses words heavily dependent on Tillich. Cf. note 86.
26. Ibid., p. 94.

biblical message in traditional terms. A radical reinterpretation was required if modern people were to believe the basic message of Scripture. For that purpose he thought the tools of Heidegger's existentialistic philosophy were especially appropriate for conveying the basic New Testament message that concerns authentic human existence. His view of revelation also falls into the third category of the Heidegger-Macquarrie "epistemology of revelation."

SCRIPTURE AND INERRANCY

In his famous 1941 programmatic essay, "New Testament and Mythology," Bultmann declared that "it is impossible to use electric light and the wireless . . . and at the same time to believe in the New Testament world of spirits and miracles."[27] Because "all our thinking to-day is shaped irrevocably by modern science," modern people find it impossible to believe the Bible in the traditional way because the Bible presents "the cosmology of a prescientific age."[28] But it is not only the challenge of natural science that makes the mythology of the New Testament incredible today. According to Bultmann there is also a "more serious challenge presented by *modern man's understanding of himself.*"[29]

From the perspectives of positivistic science and the existentialistic view of human existence, Bultmann declares that "the cosmology of the New Testament is essentially mythical in character. The world is viewed as a three-storied structure, with the earth in the center, the heaven above, and the underworld beneath. Heaven is the abode of God and of celestial beings—the angels. The underworld is hell, the place of torment."[30] But Bultmann's objections are not primarily spatial or geographical; he is not simply objecting to an "above" and a "below." His chief objection is that "even the earth is more than the scene of natural, everyday events, of the trivial round and common task. It is the scene of the supernatural activity of God and his angels on the one hand, and of Satan and his demons on the other. These supernatural forces intervene in the course of nature and in all that men think and will do."[31] The interaction of God, man, and Satan

---

27. Rudolf Bultmann, *Kerygma and Myth*, ed. H. W. Bartsch (New York: Harper & Row, 1961), p. 5.
28. Ibid., p. 3.
29. Ibid., p. 6.
30. Ibid., p. 1.
31. Ibid.

conflicts with Bultmann's positivistic view of a world controlled by natural causes and effects. The view of the interaction of God, man, and Satan on this earth, here and now, is declared an "obsolete," mythical view of the world, one that makes the kerygma "incredible to modern man."[32]

Butlmann thinks a Christian would have to be a schizoid if he were to live in the modern world and accept the obsolete mythology of the Bible. In contrast to liberalism, he does not think that mythology has to be discarded, rather, it has to be "demythologized." The kernel of truth in the New Testament message has to be removed from the husk of its mythical setting. "Demythologizing" is to be viewed as a new hermeneutical method so that by interpretation and exegesis the biblical message can be translated into a meaningful challenge to faith for modern people.

As Bultmann applied the form-critical method to the synoptic gospels in 1921 and to the gospel of John in 1941 publications, he concludes that they tell us almost nothing about history or the historical Jesus. Rather, the gospels were really the creation of the early Christian communities and reflect their devotional, theological, and apologetic needs. He concludes that "we can now know almost nothing concerning the life and personality of Jesus."[33] Primitive Christianity had turned the historical person of Jesus into a myth. Bultmann argues that only when that material is demythologized do we discover that the Bible really speaks about "eschatological events" that call for decision in the present. The incarnation and the resurrection are not real events of history, not datable events of the past; they are "eschatological events" that express the faith of the early communities and call for existential decision in the present. The resurrection, for example, is not the event that concerns the coming again to life of Jesus of Nazareth; it depicts the disciples' "rise to faith."

One could go on to illustrate Bultmann's radical rejection of the evangelical view of Scripture, but those illustrations must suffice. It is apparent that his form-critical and mythological approach to Scripture makes any reference to infallibility or inerrancy meaningless.

REVELATION IN THE NEW TESTAMENT

Bultmann's most extensive discussion of the nature of revelation was presented in his 1929 essay "The Concept of Revelation

32. Ibid., p. 3.
33. Bultmann, *Jesus and the Word* (New York: Scribners 1934), p. 8.

in the New Testament."[34] More than one-third of the essay is devoted to a "clarification of the question through an inquiry into the guiding preunderstanding of revelation." This section is very important because Bultmann actually says more about his view of revelation here than in the following twenty pages specifically devoted to the New Testament itself. In fact, the latter section largely contains a selection of "proof-texts" to support the choices made in the section on preunderstanding and clarification.

Existentialistic preunderstanding. Bultmann considers the clarification of one's preunderstanding crucial because "only a clear question will hear a clear answer."[35] We must be completely clear what we are asking of the New Testament. The clarification is carried out in three sections: first, a "provisional definition of the concept of revelation and its differentiations"; second, "the motive of the question and the character of the answer that may be expected"; and third, "a survey of the understandings of revelation in the tradition."[36]

Bultmann maintains that just as one has a preunderstanding of marriage or the state when one asks what the New Testament says about those subjects, so one has a preunderstanding of the concept of revelation when one approaches the New Testament on that subject. He distinguishes a general and a religious preunderstandng of revelation, and each of those carried a double meaning or "differentiation."

In the more general sense revelation means "the disclosure of what is veiled, the opening up of what is hidden"; and there are two major meanings: (1) "Revelation is the communication of knowledge by the word," or (2) "revelation is an occurrence that puts me in a new situation as a self, in which to be sure, there is also given the possibility of knowledge (namely, about myself in my new situation), but without regard for whether or not this knowledge becomes explicit."[37] The "religious" sense of revelation is more specific, Bultmann observes, but there are also two shades of meaning: "Here revelation means that opening up of what is hidden which is absolutely necessary and decisive for man if he is to achieve 'salvation' or authenticity; i.e., revelation here is the disclosure of *God* to man—whether this disclosure is thought to take place through the communication of knowledge, through a mediating doctrine about God, or whether it is an occurrence that

---

34. Bultmann, *Existence and Faith*, ed. S. M. Ogden. See note 7 above.
35. Ibid., p. 58.
36. Ibid., pp. 58-60; 60-65; 65-71.
37. Ibid., p. 59.

puts man in a new situation."[38] Throughout his discussion it is obvious that Bultmann's choice has been made for "an occurrence that puts man in a new situation" as a self, the third of the Heidegger-Macquarrie categories.

That leads to Bultmann's second preliminary question: "Why do we want to know what the New Testament understands by revelation?"[39] What is "the motive of the question and the character of the answer that may be expected"? Bultmann devotes considerable space to that question; existentialist presuppositions are prominent in the discussion. The knowledge of our preunderstanding is not "definitive knowledge" of revelation; if it were, we would be going to the New Testament as one would go to a museum or an exhibition. We would be mere spectators. Bultmann insists, however, that "our preliminary knowledge of revelation is only a very vague knowedge, . . . a peculiarly *not-knowing knowledge*."[40]

Bultmann amplifies this answer. What is our motive for asking the New Testament for its view of revelation?

> Thus every man knows what is at issue when we speak of revelation; and yet he does not know it either, because he can only know of it as he knows of himself and his limitation and thus always only anew and differently. Therefore, if we are able to ask concerning the concept of revelation in the New Testament only on the basis of a knowledge of our own limitation, we do not ask on the basis of a certain knowledge that we possess, but on the basis of a peculiarly *not-knowing knowledge*.[41]

What kind of *answer* must we then expect from the New Testament? The existentialistic perspectives are clear in Bultmann's response. One cannot expect an answer that is "a simple communication." Revelation in the New Testament is understood "only as a *personal address*," and he explained: "The question concerning revelation is simultaneously the question concerning man's limitation; and an answer to the question, What is revelation? can only be perceived if the questioner is prepared to let his limitation be disclosed."[42]

According to Bultmann that understanding does not involve

38. Ibid.
39. Ibid., p. 60.
40. Ibid., p. 61 (italics added).
41. Ibid., p. 63 (italics added).
42. Ibid., p. 64.

information or communication; the understanding to be "real-ized" calls for personal "resolve." Although Bultmann asserts that the preunderstanding must be questioned, it is evident that an existentialist preunderstanding already determined the an-swer. In another article Bultmann admits there are some Old Testment and New Testament passages that speak of revelation as communication, but he maintains that is not the dominant motif, and he therefore ignores it. The question concerning rev-elation and the answer to be expected is put by the person "who *knows* with that *not-knowing knowledge.*"[43]

In the third preliminary section Bultmann examines the views of revelation present in the "historical tradition."[44] Each person's preunderstanding of revelation is "always present in a specific 'historical tradition.' " One is Roman Catholic, Protestant, ratio-nalist, idealistic or Romantic, or liberal—to mention only those to which Bultmann refers. It is a brief but interesting survey of historical views. In terms of Macquarrie's three categories of knowing, Bultmann's view can be summarized by stating that he sees those historical views falling into mainly two extremes, ei-ther objectivism or subjectivism. For all their differences, Roman Catholicism and Protestantism are basically agreed that revela-tion is "the communication of knowledge or of doctrine" with the main difference between the knowledge of reason and revelation as simply one of *origin.*[45] For rationalism revelation became su-perfluous and the concept "natural revelation" was "self-contra-dictory."[46] In Romanticism or idealism, while continuing in the same Western tradition, "the feeling of creativity seems to be revelation."[47] Bultmann is critical of the "irrational features" and the "deep subjectivity" for "man does not become aware of God, but only of himself," and "he is deceived if he interprets the numinous as the divine." According to Bultmann liberalism trivi-alized the concept of revelation for "indeed, *everything* is revela-tion"; in liberalism "experience" came to be revelation. In this article Bultmann makes no mention of neo-orthodoxy.

Although disagreeing with the entire tradition on revelation, Bultmann yet sees an existentialistic concern present; all are concerned with human limitation and the revelational means of overcoming it:

43. Ibid., p. 65 (italics added).
44. Ibid.
45. Ibid., p. 66.
46. Ibid., p. 67.
47. Ibid., p. 69.

In all of these attempts to say what revelation is, the thought is maintained—even when it is distorted into meaninglessness—that it is by means of revelation that man comes to his authenticity, in which he does not simply find himself and on which he must at least reflect if it is to be achieved. It is affirmed that man understands his existence as limited, i.e., as qualified by limitation, and that being limited is something that terrifies him and makes him anxious and places his existence in question. And what is everywhere said, in one way or another, in speaking of revelation is that this limitation is provisional, that the limits can be broken through.[48]

In that statement critical of the entire Western tradition, Bultmann indicates rather clearly what he personally understands by "revelation." That is clarified in these additional comments: "For the rest, the various views of revelation are distinguished from one another according to the way man understands himself, i.e., wherein he sees the highest possibility of his being, through the realization of which he achieves his authenticity."[49] In short, Bultmann sees the basic difference between the various historical views in what man sees his *limitation* to be and what *revelation* does to meet that limitation.

Existentialistic concept of revelation. When Bultmann finally presents the concept of revelation in the New Testament, he does not engage in examination and exposition in the usual sense. The presuppositions evident in the preliminary analysis now become dominant in his conclusions, with proof-texts to illustrate each contention. It is an unusual section in several respects. Bultmann sets forth his understanding of the New Testament conception of revelation under six heads; some of them involve little more than his statement and an array of Scripture passages that he thinks supports that point.

The "what" of revelation, according to Bultmann, is "life in Christ." The New Testament indicates that man's limitation is death; hence "revelation can only be the gift of life through which death is overcome."[50] Hence the New Testament "not only says *what* revelation is, it also says *that* it is. Revelation is an *occurrence* that abolishes death, not a doctrine that death does not exist. But it is not an occurrence *within* human life, but rather one that *breaks in upon it from outside and* therefore cannot be

48. Ibid.
49. Ibid.
50. Ibid., p. 72.

demonstrated within life itself. . . . One can only believe in it."[51]
Revelation is an occurrence "that directly concerns *us*, that takes
place in us ourselves; and the word, the fact of its being proclaimed, must itself belong to the occurrence." Hence preaching is
itself revelation for Bultmann.[52]

That revelation is "an eschatological event." It does not involve
the "historical Jesus" or "Christ according to the flesh." Rather, it
"takes place in the present, in my particular present," and "the
way in which it is made present . . . is through preaching . . . by
presenting it in the form of an address."[53] It is "only *in* faith that
the object of faith is disclosed; therefore faith itself belongs to the
revelation." Bultmann summarizes the first two points: "If by
means of revelation as an occurrence wrought by God, death is
abolished and life is revealed, then 'life' is not thought of as an
objective condition in which we find ourselves, but rather as a
mode of being that we lay hold on in faith."[54]

In the third section the "content" of revelation is simply expressed by means of various synonyms; "the righteousness of
God, the forgiveness of sins, freedom, and love" are simply synonyms for "life in Christ" as the "what" and "how" of revelation.
Sin, godlessness, death are forms of inauthentic existence; life
and its synonyms are expressive of authentic being.

The most difficult question for traditional theologians to understand concerns the "content" of such revelation. To the question, What, then, has been revealed? Bultmann answered: "Nothing at all, so far as the question concerning revelation asks for
doctrine—doctrines, say, that no man could have discovered for
himself—or for mysteries that become known once and for all as
soon as they are communicated." But he continued: "On the other
hand, however, *everything has been revealed, insofar as man's eyes
are opened concerning his own existence and he is once again able
to understand himself.*"[55] That answer reminds one of Buber's explanation of the content of revelation in the divine-human encounter: "What, then, do we know of *Thou*? Just everything. For
we know nothing isolated about it any more."[56] The striking dif-

51. Ibid.
52. Ibid., p. 79.
53. Ibid.
54. Ibid., p. 80.
55. Ibid., p. 85.
56. Martin Buber, *I and Thou*, trans. R. G. Smith (Edinburgh: T. & T. Clark, 1937),
    p. 11. Cf. Karl Barth's similar response to the content of revelation question
    in *The Doctrine of the Word of God (Prolegomena)*, vol. 1, pt. 1, 2d ed., of
    Church Dogmatics, trans. G. W. Bromiley and T. R. Torrance (Edinburgh: T. &
    T. Clark, 1975), p. 132 (1st ed., p. 149).

ference, of course, is that Buber (and Barth) refer to the "Thou," whereas Bultmann refers to "I" or "me." Macquarrie's criticisms of the "I-thou" relation help to clarify this important difference.[57]

What occurs in the moment of "revelation" according to Bultmann is "authentic being," for "existence in the moment is his authentic being."[58] Revelation calls for obedience in the concrete now:

> Thus it becomes completely clear that revelation is an act of God, an *occurrence*, and not a communication of supernatural knowledge. Further, it is clear that revelation reveals *life*, for it frees man from what is provisional and past and gives him the future. Even so, it is clear that *Christ* is revelation and revelation is the word: for *these two are one and the same.*[59]

By going to the New Testament in this way, according to Bultmann, "the preunderstanding that man already has is radicalized and thereby corrected; it is not for him to break through his limits, but rather to understand himself in them."[60] Hence the knowledge of revelation is "a knowledge that must always be acquired anew and by going the long way around." There is no finished revelation, and certainly no progressive revelation; "every generation has the same original relation to revelation."

There is development only in "the conceptual explication of our preunderstanding of revelation" and in "the theological or conceptual explications of faith's knowledge of itself which has its basis in revelation." In other words, "all that develops is simply our way of talking about revelation." All explication also remains in the realm of preunderstanding: "The radicalizing only really takes place when what is said in the New Testament is truly heard."[61] Only then can one claim it and proclaim it! Hence the New Testament is not itself revelation, but becomes revelation when it is so heard: "Thus, in response to the question what the New Testament understands by revelation, it asks the counterquestion whether it itself is heard as revelation."[62] That revelational occurrence described by Bultmann is therefore clearly in the "primordial" or "essential" category of the Heidegger-Macquarrie "epistemology of revelation."

---

57. See note 20 above.
58. Ibid., p. 86.
59. Ibid., p. 87 (italics added in last line only).
60. Ibid., p. 89.
61. Ibid., p. 90.
62. Ibid., p. 91.

TILLICH'S VIEW OF REVELATION

In his *Systematic Theology* Paul Tillich sets forth an existentialist view of revelation that also fits the third of the Heidegger-Macquarrie categories. Tillich does list the Bible as one of the sources of systematic theology, but he sharply distinguishes his view of Scripture from neo-orthodoxy, European orthodoxy, and American fundamentalism and evangelicialism.

SCRIPTURE AND INFALLIBILITY

In the "Introduction" or prolegomena section of his *Systematic Theology*, Tillich indicates that the Bible is a source, but not the only source of theology; it is not the medium of revelation, for experience is that; and the norm of theology is something within the Bible, not the entire Bible.

As "sources of systematic theology," Tillich lists the Bible, church history, history of religion, and culture. He first rejects "the assertion of neo-orthodox biblicism that the Bible is the *only* source."[63] Tillich acknowledges that "the Bible is the original document about the events on which Christianity is based" and "on which the Christian church is founded."[64] Because of that, the Bible is "the basic source of systematic theology," but it is not the only source, not the major source, and not the norm.

In opposition to "neo-orthodox biblicism," Tillich asserts that "the biblical message cannot be understood and could not have been received had there been no preparation for it in human religion and culture." And, he adds, "the biblical message would not have become a message for anyone, including the theologian himself, without the experiencing participation of the church and of every Christian."[65] Furthermore, "if the 'Word of God' or the 'act or revelation' is called the source of systematic theology, it must be emphasized that the 'Word of God' is not limited to the words of a book and that the act of revelation is not the 'inspiring' of a 'book of revelations,' even if the book is the document of the final 'Word of God,' the fulfillment and criterion of all revelations."[66]

Yet the Bible is "the basic source of systematic theology" because it is the document about the events on which Christianity

---

63. Tillich, *Systematic Theology*, 1:34.
64. Ibid., 1:34, 35.
65. Ibid.
66. Ibid., 1:35.

and the church are founded. The term *document* must, however, exclude legal connotations: "The Bible is not a legally conceived, formulated, and sealed record about a divine 'deed' on the basis of which claims can be decided. The documentary character of the Bible is identical with the fact that it contains the original witness of those who participated in the revealing events." And, he emphasizes, "their participation was their response to the happenings which became revealing events through this response."[67]

When Tillich speaks of the inspiration of Scripture, he means the "receptive and creative response" of the original witnesses "to potentially revelatory facts. The inspiration of the writers of the New Testament is their acceptance of Jesus as the Christ, and with him, of the New Being, of which they became witnesses."[68] Tillich contends that "since there is no revelation unless there is someone who receives it as revelation, the act of reception is a part of the event itself. The Bible is both original event and original document; it witnesses to that of which it is a part."[69]

Such statements are found in contexts in which Tillich opposes various forms of what he calls "biblicism." "The radical biblicistic attitude" of some Protestants, he charges, "is a self-deception."[70] "Evangelical biblicism, both past and present" is unaware of this "self-deception," Tillich continues, and it "produces a 'biblical' theology which actually is dependent on definite dogmatic developments of the post-Reformation period." He suggests that "through historical scholarship the difference between the dogmatic teaching of most American evangelistic churches and the original meaning of the biblical text can easily be shown."[71]

When Tillich describes his "method of correlation," he distinguishes it from supranaturalistic, naturalistic, and dualistic methods. His rejection of the so-called supranaturalistic method hits chiefly at his understanding of the classic Christian view of Scripture: "It takes the Christian message to be a sum of revealed truths which have fallen into the human situation like strange bodies from a strange world."[72] Tillich suggests that "in terms of the classical heresies, one could say that the supranaturalistic method has docetic-monophysitic traits, especially in its valuation of the Bible as a book of supranatural 'oracles' in which human receptivity is completely overlooked."[73] In Tillich's view

67. Ibid.
68. Ibid.
69. Ibid.
70. Ibid., 1:36.
71. Ibid., 1:37.
72. Ibid., 1:64.
73. Ibid., 1:65.

"the dynamics of the history of revelation excludes the mechanis-tic-supranaturalistic theories of revelation and inspiration."[74]

Tillich distinguishes six different meanings of the "Word of God": " 'God manifest'—manifest in himself, in creation, in the history of revelation, in the final revelation, in the Bible, in the words of the church and her members. 'God manifest'—the mystery of the divine abyss expressing itself through the divine Logos—this is the meaning of the symbol, the 'Word of God.' "[75] Therefore, he contends, "if the Bible is called the Word of God, theological confusion is almost unavoidable. Such consequences as the dictation theory of inspiration, dishonesty in dealing with the biblical text, a 'monophysitic' dogma of the infallibility of a book, etc. follow from such an identification."[76] Tillich suggests that there are two senses in which one can refer to the Bible as the Word of God: "It is the document of the final revelation and it participates in the final revelation of which it is the document." But he adds: "Probably nothing has contributed more to the mis-interpretation of the biblical doctrine of the Word than the iden-tification of the Word with the Bible."[77]

For Tillich, then, the Bible (understood in the above sense) is one of the sources of systematic theology. But he firmly rejects the contention that the Bible is the *norm* of theology: "If the Bible *itself* is called the norm of systematic theology, nothing concrete is said, for the Bible is a collection of religious literature written, collected, and edited through the centuries."[78] Something within the Bible must be regarded as the canon. For Tillich this norm is "the New Being in Jesus as the Christ as our ultimate concern."[79] In the light of these largely negative statements of Tillich on Scripture and infallibility, let us turn to his existentialistic view of revelation.

MARKS OF REVELATION

As a student of Edmund Husserl, Paul Tillich began his consid-eration of "the reality of revelation" with a phenomenological approach. Tillich's preliminary discussion is similar in many ways to what we have just seen in Bultmann, but Tillich worked out the

74. Ibid., 1:143; Cf. 1:114.
75. Ibid., 1:159.
76. Ibid., 1:158.
77. Ibid., 1:158-59.
78. Ibid., 1:50.
79. Ibid.

issues more systematically and thoroughly than Bultmann did. Tillich soon recognized that "pure phenomenology" could not be employed because one cannot avoid the choice of a criterion when examples of revelation are considered. Hence Tillich proposed a "critical phenomenology," one which is "critical in form" and "existential in matter." According to Tillich that approach is "dependent on a revelation which has been received and which is considered final, and it is critical with respect to other revelations."[80]

In pursuing his critical-phenomenology of revelation, Tillich notes three "marks of revelation": mystery, miracle, and ecstasy. According to Tillich revelation is always "revelation of that which is essentially and necessarily mysterious." That means "the manifestation of something within the context of ordinary experience which transcends the ordinary context of experience."[81] Genuine mystery never ceases to be mystery. After revelation, something is known about the mystery; its reality has been experienced and our relation to it is a matter of experience, and both of these are cognitive elements. "But revelation does not dissolve the mystery into knowledge. Nor does it add anything directly to the totality of our ordinary knowledge, namely, to our knowledge about the subject-object structure of reality."[82] Tillich's view of revelation also fits into the third Macquarrie-Heidegger category of "primordial" or "essential" thinking.

Tillich enumerates three characteristics of revelation as mystery. "The mystery which is revealed is of ultimate concern to us because it is the ground of our being";[83] hence revelation is always "the manifestation of what concerns us ultimately." Second, revelation is never general; it is "invariably revelation for someone in a concrete situation of concern."[84] Revelation "grasps an individual or a group, usually a group through an individual; it has revealing power in this correlation." Hence for Tillich "there is no revelation if there is no one who receives it as his ultimate concern." Third, "revelation always is a subjective and an objective event in strict interdependence;" the objective side he calls "miracle" and the subjective, "ecstasy." Both terms are given "a radical reinterpretation." The event of revelation always occurs in the correlation of the objective "miracle" and the subjective "ecstasy." They are like the two sides of one coin. Tillich thus

80. Ibid., 1:107.
81. Ibid., 1:109.
82. Ibid.
83. Ibid., 1:110.
84. Ibid., 1:111.

opposes the traditional distinction between revelation and its subjective acknowledgement and appropriation in soteriology.

Not surprisingly, Tillich first considers the subjective side of ecstasy. *Ecstasy* literally means "standing outside one's self" but it is not to be taken in an "irrational" or "antirational" sense. Ecstasy is the state of mind in which "reason is beyond itself, that is, beyond its subject-object structure."[85] Macquarrie's third category is what Tillich has in mind. "Ecstasy occurs only if the mind is grasped by the mystery, namely, by the ground of being and meaning." Tillich contends that there is no revelation if ecstasy is not present. Without ecstasy there could only be information and that would involve the Western, metaphysical concept of revelation. "Ecstasy is the form in which that which concerns us unconditionally manifests itself within the whole of our pyschological conditions. It appears through them. But it cannot be derived from them," as he explains further:

> In revelation and in the ecstatic experience in which it is received, the ontological shock is preserved and overcome at the same time. It is preserved in the annihilating power of the divine presence *(mysterium tremendum)* and is overcome in the elevating power of the divine presence *(mysterium fascinosum)*. Ecstasy unites the experience of the abyss to which reason in all its functions is driven with the experience of the ground in which reason is grasped by the mystery of its own depth and of the depth of being generally.[86]

Tillich's view of ecstasy as a mark of revelation characterizes his criticism of the traditional Christian view of the inspiration of Scripture. "In the last analysis," he states, "a mechanical or any other form of nonecstatic doctrine of inspiration is demonic. It destroys the rational structure which is supposed to receive inspiration." As a mark of revelation ecstasy indicates that the occurrence or the experience "grasps, shakes, and moves" us.[87]

On its objective side revelation involves "miracle;" but "miracle" must be reinterpreted to eliminate any supernatural connotations. According to Tillich "miracle" refers to the " 'giving side' of a revelatory experience."[88] The supernatural implications must be overcome because neither the "manifestation of the mystery of being" nor "the ecstasy in which the mystery is received" destroys

85. Ibid., 1:112.
86. Ibid., 1:113.
87. Ibid., 1:127.
88. Ibid., 1:115.

"the rational structure of the mind by which it is received . . . [nor] the rational structure of the reality in which it appears."[89] According to Tillich, a genuine miracle involves three simultaneous conditions: the event must be "astonishing, unusual, shaking, without contradicting the rational structure of reality;" it must be "an event which points to the mystery of being, expressing its relation to us in a definite way"; and it must be "an occurrence which is received as a sign-event in an ecstatic experience."[90]

Although miracle refers to the objective side of the revelatory experience, Tillich insists that "objective miracles" are "a contradiction in terms." The objective side of revelatory experiences (miracle) and the subjective side (ecstasy) are correlative. "This strict correlation makes it possible to exchange the words" in a sort of dialectical fashion: "one can say that ecstasy is the miracle of the mind, and that miracle is the ecstasy of reality."

According to Tillich, revelation occurs in a dimension different from that of science; therefore "science, psychology, and history are allies of theology in the fight against the supranaturalistic distortions of genuine revelation." To recapitulate:

> Revelation is the manifestation of the depth of reason and the ground of being. It points to the mystery of existence and to our ultimate concern. It is independent of what science and history say about the conditions in which it appears; and it cannot make science and history dependent on itself. No conflict between different dimensions of reality is possible. Reason receives revelation in ecstasy and miracles; but reason is not destroyed by revelation, just as revelation is not emptied by reason.[91]

MEDIUMS OF REVELATION

Tillich next turns to "the mediums of revelation." He contends that "there is no reality, thing, or event which cannot become a bearer of the mystery of being and enter into a revelatory correlation."[92] That does not mean that there is a "natural revelation," for that is "a contradiction in terms."[93] Not everything is "a medium of revelation," but everything is simply capable of becoming

89. Ibid., 1:116.
90. Ibid., 1:117.
91. Ibid., 1:117-18.
92. Ibid., 1:118.
93. Ibid., 1:119.

that. Its capability lies in no "special qualities"; rather it is because "every person and every thing participates in being-itself, that is, in the ground and meaning of being."[94] That is why "almost every type of reality has become a medium of revelation somewhere." When revelation happens, however, "natural knowledge" does not result, for revelation "makes nature ecstatic and miraculous."[95]

Tillich discusses how nature, history, groups, and individuals become mediums of revelation. Finally he considers "the word as a medium of revelation." He acknowledges that "revelation cannot be understood without the word as a medium of revelation."[96] But he opposes Barth's "enlarged doctrine of the 'Word of God'" since "word of God" then loses its symbolical meaning. For Tillich "the word communicates the self-related and unapproachable experience of an ego-self to another ego-self" by way of "expression and denotation."[97] In revelation language has "a denotative power which points through the ordinary meaning of the words to their relation to us."[98] "Being precedes speaking," he contends, "and the revelatory reality precedes and determines the revelatory word."[99] Therefore the words of Scripture cannot be considered revelatory in themselves, not even the Ten Commandments or the words of Jesus.

ORIGINAL AND DEPENDENT REVELATION

Tillich also distinguishes between "original and dependent revelation." An original revelation is one in which the constellation of miracle and ecstasy occurs for the first time. A dependent revelation is one in which "the miracle and its original reception together form the giving side, while the receiving side changes as new individuals and groups enter the same correlation of revelation."[100] In that sense Tillich refers to an original revelation when Peter encountered Jesus, who became the Christ in that event. That original revelation can become a dependent revelation for us, but it is not revelation as such. He contends, therefore, that "the history of the church . . . is the locus of continuous dependent revelations."[101] Prayer and meditation are also revelatory

94. Ibid., 1 118.
95. Ibid., 1:119.
96. Ibid., 1:122.
97. Ibid., 1:123.
98. Ibid., 1:124.
99. Ibid., 1:125.
100. Ibid., 1:126.
101. Ibid., 1:127.

according to Tillich for "the marks of revelation—mystery, miracle, and ecstasy—are present in every true prayer." Although Tillich refers to prayer as "speaking to God and receiving an answer" in the ecstatic experience, yet he considers it "blasphemous and ridiculous" to think of prayer in terms of a "conversation betwen two beings." What happens in prayer is entirely on the subjective side according to Tillich's view.

Knowledge of revelation for Tillich is "essential" in character, as it was for Bultmann and Macquarrie. Revelation never renders information; hence the most accurate expression is "revelatory knowledge," knowledge of revelation . . . does not imply factual assertions. . . ."[102]; it has a gift like character.

CRITERION OF REVELATION

Tillich also discusses the criterion of revelation, and he distinguishes between "actual and final revelation." Every actual revelation is "necessarily final revelation" because "the person who is grasped by a revelatory experience believes it to be the truth concerning the mystery of being and his relation to it."[103] Tillich acknowledges Jesus Christ as the final revelation, not on the grounds of its factuality, but on the grounds of his own criteria. For Tillich "a revelation is final if it has the power of negating itself without losing itself."[104] Jesus did that by becoming the Christ, "that is, by sacrificing himself"; thereby "he affirms that he is the bearer of the final revelation" or "the 'Son of God' in classical terms." According to Tillich, Jesus is "the Christ as the one who sacrifices what is merely 'Jesus in him. The decisive trait in his picture is the continuous self-surrender of Jesus who is Jesus to Jesus who is the Christ."[105]

Correlation also is crucial here for Tillich. "The Christ is not the Christ without the church, and the church is not the church without the Christ. The final revelation, is correlative."[106] For Tillich "the history of revelation and the history of salvation are one history."[107] That means that "revelation can be received only in the presence of salvation and salvation can occur only within a correlation of revelation."[108] Thus we see that Tillich reaches basi-

102. Ibid., 1:130.
103. Ibid., 1:132.
104. Ibid., 1:133.
105. Ibid., 1:134.
106. Ibid., 1:136-37.
107. Ibid., 1:144.
108. Ibid.

cally the same conclusion that Bultmann did. Revelation is described in terms of the third category of Heidegger-Macquarrie; it involves "essentialist thinking" and "gift-like knowledge." The classic Christian view of Scripture as God's authoritative revelation is discarded as a remnant of Western "calculative thinking."

EVALUATION AND CRITIQUE

In the effort to understand what existentialist theologians think about Scripture and inerrancy, we have had to give considerable attention to their conception of revelation, the "revelatory experience." As I now turn to evaluate their views, I shall do so under these four headings: in Schleiermacher's line, caricatures of evangelical views, philosophy and theology, and an evangelical epistemology of revelation.

Because the existentialists restrict revelation to a human experience exclusively on the horizontal level, I suggest that they represent a neo-liberalism in Schleiermacher's line of Enlightenment theology. The existentialist critique of evangelical views of Scripture, inspiration, and infallibility are generally set forth in the form of caricature. That calls for specific comment. Next the relationship of theology and philosophy calls for consideration, both with respect to existentialist and evangelical theologians. Finally, I shall sketch the outline of an evangelical epistemology of revelation. Since the Macquarrie-Heidegger categories do not really locate the evangelical view, it is necessary to clarify those fundamental issues. That is doubly necessary because existentialist theologians mistakenly place the evangelical position in the subject-object category of calculative thinking and objective knowledge.

IN SCHLEIERMACHER'S LINE

Friedrich Schleiermacher, the father of liberal theology, redefined revelation when he applied the term to every original and new intuition. He also applied "inspiration" exclusively to a human activity. The existentialist view of revelation, cast in the thought forms of existentialism, stands in this Schleiermacher line of Enlightenment thought.

We have seen that the existentialist theologians found it very difficult to present a lucid statement of their understanding of revelation. Macquarrie's "epistemology of revelation" proved helpful in depicting the category of "essential thinking" and "gift-like knowledge" in locating the "revelatory experience." Revelation involves neither a subject-object relationship nor a subject-subject relationship; rather, a mode of thinking is involved "in which I would be subject to that which is known," and in it "I am transcended, mastered, and, indeed, known myself."[109] One waits and listens in a meditative mood for an "occurrence of being." The "revelatory experience" is analagous to the insights and intuitions of religion and poetry. Hence revelation is located within the range of human cognitive experience, even though unique.

In the existentialist view of revelation there is no vertical dimension. The revelatory experience may involve an element of transcendence, but that is only an aspect of human self-transcendence. In Kantian terms, revelation involves the transcendental but not the transcendent. The living God does not reveal Himself to human subjects. Bultmann candidly labels that vertical perspective "mythology," and Tillich refuses to speak of God as "a Being." If the term *God* is used, the existentialists do not mean "a divine Being" but simply "being." Macquarrie's three criticisms of the "I-thou" relationship in the subject-subject category made that point crystal clear.[110] Even interpersonal terms are inappropriate to the revelational event contemplated by existentialists as occurring within a human subject.

Hence the existentialist conception of revelation, as well as of inspiration, continues the line of Schleiermacher's liberalism and subjectivism. In such horizontal views of revelation *inerrancy* has little relevance. We have noted that the existentialists rarely mention that term, and *infallibility* occurs only for the sake of emphatic rejection. If reference to God, angels, Satan, and demons is evidence of mythology, it is apparent that the rejection of infallibility and inerrancy is really radical. From a form-critical perspective Bultmann concluded that we can know almost nothing of history or the historical Jesus; that conclusion simply highlights the irrelevance of any question concerning the trustworthiness of Scripture.

Of course, the role of existentialist philosophy leads to significant differences from Schleiermacher. The father of liberalism emphasized feeling whereas the neo-liberal existentialists emphasize the will and the call for decision. The hermeneutical perspectives of the existentialists also owe much to the early Schleiermacher. The hermeneutical question that Bultmann thinks opens the text of Scripture is this one: What does it say

109. See note 22.
110. See note 20 in text.

about human existence? And when Tillich uses the terms "mystery, miracle, and ecstasy" as marks of revelation, he gives those terms radically new meaning. Everything supernatural is excluded; those terms describe the psychological features of the horizontal revelatory experience.

The existentialist theologians also reject any revelational content in the sense of information, communication, or message. Revelation does not convey good news; it conveys no news at all. Words are needed to express or describe the revelatory experience, and events, like almost everything else, can become the media of revelation. Yet the only knowledge of revelation is "self-knowledge," the human awareness that is part of authentic being. According to Bultmann, revelation reveals no doctrines but rather opens a person's eyes to his own existence and enables him to understand himself.

Because there is no revelation apart from the revelatory experience, existentialist theologians do not distinguish between revelation and response. The revelatory experience is always part of "soteriology," and quotations marks are needed because that "soteriology" is also exclusively horizontal. It would be interesting to evaluate the existentialist view of revelation from a soteriological perspective. The "revelatory experience" may have more in common with such soteriological concepts as regeneration, conversion, faith, or illumination, than with revelation in traditional Christian terms.

Therefore it is extremely difficult to compare the existentialist view of revelation with that of historic Christianity. Radically different views are involved, not only of revelation, but of Christianity itself. If J. Gresham Machen, facing the old liberalism, found it necessary to speak of "Christianity and Liberalism,"[111] we are compelled to be equally forthright in confronting the neo-liberalism of existentialist theology. In the theologies of Bultmann, Tillich, and Macquarrie we see Pelagian man urged to make decisions for the sake of authentic being. A psychologically well-adjusted person who makes his own decisions distinct from the crowd is certainly needed in today's world. But to make that the heart of the gospel is to secularize it. Paul's warning to Galatian Christians must be voiced with even greater urgency today. The existential theology of Bultmann, Tillich, and Macquarrie proclaims "a different gospel—which is really no gospel at all" (Gal. 1:6-7, NIV).

111. J. Greshman Machen, *Christianity and Liberalism* (Grand Rapids: Eerdmans, 1923).

CARICATURE OF EVANGELICALISM

It is often difficult to represent the position of one's opponent accurately when basic presuppositions and theological viewpoints differ radically. That is understandable. This evaluation of the existentialist theologians is made by one who operates with quite different presuppositions and who holds to an evangelical-Reformed theology. I have tried to be accurate and fair in representing existentialist theology, but ultimately the reader will have to judge whether I have succeeded.

But have the existentialist theologians been fair to their opponents? Have they accurately presented the evangelical views that they so vigorously reject? Or have they caricatured their opponents? In my opinion caricature has dominated the sections in which Bultmann, Tillich, and Macquarrie oppose traditional views of Scripture, inspiration, and infallibility.

It is understandable that from their perspective the existentialist theologians describe the Bible in words reminiscent of Schleiermacher. Scripture is referred to as the sacred writings of the community of faith or as a collection of religious literature. Similarly, inspiration is referred to in ways paralleling Schleiermacher, who employed the analogy of literary and artistic inspiration. I am not referring to such language as caricature, although I disagree with it.

Caricature emerges, I contend, when one's opponents are regularly referred to as biblicists, ultraconservative biblicists, or absolutizers of the Bible. Caricature is present when one knows only of mechanistic and dictation views of inspiration and when one speaks of dishonesty and self-deception. Although Tillich and Macquarrie also refer to "neo-orthodox biblicists," the opponents generally are European orthodoxy and American evangelicalism. Apparently those who subscribe to the historic Protestant confessions and the Chicago Statement of 1978 are considered "ultraconservative biblicists." Therefore I refer simply to the caricature of evangelicalism in this section.

Not one of the three theologians examined in this essay sets forth the evangelical position fairly and accurately. Brief pejorative statements are common. Is it really characteristic of evangelicals that they take the Christian message to be "a sum of revealed truths which have fallen into the human situation like strange bodies from a strange world"?[112] Do evangelicals view the

112. See note 72.

Bible "as a book of supranatural 'oracles' in which human receptivity is completely overlooked"?[113] Do evangelicals really espouse "mechanistic-supranaturalistic theories of revelation and inspiration" in which "the dynamics of the history of revelation"[114] is excluded? Is it really true that one who confesses that Scripture is the Word of God is forced to "such consequences as the dictation theory of inspiration, dishonesty in dealing with the biblical text, a 'monophysitic' dogma of the infallibility of a book, etc."?[115] Are those the views of John Calvin, Abraham Kuyper, Herman Bavinck, B. B. Warfield, and other evangelical theologians? Were they dishonest or deceived? One ought not to need a straw man to win an argument!

Macquarrie was the only one of our three existentialist theologians who presented a few arguments against the infallibility of the Bible. But the arguments he suggested indicate that he had only a superficial acquaintance with the evangelical position.[116] Of course, all human activity is imperfect and subject to criticism. That is also true of evangelical theology. One can generally profit from the honest criticism of one's opponents, including the existentialist theologians. But one grows weary of caricature.

Evangelical Christianity has been unfairly criticized ever since the Enlightenment and the rise of liberalism. Neo-orthodox theologians continued the caricature of the evangelical doctrine of Scripture, and now the neo-liberal or existentialist theologians do the same. Are they simply repeating tired clichés? Or have their presuppositions and their chosen positions blinded them to the evangelical position? In the final section of this critique I shall sketch what I understand by an evangelical epistemology of revelation. The evangelical view is not the simplistic position that has been caricatured by the existentialist theologians.

THEOLOGY AND PHILOSOPHY

The history of theology frequently reflects the subtle influences of alien thought, especially from science and philosophy. Bultmann, for example, shows the crucial influence of positivistic science and existentialist philosophy. From the perspective of positivistic science he rejected the entire framework of Scripture as mythological and approached the biblical message from existen-

113. See note 73.
114. See note 74.
115. See note 76.
116. See note 14.

tialistic presuppositions. Tillich and Macquarrie worked from similar perspectives.

That approach of the existentialist theologians raises hermeneutical questions with new urgency, for evangelical theologians no less than for others. Hermeneutical questions in the interpretation of Scripture pose some of the most basic philosophical issues today. At this point I can raise only two serious objections to the use of existentialist philosophy and pose a question for evangelical theologians.

At least two basic features of existentialism disqualify it for use in Christian theology. The claim that existence precedes essence conflicts directly with the biblical doctrine of creation. As Sartre bluntly expressed the first principle of existentialism: "There is no human nature, because there is no God to have a conception of it. . . . Man is nothing else but that which he makes of himself."[117] The biblical doctrine of God's creation of Adam and Eve in His own image indicates that created essence precedes historical existence. Furthermore, existentialism operates with a Pelagian view of man. The results are twofold: the existentialist theologians do not acknowledge the radical effects of sin as guilt before God even though they speak of finitude, limitation, alientation, estrangement, and death; at the same time, they exaggerate the capacity of men and women to make the decisions that really lead to authentic being. In short, denying the biblical doctrine of creation and the Fall, they underestimate the human predicament and they overestimate human ability to reach authenticity. Thus they have emasculated the gospel and restricted it to the horizontal dimension of psychologically well-adjusted personhood. By means of existentialistic preunderstandings and a horizontalized conception of revelation, the existentialist theologians have distorted the good news of Scripture even though they claim Scripture as a source for theology.

What happens in existentialist theology has happened repeatedly to other theologians by means of alien philosophical influences. The same threat exists today and evangelicals are not immune to the danger. Candor requires that evangelicals also face the philosophical questions forthrightly. Throughout history evangelical theologians have employed Aristotelianism or Scottish realism in the theological enterprise; others have depended upon Descartes or other philosophers. Protestant Scholasticism provides warning against such syntheses. Today the infallibility-

117. See note 4.

inerrancy debates within evangelicalism highlight the importance of facing philosophical questions with renewed urgency. The importance of hermeneutical questions is becoming more clear, and heremeneutics cannot operate without facing philosophical issues.

It is a disturbing fact that people who may agree in confessing the inerrancy of Scripture may still differ in their interpretations of Scripture to such a degree that their agreement on inerrancy is practically nullified. A synthesis of Christianity with an alien philosophy can undercut the significance of theological agreements. What appears so clearly in existentialist theology ought to provide a warning to evangelicals as well in facing the relation of theology and philosophy. Thoroughly Christian philosophical perspectives are needed.

AN EVANGELICAL EPISTEMOLOGY OF REVELATION

According to existentialist theologians the confession that Scripture is the authoritative Word of God necessarily involves the Western tradition of the subject-object category of calculative thinking and objective knowledge. I have already indicated that I disagree with that contention. There have been various theological syntheses of Christianity with various kinds of Western philosophical thought, but the biblical message is not an essential part of that Western tradition. The other two Heidegger-Macquarrie categories do not appropriately describe evangelical theology either. Hence I shall conclude this essay with a sketch of a fourth category in the "epistemology of revelation." It can be called "believing thought and heart knowledge," and it calls for some amplification.

I view this section as my most comprehensive critique of the existentialist view of revelation. I shall refer, of course, to God as revealing Himself in history and to God's actions in bringing sinners to faith in Christ; whereas Bultmann may call that "mythology," I am convinced that it is essential to authentic Christianity. Furthermore, all distinctions made below are drawn from Scripture and should be judged by that norm.

Subject—revelation—subject. If this "epistemology of revelation" is to speak to the issues raised by existentialist theology, it will have to include reference to both revelation and response. In this first section the focus is on revelation; in the second the focus is on the response, the soteriological dimension.

Revelation is the means by which the divine Subject, the triune

God, communicates to human subjects. When God inscripturates His revelation, there is the sinful possibility that the human subject will consider such revelation as an object that can be handled, used, manipulated, and probed in an "I-it" relationship. All theology faces that temptation; in my judgment the three existentialist theologians considered in this essay have succumbed to that temptation. Because that is not what God intends, I have not called revelation an object. Rather, I refer to "Subject—revelation—subject." Let me briefly amplify that.

Revelation originates with the divine Subject, the living, triune God, who created the world and made man and woman in His own image. As image bearers of God, they were created in fellowship with God and were dependent upon His revelation. Revelation was conveyed by means of the entire creation that manifested the glory, everlasting power, and divinity of the Creator (Ps. 19; Rom. 1:18-32; cf. Acts 14:14-17; 17:24-28) as well as by means of the oracles of preredemptive special revelation (Gen. 1:28-30; 2:16-17). Created receptive for God's revelation, Adam and Eve responded in obedient love; they knew God and loved Him with all their hearts. Indeed, as Calvin expressed it: "Nearly all the wisdom we possess, that is to say, true and sound wisdom, consists of two parts: the knowledge of God and of ourselves."[118] These two parts are so interrelated and correlative that one does not have the one without the other.

When the human subjects Adam and Eve rebelled against God and disobeyed His revealed command, new needs arose from their guilt, alienation, and sin. In His mysterious love God began a complex redemptive-revelatory process for the salvation of His children. Special revelation by word and deed accompanied the redemptive process of providing salvation through Jesus Christ, the Son of God incarnate. That revelation was rooted deeply in history, in the history of the patriarchs, the Israelites, and finally in Jesus Christ. By means of various modes of revelation God made known His works, His promises, His will, Himself to the descendants of Adam. That original special revelation came by means of theophany ("external manifestation"), prophecy ("internal suggestion"), and inspiration ("concursive operation").[119] Under the inspiration of the Holy Spirit, that original special revelation was partially inscripturated as canon for Israel, the covenant

---

118. John Calvin *Insitutes of the Christian Religion* 1.1.1.
119. I am using the terms suggested by B. B. Warfield in "The Biblical Idea of Revelation," *The Inspiration and Authority of the Bible* (Philadelphia: Presbyterian & Reformed, 1948), pp. 71-102.

people of God, so that the entire Old Testament existed when Jesus began His redemptive-revelatory work. From the abundance of revelation in and through Jesus Christ, the Holy Spirit led the New Testament writers to inscripturate selectively (cf. Luke 1:1-4; John 20:30-31; 21:25) the rest of the canon of Scripture.

Scripture did not drop ready-made from heaven; it was the product of a long, complex history in which human authors driven by the Holy Spirit (2 Pet. 1:20-21) produced the writing that is "God-breathed" (2 Tim. 3:16). The Bible is a book, and it can be handled (sinfully!) as an object, but it is in fact the Word of the living God. Scripture is the revelation of the Creator-Redeemer to His fallen subjects to call them back into His fellowship and service. Scripture reveals the message of creation, fall, redemption; but the message is conveyed to reform, redirect, and restore. Scripture was not meant to be merely an informing object; it is God's great love letter centering in Jesus Christ (Luke 24:27, 44; John 3:16; 5:39). Scripture calls God's alienated creatures to heart knowledge, which involves fellowship and communion with Him, the triune, living God. Of course as the redemptive message is disclosed Scripture reveals the anger and judgment of God upon all sin and disobedience. Although Scripture is a book in our history, it conveys God's address to us now, which calls for our obedient response; Scripture addresses us Person to person. Hence an evangelical epistemology of revelation emphasizes "Subject—revelation—subject" when the revelation side of the equation is contemplated. We must next consider the response side, in which the order is reversed: subject—revelation—Subject.

subject—revelation—Subject. As already noted, when God created us in His image, He made us receptive to His revelation. Romans 1 indicates that the revelation in the creation continues to impinge upon everyone, and everyone is accountable for suppressing (1:18) the knowledge of the Creator conveyed by that revelation. But fallen creatures have no hope except through the gospel of Jesus Christ (Rom. 1:16-17; 3:21; 10:14-15).

Scripture reveals the message of Jesus Christ, the good news of the gospel. Scripture does indeed convey news, the good news of God's salvation-history accomplishments that culminate in the life, ministry, death, and resurrection of our Lord Jesus Christ. Yet a sinner is incapable of responding to the overtures of God's love revealed through the Scriptures without the regenerating work of the Holy Spirit.

Regeneration by the Holy Spirit brings one from death to life;

He turns human hearts from disobedience to obedience, from hatred to love of God and neighbor. When the Spirit's regeneration produces faith and confession in the believer, he comes to know the living God as He has revealed Himself in Scripture. The internal testimony of the Holy Spirit in a believer's heart leads to a deep-rooted conviction that what the Scriptures say and claim is true. Revelation from God is the means to fellowship with God. Through the ongoing illumination of the Holy Spirit, a believer grows in understanding Scripture and in more fully understanding the Creator-Redeemer God, as well as himself as God's creature and the world as God's creation. Through the Spirit's soteriological work in sinners, Scripture functions as the revelational means for restoring them to fellowship with the Creator-Redeemer God in building Christ's church and extending God's kingdom.

An evangelical "epistemology of revelation" thus involves "believing thought" and "heart-knowledge." That marvelous process moves from the divine Subject via revelation to the human subject; and the fallen human subject through the Spirit's agency moves via revelation to the revealing Subject. What a far cry that is from an "I-it," subject-object relation of calculative thought! If one is looking for authenticity and life this is where it is to be found—in the authoritative Scripture revealing Father, Son, and Holy Spirit.

8. Recent Roman Catholic Theology

Robert L. Saucy

Modern Roman Catholic biblical and theological scholarship has come to share much the same opinions toward the Scripture as its liberal Protestant counterpart. Because of the monolithic structure of the church and its traditional belief in the infallibility of its teaching, the abandoning of the high view of inspiration was slower in coming among the Catholic ranks. But the attempt to modernize the church has opened the door for the widespread historical-critical understanding of Scripture, which leaves the Bible something less than a divinely inspired, inerrant Word from God.

In seeking to understand something of the underlying theological concepts that have been influential in that new understanding of Scripture, we have chosen to look at the thought of two prominent Catholic theologians—Hans Küng and Karl Rahner. Our desire will be to set forth as much as possible the various aspects of their thought concerning the nature of Scripture, although the real causal relationships between those concepts are difficult to explicate. Before analyzing their theology, a brief historical sketch will be helpful to set the stage for their position within Catholic thought.

ROBERT L. SAUCY, A.B., Westmont College; Th.M., Th.D., Dallas Theological Seminary, is professor of systematic theology at Talbot Theological Seminary, La Mirada, California. His writings include *The Church in God's Program* (1972) and *The Bible: Breathed from God* (1978).

RECENT HISTORY ON THE CATHOLIC VIEW OF SCRIPTURE

VATICAN I TO THE MODERNIST CONTROVERSY

Vatican I marked the time of the first real encounter of the Roman Catholic Church with the rising Protestant critical approach toward the Bible. Up to that point the church had been accustomed to thinking of Scripture as divinely inspired and inerrant. In the face of some non-Catholic biblical studies that tended to lower the religious value of Scripture, Vatican I took a defensive posture that reaffirmed inspiration as noted at the Council of Trent, with the added emphasis upon the divine authorship. More important as evidence of the official ecclesiastical attitude than the pronouncement of Vatican I (1870), however, was the encyclical of Leo XIII, *Providentissimus Deus* (1893). That document was primarily negative, reflecting "hostility and distrust of higher criticism" and the work of non-Catholic scholars.[1] Nevertheless, the Pope showed at the same time an awareness "of the advantages of scientific linguistic and exegetical studies," indicating a cautious openness toward new biblical studies.[2]

THE PERIOD OF THE MODERNIST CONTROVERSY

Whatever tendency there may have been toward new ideas with regard to the Scriptures received a major setback in the modernist crisis. It was described as "the third crisis regarding the Bible" (the first being the Protestant Reformation, answered in Trent, and the second, Enlightenment rationalism, rejected in Vatican I), and, as Megivern notes, this crisis was different from the previous two. Now "the 'enemies' were not outsiders but insiders."[3] Expressed particularly in the writings of Alfred Loisy, modernism was using the new approach of German Protestant higher criticism. Pius X, seeing in that a threat to the fundamental faith of the church, came down hard against the new movement and its leaders. The official condemnation came in 1907 with the decree of the Roman Inquisition, *Lamentabili*, and the papal encyclical, *Pascendi*. Because of the threat to the faith caused by the new critical methods, they were condemned in toto rather than mak-

---

1. James J. Megivern, ed., *Bible Interpretation: Official Catholic Teachings* (Wilmington, N.C.: McGrath 1978), p. xxi.
2. Raymond E. Brown, "Church Pronouncements," in *The Jerome Biblical Commentary*, ed. Joseph A. Fitzmyer and Raymond E. Brown, 2 vols. (Englewood Cliffs, N.J.: Prentice-Hall, 1968), 1:625.
3. Megivern, p. xxii.

ing any distinction between "the possible intrinsic validity of these approaches and the Modernist theological misuse of them."[4] As a follow up of this initial action, the Pontifical Biblical Commission began to issue official statements on many finer points regarding biblical authorship and interpretation. Its tone was so negative that "Catholic scholars got the message that new ideas, especially if imported from Protestant critics, were unwanted by Rome."[5] The years immediately following that response to modernism were relatively sterile with regard to changes in biblical studies. Nevertheless the period between the two world wars was a time of quiet growth during which the climate was changing in preparation for a new outlook.

THE RECENT ERA AND VATICAN II

Signs of a change in Rome's stance toward critical biblical studies appeared in 1941 when the Biblical Commission "condemned an overly *conservative* distrust of modern biblical research."[6] The Magna Charta for so-called progress in biblical studies came two years later in 1943 with the encyclical of Pius XII, *Divine Afflante Spiritu*. According to the Catholic biblical scholar Raymond Brown, in this statement the church

> made an undeniable about-face in attitude toward biblical criticism. The encyclical . . . instructed Catholic scholars to use the methods of a scientific approach to the Bible that had hitherto been forbidden to them. Within about ten years teachers trained in biblical criticism began to move in large numbers into Catholic classrooms in seminaries and colleges, so that the mid-1950's really marked the watershed. By that time the pursuit of the scientific method had led Catholic exegetes to abandon almost all the positions on biblical authorship and composition taken by Rome at the beginning of the century.[7]

The new mood, however, was not welcome on all fronts. When Pius XII died in 1958, conservatives sought to reverse the trend. The Congregation of Seminaries expressed negative reaction toward a new textbook issued by the progressives. Attacks were

---

4. Brown, "Church Pronouncements," 1:625.
5. James T. Burtchaell, *Catholic Theories of Biblical Inspiration Since 1810* (Cambridge: Cambridge U., 1969), p. 232.
6. Brown, "Church Pronouncements," 1:625.
7. Raymond E. Brown, *Biblical Reflections on Crises Facing the Church* (New York: Paulist, 1975), pp. 6-7.

made publicly against certain scholars and two were removed from their teaching positions at the Pontifical Biblical Institute. In 1961 the Holy Office issued a warning against questioning certain historical and objective truth of Scripture. That negative approach was reflected in the first draft of the schema "The Sources of Revelation" prepared for the forthcoming Vatican II in 1962. Because of the personal intervention of John XXIII, however, the conservative position did not prevail. Vatican II adopted a final schema on revelation in 1965 under Paul VI that, although relatively conservative and somewhat ambiguous at certain points for the sake of conciliation, clearly placed the Catholic Church on the side of the modern critical approach to the Bible. The "Instruction on the Historical Truth of the Gospels," issued one year earlier in 1964, likewise explicitly endorsed the critical understanding of the nature of the gospels. The new critical approach to Scripture entailed the revision of the doctrines of revelation, inspiration, and inerrancy. Those changes are reflected briefly in the schema, but their full import is evident in the theologies of Hans Küng and Karl Rahner.

THE THEOLOGY OF HANS KÜNG AND THE SCRIPTURES

Despite the revocation of his status as an official Catholic theologian in December 1979, Hans Küng continues as one of the most prominent and influential forces within the Roman Catholic church. The prestigious platform of a professorship at the University of Tübingen and above all his significant writings, including the monumental *On Being a Christian* and *Does God Exist?*, make Küng one of the most highly regarded theological voices in the world today. His concern with the broad fundamental issues of theology and the Christian faith, coupled with an explicit concern for ecumenical dialogue, give him a respected hearing in all theological discussions. Nor is his influence limited strictly to professional theologians. Many of his works are written to include the educated laity and have been successful in attaining a wide readership. Küng's understanding of the nature of the Scriptures is thus an influential force shaping the thought of the church at large.

THE STARTING POINT OF MODERNITY

Küng's theological endeavor is shaped by a passionate concern to do theology for modern man. He is interested not simply in answering the question of what it means to be a Christian. Rather he is concerned with what it means to be a Christian today, given the contemporary situation of man. In Küng's opinion the traditional "neo-scholastic theology" of the First Vatican Council is no longer adequate. Even Vatican II, although effecting some beneficial changes in the areas of inner-church reform and the relation of the Roman church to outsiders, did not really deal with fundamental questions posed for theology by the modern world. Because of the domination of the Council by "the curial apparatus," according to Küng, a "genuine reflection on theological foundations could not take place." Instead "the foundation appeared once again to be given in defined or undefined traditional doctrinal elements."[8] It was evident, however, even at the Council that that traditional foundation was under attack and subsequent events have further exposed its critical defects that threaten the stability of the "entire edifice of traditional doctrine."[9]

What is needed according to Küng is a restructuring of theology around "two poles" or, as he describes it, an "elliptical movement of . . . theologizing."[10] Such a two-pole theology entails thinking through and expressing the original Christian message within the human situation of our time. Küng offers the following explanation of that theological enterprise:

> In our current decade it has become increasingly evident that the only theology (primarily systematic and especially dogmatic theology) that could survive the future would be one that was daringly able to blend two vital elements in a nontraditional and highly convincing manner. These two elements are a "return to the sources" and a "venturing forth on to uncharted waters," or to put the matter less poetically, a *theology* of *Christian origins and center enunciated with the horizon of the contemporary world.*[11]

He then proceeds to show how it is distinguished from traditional, dogma-based Catholic theology:

> Such a theology is essentially different from those which envision Church dogmas as the *terminus a quo* and *terminus ad quem* of systematic theology. Such theologies reiterate in positivistic fashion dogmas that have become questionable while attempting to

8. Hans Küng, "Toward a New Consensus in Catholic (and Ecumenical) Theology," in *Consensus in Theology?* ed. Leonard Swidler (Philadelphia: Westminster, 1980), p. 2.
9. Ibid.
10. Ibid., p. 4.
11. Ibid., pp. 2-3.

demonstrate their validity on the basis of Scripture and tradition, attempting to make them more palatable to contemporary humanity by the use of transcendental or other speculative methodologies.[12]

It is obvious that Küng is calling for more than the conveyance of the traditional Christian theology in updated language. He is concerned with rethinking the message. "In this process," he notes, "we cannot simply 'utilize' an already well-known, purportedly timeless, eternal message. Instead, it calls for a new 'translation' of this message in terms of our own world of experience."[13]

In using "our world of experience" as one of his "poles" for doing theology, Küng is prepared to accept the modern outlook of "critical rationality" as the starting point of the theological method so long as it is truly critical of itself and does not extend its methods beyond where they properly apply.[14] Apparently in the recognition that modern man through critical rationality is able to understand his world, Küng argues for beginning theology with questions structured by modern man. Rejecting a theology that begins vertically, from above, he calls for starting "as consistently as possible 'from below,' from man's first questions, from human experience" in order to give a rational justification of faith today.[15]

The extent of Küng's acceptance of the modern world view is evidenced in his view of God. We must no longer talk of Him in the same way, but rather "learn to speak with great care in a new way of God."[16] "We must keep in mind the *modern outlook* which enables both believers and unbelievers to purify and deepen their understanding of God."[17] Three characteristics of that modern outlook that should shape theology are particularly noteworthy:

> The present-day understanding of God presupposes the *scientific explanation of the world:* weather and victories in battle, illnesses and cures, fortune and misfortune of individuals, groups and nations are no longer explained by the direct intervention of God, but by natural causes. . . .
>
> The present-day understanding of God presupposes the modern *understanding of authority:* no truth is accepted without being sub-

12. Ibid.
13. Ibid., p. 12.
14. Hans Küng, *On Being a Christian,* trans. Edward Quinn (Garden City, N.Y.: Doubleday, 1976), p. 85.
15. Ibid., p. 83.
16. Ibid., p. 79.
17. Ibid., p. 81.

mitted to the judgment of reason, merely on the authority of the Bible or tradition of the Church, but only after a critical scrutiny. . . .

The present-day understanding of God presupposes the modern *shift of awareness from the hereafter to the here and now:* as a result of the process of secularization, the autonomy of earthly systems (science, economy, politics, state, society, law, culture) is increasingly not merely known in theory but realized in practice.[18]

The acceptance of modern man's critical rationality that leads to the above picture of God obviously requires certain corresponding conclusions with respect to the Scriptures. For one thing, all reference to God's direct intervention into the world of nature or history is ruled out. According to Küng, the modern understanding of God "must start from a coherent understanding of reality. . . . There is no action of God *alongside* world history, but only *in* the history of the world and of man's activity."[19] As a consequence "demythologizing is inescapable."[20] There is no question of presenting as historical facts in theology, preaching or catechesis, biblical happenings and ideas that have proved to be myth, saga, legend, symbol, image, still less of imposing them on the faithful as truths of faith, binding for all time.[21] Those mythological elements reveal something of the faith of the people of Israel and the early Christian community in response to events about which we can know little today historically. It is only the expression of their faith that retains significance for us today.[22]

All theology to be influential with modern man must be based on scientific historical-critical investigation of the Scriptures.

Only a theology that seriously considers and, as far as possible, attempts to solve those problems enunciated by history can be seen as functioning at the level of critical awareness current among those (in the West *and* the East) who have undergone a Western education. Only such scientific theology stands on a par with the scholarly period of our time.[23]

THE MEANING OF REVELATION AND TRUTH

A seemingly necessary corollary to the general acceptance of a modern historical-critical approach to the Scriptures is the expla-

18. Ibid., pp. 81-82.
19. Ibid., p. 295.
20. Ibid., p. 413.
21. Ibid.
22. Ibid., p. 416.
23. Küng, "Toward a New Consensus," p. 7.

nation of revelation as nonpropositional. In words reminiscent of the neo-orthodox terminology of Barth, Küng speaks of the only "absolutely reliable reality" as "God Himself as He has spoken and acted for believers through Jesus Christ."[24] That revelation of God is always mediated through human experience and thus, although it is not a human product, it is always a correlate to the subjective experience of man. Küng explains the relationship noting that "for the Christian faith, Jesus is the definitive revelation of God in the history of Israel because He was so experienced by His first disciples (subjectively) and He was such for them (objectively). The subjective and objective moments belong together."[25]

The subjective experience on the human side is not, however, a clear receptor of the divine Word, for the experience entails an inherent and immediate interpretation of the revelation.

> No experience—of love, but also of revelation, salvation and grace—is ever "pure," but only interpretively given, even if this is not a matter of reflection from the outset. Every experience is already accompanied by elements of interpretation. At the same time this experience is enriched by further interpretive elements and finally verbalized in specific conceptual or figurative statements of the interpretation (interpretament), which can affect the original experience by deepening or leveling it.[26]

The "interpretive elements" that accompany the experience include "general interpretive frameworks or theoretical models of understanding (paradigms) of which we are more or less conscious."[27] Those interpretive frameworks are derived from the individual's personal historical situation that obviously differs not only between historical eras but even somewhat between contemporary individuals. How that concept of revelation and divine truth affects Küng's understanding of the Bible is apparent in the following statement:

> Thus, not only the experiences from the history of Israel but also the experiences of Jesus were from the outset interpreted differently by the biblical authors. The basic common experience of salvation from God in Jesus was depicted in the Synoptics, in the Pauline and Johannine writings, in very distinct sets of questions

---

24. Hans Küng, *The Church—Maintained in Truth*, trans. Edward Quinn (New York: Seabury, 1980), pp. 44-45.
25. Küng, "Toward a New Consensus," p. 5.
26. Ibid.
27. Ibid., pp. 5-6.

and conceptual forms utilizing varying patterns of thought and speech. They write within the interpretive frameworks of their environment and socio-cultural milieu of their age. These figurative and conceptual models and descriptions stem from a completely different world of experience that no longer speaks directly to us today, but which we must interpret anew.[28]

Küng argues that such a concept of the revelation of divine truth is actually supportive of a proper understanding of faith. This proper understanding is only in the fact that the reality of God and His truth lie behind the varied statements "that the invitation to faith can actually be justified. . . . Faith cannot be 'proved' in the same way as other things are proved. . . . If someone has to cope with the reality of God, he cannot have the assurance that is provided by ordinary reality."[29] Thus Küng appears to tell us that any equation of ordinary reality with the revelation of God, be it the human language of Scripture or a miraculous intrusion into history, would tend to diminish the experience of faith, which alone can provide true security.

Although the revelation of God comes to man only through fallibly interpreted experience, God's truth does get through to the church. That fact according to Küng is vouchsafed by the Lord Himself in the promise of the presence of the Spirit of truth (John 14:16-17; cf. 1 Tim. 3:15). "In the face of all human failings and mistakes, God's truth proves to be stronger and because the message of Jesus continually produces faith, so that Jesus remains in the community of believers and His Spirit constantly guides them afresh into the whole truth."[30] Thus there is, through the varied expressions of the experience of revelation, a unified truth that shines through. He who accepts God's call through the different and fallible human words by the Spirit of truth comes to know "quite clearly and unequivocally what is decisive in the Christian message. In all words, he grasps the word, in the different Gospels the one Gospel."[31]

Such an understanding of the maintenance of truth in the midst of human expressions, none of which can be identified as truth per se, raises the question of Küng's meaning of the word *truth*. He provides an answer of sorts in his comparison of faith to love. As love is not finally dependent on its expression in infalli-

---

28. Ibid., p. 6.
29. Küng, *The Church* pp. 13-14.
30. Ibid., pp. 14-15.
31. Küng, *On Being a Christian*, p. 467.

ble statements, neither is faith. "Faith is not completely expressed in proposition. True faith is maintained even through untrue propositions."[32]

THE INSPIRATION AND INERRANCY OF THE BIBLE

As noted above, Küng's view of revelation leads to a clear distinction between God's revelation and the words of the Bible. He adamantly denies any identity of the two and declares, "The revelation of the Old and New testaments cannot in any case be simply identified with Scripture. Scripture is not revelation: it attests revelation."[33] In a similar statement he says, "The Scriptures are not themselves divine revelation. They are merely the human testimonies of divine revelation in which the humanity, independence and historicity of the human authors always remain intact."[34]

The total humanity of the biblical authors with the notation of their limitation and fallibleness is a recurring theme in Küng's discussion of the Bible. "The *truth of Scripture* . . . reaches man without any violence *through the humanity*, historicity, and frailty of the human authors."[35] *"The Bible is not simply God's word: it is first of all and in its whole extent man's word, the word of quite definite individuals."*[36] The humanness of the word involves all kinds of errors. Because the Bible "is unequivocally *man's word* . . . it is not without shortcomings and mistakes, concealment and confusion, limitations and errors."[37] The biblical authors witness to faith "in all human frailty, relativity and limitedness, in frequently halting speech and with utterly inadequate terminology."[38] The distance between Küng's understanding of the Scriptures and the traditional view of their nature as the inspired Word of God is clearly seen in this description of the pure humanness of the authors:

> Thus the human weakness, autonomy, and historicity of the biblical writers remain completely untouched. They are never at any time made inerrant, almost superhuman: which would mean that they were not really human at all, but tools, without will and without

32. Küng, *The Church* p. 46.
33. Hans Küng, *Infallible? An Inquiry,* trans. Edward Quinn (Garden City, N.Y.: Doubleday, 1971), pp. 216-17.
34. Küng, *On Being a Christian,* p. 466.
35. Ibid (italics in original).
36. Ibid., p. 467 (italics in original).
37. Ibid., p. 463 (italics in original).
38. Ibid., p. 465.

responsibility. The operation of the Spirit excludes neither defects nor faults, excludes neither concealment nor dilution, neither limitation nor error. The testimonies of the New Testament, however much they all proclaim the God who acts on us through Jesus Christ, are neither uniform nor of equal value; there are brighter and darker, more clear and less clear, stronger and weaker, more original and more derivative testimonies: all in all, supremely variable testimonies, which can diverge, contrast and—up to a point—contradict one another.[39]

Because of these limitations of the biblical authors we today have the responsibility to examine their writings in the light of the modern understanding of reality, with our scientific historical-critical methods making corrections if necessary. In light of the humanness and the historical conditionedness of the biblical writings we are "compelled to examine ideas of former centuries, to take up the justified concerns which they express and make them our own, and—where necessary—critically but cautiously to correct their language and imagery if today these are misleading or liable to be misunderstood."[40]

As we have seen in the above-mentioned citations Küng's concept of the origin of the Scriptures excludes any idea of the participation of the Spirit in their actual production. In the writing of Scripture, humanity always remains "intact." The truth of Scripture reaches man "without any violence *through* the humanity . . . of the human authors." It comes in "unrestricted human historicity."[41]

Küng acknowledges that the traditional view of Scripture include the concept of inspiration by the Spirit by which was understood the Spirit's control of the human writers so that the final product was equivalent to God's Word and thus free from error. In a manner not uncommon to the critics of that view, Küng tends to set forth the traditional view as a mechanistic operation that diminishes any human involvement to that of a passive instrumentality. The traditional view, Küng says, makes "the authors of the books of the Bible . . . appear as unhistorical phantom beings through whom the Holy Spirit effects everything directly."[42]

It is not, however, simply an aversion to a one-sided view of inspiration that Küng rejects. It is the traditional concept of

39. Küng, *Infallible?* p. 217.
40. Küng, *On Being a Christian*, p. 464.
41. Küng, *Infallible?* p. 217.
42. Ibid., p. 209.

inspiration as a unique work of the Spirit on the writers of Scripture that can no longer be accepted. Describing the traditional view as a "later theory," Küng states; "If today the misleading term 'inspiration' of Scripture is to be used at all, it must certainly not be understood in the sense of that later theory of inspiration which conceives the activity of the divine Spirit as a miracle limited to certain particular acts of writing on the part of an apostle or a biblical author."[43] Küng admits that 2 Timothy 3:16 (which he describes as "a single, late text of the pastoral epistles—which, as is well-known, are not by Paul"), is "a statement in Hellenistic style" similar to the traditional view of the church. But he dispenses with it simply with the comment that "anyway [it] does not imply a mechanistic theory of inspiration,"[44] a comment with which the advocates of the traditional view would gladly concur.

The "*traditional view* of a kind of mechanical inspiration," in Küng's mind, "has been increasingly *shaken* by the historical-critical study of the Old and New Testaments."[45] In its place he proposes an inspiration that encompasses the entire process of composition of Scripture, its proclamation and reception in faith.

> The whole course of the origin, collecting, and transmission of the word, the whole process of accepting in faith and handing on the message in proclamation, is under the guidance and disposition of the Spirit. Not only the history of the recording, but the whole pre and posthistory of Scripture altogether is in this sense "inspired" by the Spirit: not dictated by the Spirit, but Spirit-effected and Spirit-filled.[46]

Küng's understanding of the inspiration of the Scripture is thus in harmony with his comprehensive theology of the nature of God and His revelation to the world and human history. Beginning with the modern outlook that excludes God from any direct activity within the empirical world, revelation must of necessity be denied an identifiability with any objective realities in human history. It can only come in a "hidden way."[47] The necessary corollary to that theology of God and His revelation can only be a Bible of fallible human words.

43. Küng, *On Being a Christian*, p. 465. See also Küng, *Infallible?* p. 216.
44. Küng, *On Being a Christian*, p. 465.
45. Ibid., p. 464.
46. Küng, *Infallible?* p. 216.
47. Ibid., p. 217.

THE THEOLOGY OF KARL RAHNER AND THE SCRIPTURES

Karl Rahner stands as a giant among Catholic theologians, respected both inside and outside of the Roman church. When both the range and depth of his writings are considered, few theologians can be considered his peer. He has written on a vast array of subjects, many of which are not strictly theological. Nevertheless his primary interest has been contemporary theological problems, which he confronts with true profundity. His theology is marked by a tendency to affirm the essential traditional ideas while presenting them in new and creative forms. His thinking is truly systematic, with his view of God and His revelation being intrinsic to all of theology.

ANTHROPOLOGICAL STARTING POINT

Like Küng, Rahner is concerned with doing theology for modern man. Too often, he notes, twentieth-century Catholic theology has been introverted and has followed its own interests rather than having a pastoral concern to answer the questions of contemporary man. To perform that function Rahner demands that the experience of man be placed alongside the revealed truth of Christianity as the two foci of theological concern.[48] According to Burke, the focus on man has become increasingly dominant in Rahner's works. "Rahner's early and laborious reexamination of the sources of (and historical 'developments' in) Catholic theology is no longer so dominant in his later attention in theology. Since Vatican II, Rahner's attention seems to focus much less upon the supposedly definitive past and more upon the contemporary human person, the self-consciousness of the man of today."[49]

Rahner's desire to include modern man in the theological enterprise means more than making theological truth practical for life. It means beginning with modern man's understanding of his world. Theological formulas must "speak to modern man immediately within his own sphere of thought and from his own experience. They must—as far as possible— . . . make use of such presuppositions as are self-evident to modern man."[50] Such language is indicative of the impact of Rahner's education in "the

---

48. Karl Rahner, "Theology (I: Nature)," *Sacramentum Mundi.* 6(1970): 244-45.
49. Ronald Raymond Burke, "Rahner and Revelation" Ph.D. diss., Yale University, 1974, p. 13.
50. Karl Rahner, "Die Forderung nach einer 'Kurzformel' des Christlichen Glaubens," in *Schriften zur Theologie*, vol. 3, pp. 154-55, cited by Burke, "Rahner and Revelation," p. 31.

person centered philosophies developed by *Menschen Von Heute*—such as the existential, transcendental, and personalist philosophies."[51] Of particular significance in that training were the phenomenological and existential concepts of Heidegger, under whom Rahner studied. Robertson notes that "Rahner follows Descartes, Kant, and Heidegger in focusing upon the subject and his act of self-knowledge as the key access to knowledge of the real."[52] The influences of those ideas is readily seen in the concept of a universal transcendental revelation that will be discussed later.

Using modern man's presuppositions means among other things for Rahner the acceptance of evolution. The transcendental question of Christology is located in man who has a historical concreteness that Rahner defines as "the situation of an evolutionary view of the world." He goes on to say, "We are proposing thereby the evolutionary view of the world as a given, and we are asking whether Christology is compatible or can be compatible with it and not vice versa."[53]

The impact of an evolutionary view upon Rahner's understanding of Scripture is readily apparent in his discussion of the "primal revelation" in the first chapters of Genesis:

> How is one to conceive of this revelation to the "first parents," when they lived perhaps two million years ago, originated from the animal world by evolution and so must be imagined as "primitive" beings? And yet they are supposed to recognize the path of "supernatural salvation." Furthermore what is one to make of this account if, with some justification, one assumes a state of polygenism with regard to the origins of mankind?[54]

Rahner concludes his questioning of the Genesis record by rejecting its traditional meaning in favor of the understanding of modern man. "The portrayal of the original revelation," he summarizes, "is located in a traditional framework of meaning and ignores too many questions to allow a contemporary reader to make sense of it."[55]

In harmony with evolution, Rahner, like Küng, views the universe as closed to direct divine intervention. According to Rahner,

51. Burke, p. 26.
52. John C. Robertson, Jr., "Rahner and Ogden: Man's Knowledge of God," *The Harvard Theological Review* 63 (1970): 380.
53. Karl Rahner, *Foundations of Christian Faith*, trans. William V. Dych (New York: Seabury, 1978), p. 178.
54. Karl Rahner, *Theological Investigations*, trans. David Morland, 16 vols. (New York: Seabury, 1961-79), 16:194.
55. Ibid., 16:195.

the modern period has changed the viewpoint of the world. It "has been transformed and deepened to an extraordinary degree and the whole situation has altered." In the modern understanding, "the world has become a self-contained whole which is not open to God at particular points and does not flow into the divine sphere; it does not experience the impact of divine causality at specific individual points which are open to human observation (prescinding for the moment from the supernatural history of salvation)."[56] As a result of that modern view of the world, "direct human perception of God is impossible and only indirect knowledge lies open to man."[57] Thus Rahner's acceptance of that understanding of the world, including the evolutionary perspective, has determinative bearing on his theology of revelation and the nature of the Bible.

THE MEANING OF REVELATION

Rahner discusses revelation in two aspects—universal transcendental revelation and special categorical revelation. Those are both really one revelation, namely, the self-communication of God in grace. The latter aspect merely objectifies and interprets the former, primary aspect.

The universal transcendental revelation is based upon the understanding of man as a transcendent being. Human experience is not exhausted in the realm of the finite. Man inevitably asks questions that transcend his finiteness. In so doing he shows himself to be a transcendent being. Rahner explains, "In the fact that he experiences his finiteness radically, he reaches beyond this finiteness and experiences himself as a transcendent being, a spirit."[58]

As a transcendent being man shows himself to be grounded in infinite being itself. Man's "conscious activity is grounded in a pre-apprehension *(Vorgriff)* of 'being' as such, in an unthematic but ever-present knowledge of the infinity of reality."[59] That knowledge, however, is not due to man but to that reality that makes itself known. Rahner notes:

> This pre-apprehension as merely a question is not self-explanatory, it must be understood as due to the working of that to which man is open, namely, being in an absolute sense. . . . Whenever man in his

56. Ibid., 16:169-70.
57. Ibid., 16:172.
58. Rahner, *Foundations*, p. 32.
59. Ibid., p. 33.

transcendence experiences himself as questioning, as disquieted by the appearance of being, as open to something ineffable, he cannot understand himself as subject in the sense of an *absolute* subject, but only in the sense of one who receives being, ultimately only in the sense of grace.[60]

The experience of the ultimate mysterious being itself is a continual universal experience of all men as transcendent beings.

When that understanding of man and ultimate reality is translated into theological language it refers to the revelatory self-communication of God to all human beings. There is a real communication of God in "his own being, . . . a communication for the sake of knowing and possessing God in immediate vision and love,"[61] which is universal. "Man is the event of a free, unmerited and forgiving, and absolute self-communication of God."[62]

Because for Rahner that revelation of God is never simply objective but rather takes place in the subjectivity of human transcendental experience, the revelation is therefore of the same nature as that revealed in Christ. Expressing universal revelation in terms of Christian doctrine, Rahner says: "This is . . . the communication of God's Holy Spirit, the event of immediacy to God as man's fulfillment is prepared for in such a way that we must say of man here and now that he participates in God's being; that he has been given the divine Spirit who fathoms the depths of God; that he is already God's son here and now, and what he already is must only become manifest."[63]

Universal transcendental revelation in the transcendent existence of the human spirit inevitably leads to the objectifying self-interpretation of the experience. That brings us to Rahner's second aspect of revelation, namely, special categorical revelation. Such self-interpretation takes place first in all that man does in his history. But it becomes increasingly an explicit religious self-interpretation of the transcendental experience of God. It is the latter specifically categorized in religious themes that constitutes the history of revelation in the usual sense of that word, according to Rahner.[64] Such special categorical revelation takes place at

---

60. Ibid., p. 34.
61. Ibid., pp. 117-18.
62. Ibid., p. 116.
63. Ibid., p. 120. Although such a statement appears to teach universal salvation, a theme recurring frequently in the theology of Rahner, it must be noted that he does leave open the possibility of a radical rejection of God. Cf. *Foundations*, pp. 99-104, 443-44.
64. Ibid., p. 155.

times in all religions, but it is in Christ that we find "the full and unsurpassable event of the historical self-objectification of God's self-communication to the world," which therefore stands as the criterion for understanding all transcendental experience of God.[65]

From the foregoing discussion of Rahner's viewpoint of revelation it becomes evident that revelation can never be equated directly with anything objective in this world. A theological proposition, Rahner asserts, cannot "by itself . . . be the object of revelation since, as an inner worldly state of affairs, it is in principle open to secular human understanding and is thus not the right sort of object to be revealed in a personal, divine self-disclosure."[66] Revelation, in fact, does not mean an increase in knowledge about God in the ordinary sense of that term. Rather, it means the "deepening perception of God *as* mystery . . . the growing awareness that we are involved with the permanent mystery."[67] As Burke explains, revelation according to Rahner belongs to a level of human existence that cannot be conveyed in words: "The basic reality or event of revelation is claimed to be not a matter of words, but a matter of life. It is of such existential subtlety and significance that it cannot be adequately articulated."[68]

One further aspect of Rahner's concept of revelation is its continuance in the church. With the coming of Christ and the end of the apostolic era, revelation can be considered "closed" in the sense of a never-to-be-replaced climax of God's self-communication to the world.[69] But that "closed" revelation has been committed to the church that, because of its faith in the revelation, is "in possession of the revealed Reality itself."[70] Apostolic succession does not mean that the apostles handed on only propositions about their faith (Rahner's understanding of the apostolic writings), but they bequeathed the reality behind their words, namely, the Spirit Himself. Thus the same things that belonged to the apostles now belong to the church. The experience of the church is "in principle the same as that of the Apostles . . . it is an experience, resting on that of the Apostles and prolonging *theirs*."[71] By virtue of that "*successio apostolica*," the church can explicate the

65. Ibid., p. 157.
66. Rahner, *Theological Investigations*, 16:182.
67. Ibid., 16:238.
68. Burke, p. 135, n. 200.
69. Rahner, *Theological Investigations*, 1:49.
70. Ibid.
71. Ibid., 1:68.

apostolic traditions deducing new propositions that are equally revelation.[72] As we will see, that concept of revelation in the church allows Rahner to deny the absolute inerrancy of the Scripture and yet claim an infallible guide beyond individual subjectivism in the church.

THE MEANING OF INSPIRATION AND INERRANCY

The meaning of the inspiration of Scripture is for Rahner intrinsically involved in his concepts of revelation and the church. God's self-communicaton in revelation reached its final and irreversible form in Jesus Christ crucified and risen. That revelation became explicit and thematic in the expressions of faith in Christ in the early church, which expressions constitute the Scriptures.

Because of its relation to the event of Christ, the church of the apostolic age was the "object of God's activity in a qualitatively unique way which is different from his preservation of the church in the course of history" and is therefore normative.[73] The Scriptures as the objectification of the apostolic church are the means by which the normative characteristics of the early church are preserved for the church of history. Thus the Scriptures do not stand over the church as a norm. They are rather the expression of the original normative church; both are together the effect of the Christ event.

It is in that union with founding of the church that Rahner locates the meaning of the Spirit's work of inspiration. He explains:

> If God wills the original church as an indefectible sign of salvation for all ages, and wills it with an absolute, formally pre-defining and eschatological will within salvation history, and hence if he wills with this quite definite will everything which is constitutive for this church, and this includes in certain circumstances scripture in a preeminent way, then he is the inspirer and the author of scripture, although the inspiration of scripture is 'only' a moment within God's primordial authorship of the church.[75]

As we have seen in the discussion of Rahner's view of revelation, the work of inspiration cannot involve the direct communication of God's Word in human words. The Scriptures can only be

72. Ibid., 1:58-59.
73. Rahner, *Foundations*, p. 374.
74. Ibid., pp. 372-73.
75. Ibid., p. 375.

human witness to a nonpropositional revelation. As human witness they contain the historical and cultural conceptual horizons of their authors, some of which are incorrect factually.[76] Any inerrancy of Scripture must be understood only in the intent of the unified whole. Individual statements are true only as they are part of the whole that witnesses to the truth of God's action in Christ. "We must read every individual text within the context of this simple whole in order to understand its true meaning correctly. Only *then* can it be understood in its real meaning, and only then can it be really grasped as 'true.' "[77]

Rahner admits that such a view of Scripture with its denial of an inerrant inspiration removes the Scripture from being the sole authority. He correctly notes that "one cannot abandon the principle of an absolute verbal inspiration of Scripture, as in fact has happened, and still maintain the principle of Scripture alone in the sense which it had at the time of the Reformation."[78] In light of that departure from an inerrant inspiration, two alternatives for authority remain: "man's . . . ultimate, inescapable and existential experience of the Spirit," or the authoritative teaching office of the church. As a Catholic, Rahner opts for the second and finds in Christ's promise of the perpetuity of the church ground for believing in the infallibility of the church's voice as it explicates its normative tradition.[79] Thus for Rahner the church can provide that authority that his view of errant inspiration takes away from Scripture.

CRITIQUE

We have sought to set forth the primary theological concepts related to the positions of Küng and Rahner regarding Scripture. As mentioned in the introduction, the specific relationship of those theological viewpoints to the belief in an errant Bible is not always evident. Which of the positions actually contribute to the position of errancy and which are constructed on the basis of that belief is difficult to determine. The choice to accept the modern world's view of reality, with its canons for so-called scientific historical criticism, as a starting point stands in some sense as a general presupposition that inevitably leads to the conclusion of an errant Scripture. On the other hand, it could reasonably be

76. Ibid., p. 376.
77. Ibid.
78. Ibid., p. 362.
79. Ibid., pp. 362-65.

argued that ideas such as the nonpropositional nature of revelation and truth flow from the rejection of Scripture as equal with God's revelation, which itself is based on a previous determination of Scripture errancy. Whatever the exact nature of their relationship, those various theological concepts form a unified system that in the minds of Küng and Rahner includes an errant Bible.

A more crucial question concerns the validity of those theological ideas linked to the doctrine of errancy. Despite errancy's undermining of the Bible's position as an infallible norm, Scripture's supremacy as a criterion of truth still remains among those who profess allegiance to Christ. It is therefore according to that criterion that the truth claims of all theological ideas must be judged.

THE MODERN WORLD VIEW

As we have seen, the desire of both Küng and Rahner to do apologetic theology for modern man causes them to use his understanding of reality as the framework for theology. They desire to begin theology from below, rather than with a revealed Word from above. The present human empirical experience is somehow revelatory of the *true* nature of reality with which theology must relate and is, in fact, a "constitutive element in our understanding of God's revelation."[80] Inherent in that assumptive starting point is the common belief that the Bible involves a conceptual system that is alien to that of modern man. A correlative assumption, of course, is that our modern view is superior in its reflection of reality.

Several concerns are raised by that whole approach. In the first place, it may be asked if the "human experience" of the biblical world is really substantially different from modern experience. Sloyan rightly questions the assumed dichotomy, asserting:

> Part of the problem is that "traditional Christian experience" includes patterns of thought and language that, despite being centuries old and scarcely comprehensible in the terms of their initial framing, are *also* part of "our human empirical experience." Hence it is false to set them against one another as mutually exclusive. The age-old pain of humanity is alienation: from oneself, from the community, from God. Yet if revealed truth and reconciliation have

---

80. Küng, "Toward a New Consensus," p. 12.

been held out and accepted in a language characteristic of no other human experience, it remains valid language from the fact that God has been perceived and reconciliation accepted. This seems to be the chief weakness of the supposition of Küng . . . that human empirical experience has no capacity to include traditional Christian experience.[81]

When one examines the experience of man throughout history, it becomes evident that it is not so much the experience that changes, but the interpretation of that experience. Therefore, it may be asked, Does not the difference that Küng makes so formative for his rejection of traditional doctrine rest on the fact that biblical man spoke of God as directly active in the world whereas modern man excludes Him? If such is the case, by what criterion can we assume that the modern view more truthfully reflects ultimate reality? In a world of increasing human experience of the spirit world, there seems to be no basis for denying the biblical picture of direct divine activity.

The assumption of modern man's view of reality as a construct of theology also raises the question of the noetic effect of sin. Küng's belief in a sort of neutral historical criticism to find the true historical picture of Christ and, to some extent, Rahner's concept of a universal revelation both suggest that the mind of modern man is capable of attaining and acknowledging objective truth concerning divine activity. Küng writes: "Does historical-critical Jesus research presuppose faith? No. Even the unbeliever can carry out objective research on Jesus. . . . The presupposition of historical research therefore is not belief or unbelief, still less indifference, but certainly an open-mindedness in principle toward everything that comes to us from this frequently disturbing figure."[82] In this assumption of the unbeliever's objectivity no cognizance is taken of the biblical teaching that the human heart and mind are darkened by sin (cf. Rom. 1:21; Eph. 4:17-18; Tit. 1:15). The canons of much of the so-called scientific historical criticism based on the modern, antisupernaturalistic world view can hardly be expected to draw truthful conclusions concerning the life of the incarnate Son of God. We are compelled to agree with the criticism of Küng offered by his fellow Catholic theologian Avery Dulles: "He seems to exaggerate the capacities of a

---

81. Gerard Sloyan, "Jesus of Nazareth: Today's Way to God," in *Consensus in Theology?* ed. Leonard Swidler (Philadelphia: Westminster, 1980), p. 55.
82. Küng, *On Being a Christian*, p. 164.

theologically neutral historical-critical method to grasp the reality of Jesus."[83]

The proper involvement of the modern scientific world in theology raises the question of the true task of theology. The words of the Muslim professor Seyyed Hossein Nasr are apropos to all who claim to be engaged in theology.

> Theology is after all literally "the science of God." It should explain the temporal with reference to the Eternal and not the Eternal in the light of temporality which is made to sound very *real*, central, and important by being baptized as the human condition, the modern world, or urgent human problems. There is not more urgent a human problem than the task to distinguish between the real and the Eternal on the one hand and the illusory and ephemeral on the other.[84]

To allow the common experience of a humanity that has turned its back on God and walks in the stultifying darkness of the absence of His light to be the interpreter of divine revelation is to distort the voice of God and make theology harmonize with experience rather than to bring that experience back under the lordship of God. That transformation, which took place first among Protestants, has had devastating results toward the Scriptures. Henry notes: "While Protestant modernism contended that twentieth-century man can still be Christian, it elevated empirical verifiability as decisive for truth; forsaking transcendent revelation and external miracle. . . . By subordinating revealed theology to empirical inquiry, the modernist era . . . abandoned the scriptural verification of invisible spiritual realities and excluded any fixed or timeless Word conveyed by biblical revelation."[85] Experience, including that of modern science, must be explained in the light of a theology based on a revelation from God and not vice versa. "It is not theology which must surrender itself to modern science and its findings. Rather it is modern science which must be critically appraised from the metaphysical and theological points of view and its findings explained in this light."[86] That is not to deny the need of theology to deal with the factual data of modern scientific research. History reveals only

83. Avery Dulles, "Ecumenism and Theological Method," in *Consensus in Theology?* p. 47.
84. Seyyed Hossein Nasr, "A Muslim Reflection on Religion and Theology," in *Consensus in Theology?* p. 113.
85. Carl F. H. Henry, *God, Revelation and Authority*, 6 vols. (Waco, Tex.: Word, 1976-83), 4:20.
86. Nasr, "A Muslim Reflection on Religion and Theology," p. 115.

too clearly the dangers of an obscurantist attitude on the part of theology. Nevertheless to accept uncritically the modern outlook with its evolutionary underpinnings is to allow the fallen human mind to dictate the criteria of facticity for the words of Scripture. Such an approach not only destroys the words' ultimate authority but transforms the real nature of theology as well.

The blending of modern human experience with biblical faith has been the goal of Protestant theology since the eighteenth century. The issues of modernity that challenged first the liberals and then the neo-orthodox are precisely the same ones confronting the Catholic church today.[87] The success of the Protestant venture is summed up by Gilkey with this assessment: "At present, while Protestant theology offers two and possibly three creative options, it seems neither to be producing, nor to have the prospect of producing, any powerful synthesis of modernity and the gospel that can support and enhance Christian life for our time."[88] Such a record bodes little hope for the modern Catholic prospect and, in fact, should challenge the validity of the attempt.

THE VALIDITY OF THE HISTORICAL-CRITICAL METHOD

One of the key points at which the presupposition of the modern outlook impinges on theology is the use of the historical-critical method in the exegesis of Scripture. Küng in particular insists that a valid systematic theology must be constructed on such an exegetical base. The question is immediately raised as to whether such a critical method can provide a reliable word upon which to construct a normative theology. According to the apostle Peter, Christianity is not based on myths but on historical reality, particularly the life and work of Jesus Christ. Because the critical approach taken by Küng and Rahner demands that we demythologize the gospels, can it at the same time assure us of the historical data? Küng is optimistic that it can, declaring that "a scholarly answer to the question about the Jesus of history is again regarded as possible today in a new form and within certain limits."[89] Others, however, are not so sure. Lindbeck argues that Küng's "judgement is possible, if at all, only when one confines attention to continental, and especially German biblical studies." He points to differing views and concludes that "Küng's method-

87. Langdon Gilkey, *Catholicism Confronts Modernity* (New York: Seabury, 1975), p. 13.
88. Ibid., p. 14.
89. Küng, *On Being a Christian*, p. 157.

ological proposal insofar as it depends on a positive scholarly consensus seems premature."[90]

The whole problem of establishing a solid criterion for theology on the basis of the historical-critical method is raised in Van Buren's reaction to Küng. Noting that the nineteenth-century quest for the historical Jesus ended up in "a Jesus of their own nineteenth century," he acknowledges his preference for today's researchers' Jesus as a "first-century Palestinian Jew." But he adds, "We are still learning so much these days about Judaism in the first century . . . that I hardly want to base my faith on such tentative hypotheses. Biblical scholars have taught me to be cautious about their tentative conclusions."[91]

The comments of Van Buren point out the fatal flaw in the higher critical methodology undergirding the biblical understanding of theologians such as Küng and Rahner. A system based upon certain presuppositions of human experience and reason will inevitably yield conclusions conditioned by those same factors, and therefore it will be variable according to the dominant cultural mood.

NONPROPOSITIONAL REVELATION

The idea of revelation as personal self-disclosure that is nonpropositional contributes significantly to the recent Catholic understanding of the Scriptures. Burtchaell reveals a major source of influence promoting that concept, which is admittedly a change from a previous belief in a propositional revelation, when he says, "No one should gainsay that Rudolf Bultmann's existential, non-contentual understanding of revelation has been one of the chief stimuli to Catholic thought on our subject." He goes on to add, however, that Catholics are reluctant to follow his theory completely.[92]

The theory of a personal, nonpropositional revelation deserves rejection on many counts. At the outset it should be noted that it not only contradicts the testimony of the scriptural writers (cf. Jer. 1:6-9; 1 Thess. 2:13), but it denies the biblical portrait of God as a God who speaks words (cf. Isa. 51:16). Moreover, the words of Jesus must certainly be considered propositional in nature, and

---

90. George Lindbeck, "The Bible as Realistic Narrative," in *Consensus in Theology?* pp. 82-83.
91. Paul M. Van Buren, "Historical Thinking and Dogmatics," in *Consensus in Theology?* p. 95.
92. Burtchaell, *Catholic Theories of Biblical Inspiration,* p. 278.

He claimed that His words came from the Father (cf. John 14:10, 24). Henry notes the disparity between the God of Scripture and the God implied by the exclusion of propositional revelation:

> If one believes in a sovereign divine mind and will, in God who personally speaks and conveys information and instruction, then the presuppositions of scriptural inspiration lie near at hand. But if one believes rather in the modern philosophies of Kant, Heidegger, Ayer and others who exclude objective cognitive knowledge of God, not to mention propositional-verbal divine revelation, then all reference to God who communicates truths must be compressed in advance into a high-flown metaphor representing something other than verbal information. But the God of Moses, Isaiah and Jeremiah, the God of Paul and Peter and John, appears not only as the divine commentator on his present doings, but as one who speaks also of his future purposes and of his past creation of man and the world, and who conveys precise verbal instruction concerning these matters.[93]

In addition to contradicting the plain teaching of Scripture concerning its own nature (a teaching that cannot be set aside without logically undermining the reliability of its total message), the theory of nonpropositional revelation has been rightly attacked as ending in a subjectivism that is ultimately not controlled by objective reality. Küng shows himself to be an example of that when he writes: "in the Christmas, miracle, Easter and judgment stories, the main interest is not in what really happened or will happen at that point—of which we often know very little—but in the practical question of *what it means for us:* on which there is always scope for fresh critical thinking in each individual and social stituation."[94] Such subjectivism inevitably leads to theological relativism and skepticism.[95]

The effect of a theology of nonpropositional revelation upon practical religious life has been cogently pointed out by Langdon Gilkey in his analysis of neo-orthodoxy. Gilkey notes that that earlier Protestant theology was attempting to build its system on the same foundation as we have seen in Küng and Rahner. It was a desire to synthesize the presuppositions of the modern world with a transcendent God and His acts of salvation. Neo-orthodoxy, according to Gilkey, "accepted a great deal of its own liberal inheritance and so many of the basic assumptions of the modern

93. Henry, 3:428.
94. Küng, *On Being a Christian*, p. 416.
95. For an excellent discussion of this whole question see Henry, 3:248-487.

world view." Included in those were a "naturalistic account of all space-time events" (which excluded "miraculous divine interventions"), historical relativity with regard to the Scriptures, and evolution. That resulted in an approach to the Bible much like that of modern Catholicism. "Whatever revelation might mean, it did *not* mean the communication of the divine information about space-time events. . . . No more for them than for liberals did the Bible communicate information about 'matters of fact'. . . . Rather . . . scripture mediates its truth existentially to Christian faith. . . . Biblical doctrines . . . are reflections on an existential encounter with God in his Word."[96] From that explanation of Gilkey the dependency of modern Catholic thought upon Protestant neo-orthodoxy is strikingly apparent.

The problem with such a theology, however, is that it could not foster and sustain faith for the ordinary person. By excluding God from the ordinary events of human history it demanded a schizophrenic approach to life. "It attempted to accept the secular world *secularly,* but to retain the Biblical and orthodox worlds *religiously.*"[97] At the heart of that dualism was the failure to let God speak propositionally in this world. As a result it was impossible to foster a convincing belief in the reality of a transcendent God. Gilkey explains the failure when he writes:

> Neoorthodoxy frequently seemed to be dealing with and talking about events, categories, forces, and factors which were invisible, inaudible, unknowable, and surely undemonstrable to anyone outside of the circle of faith, and so to have a structure of discourse relevant, meaningful, and valid *only* if faith is presupposed. Its language was thus radically unconnected with the ordinary structures and language of secular life. It had, perhaps rightly, fixed its hope on the transcendent God rather than on anything in his visible creation, and placed its trust in God's Word rather than in all the wayward opinions of his creatures. But it seemed to be forced thereby to inhabit its own separated, irrevelant, and so apparently illusory world.[98]

A SUBJECTIVE TRUTH

An inherent corollary to a nonpropositional view of revelation is a nonpropositional view of truth. It is difficult to avoid the

96. Langdon Gilkey, *Naming the Whirlwind: The Renewal of God-Language* (Indianapolis: Bobbs-Merrill, 1969), p. 83.
97. Ibid., p. 84.
98. Ibid., p. 88.

conclusion that such a position ultimately obfuscates objective truth, making it impossible to distinguish from subjective opinion.

In his denial of the infallibility of the church Küng includes the sweeping statement that truth lies beyond all human institutions and propositions, including those of Scripture. In his words, "not only has the plane of institutions and authorities been penetrated but also that of propositional truths, in order—if necessary through very varied statements—to point to one and the same reality which lies behind the individual statements and alone gives them their truth."[99] For him only such a concept of truth can finally justify the meaning and demand of faith. "It is only in the light of this reality, lying behind all talk of faith," he argues, "that the invitation to faith can actually be justified. . . . Faith cannot be 'proved' in the same way as other things are proved." The person of faith "cannot have the assurance that is provided by ordinary reality."[100] For Küng, truth is maintained in spite of "all human failings and mistakes."[101] The failure to accept such a reality is "ultimately a lack of faith."[102]

Rahner, likewise, speaks of truth in a way that transcends that worldly objectivity. In a discussion of the statements of the Old Testament, some of which Rahner believes do not correspond to actual reality, he nevertheless argues that "they can and should be rightly described as true in the sense of truth which consists in the open-ended movement to God arising from God's own self-communication and the grace and revelation it contains. Thus, to put the matter briefly, inner-worldly error can lead to absolute truth. This error must then be itself 'true' because it is taken up into the movement directed to the absolute divine reality."[103] As we have seen, Rahner's whole concept of a nonpropositional revelation necessitates such an understanding of truth.

In place of and standing contrary to any propositions, truth is viewed as finally related to God and His personal self-disclosure in Christ. "Facts" and "truths" are not ultimately decisive because we believe "in God and in him whom God has sent."[104] Since Christ is the truth, the question of truth is not one of doctrines but of "discipleship in the Spirit of Jesus Christ."[105]

99. Küng, *The Church*, p. 13.
100. Ibid., pp. 13-14.
101. Ibid., p. 15.
102. Küng, *Infallible?* p. 176.
103. Rahner, *Theological Investigations*, 16:185.
104. Küng, *The Church*, p. 45.
105. Ibid., p. 28.

In no way must any claim for the propositional truth of Scripture be allowed to eclipse the reality of God's truth in Christ. The question remains, however, whether the personal expression of truth in Christ can be divorced from the propositional truth of Scripture and still retain an objective quality for man. Christian discipleship most certainly entails following the true Christ and involves knowing something of His objective reality. If the Scriptures are a mixture of historical facts and myths, how can one be sure that he is not, in fact, following only a humanly contrived image rather than the personal revelation of God? Surely our cognitive understanding of Christ and His saving work has a controlling influence on the validity of any professed discipleship. The acuteness of that problem for those denying the inerrant propositional truth of the Scriptures is only too evident as one remembers the various images of Jesus propounded throughout the quest for the real, historical person.

The problem is apparent also in Küng's own admission of a hermeneutical circle in the search for theological truth. On the one hand he argues that the magisterium of the church "is under the word of God and consequently is open to criticism in the light of the normative criterion of Scripture." In saying that, Küng is denying the possibility of the church's being an infallible norm of truth. But because of his view of the Scripture, it likewise cannot be that norm. Anyone who "simply makes the gospel the ultimate criterion," according to Küng, "is in danger of lapsing into an emotional subjectivism: with the aid of the historical-critical method he makes light of the ultimate authority of faith." Thus because of a nonpropositional view of revelation and truth the Bible, although referred to as the source and norm of faith, is in fact deprived of that status. On the other hand, because of human fallibility no theologian or church can be that norm either, which leaves us without such a criterion of truth. Küng concludes, "It seems as if a hermeneutical circle cannot be avoided in practice." The interpreter must subject his faith to the norm of Scripture and at the same time subject the Scripture to the critically scientific methods of modern culture.[106]

For an infallibility in religious authority Küng applies that concept neither to the church nor the Bible, but only to God who encounters the believer in Christ, which results in certainty of religious truth. Such nonpropositional encounter truth has never been able to demonstrate how it contains more than the fact of a

106. Ibid., p. 42.

subjective experience rather than truth of objective reality about God. After analyzing Küng's concept of infallible truth and the certainty of faith, Obitts rightly concludes that he does not attain to either of those because of his exclusion of propositional truth.

> The distinction between evidenced belief and divinely authorized belief should not be blurred if the concept of infallibility is to have a viable meaning in the logic of religious faith. The believer's experience of God in Christ as he responds in love to the proclamation of the gospel, as Küng describes it, is certainly evidence for something. But only God or those whom He has informed infallibly know for sure. Such information is never experienced, for it is the interpretation of experience. To be infallible, therefore, its veracity would have to be based on divine authority; its evidence cannot be ascertained by the believer. How such information could be available to the believer nonpropositionally is not clear. Certainly Küng has not explained how it could be available.[107]

The concept of a nonpropositional truth that both Küng and Rahner assert and that is inherently linked to an errant Scripture can never provide a ground of objective truth. With such, Christianity must logically give up its claim to absolute truth and sink to the status of just another human religion.

THE FINAL AUTHORITY OF THE CHURCH

We have seen how for both Küng and Rahner the authority of Scripture is bound up with the teaching voice of the living church. Although they refer to the Scripture as the norm of divine truth, by placing their infallible or, in the case of Küng, their indefectible interpretation in the hands of the church, they effectively transfer the final authority to the church.

The traditional concept of the infallibility of the church has been modified by both theologians. As noted, Küng prefers to speak of an indefectible rather than an infallible church. The church, he insists, has made obvious errors throughout the course of history. But the promise of the Spirit guarantees that it will not ultimately defect from the truth. There is "a fundamental *remaining* in the truth in spite of all ever possible errors.[108] Rahner, on the other hand, argues for the infallibility of the

---

107. Stanley Obitts, "Religious Certainty and Infallibility: A Discussion with Hans Küng," in *Toward a Theology for the Future*, ed. David Wells and Clark Pinnock (Carol Stream, Ill.: Creation House, 1971), p. 290.
108. Küng, *Infallible?* p. 185.

church, but interprets it in an evolutionary, relativistic sense. Statements of dogma must be interpreted in their historical context and only in such contexts are they true. Different times and conditions call for different interpretations. For both Küng and Rahner, therefore, the authority of the church is reduced to pronouncements of relative truth. Nevertheless, the authority of the church assumes new utilitarian import with the defection from an inerrantly infallible Bible. In their minds it yet provides a unified authority transcending individual subjectivity.

The substitution of the authority of the church for that of the Scriptures runs afoul on both biblical and historical grounds. The Scripture does not teach the organic unity of the inspired writings and the church as propounded in the Roman theory. Rather than fusing the Scriptures with the church and making the Word nothing more than the expression of the faith of the church, the Bible teaches a uniqueness of its writings, which stand as an objective norm over the church. It was the writers of Scripture who received direct revelation and the special influence of the Holy Spirit, not the church. The inspired writers were immediately instruments of the Holy Spirit *for* the church and not *as* the church. The uniqueness of the biblical writers and consequent relation to the church has been noted by Cullmann.

> There is an apostolic tradition which is norm because it rests upon eyewitnesses chosen by God, and because Christ speaks directly in it, and there is a post-apostolic tradition which is a valuable help for the understanding of the divine Word, but is not to be regarded as a norm. While accepting humbly the *exegetical and dogmatic directives* of the Church and its teachers, we must be ready to set ourselves directly before the testimony of the apostles, as the apostles themselves were confronted directly with the divine revelation (Gal. 1:12), without any intermediate interpretation.[109]

Because of the uniqueness of those directly involved in revelation and inspiration, their teaching must remain normative to the church; they cannot be replaced or succeeded by later church teachers. To be sure, the Holy Spirit continues His work in the church in the sense of illumination and interpretation, but not in inspiration. With specific reference to an apostle, Cullmann correctly notes that "he must continue *himself* to fulfill his function in the Church of today: *in* the Church, not *by* the Church, but *by*

109. Oscar Cullmann, "The Tradition," in *The Early Church*, ed. A. J. B. Higgins (London: SCM, 1966), p. 86.

his word . . . in other words, by his writings."[110] That relationship is borne out by the Lord's reference to future generations of the church as "those . . . who believe in Me through their word," that is, the word of the apostles, not of the church. The continual appeal to the Scriptures as the final count of authority by both Jesus and the biblical writers (cf. Matt. 4:4; Mark 12:24), along with the ejection of the extrabiblical traditions that could be viewed as the interpretation of the religious community of that time (Mark 7:1-13), confirms the normative position of the sacred Scriptures as standing above and not fused with the later interpretations of the community.

Not only the teaching of Scripture, but the history of the Roman church itself refutes any idea of its infallibility. Küng himself states that "the errors of the ecclesiastical teaching office in every century have been numerous and indisputable."[111] Although he argues that the church cannot fundamentally depart from truth, he lists the church's teaching of "no salvation outside of the Church" as one of the errors. His meaning of apostatizing therefore remains questionable for what, if not the unjustifiable exclusion from salvation, "would approximate a fundamental departure from Christ's truth"?[112] In short, the record of the church with its various conflicting pronouncements and frequent aberrant walk, necessitating reformative steps, provides no basis for use of the church as a final criterion to determine truth in an errant Bible. Without an inerrant Scripture, we are left without an objective, historical, inerrant authority.

CONCLUSION

The positions of Küng and Rahner represent the result of a gradual erosion of the traditional views of Rome. Various tactics of compromise were used along the way to retain the traditional understanding of inerrant, propositional truth. Some sought the security of inerrancy by limiting it to matters of faith and morals. Later is was explained in terms of authorial intent. According to that view, much of what was unacceptable to modern understanding was to be interpreted as literary forms in which the author couched inerrant truth. Thus one could interpret problem passages as mythical or poetic without impugning the writer with

---

110. Ibid., p. 80.
111. Küng, *Infallible?* p. 32.
112. Henry, 4:226.

scientific error. None of those devices was able to stem the tide. The logic of the very principles of critical rationality that the compromises sought to appease eventually swept to dominance. There was no way that error, even in religious teaching, could be excluded from the ancient writers given the canons of modern understanding.

The modern Catholic understanding of the Scriptures has thus traveled the same road as that of much of contemporary Protestantism. The attempt to synthesize the modern understanding of reality with the Scriptures, while commendable in its aim of relevancy, proved fatal for the ultimate authority of the Bible. By subjecting the Scriptures to the modern, critical rationality, they were reduced to a fallible human record of religious experience rather than the revealed Word from God. God's speech was limited to a nonverbal experience that defies authoritative interpretation by fallible man.

The portrait of recent Roman Catholic bibliology therefore points out the dangers of seeking to divide human experience into two worlds—one empirical, ruled by the canons of autonomous human rationality and another religious, ruled by the canon of Scripture. Human experience is ultimately wholistic and must have one final authority. Either God has inerrantly revealed truth, which controls the interpretation of all of reality, or we are left with our own human understanding as the final source of meaning.

9. Process Theology and Inerrancy

Norman L. Geisler

Fundamental to our belief that the Bible is the Word of God is our belief in God. Orthodox Christianity is based in traditional theism. The classic representatives of that theism were Augustine, Anselm, and Aquinas. The Reformers also accepted this basic view of God. But with the rise of a modern process view of God there has come a serious challenge to the traditional theism and therefore its view of biblical inspiration. For as one can readily see, how one views Scripture authority will be determined by how one views the nature of God. Stated another way, the meaning of the affirmation "the Bible is the *Word* of God" will be determined by the kind of *God* connected with that Word.

TRADITIONAL AND PROCESS VIEWS OF GOD COMPARED

Before we can see the implications of classical theism versus neo-classical (or process) theism on one's view of Scripture, we will examine briefly what each believes.

Because the works of Augustine and Anselm were best systematized by Thomas Aquinas, we will use his *Summa Theologica* as the expression of classical theism.

NORMAN L. GEISLER, A.B., Wheaton College; M.A., Wheaton Graduate School; Th.B., Detroit Bible College; Ph.D., Loyola (Chicago) University, is professor of systematic theology at Dallas Theological Seminary, Dallas, Texas. Among his numerous books are: *General Introduction to the Bible* (1968), *From God to Us* (1974), ed. *Inerrancy* (1979), ed. *Biblical Errancy: Its Philosophical Roots* (1981), and *Decide for Yourself: How History Views the Bible* (1982).

CLASSICAL THEISM

For Aquinas the central metaphysical attributes of God are aseity, necessity, simplicity, infinity, immutability, eternality, and unity. Of course God is held to be omniscient, omnipotent, omnipresent, loving, just, and merciful as well. However, we are concerned here with the nonmoral, or metaphysical, attributes.

For Thomas every being cannot be contingent or dependent.[1] Ultimately there must be one being that is necessary or independent. That is, every being that receives its existence from another must get it ultimately from a Being that self-exists. That necessary, uncaused, self-existent Being is what is meant by the aseity of God.

Further, every contingent being is subject to change. And what can change has both an actuality and a potentiality (to change). But the ultimate cause of all changing beings is pure actuality with no potentiality to change. Hence, from aseity follows immutability.[2]

Likewise from aseity flows simplicity. For if God is pure actuality (with no potential) then He has no parts or principle of division within Him.[3] The same logic demands that God cannot be temporal (or spatial). For time (and space) involves some kind of change and, as we seen above, a self-existent God cannot change. God is pure act, and pure act has no potential to change.[4] In fact, since pure actuality is unlimited as such (potentiality being the principle of limitation), a self-existent being must be infinite (literally, *not*-finite). And there can be only one such unlimited being. Other beings can *have* being; but only one can *be* being itself.[5] So for Aquinas, God is pure *esse* (existence); all other beings have being only by receiving their being from God, according to their own limited potential.

At least two other important attributes flow from the understanding of God as the self-existent "I Am" (cf. Ex. 3:14): God's omnipotence and His omniscience. For Aquinas, if God is infinite (unlimited) actuality and the actualizer of everything else that exists (which takes power to do), then it follows logically that He must have infinite power.[6] Likewise, if God knows anything (and

1. Thomas Aquinas *Summa Theologica* 1. 2. 3 (A. Pegis translation).
2. Ibid. 1. 9. 1.
3. Ibid. 1. 3. 7.
4. Ibid. 1. 10. 2.
5. Ibid. 1. 11. 3-4.
6. Ibid. 1. 7. 1; and 1. 25. 2.

He must know something, because it took intelligence to create the world and intelligent beings), then God must be infinitely intelligent.[7] That can be seen from remembering that God is simple, that is, He has no parts (and a being with no parts cannot be partly anything). Whatever God is, He must be that infinitely, simply, eternally, and necessarily because that is the kind of Being He is by His very nature.

Aquinas was not alone in his view of the attributes of God. Substantially, it is the view of Augustine before him and Calvin after him.[8] It is in essence the view of the orthodox Princetonians, such as Hodge and Warfield. And with few significant modifications it is the view of the most modern evangelical theologians. But with the rise of process theology the situation has changed considerably. And it is understandable that with a change in the view of God there will come a concomitant change in the meaning of the affirmation "the Bible is the Word of God." Again, process theology is a case in point.

NEO-CLASSICAL OR PROCESS VIEW OF GOD

The ancient origins of process theology go back to Heraclitus (500 B.C.) and to Plato (d. 347 B.C.).[9] The most significant forerunners in the modern world were Hegel (d. 1831) and Henri Bergson in his *Creative Evolution* (1907). The real shift began, however, when Alfred North Whitehead combined the growing belief in evolution with the newly conceived view of relativity into his famous *Process and Reality* (1929). We will begin our discussion here with Whitehead's process view of God.

Simply put, Whitehead's process view of God is nearly the antithesis of classical theism. For Whitehead, God is not being but is becoming. He is not immutable but changing. God is not pure actuality; He is a combination of actuality and potentiality. God is not monopolar; He is bipolar. He is not actually infinite but is limited. God is not an eternal being; He is temporal.[10] Indeed for Whitehead, God is not an immaterial spirit; the changing

7. Ibid. 1. 2. 3 ("fifth way").
8. See Augustine *City of God* 8. 6; 11. 2, 5, 10; 12. 2; compare John Calvin *Institutes of the Christian Religion*, chaps. 1, 11-13.
9. For a more detailed discussion on the background and nature of process theology see my article "Process Theology," in *Tensions in Contemporary Theology*, Stanley Gundry and Alan Johnson, eds. (Chicago: Moody, 1976), pp. 237-86.
10. See Alfred North Whitehead, *Process and Reality* (New York: Macmillan, 1929), pp. 44-45, 520-33. (Hereafter called *PR*.)

world is God's "body." Hence, God is not an absolute and necessary being; God is actually a relative and contingent being.

Needless to say, Whitehead's God is neither omniscient nor omnipotent in the traditional sense of those attributes. In fact, God is not really in sovereign control of the world: He is working more in cooperation with it. For Whitehead, God is not even Creator of the world (ex nihilo); He is more a director of world affairs. God does not relate to the world as a being independent of it, for God is really involved in an interdependent way with the world.[11]

The rationale for rejecting the traditional view of God for the process view is stated most forcibly by Shubert Ogden and Charles Hartshorne. Their objections are in the form of five antinomies.

First, the antinomy of creation.[12] That alleged contradiction in classical theism is as follows. God is a necessary being, but His will is one with His essence, because God is also simple. (According to classical theism creation is said to flow freely from God's will.) However, Ogden insists that God cannot have both a necessary will and a free creation. If God necessarily willed creation as His nature demanded, then creation did not flow freely from His will. Thus, Ogden believes the traditional theistic view of God is contradictory.

Second, the antinomy of service.[13] According to Ogden there is no meaningful sense in which a traditional theist can really serve God. For service is doing something *for* God. But if God is already absolutely and immutably perfect then there is nothing anyone can do *for* Him. What can you give to the Being who literally has everything? In Ogden's words the God of Aquinas is "statically completed Perfection." So there is nothing we can do to add to Him.

Third, the antinomy of relationship.[14] Perhaps the most often stated of the alleged contradictions in traditional theism is the one that insists the God of Aquinas is unrelatable to the world. As an analysis of relationship reveals, all genuine relationships involve give and take, or mutual dependence. But according to classical theism God is in no sense dependent on the world. He is completely independent of the world; the world is completely de-

11. Ibid., pp. 340, 518, 529.
12. Shubert Ogden, *The Reality of God and Other Essays* (New York: Harper & Row, 1966), p. 17.
13. Ibid., p. 17.
14. Ibid., p. 18.

pendent on Him. If so, argues Ogden, then the God of theism is unrelatable to the world. He cannot really act or interact with the world such as the God described in the Bible does.

Fourth, the antinomy of supreme reality. That antinomy is offered by Charles Hartshorne as follows:

> Another customary antinomy was that the supreme reality, taken to be absolute, must be either all-inclusive or not all-inclusive. The supposition of inclusiveness involves a choice between the contradiction that constituents which could have been otherwise contribute to a totality which could *not* have been otherwise and the contrasting absurdity that neither the totality nor the constituents could have been otherwise, and thus that everything is absolute— wherewith both relativity and absoluteness lose all distinctive meaning. The supposition that the supreme reality is not all-inclusive implies that it is but a constituent of the totality, and so not the supreme reality after all.[15]

Fifth, the antinomy of contingent truth. That rejection of traditional theism is stated by Hartshorne this way:

> In those systems there was often the contradiction of a God held to be without accidental properties, although having knowledge of contingent truth. Thus he knows that a certain world exists which might not have existed; but surely had it not existed, he would not have known it to exist; hence he has knowledge which he might not have had. And still, none of his properties or qualities was admitted to be contingent![16]

IMPLICATIONS OF WHITEHEAD'S PROCESS VIEW FOR SCRIPTURE

Since Whitehead is not only the systematic fountainhead of process theology but also wrote on its relation to Scripture, it is only fitting to begin our analysis with him. The book in which he explicitly treats the topic is entitled *Religion in the Making* (1926).

Again we begin with Whitehead's view of God. And as we shall see, it has radical implications with regard to his view of Scripture.

WHITEHEAD'S CONCEPT OF GOD

According to Whitehead there are three main concepts of God:

---

15. Charles Hartshorne, *Creative Synthesis and Philosophic Method* (La Salle, Ill.: Open Court Publ., 1970), p. 48.
16. Ibid., p. 48.

1. The Eastern Asiatic concept of an impersonal order to which the world conforms. This order is the self-ordering of the world; it is not the world obeying an imposed rule. The concept expresses the extreme doctrine of immanence.

2. The Semitic concept of a definite personal individual entity, whose existence is the one ultimate metaphysical fact, absolute and underivative, and who decreed and ordered the derivative existence which we call the actual world.

3. The Pantheistic concept of an entity to be described in the terms of the Semitic concept, except that the actual world is a phase within the complete fact which is this ultimate individual entity. The actual world, conceived apart from God, is unreal. Its only reality is God's reality. The actual world has the reality of being a partial description of what God is. But in itself it is merely a certain mutuality of "appearance," which is a phase of the being of God. This is the extreme doctrine of monism.[17]

He rejects all of those, including the Semitic view, and says that "for most Christian Churches, the simple Semitic doctrine is now a heresy, both by reason of the modification of personal unity and also by the insistence of immanence." Modifications in the Semitic concept of God, says Whitehead, were made by both Jesus and the apostle John.

> But even here important qualifications have to be made. Christ himself introduces them. How far they were then new, or how far he is utilizing antecedent thoughts, is immaterial. The point is the decisive emphasis the notions receive in his teaching. The first point is the association of God with the Kingdom of Heaven, coupled with the explanation that "The Kingdom of Heaven is within you." The second point is the concept of God under the metaphor of a Father. The implications of this latter notion are expanded with moving insistence in the two Epistles by St. John, the author of the Gospel. To him we owe the phrase, "God is love."
>
> Finally, in the Gospel of St. John, by the introduction of the doctrine of the Logos, a clear move is made towards the modification of the notion of the unequivocal personal unity of the Semitic God.[18]

Just what is it that Whitehead objects to in the Semitic concept of God? "The Semitic God is omniscient; but in addition to that, the Christian God is a factor in the universe." To support the

---

17. Alfred North Whitehead, *Religion in the Making* (New York: Macmillan, 1926), pp. 66-67. (Hereafter called *RM.*)
18. *RM*, p. 71.

later point Whitehead quotes one of the extrabiblical (apocryphal) sayings of Christ from second-century Egypt: " 'Cleave the wood, and I am there.' This is merely one example," says Whitehead, "of an emphatic assertion of immanence, and shows a serious divergence from the Semitic concept."[19]

Another attribute of the theistic God that comes under the Whiteheadian attack is aseity. He writes, "There is no entity, not even God, 'which requires nothing but itself in order to exist.' "[20] Likewise, God's necessity and independence from the world is rejected in these words: "Apart from God, there would be no actual world; and apart from the actual world with its creativity, there would be no rational explanation of the ideal vision which constitutes God."[21] Also, God's infinity and unlimited goodness are dismissed in bold strokes: "The limitation of God is his goodness. He gains his depth of actuality by his harmony of valuation. It is not true that God is in all respects infinite. If He were, He would be evil as well as good. Also this unlimited fusion of evil with good would mean mere nothingness. He is something decided and is thereby limited."[22] In fact, Whitehead believes that all actual things are finite. For "to be an actual thing is to be limited."[23]

What then is God if not the infinite, sovereign Creator of the universe? Whitehead answers, "God is that function in the world by reason of which our purposes are directed to ends which in our own consciousness are impartial as to our own interests."[24] Further, God is the actual realization (in the world) of the ideal world. In his words, "the kingdom of heaven is God."[25] Now it must be remembered that for Whitehead the world is all there is. For "the temporal world and its formative elements constitute for us the all-inclusive universe."[26] Thus it follows that Whitehead's God is actually nothing more than the order and value of the actual world. He writes, "He is not the world, but the valuation of the world."[27] Again he says, "The order of the world is no accident. There is nothing actual which could be actual without some measure of order. . . . this creativity and these forms are together

19. *RM*, p. 71.
20. *RM*, p. 104.
21. *RM*, 150-51.
22. *RM*, p. 147.
23. *RM*, p. 144.
24. *RM*, p. 151.
25. *RM*, p. 148.
26. *RM*, p. 87.
27. *RM*, p. 152.

impotent to achieve actuality apart from the completed ideal harmony, which is God."[28] In that way God functions as the ground for creativity that is necessary for the attainment of value in the world. For "God, as conditioning the creativity with his harmony of apprehension, issues into the mental creature as moral judgment according to a perfection of ideals."[29] And, "Thus the purpose of God in the attainment of value is in a sense a creative purpose. Apart from God, the remaining formative elements would fail in their functions."[30]

With Whitehead's view of God in mind let us turn to an exposition of his view of dogma. Dogmas are the outer and balancing side of Whitehead's famous statement that "religion is what the individual does with his own solitude."[31] Thus religion is primarily individual, and the dogmas of religion are clarifying modes of external expression. That is, "expression, and in particular expression by dogma, is the return from solitariness to society. There is no such thing as absolute solitariness. Each entity requires its environment. Thus man cannot seclude himself from society."[32] In view of that, "A dogma is the precise enunciation of a general truth, divested so far as possible from particular exemplification. Such precise expression is in the long run a condition for vivid realization, for effectiveness, for apprehension of width of scope, and for survival."[33] Or, more briefly, "The dogmas are statements of how the complex world is to be expressed in the light of the intuitions fundamental to the religion."[34]

For Whitehead there is an important relationship between dogma and religious experience: "The dogmas of religion are the attempts to formulate in precise terms the truths disclosed in the religious experience of mankind. In exactly the same way the dogmas of physical science are the attempts to formulate in precise terms the truths disclosed in the sense-perception of mankind."[35] It is for that reason that he believes "religions commit suicide when they find their inspirations in their dogmas. The

28. *RM*, p. 115.
29. *RM*, p. 114.
30. *RM*, p. 110.
31. *RM*, p. 58.
32. *RM*, p. 132.
33. *RM*, p. 122.
34. *RM*, p. 133-34.
35. *RM*, p. 57.

inspiration of religion lies in the history of religion. By this I mean that it is to be found in the primary expressions of the intuitions of the finest types of religious lives."[36] Thus "a dogma which fails to evoke any response in immediate apprehension stifles the religious life."[37] And it is for that same reason that "idolatry is the necessary product of static dogmas."[38] For when the dogma no longer evokes a response to God then it becomes, accordng to Whitehead, an end in itself—a dead, idolatrous end.

Perhaps the most important dimension of Whitehead's view of dogmas is their limited and temporal nature. He contends that "in their precise forms they are narrow, limitative, and alterable: in effect untrue, when carried over beyond the proper scope of their utility."[39] In fact Whitehead argues:

> You cannot claim absolute finality for a dogma without claiming a commensurate finality for the sphere of thought within which it arose. If the dogmas of the Christian Church from the second to the sixth centuries express finally and sufficiently the truths concerning the topics about which they deal, then the Greek philosophy of that period had developed a system of ideas of equal finality.[40]

So "a dogma—in the sense of a precise statement—can never be final; it can only be adequate in its adjustment of certain abstract concepts. But the estimate of the status of these concepts remains for determination."[41] Thus from time to time dogmas must be modified by new experience. "Religion, therefore, while in the framing of dogmas it must admit modifications from the complete circle of our knowledge, still brings its own contribution of immediate experience."[42]

In view of the above-described nature of dogma, Whitehead believes that dogmas do not have a normative function. They cannot be used to limit or negate other ways of approaching the same subject. The reason he gives for that is:

> You cannot rise above the adequacy of the terms you employ. A dogma may be true in the sense that it expresses such interrelations of the subject matter as are expressible within the set of

36. *RM*, p. 138.
37. *RM*, p. 132.
38. *RM*, p. 142.
38. *RM*, p. 140.
40. *RM*, p. 126.
41. *RM*, p. 126.
42. *RM*, p. 77.

ideas employed. But if the same dogma be used intolerantly so as to check the employment of other modes of analyzing the subject matter, then, for all its truth, it will be doing the work of a falsehood.[43]

The latter statement raises the whole question of the nature and adequacy of religious language, to which we now turn.

WHITEHEAD'S CONCEPT OF LANGUAGE

According to Whitehead, language is like a sacrament. He writes: "Expression is the one fundamental sacrament. It is the outward and visible sign of an inward and spiritual grace."[44] Language is an outward sign of an inward reality: the religious experience itself.

> But the expressive sign is more than interpretable. It is creative. It elicits the intuition which interprets it. It cannot elicit what is not there. A note on a tuning fork can elicit a response from a piano. But the piano has already in it the string tuned to the same note. In the same way the expressive sign elicits the existent intuition which would not otherwise emerge into individual distinctiveness.[45]

But the basic intuitions that language evokes are deeper and more profound than the language is capable of expressing. In short, "We know more of the characters of those who are dear to us than we can express accurately in words. We may recognize the truth of some statement about them. It will be a new statement about something which we had already apprehended but had never formulated."[46] Thus it is that "the importance of rational religion in the history of modern culture is that it stands or falls with its fundamental position, that we know more than can be formulated in one finite systematized scheme of abstractions, however important that scheme may be in the elucidation of some aspect of the order of things."[47]

For Whitehead the essence of it all is this: language is inadequate to express the reality of that which it is an evocative sign. That is especially true of religious language because of the uniqueness of God. For whereas in ordinary language we speak of

43. *RM*, p. 126.
44. *RM*, p. 127.
45. *RM*, p. 128.
46. *RM*, p. 123.
47. *RM*, p. 137.

particular parts of the world, in religious language the whole world (i.e., God) is the object. Of language in general Whitehead writes, "A language is not a universal mode of expressing all ideas whatsoever. It is a limited mode of expressing such ideas as have been frequently entertained, and urgently needed, by the group of human beings who developed that mode of speech."[48] Elsewhere he adds, "Deficiencies of language stand in the way inexorably. Words and phrases must be stretched toward a generality foreign to their ordinary usage; . . . they remain metaphors mutely appealing for an imaginative leap."[49] The reason for that is that "language is thoroughly indeterminate, by reason of the fact that every occurrence presupposes some systematic type of environment." Thus "a precise language must await a completed metaphysical knowledge."[50] That is, of course, what Whitehead hoped to do in his process metaphysic. However, he recognized that because reality is in constant evolutionary flux and because the basis of meaning is experience, the meaning of words is subject to continual change. That is true not only about the world but also about God, because God's actuality is identified with the changing world.

WHITEHEAD'S CONCEPT OF TRUTH

Another factor fundamental to the whole topic of language, dogma, and Scripture is the matter of truth. In fact, Whitehead's view of truth is, from an evangelical point of view, perhaps the most crucial of all. In what sense is the Bible *true* for Whitehead? But first of all, what is truth? Broadly speaking truth is defined as the conformity of appearance with reality. But for Whitehead there are different levels of truth. "Thus, on the most basic level, the question of truth has to do with the conformity of affective tone in perceived actualities and those who perceive them."[51] In short Whitehead believes that there is some basis in a red object for what perceivers generally perceive as red. The "second level of truth-relation depends on the bodily sensibilities of a particular species." In other words, "appearances can be classified as 'true' when they correspond with the normal experience of a well-conditioned member of the species."[52] For example, the traffic signal

48. *RM*, p. 33.
49. *PR*, p. 6.
50. *PR*, p. 18.
51. Lyman Lundeen, *Risk and Rhetoric in Religion* (Philadelphia: Fortress, 1972), p. 177. Compare Alfred North Whitehead, *Adventures of Ideas* (New York: Macmillan, 1933), p. 247.
52. Lundeen, p. 177.

can be said to be red because normal people perceive it so even though some (color-blind) members of the race do not perceive it that way.

There is a third level of truth-relations that illuminates cultural symbols. "On this level, the truth-relation is quite indirect and does not depend on any causal connection between symbol and meaning, other than cultural association."[53] Whitehead calls conformity on that level "symbolic truth."[54] Those symbols have both an objective and subjective function. That is, they are partly descriptive but primarily evocative. Symbolism is required by the dynamic and creative dimensions of reality. In Whitehead's view both the speculative generalization and the empirical data are necessary for meaningful language. But "those societies which cannot combine reverence to their symbols with freedom of revision, must ultimately decay either from anarchy, or from the slow atrophy of a life stifled by useless shadows."[55] Religious language is also symbolic. That is, it is not to be understood literally but only "analogously" or metaphorically. "Words function between the limits of complete precision and radical equivocation."[56] However, Whitehead does not consider religious words purely noncognitive. They "verge on equivocation and sheer contradition, but they continue to function in a meaningful way expressing a partial grasp of realities, and by maintaining the tentative and approximate character of all knowledge and expression."[57] Thus there is some element of truth in religious language, however inadequately expressed.

In view of the inherent inadequacy of language and of the processive nature of reality, truth statements must always be understood as in the state of progress and capable of revision. For "progress in truth—truth of science and truth of religion—is mainly a progress in the framing of concepts, in discarding artificial abstractions or partial metaphors, and in evolving notions which strike more deeply into the root of reality."[58] Thus any given formulation of truth in one context may be false in another. In Whitehead's words, "this example brings out another fact: that a one-sided formulation may be true, but may have the effect of a lie by its distortion of emphasis."[59] In summation, religious

53. Ibid., p. 177.
54. Whitehead, *Adventures of Ideas*, p. 248.
55. Alfred North Whitehead, *Symbolism: Its Meaning and Effect* (New York: Capricorn, 1959), p. 88.
56. Lundeen, p. 185.
57. Ibid., p. 186.
58. *RM*, p. 127.
59. *RM*, p. 123.

truths are generalizations of particular experiences. "Religion starts from the generalization of final truths first perceived as exemplified in particular instances. These truths are amplified into a coherent system and applied to the interpretation of life. They stand or fall—like other truths—by their success in this interpretation."[60] But in the final analysis truth is not uni-leveled. It is variegated and multi-aspected. Religious language is perspectival. To borrow a phrase from another, Whitehead's view is a kind of "poly-mythic organicism." That is, there are many different (and even differing) linguistic ways (symbols) to evoke an experience with the organic whole of the universe (i.e., God).

WHITEHEAD'S VIEW OF SCRIPTURE

Whitehead has some high compliments for the Scriptures. He says, "The Bible is by far the most complete account of the coming of rationalism into religion, based on the earliest documents available."[61] However, our evangelical enthusiasm is dampened when we remember that he believed "rational religion emerged as a gradual transformation of the preexisting religious forms."[62] Like most modern thinkers Whitehead is not immune to the rationalistic and naturalistic inroads of negative higher criticism. He accepts the alleged antithesis between John and Paul, saying, "If the modern world is to find God, it must find him through love and not through fear, with the help of John and not of Paul."[63] He believes that at the hands of the apostle Paul, who ". . . had no first-hand contact with the original teaching . . ." of Christ, "something was added and something was lost; but fortunately the Gospels also survive."[64] Despite his backhanded compliment for the gospels Whitehead believes the Sermon on the Mount ". . . represents rationalism derived from direct intuition [of Christ] and divorced from dialectics."[65] As for the gospel records, they are no more than ". . . a peculiarly vivid record of the first response to it [Christ's life] in the minds of the first group of his disciples after the lapse of some years, with their recollections, interpretations, and incipient formularizations."[66]

In Whitehead's view much of the Old Testament does not fare

60. *RM*, p. 120.
61. *RM*, p. 29.
62. *RM*, p. 32.
63. *RM*, p. 73.
64. *RM*, p. 29-30.
65. *RM*, p. 57.
66. *RM*, p. 55.

as well as the New. Despite what he thinks are some noble psalms, "the other side comes out in the psalms expressing hate, psalms now generally withdrawn from public worship. The glorification of power has broken more hearts than it has healed." Indeed, some psalms are even barbaric wherein "there is the glorification of power, magnificent and barbaric." To that Whitehead adds, "I suppose that even the world itself could not contain the bones of those slaughtered because of men intoxicated by its attraction."[67] Whitehead's rejection of what he considers to be an imperial kind of (Semitic) theism leads him to other excesses in his criticism of the worship of the supreme God in the psalms. Commenting on Psalm 24, he says: "Magnificent literature! But there is no solution here of the difficulties which haunted Job. This worship of glory arising from power is not only dangerous: it arises from a barbaric conception of God."[68] Likewise, "There is also throughout the book [of Job] the undercurrent of fear lest an old-fashioned tribal god might take offense at this rational criticism."[69]

SHUBERT OGDEN'S PROCESS VIEW OF SCRIPTURE

Before we analyze the relation of process theology and Scripture we should point out what another significant process theologian, Shubert Ogden, says with regard to the Scriptures.

REJECTS ORTHODOX VIEW OF SCRIPTURE

Ogden recognizes but rejects the view that "what the Bible says, God says." He writes:

> In Protestant orthodoxy, then, the developed doctrine of the verbal inspiration of the canonical writings entailed the assertion of their uniform authority, and thus made it possible to claim without qualification that "what Scripture says, God says." But, with the emergence of Protestant liberal theology and its commitment to the historical-critical method, as well as its insistence that Scripture neither is nor can be a sufficient authorization for the meaning and truth of theological assertions, this claim was abandoned, never again to be made by those who have led in the subsequent important developments in Protestant theology.[70]

---

67. *RM*, p. 54.
68. *RM*, p. 54.
69. *RM*, p. 49.
70. Shubert Ogden, "The Authority of Scripture for Theology," *Interpretation* 30, no. 3(July 1976):257.

ACCEPTS NEGATIVE HIGHER CRITICISM

Ogden believes that theology is necessarily dependent on negative higher criticism. He believes that " 'the historic, apostolic Christ,' just like 'the historic, biblical Christ,' is every bit as historical as 'the so-called historical Jesus,' and to this extent there is no escaping the dependence of theology on the work of the historians. On the contrary, we must insist that historical-critical inquiry is *theologically* necessary and legitimate."[71]

SEES A CHRISTOLOGICAL "CANON" WITH THE BIBLE

> Given our present historical methods and knowledge, the locus of the canon—in the early church's own sense of the apostolic witness—cannot be the writings of the New Testament as such but can only be the earliest traditions of Christian witness accessible to us today by historical-critical analysis of those writings. Specifically, the canon of the church, and hence also the highest authority for theology, must now be located in what form critics generally speak of as the earliest layer of the Synoptic tradition, or what Marxsen in particular refers to as "the Jesus-kerygma," as distinct both from "the Christ-kerygma" and from "the mixed form of the Jesus-kerygma and the Christ-kerygma" that we find expressed in the writings of the New Testament. Accordingly, the witness to which theological assertions must be appropriate is not the *scriptural* witness typically spoken of in most postliberal Protestant theology, but rather, the *apostolic* witness, which is to be discerned by critical interpretation of this earliest layer of Christian tradition or kerygma.[72]

REJECTS APOSTOLIC AUTHORSHIP OF NEW TESTAMENT BOOKS

Given his acceptance of negative higher criticism it is not surprising to hear Ogden say, "It is now commonly acknowledged that none of the New Testament writings, in its present form, was authored by an apostle or one of his disciples. Even the authentic letters of Paul come from one who was only indirectly an apostle in this sense, in that he was not a witness of Jesus' earthly life, having seen only the risen One."[73] Quoting Marxsen's words Ogden believes "the norm for the church, therefore, is not the New Testament but, rather, the *apostolic witness.* This witness is, of course, found in the New Testament, but it is not identical with

71. Ibid., p. 256.
72. Ibid., p. 258.
73. Ibid., p. 251.

the New Testament. In the strict sense only the apostolic testimony to Jesus as the Divine revelation can be described as canonical."

REJECTS THE BIBLE AS THE SUPREME AUTHORITY

Traditionally Protestants have held to Scripture as the supreme authority for faith and practice. Ogden clearly rejects that historic position,[74] writing:

> We today must indeed recognize a higher theological authority than the canon of Scripture, and hence can no longer maintain that Scripture is in some sense the sole primary authority for Christian theology. The theological authority of Scripture, great as it may be, is nevertheless a limited authority, in that it could conceivably be greater than it is—namely, as great as that of the apostolic witness by which it itself is and is to be authorized.[75]

REJECTS THE BIBLE AS THE SOLE AUTHORITY FOR FAITH

Not only does Shubert Ogden reject the Bible as the supreme or final authority for the Christian faith but he does not even see it as the sole source for faith. Thus he insists:

> Most discussions of our question have proceeded on the assumption that to determine what is or is not a theological authority is *eo ipso* to determine what is or is not a sufficient authorization for the meaning and truth of theological assertions. Thus it is commonly inferred that, if Scripture is in any sense the sole primary authority for Christian theology, Scripture is also in some sense the sole sufficient authorization that the claims of Christian theology are meaningful and true. My contention, however, is that this assumption is unfounded and that the common inference concerning Scripture as a theological authority must be rejected.[76]

Ogden's view at this point is very Catholic, as the following excerpt shows:

> Therefore, we have every reason to accept the further conclusion that Marxsen draws with characteristic candor: . . . the alternative stated again and again from the Protestant side ever since the Reformation is no genuine alternative at all. According to the traditional formulation, we Protestants maintain *"sola scriptura"*

74. Ibid., p. 252.
75. Ibid., p. 252.
76. Ibid., p. 252.

(canonical Scripture alone), while the Catholics hold to "Scripture and tradition." But that is not a real alternative; for whoever admits *"sola scriptura"* (Scripture alone), which is to say, the New Testament canon of Athanasius and the Synod of Rome, thereby also always admits tradition, the decision of the church. . . . Given the alternative, "Scripture alone" or "Scripture and tradition," the Roman Catholic Church undoubtedly has the better position; for (this I say quite sharply) whoever admits *sola scriptura*, in the sense of holding that the canonical New Testament is the sole norm, rule, and standard, goes the way of the Roman Catholic— only not as consistently.[77]

BIBLE HAS ONLY FUNCTIONAL (CHRISTOLOGICAL) AUTHORITY

Besides not believing that the Bible is either the supreme or sole authority for faith, Ogden does not believe it has *any* authority at all. He contends this

> . . . point can be made by observing the general distinction between *de facto* and *de jure* authority. Authority may be said to exist *de facto* whenever one person recognizes another, or some agent or instrument of another, as having the right to command or to act as regards his own action or belief. Thus Scripture may be said to have a *de facto* authority for theology whenever a theologian recognizes that the writings of the canonical authors are entitled to function as a standard or norm for determining the appropriateness of his assertions to the Christian witness of faith. . . . Moreover, not even Scripture is understood to be an exception to this rule when it, in turn, is claimed to have unique theological authority; for, according to the so-called material principle of the Reformers, it is Christ alone who authorizes Scripture as *norma-normans, sed non normata.* Just because Scripture is uniquely normative over all other theological sources or norms it itself ultimately stands on the same level as those who are subject to its authority *vis-à-vis* Jesus the Christ.[78]

What then is the authority of the Bible? It is a function but not an essential authority. It is an authority insofar as it brings Christ to us. Ogden writes:

> In this connection, it may not be entirely misleading to recall that a somewhat similar point was made by the older orthodoxy concerning the "perfection" of Scripture. This perfection, it was

77. Ibid., p. 253.
78. Ibid., p. 246.

claimed, . . . a perfection with respect to the end of man's salvation, and so to witnessing to all that is necessary to the attainment of that end. By analogy with this claim, we may say that the authority of Scripture, also, can only be an . . . authority with respect to the end of bearing the distinctively Christian witness of faith and, therefore, so far as theology is concerned, an authority for determining the appropriateness of its assertions.[79]

If we were to ask, How can Christ be the authority for the true canon within Scripture when what we know about Christ comes from the canon of Scripture? Ogden would reply that Christ and Scripture are dependent on each other, for "even though it is solely the Christ meant in these traditions who authorizes what they say, it is solely through what they say that we have directly to do with the Christ who is the source of their authority and, through them, all other theological authority."[80]

PROCESS THEOLOGY'S VIEW OF GOD AND SCRIPTURE

In order to see more fully the kinds of implications that can and have been drawn by process theologians about the Bible it will be helpful to look briefly at the contribution of other process theologians.

GOD THE COSMIC PERSUADER

The primary process motif Lewis Ford borrows from Whitehead and with which he approaches Scripture is that of God as the persistent persuader who seeks to lure the universe toward increasing value. According to Ford, Whitehead admired Plato's belief that "the divine element in the world is to be conceived as a persuasive agency and not as a coercive agency." That, Ford believes, is "one of the greatest intellectual discoveries in the history of religion."[81] Ford honestly acknowledges that kind of explanation does not square with all the facts of Scripture, but that does not dissuade his systematic efforts. He writes:

Our justification for the appeal to divine persuasion is broadly philosophical: its inherent reasonableness, its applicability to all we know about the world we live in, and its consonance with our

79. Ibid., p. 245.
80. Ibid., p. 255.
81. Lewis Ford, "Biblical Recital and Process Philosophy," *Interpretation* 26, no. 2(April 1972):198.

best ethical and religious insights. As such, it is at least a partially alien criterion by which to appreciate biblical traditions, since their understanding of divine power is rather different. Therefore we cannot propose divine persuasion as a unifying theme whereby all Old Testament traditions can be systematically correlated. We can recommend process theism, however, for the hermeneutical task of translating these traditions into a systematic context appropriate to our contemporary situation, without thereby losing Israel's peculiar witness to the action of God in her history.[82]

PROCESS VIEW OF THE DOCTRINE OF CREATION

Ex nihilo creation is rejected because it is coercive. Ford writes:

> Quite apart from biblical precedents, the temptation to interpret God's role in creation by means of coercive power is extremely great. If the entire created order is dependent for its existence upon his will, then it must be subject to his full control. . . . Insofar as God controls the world, he is responsible for evil: directly in terms of the natural order, and indirectly in the case of man.[83]

Instead of the coercive terms of *ex nihilo* creation we must think of creation in persuasive terms: "Conceived in terms of persuasion, creation is the shaping and structuring of that which already exists into newer and richer forms." Furthermore, ". . . the Old Testament traditions concerning creation, whether in P, J, Second Isaiah, or The Psalms, do not insist upon *creatio ex nihilo*, though this is expressed in later passages such as II Maccabees 7:28." Basically "the *ex nihilo* doctrine is a protective gesture designed to safeguard the essential goodness of God's creation and man's responsibility in the fall."[84]

How then is God related to the world if not as Creator of it? The answer is: God is not Creator but companion of the world. For "God is not the cosmic watchmaker, but the husbandman in the vineyard of the world, fostering and nurturing its continuous evolutionary growth throughout all ages." God "is the companion and friend who inspires us to achieve the very best that is within us. God creates by persuading the world to create itself."[85] In brief, God is not in absolute control of the universe. For "if God's

82. Ibid., p. 209.
83. Ibid., p. 201.
84. Ibid., p. 203.
85. Ibid., p. 202.

control over the world is absolute such that it is independent of all creaturely contingencies, then God's activity may flow directly from his unchanging nature which is wholly necessary and self-sufficient."[86]

PROCESS VIEW OF THE DOCTRINE OF PROVIDENCE

The doctrine of divine providence is also recast in terms of persuasion. Ford writes:

> From the standpoint of divine persuasion, providence is simply another way of looking at God's guidance of the historical process already manifest in creation. Classical omnipotence, however, in affirming God's sovereign control over the future, must look for a final break with the ambiguities of history in which God's goodness is unambiguously made manifest.[87]

PROCESS VIEW OF PROPHECY

One of the consequences of the process view of God is that predictive prophecy is eliminated, at least in any infallible sense.

> Divine providence cannot be understood as the unfolding of a predetermined course of events. Prophecy is not prediction, but the proclamation of divine intent, dependent for its realization upon the continued presence of those conditions which called forth that intent and upon the emergence of the means whereby that intent may be realized. Isaiah's proclamation of the destruction of Judah was dependent upon the further, persistent opposition of Israel to God's commandments and upon the power of Assyria. God becomes the great improvisor and opportunist seeking at every turn to elicit his purpose from every situation: if not by the hand of Sennacherib, then by the hand of Nebuchadnezzar.[88]

In that sense "history is quite contingent and open-ended in its making, but it becomes the way in which God achieves his purposes in one way or another." For "if the nation of Israel will not actualize his redeeming purpose for man, then the task must be reserved for the faithful remnant, and if the faithful remnant fails, then that purpose may become focused upon a single carpenter from Nazareth."[89] But God persists in His persuasion until

86. Ibid., p. 207.
87. Ibid., p. 205.
88. Ibid., p. 206.
89. Ibid., p. 206.

He accomplishes the maximal good possible. However, God is not in sovereign control of history but is in a continual dialogue with it. In Ford's words:

> God proposes and the world disposes. The creature may or may not embody that divine urge toward greater complexity, but insofar as that ideal is actualized, an evolutionary advance has been achieved. This process is directed but not controlled, for the necessary self-activity of the creature requires spontaneity of response. . . . Not only we ourselves but the entire created order, whether consciously or unconsciously, is open to this divine persuasion, each in its own way.[90]

Thus it is just as true to say that history shapes God as it is that God shapes history. For "history need not be solely an immanent process which can at best point only symbolically to the divine, for that historical involvement may also shape the concrete actuality of God himself."[91] So even God cannot predetermine the future. For "historical development is completely open-ended, for process thought does not impose any particular pattern of historical development upon history, since God is ever resourceful in finding new perfections for creation to strive for."[92]

PROCESS VIEW OF THEODICY

If God is not in omnipotent control of the world how can He overcome evil? The answer is that even God cannot guarantee in advance the outcome, but He keeps pressing on. For "divine persuasion responds to the problem of evil radically, simply denying that God exercises full control over the world. Plato sought to express this by saying that God does the best job he can in trying to persuade a recalcitrant matter to receive the impress of the divine forms."[93]

If one wonders just how God can influence without determining the outcome of world events the answer lies in the luring power of God. For "God furnishes the initial direction, but the creature is responsible for its own actualization, whether for good or for evil."[94]

But just how can there be any certainty of the outcome if God

90. Ibid., p. 203.
91. Lewis Ford, *The Lure of God* (Philadelphia: Fortress, 1978), p. 28.
92. Ibid., p. 27.
93. Ford, "Biblical Recital and Process Philosophy," p. 202.
94. Ibid., pp. 202-3.

is not in sovereign control? In a frank admission one process theologian writes, "Sure of the direction, possibly, yes. But the details of the aim, the specificity of the aim, this is the individual's decision and choice and knowledge alone." For "during that process God, as it were, has to wait with bated breath until the decision is made, not simply to find out what the decision was, but perhaps even to have the situation clarified by virtue of the decision of that concrete occasion."[95]

The only other alternative that process theologians see to that solution is a completely determined and closed future. For if man is free then God cannot know the future until it actually happens. As Ford puts it, "God's generic attributes are necessary and his steadfast purpose is everlasting, but his experience and concrete activity are also dependent upon the contingencies of the world." That is, "God knows all there is to know, but if the future is genuinely open-ended, awaiting contingent creaturely actualization, it is not yet 'there' to be known." For "God knows all actualities as actual and all possibilities as possible, but to 'know' a future possibility as if it were already actual would be to know something which is not the case, and this would be to know falsely." Thus "God's omniscience, his total experience of the world, is constantly growing and being enriched by the world's growth."[96]

PROCESS VIEW OF REVELATION

Process theologians have delineated the sense in which they are willing to talk of the Bible as a divine "revelation." Although Ogden does admit there are passages in the Bible that support the orthodox view of revelation, he hastens to add, "Scripture does not characteristically appeal to revelation as providing special knowledge of God's existence and nature."[97] For "*what* Christian revelation reveals to man is nothing new, since such truths as it makes explicit must already be known to him implicitly in every moment of existence."[98]

There does seem to be agreement among process theologians that the evangelical view of propositional revelation is wrong.

---

95. Bernard Loomer, "A Response to David R. Griffin," *Encounter* 36, no. 4(Autumn 1975):365.
96. Ford, "Biblical Recital and Process Philosophy," p. 208.
97. Shubert Ogden, "On Revelation," in *Our Common History as Christians* (New York: Oxford U., 1975), p. 272.
98. Ibid., p. 287.

Henry Wieman writes, "Let us now turn back again to the first distinction we made, that the revelation is not any set of propositions about God but is the actual presence of the saving and sustaining power. This being the case, the teaching of the New Testament writers about the revelation should not be identified with the revelation itself."[99]

What then is revelation according to the process view? The various answers follow closely those of many neo-othodox theologians. Revelation is a saving act of God. As Bernard Loomer puts it, "There is no revelation that does not involve salvation to one degree or another."[100] Wieman speaks of revelation as fellowship or communion with God.[101] In agreement with that David Griffin notes that ". . . for an event to become a revelation it must be *received* as such by someone. By definition, a revelation must be a revelation to someone, whereas an act of God is what it is independently of any person's recognition of it."[102] Trying to find some common ground between the admittedly radically different views of Barth and Tillich on that point, Wieman suggests, "They all agree implicitly that the communion which occurred in the fellowship of Jesus was and is the event necessarily involved in the revelation. But they fail to see that it is the very revelation itself."[103]

One of the more creative naturalistic explanations of revelation in terms of Whiteheadian metaphysics is offered by Jerry Korsmeyer. He suggests that "revelation" is akin to physical resonance. He writes, "In keeping with Whitehead's premise to start from human experience in the world, I propose as a model for revelation an analogy with the physical phenomenon of resonance." He describes reasonance as "a physical phenomenon shown by a vibrating system, which responds with maximum amplitude under the action of a force applied with a frequency that is a natural frequency of the vibrating body."[104]

Thus, "Insofar as each creature's final subjective aim is in accord with God's aim there is a resonance in which the effect of God's presence is maximized. This phenomenon, I suggest, may be

99. Henry N. Wieman, "The Revelation of God in Christ," *Process Studies* 10, 1-2 (Spring-Summer 1980):2-17.
100. Loomer, "Response to David R. Griffen," p. 362.
101. Wieman, "The Revelation of God in Christ," p. 16.
102. David Griffin, "Relativism, Divine Causation, and Biblical Theology," *Encounter* 36, no. 4(Autumn 1975):345.
103. Wieman, "The Revelation of God in Christ," pp. 13-14.
104. Jerry Korsmeyer, "A Resonance Model for Revelation," *Process Studies* (1976):195.

consciously felt as God's initiative. When one responds to it, an interpersonal communion is formed which we call revelation." From the process point of view the model seems to be a good one because "the resonance model safeguards the theologian's insistence that the initiative lies with God but that the individual is self-creating in forming the intersubjective communion that is revelation."[105]

PROCESS VIEW OF MIRACLES

Some process theologians distinguish between "general revelation" and "special revelation." Says Griffin, "General revelation would occur whenever someone correctly interprets an event in such a way as to learn something of God."[106] A special act of God or "miracle" occurs when the subjective aim or an event in the world agrees to a high degree with the subjective aim given it by God's initial persuasive lure. "That is, the subjective aim of the one event may conform almost exactly with the ideal aim received from God, while the subjective aim of the other may diverge as far as possible from the ideal impulse it received from God."[107]

In no way should the coalesence of the divine and human events be considered the result of divine causality. For, Griffin argues, "regarded from this perspective, no reference to God's causation is needed." For such would be a deterministic interruption into the free and open process of the universe. However, he insists that it is appropriate to call them "special revelations of God" since ". . . they are events (1) in which the divine initial aims can, if actualized, account for a unique aspect of the events, (2) in which the initial aim is indeed actualized to a high degree and thereby allowed to be extraordinarily effective, and (3) in which the content of the initial aim, and therefore the subjective aim, reflects the general divine aim to an extraordinary degree."[108]

Griffin is frankly aware that view assumes a naturalistic perspective. He offers the following brief reasons for his view:

> Also, the liberal position is taken for granted here that this must be done, if at all, without positing occasional interruptions of the normal course of events. The affirmation of such interruptions is

105. Ibid., pp. 195-96.
106. Griffin, "Is Revelation Coherent?" *Theology Today* 28, no. 3(October 1971):294.
107. Griffin, "Relativism, Divine Causation," pp. 351-52.
108. Ibid., pp. 353-54.

increasingly incredible; it would violate one of the axioms of modern historiography, and hence put the Christian historian outside the circle of recognized historians (which would be unfortunate if it is unnecessary); and, in application to Jesus, it would imply a docetic rejection of his full humanity.[109]

Given the naturalistic stance of process theology it comes as no surprise to hear the resurrection of Christ explained by Wieman as a subjective experience of the disciples. Here are his words:

> After the crucifixion came the resurrection. The resurrection was an experience the disciples had three days after the terrible shock of Jesus' death on the cross. It took that long for the numbness of the shock to wear away so that they could again respond to one another and to the past in the way that they had done in the living fellowship with Jesus. So vivid and so powerful was this recovery of the kind of interchange with one another that they had had when Jesus was alive with them that it produced the feeling of his actual presence with them in bodily form. Many have had this experience after the death of someone deeply involved in their lives. Either they had this psychological illusion, which would be very natural, or, what is more likely, when they tried to tell of their experience the only way they could tell it was in words that led others to think they were speaking of the bodily presence. This would be most likely to happen after the story had passed through many mouths in an age that believed bodies rose from the dead.[110]

AN EVALUATION OF THE PROCESS VIEW OF SCRIPTURE

It is evident in view of the foregoing discussion that there is a great gulf between the process and evangelical view of Scripture. Theologians on both sides can see the gulf. The question then is this: On what side of the gulf should one be standing? The answer to that has many dimensions and several approaches, as we shall now discuss.

A HISTORICAL EVALUATION

If one were to judge process theology regarding God and Scripture in terms of historic Christian theologians and confessions of faith, it would be found seriously wanting. Its views of God, revelation, miracles, Christ, and the Bible are simply not those of

109. Ibid., p. 349.
110. Wieman, "The Revelation of God in Christ," p. 6.

orthodox Christianity or its great teachers (e.g., Augustine, Anselm, Aquinas, or Calvin). In fact, in many areas the process theologians themselves admit that. Traditional theistic Christianity believes in a transcendent, sovereign God who created the world *ex nihilo*, who on occasions interrupts its regular patterns with miracles, who in the Person of Christ came in human flesh, and who supernaturally inspired the propositional revelation of Scripture. Since it is generally acknowledged by scholars on both sides of the debate that that is what Augustine, Anselm, Aquinas, and the Reformers believed, there is no need to labor the point. Process theology is not in line with the historic position of the mainstream of Christian theologians and creedal statements through the Reformation. So whatever else may be said in favor of the position, *process theology is not the mainline, historic Christian position.*

A BIBLICAL EVALUATION

Despite the regular appeal to the biblical anthropomorphic descriptions of God as changing, no process theologian of which I am aware accepts all that the Bible teaches about God, Christ, miracles, and the origin of Scripture. Most often, by their own admission, process theologians reject much of Scripture. Whitehead rejects the Old Testament concept of God, speaking of it as a barbaric glorification of power. Ogden follows Bultmann in demythologizing the gospels. He rejects the orthodox doctrine of inspiration, accepts negative higher criticism, and rejects the apostolic authorship of even some New Testament books that claim to be so authored. In fact, Ogden does not even accept *sola Scriptura.*

Lewis Ford lashes out against the biblical concept of God as sovereign Creator, the concept of predictive prophecy, and divine determination of the future. In his own words his view involves "at least partially alien criterion by which to appreciate biblical traditions, since their view of divine power is rather different."[111] In a perhaps overly frank reaction against the biblical picture of God's supremacy one process theologian even refers to God as "a big bully."[112]

One of the more honest acknowledgments of Whitehead's deviation from the biblical position came in a friendly analysis of his

---

111. Ford, "Biblical Recital and Process Philosophy," p. 21.
112. Lyman T. Lundeen "The Authority of the Word in a Process Perspective," *Encounter* 36, no. 4(Autumn 1975):285.

use of Scripture. First, Frederic R. Crownfield lists his factual findings:

> Of the 119 references, 48 per cent are to the Old Testament, 52 per cent to the New. Most often referred to in the O. T. are Genesis (15 times), I Kings (8 times) and Psalms (7 times). Some 64 per cent of the O. T. references are to narratives. In the New Testament the Gospels account for most of the references (45, or 72 per cent). The Pauline Epistles (raising no questions about II Thess.) account for 8, I John for 4. Among the Gospels Matthew is the favorite (29 references, almost half the total for the N. T.), with John second (10 references). Mark seems never to be noticed, reflecting the fact that prior to the rise of modern critical theories Augustine's slighting comment about the second gospel led to its general neglect.[113]

After an impressive survey of the facts, Crownfield makes some revealing comments on the way in which Whitehead uses Scipture. He notes: "He uses the Biblical material in various ways: often as an illustration of the point he is trying to make, but frequently simply as the source of a telling phrase which *he uses in his own way, without regard to its original meaning* (item 55). He uses the same passage to make quite different points." In a final note Crownfield adds, *"There is nothing in this study to indicate that Whitehead got any of his philosophical or religious ideas directly from his contact with the Bible."*[114] To that we might add that most other process theologians are subject to the same basic criticism. In a word, whatever else may be said in favor of the view, *process theology is definitely not a consistent biblical position.*

A PHILOSOPHICAL EVALUATION

The comments here will fall into two categories. First, we shall offer a brief response to the process critique of traditional theism. Then, we shall subject some of the basic premises on process theology to philosophical analysis.

Is traditional theism incoherent? According to Ogden* there are basic contradictions with the traditional theistic view of God. Let us briefly examine his alleged antinomies.

---

113. Frederick R. Crownfield, "Whitehead's References to the Bible," *Process Studies* 6, no. 4(Winter 1976):277.
114. Ibid., p. 278 (italics added).
   *For an excellent evaluation of Ogden's theology see the recent Boston University dissertation by Dr. David Beck, *Shubert Ogden on the Relationship Between Theology and Philosophy* (1980).

First of all, let us look at the antinomy of creation. It is true that traditional theists believed that God was necessary and simple and that His will was one with His essence. But does it follow that God must necessarily create? Aquinas did not think so. He explicitly addresses that issue in these words: "As to things willed by God, we must observe that He wills something of absolute necessity; but this is not true of all that He wills." For example, "God wills the being of His own goodness necessarily. . . . But God wills things other than Himself in so far as they are ordered to His own goodness as their ends."[115] For although God wills necessarily His own goodness, He does not necessarily will things willed because of His goodness; for it can exist without other things."[116] That is, God is necessary existence, and He must necessarily will His own existence. All other things are contingent existence, and God does not have to will them necessarily. Thus the "divine knowing has a necessary relation to the thing known; not the divine willing, however, to the thing willed. The reason for this is that knowledge is of things as they exist in the knower; but since "all other things have a necessary being inasmuch as they exist in God, but no absolute necessity to be necessary in themselves, it follows that God knows necessarily whatever He knows, but does not will necessarily whatever He wills." But how is it that God's knowledge of creation can be necessary without creation's being necessary? Aquinas answers: "It is not natural to God to will any of those other things that He does not will necessarily: and yet it is not unnatural or contrary to His nature, but voluntary."[118] That is to say, whatever is in the nature of God is there necessarily, but it is not in the nature of God that everything flow from Him with necessity. Therefore, God can be a necessary Being and yet creation can flow from Him freely. Thus traditional theism is not hereby incoherent, as Ogden claims.

The second antinomy is that of service. Is it true that there is no significant sense in which our service can be *for* God? Certainly if *for* means to *add to the nature or perfection of* an absolutely perfect God then no service can be *for* God. The absolutely perfect theistic God needs nothing to enrich His *nature*. However, that does not mean that service is not in any significant sense *for* God. It may be that God does not *need* our service but that He *wants* it.

115. Thomas Aquinas *Summa Theologica* 1. 19. 3.
116. Ibid., reply to objection 2.
117. Ibid., reply to objection 6.
118. Ibid., reply to objection 3.

Why does God want our service? For one thing He wants it *for* His glory. So although our service does not add to God's attributes, it nevertheless does add to His glory. Glory is the outward manifestation of the inward character of God. Glory is to God what a magnifying glass is to a beautiful object; it does not change the nature of the object, but it does *exalt it in the viewer's eyes.* Thus it is with our creaturely service for the Creator. We cannot add to His essence, but we can enhance His character before the universe. In terms of the popular adage "What do you give to someone who has everything?" the response is admiration. And what can we give to the God who already has (is) everything? Give Him worship! For "true worshipers will worship the Father in spirit and truth, for such the Father seeks to worship him" (John 4:23, RSV). In a significant sense, then, we can render service *for* God. But to think that mere creatures can do more *for* God, such as changing His nature, is sheer vanity.

We consider now the third antinomy, that of relationship. Is it true that all genuine relationships involve mutual dependence? It may be true that all *human* relationships involve mutual dependence, but it is gross misuse of anthropomorphism to assume that God is human. The only way Ogden's antinomy would succeed is if it were to beg the question in favor of process theology by assuming that God is finite and dependent. But if one already assumes the truth of a process view of God as an objection against the nonprocess view of God then he has committed *petitio principi.*

When the issue of meaningful relationships is stated differently the antinomy vanishes. Let us define all meaningful relationships between persons as loving relations. And let us define a two-way loving relationship as one in which both parties give and receive love. In that sense there is no contradiction involved in God's loving us and in our loving God, so long as we remember that "we love, because He first loved us" (1 John 4:19, NASB). The difference is that we *need* love but God only *desires* it. So God loves and desires to be loved; that is all that genuine interpersonal relations demand. To insist that God *needs* to be loved before He can have a genuinely personal relationship is to demean His perfect love to the level of our finite love. Thus in the process view of God it is wrong to affirm with Scripture that "God *is* love." It would be more appropriate to say, "God is *in need of* love!"

Fourth, we consider Hartshorne's antinomy of supreme reality. Does it follow that either God must include all reality or else He cannot be supreme? The answer is: it all depends on what is meant by "include all reality." If one means God must include all reality *in His being* (essence) then the theist's answer is no. Further, if that is the meaning then Hartshorne has already begged the question in favor of panentheism (process theology) by assuming from the outset that theism is wrong because panentheism is right, that is, because God must include all reality in Himself.

There is, however, another possible way in which God can be supreme and still "include all reality." He can include all reality either in Himself or else *in His power.* That is, if God created all reality *ex nihilo* (as theists claim), then He "includes all reality" either in essence or else in His creative control. To put it another way, "all reality" pre-exists in God either actually (as does His own essence) or potentially (as does the creation). And when God actualized that potentiality (i.e., when He created the world) it existed in His sovereign control. Hence, He is supreme and Hartshorne's objection fails.

Actually, one could object as well to Hartshorne's use of the word *reality.* God is "all reality" in one sense and is not in another. God is all reality in the sense of the *source* and sustainer of all but not in the sense of the *substance* of all reality. That is, there are *other* realities than God, but they do not constitute *more* reality than God. For when the teacher teaches the class there is not more knowledge; there are simply more who know. Likewise, when God created (finite) beings there was not more being, there were simply more who had it. God *is* pure being (being itself); all other things *have* being by causal (creational) dependence on Him.

In response to the fifth antinomy, that of contingent truth, the theist may point out that all of God's knowledge is necessary, even His knowledge of the contingent. Simply because the *event* is contingent does not mean that God's *knowledge* of it is contingent. Certainly the theistic God of Augustine and Aquinas has no problem knowing everything that can be known (both actual and possible) in a necessary way, because He is a simple and eternal being for whom there is a simultaneous and eternal presence of all that He knows.

The necessity of God's knowledge can be seen from considering His omniscience alone. For omniscience places necessity on all events, because an omniscient mind cannot be wrong about what it knows. So whatever God knows about the future *must* (of necessity) come to pass. That does not mean, however, that God forces or coerces all events to happen. It means simply that He knows *necessarily* and eternally (presently) it will happen, even if it results from finite free choice. As Aquinas puts it, "It is manifest that contingent things are infallibly known by God, inasmuch as they are subject to the divine sight in their presentiality; and yet they are future contingent things in relation to their own causes." So then, "things known by God are contingent because of their proximate causes, while the knowledge of God, which is the first cause, is necessary."[119] So here too the alleged antinomy fails. Theism is not incoherent.

Our conclusion is that process theologians have not shown any incoherence in traditional theism. On the contrary, their arguments, if anything, have shown an inferiority in process theism. For they have insisted that God must be imperfect, dependent, and human in order to be God. In other words, God must be like man in order to be God. In that regard the saying has come true of process theologians—God has made men in His image, and they have returned the compliment!

IS PROCESS THEOLOGY INCOHERENT?

It is unfair simply to assume the truth of our position (traditional theism) in order to criticize process theology. What seems to us to be more appropriate is to criticize it on its own ground. Thus we will ask the question, Is process theology coherent? Can it make good some of its central claims in a self-consistent way? Our discussion will focus on two central concepts, God and truth.

Process theology's concept of God. It is a strange irony that the process theologian has attacked the theist's concept of a necessary God and a contingent world as incoherent. For process theologians themselves speak of God (in His primordial pole) as being necessary and then proceed to tell us that His other pole is contingent. They say God is eternal, unchanging, and necessary in His primordial pole and yet He is temporal, changing, and contingent in His consequent pole. Now if necessity-contingency (and the like) are mutually exclusive categories when used by theists to speak of the relation of God and the world, then *how much more are they incompatible when both are placed within the very bipolar nature of God!* The antinomy of contradiction of Creator and creation is not resolved by combining the necessary Creator and the contingent creation into one being, is it? Surely if there is an antinomy in theism because of those mutually exclusive cate-

119. Ibid., 1. 14. 13, reply to object 1. See also Augustine *City of God* 5. 9.

gories, then process theology is incoherent, a fortiori.

There are several possible ways out of that incoherence for process theology. First, process theologians could disclaim any sense of nontemporal necessity in the universe. That is, they could deny the "primordial nature" of God. In that case there would be nothing to account for permanence and order in the world. Further, that would mean that literally "all is change." But if all were change then even the sentence "all is changing" would have no stable meaning by which one could understand what process theologians mean by their position. That basic incoherence is stated dramatically in Hartshorne's own words when he admits, "Relativity is the absolute principle. . . ! Indeed, it is as absolute as absoluteness." And, "if there is an eternal Being, it is some ultimate form of becoming."[120] But if all is relative and changing then their very position would be incoherent for they could not even state it without implying that something does not change (namely, the meaning of the statement of their position). Furthermore, one cannot simply posit relativity as absolute (nonrelativity) without contradiction. At a minimum such a position has sacrificed coherence.

Another option process theologians might take is to argue that God's necessity and nontemporality are conditioned by the contingent, temporal world. That is, there is a mutual dependence of God on the world and of the world on God. Now it seems to me that is indeed what many process theologians are saying. And why can it not be so? The answer again is: It seems to be an incoherent or contradictory position. How can God be dependent on that which depends on Him? How can God be the cause of that which is causing Himself? An obvious process response might be: He is not the cause *in the same sense* in which the world is causing Him. But if that is the case, then there must be some sense in which God is *completely independent* of the world's causality. For if God is somehow completely independent of the world, and not causally dependent on the world, then process theology collapses back into the theistic concept of a God who is causally independent of the world.

Perhaps the best way to understand the incoherence of process theology is to ask this question: If the whole world (God's consequent nature) were to go out of existence would there be any reality left to God? If they say no then it is obvious that God is really totally contingent and dependent and in no sense necessar-

120. Hartshorne, *Creative Synthesis*, pp. 46-47.

ily independent. But that is both contrary to their claim and to the fundamental principle that every event (or series of events) has a cause. If on the other hand they answer yes, there would be something left to God if the whole actual world were to perish completely, then they are really traditional theists in disguise! For in that case they believe there is behind the whole changing world a necessary, unchanging, and eternal being who is independent of that world. In summary, the only way to make the process view coherent is to transform it into theism.

Process theology's concept of truth. According to process theology truth is changing and relative. There are no absolute and infallible dogmas that are not subject to the flux of time. As Ogden puts it,

> Prior to the development of modern historical consciousness, it could be assumed that agreement with the received understanding of an allegedly infallible Scripture or dogma was a sufficient test of the appropriateness of a theological statement. But we now realize only too well that Scripture and dogma themselves, as well as any supposed understanding of them, are so thoroughly historical as to render any such test insufficient.[121]

He adds, "And for the same reason, we now recognize that what one epoch or culture accepts as criteria of meaning and truth by no means needs to be accepted by another. As a matter of fact, aware as we are that . . . even in logic and mathematics, we know that even the most fundamental conditions of understandability may be subject to change."[122] Even basic statements such as "I exist" are not necessarily true "since it is true and can be true only contingently."[123] Charles Hartshorne does not blush to admit that "a consequence of this view which troubles some is that it conflicts with the venerable dogma that 'truth is timeless.'" Why, we may ask, is that so? Hartshorne says it is so because "specific forms cannot be eternal or unalterable."[124] In short, truth is a characteristic of propositions. A proposition is true if it corresponds to reality and false if it does not. But because reality is changing, the truth of a proposition changes with the change in reality.

121. Shubert Ogden, "What Is Theology?" *Journal of Religion* 52, no. 1(January 1972):26.
122. Ibid.
123. Shubert Ogden, "The Criterion of Metaphysical Truth and the Senses of 'Metaphysics,'" *Process Studies* 5, no. 1(Spring 1975):47.
124. Hartshorne, *Creative Synthesis*, p. 135.

In that regard some Whiteheadians see a similarity between their mentor and Ludwig Wittgenstein, who held that meaning is based in changing forms of life. As applied to the interpetation of Scripture the conventionalist theory of meaning would take on a form as follows: "Since propositions elicited by the text tend to be felt in ways which lead to the entertaining of allied propositions with slightly different subjects or forms of definiteness, *meaning is cumulative and thoroughly temporal.*"[125] Briefly stated, meaning is based in temporal and changing experience, and since truth statements must be meaningful it follows that truth too is temporal and changing.

Process theologians are not unaware of the problematic nature of their theories of meaning and truth and have struggled to make them coherent. John Cobb, for example, confesses, "I expressed my own acquiescence in this relativistic understanding to a considerable degree. It is because no philosophy can be regarded as philosophically absolute." Nevertheless, he continues, "in Whitehead's vision the relativity of philosophies need not have so debilitating an effect as some views of the relativity of thought suggests." Why? Because "he understands the relativity of philosophies as closely analogous to the relativity of scientific theories." That means that even though the Newtonian scheme of understanding the world is now surpassed, nevertheless, "the Newtonian scheme is recognized as having a large measure of applicability." So "Whitehead believed that the situation in philosophy is similar. No philosophical position is simply false. Every serious philosophy illumines some significant range of human experience." However, adds Cobb, "in the nature of the case no system of thought is final. All must wait enlargement at the hands of the future."[126]

Cobb's last statement points up the basic incoherence of the process view of truth. How could Cobb possibly know that "all [philosophies] must wait . . . the future?" Is Cobb omniscient? If not, then he is either special pleading or incoherent. He is special pleading if he means that "all philosophies must change *except* the one (his) that enables him to make this kind of statement." Or, Cobb is incoherent if he actually means "all philosophies must change *including* the one (his)) that says all philosophies must change." That statement is as self-defeating as claiming, "I can-

125. Barry A. Woodbridge, "An Assessment and Prospectus for a Process Hermeneutic," *Journal of American Academy of Religion* 47, no. 1(March 1979):124.
126. John Cobb, *A Christian Natural Theology: Based on the Thought of Alfred North Whitehead* (Philadelphia: Westminster, 1965), pp. 107, 20-21, 108-9.

not utter a word in English."

It seems to me that process theologians make a significant mistake when they speak of truth as relative. In fact, there is a sense in which all truth is absolute. Let me explain. A relative truth would be one relative to a certain time, space, or person; but it would not necessarily hold for all time, space, and persons. For example, it would seem that the statement "the pencil is to the left of the pad" is only a relative truth because its truth depends on *where* one is standing. And if one removes the pencil then it also depends on *when* one observed it. However, that is not the case. For the statement really means: "From my vantage point at this time the pencil is to the left of the pad." And that statement is true at all times and all places for all people. For example it is true before, during, and after I make the statement that when I am observing the pen to the left of the pad that "the pen is to the left of the pad." Also, that statement of my observational standpoint is true in Moscow and London as well as in outer space. It is true everywhere and at all times that when I so observe the pen it is as stated.

Likewise, so-called subjective statements, such as "I feel sick," are really absolute truths. For it is true for everyone everywhere that I said, "I feel sick," at such and such a time and place. That truth will never change for all eternity. Simply because conditions change does not mean that truth about a previous condition changed. For example, "Richard Nixon is the President of the United States of America" (said in 1970) was, is, and always will be true. There will never come a time when it will not be true that Nixon was president in 1970. Furthermore, it is just as true for Russians and Chinese as it is for Americans. It is a truth for everyone everywhere for all time that Nixon was president in 1970. Hence, truth is absolute. There is no such thing as relative truth.

As a matter of fact, it is incoherent to claim that "all truth is relative." For if all truth were relative and changing then the very statement "all truth is relative" would be either nonrelative or relative. If it is nonrelative then *all* truth is not relative, for there is at least this one statement that is not relative (and if there is one, why not more?). If on the other hand the statement "all truth is relative" includes itself, then the statement is incoherent because the meaning changed while it was being made. Hence, the meaning of the statement is not even the same for the author (to say nothing of the hearer) from the time it began to the time it was finished. But what has many different meanings in process has no stable meaning. Hence, the statement is incoherent in meaning.

For the sake of simplicity and clarity let us state the incoherence of the process view of truth: "All truth is in process *including* the truth that all truth is in process." That of course is self-defeating. And to say that "all truth is in process *except* the truth that all truth is in process" is special pleading. Likewise, it is self-defeating to claim that human language is inadequate to express truth. That very statement ("human language is inadequate to express truth") is assumed to be an adequate expression of truth. If not, it is pointless. If so, it is self-destructive. In this regard one must reject the Whiteheadian rejection of the literal element in religious language. A language that negates all univocal forms in favor of "symbols" or "metaphors" that are evocative but not truly descriptive of God is inadequate. In fact, it is self-defeating to claim that "no talk about God can be taken literally," because that very statement is one about God that the author intends to be taken literally. Otherwise, it makes no sense. So here too we may conclude that whatever other values it may have, *process theology is philosophically incoherent.*

EVANGELICALS AND PROCESS THEOLOGY

Evangelicals have not been immune to the influence of process theology. Clark Pinnock has expressed his belief that God is not eternal or immutable in the classical sense.[127] Jack Rogers revealed his desire that we emulate process theologians' approach to Scripture.[128] Donald Bloesch also accepts a process view of God.[129]

A most explicit statement of an "evangelical" process theologian's view of Scripture comes from the Wesleyan Paul A. Mickey. In his chapter "The Holy Scriptures" in his recent book,[130] he clearly disavows his belief in inerrancy and defends essentially

---

127. Clark Pinnock, "The Need for a Scriptural, and Therefore a Neo-Classical Theism," in *Perspectives on Evangelical Theology,* ed. Kenneth Kantzer and Stanley Gundry (Grand Rapids: Baker, 1979).
128. See Jack Rogers and Donald K. McKim, *The Authority and Interpretation of the Bible* (New York: Harper & Row, 1979), p. 460, which says: "Presbyterians need a confessional centrist theology that takes the authority of the Bible as seriously as did the Princeton theologians and Barth. They equally need a method of interpreting Scripture that takes scholarly study of the Bible's historical context and our own cultural setting as seriously as do, for example, liberation and process theologies."
129. See Donald Bloesch, *Essentials of Evangelical Theology* (New York: Harper & Row, 1979), 1:24-46.
130. Paul A. Mickey, *The Essentials of Wesleyan Theology* (Grand Rapids: Zondervan, 1980).

the same view taken by Jack Rogers.[131] He speaks of the Bible as "a dynamic witness and revelation of God's purpose" (p. 94). He believes God " 'inspired' the authors" in a dynamic "mouth-to-mouth 'inspiration.' " That is, "God breathed out wisdom, and the human authors inhaled or breathed it in" (p. 105). What the authors wrote was not inerrant but only "accurate" (p. 114). Indeed, even that "accuracy" does not include "the facts of science," but "the proper scope for the authority of Scripture pertains to the matters of faith essential for salvation" (p. 113). Even the "initial receiving of inspiring of God's Word is not *a priori* exempt from the possibility of error" (p. 119).

That is not a surprising conclusion for Mickey to take in view of his rejection of the historic Christian view of an eternal and immutable God in favor of attributes such as "integrity" and "supremacy" (pp. 46, 47).

Mickey does not clearly reveal that he is a process theologian in the chapter of his book. His true colors fly, however, in the paper he gave to the American Academy of Religion. Here Mickey draws explicitly from Whitehead and comes to the astounding conclusion: "I am suggesting that informally and now perhaps in a more formal fashion the evangelical community will come to appreciate the benefits of a process perspective not only for a theology of the inspiration of Scripture but also for the larger task of writing theology in general."[132]

The new *International Standard Bible Encyclopedia* is also infected with process thought when it claims that God has neither simplicity nor eternity in the Augustinian sense.[133]

Also Stephen T. Davis, who wrote a book denying inerrancy,[134] has come out against the traditional view of God's eternity and in favor of a temporal process view, saying, "I do not know what is meant by the claim that God is outside of time. I believe that God is 'in' time, i.e. is a temporal being, just as I am: he too has a past, present, and future; today is '8 April 1977' for God just as it is for me."[135]

The ray of hope on the evangelical horizon is the recent conver-

131. Ibid., p. 118.
132. This paper is available through *Theological Students Fellowship* and is entitled "A Process Perspective as an Option for Theology of Inspiration."
133. See "Eternity," in *International Standard Bible Encyclopedia*, ed. Geoffrey W. Bromiley (Grand Rapids: Eerdmans), 2:162-64.
134. Stephen T. Davis, *The Debate About the Bible* (Philadelphia: Westminster, 1977).
135. Stephen T. Davis, "Divine Omnipotence and Human Freedom," *Religious Studies* 15, no. 3 (September 1979): 315.

sion of a process theologian, Royce G. Gruenler, to a thoroughgoing evangelical position. His penetrating critiques of process theology are set forth in a forthcoming book on the topic.[136] It is sincerely hoped that his experience and insight will help stem the tide toward process thought among evangelicals.

SUMMARY AND CONCLUSION

Process theology has definite implications for one's view of Scripture. For if God is finite, changing, and is neither in control of nor knowledgeable of the future, therefore there is no infallible, unchanging word from God. A changing God cannot utter changeless truths. In view of that it is indeed disappointing to hear evangelical theologians deny some of the traditional attributes of God. The logic of denying God's essential attributes will lead ultimately to a denial of some aspect of God's Word. That could be a factor in the denial of inerrancy by some contemporary evangelicals such as Jack Rogers, who pleads for a "method of interpreting Scripture that takes scholarly study of the Bible's historical context and our own cultural setting as seriously as do . . . process theologies." That would surely be a fatal error for evangelicals to make. If we take the relativity of setting *as seriously* as process theologians, then we will end up with a process view of truth and/or of God. And there is no way evangelicals can consistently maintain an infallible and inerrant Word from a fallible and errant God.

---

136. See Royce G. Gruenler, *The Inexhaustible God: Biblical Faith and the Challenge of Process Theism* (Grand Rapids: Baker, 1983).

10. The Functional Theology of G. C. Berkouwer

Hendrik Krabbendam

INTRODUCTION

G. C. Berkouwer is easily the most prominent theologian to foster opposition to the doctrine of inerrancy in the Reformed and evangelical camp today. His influence has been pervasive on both sides of the Atlantic. In Europe his position is espoused by most, if not all, of the members of the theological faculty of the Free University in Amsterdam, at times in an even more radical form. In recent years Herman Ridderbos also has adopted Berkouwer's approach to Scripture.[1] In America Jack Rogers has come to share Berkouwer's thinking and is now his unofficial spokesman, busily engaged in disseminating his views in a variety of very readable publications, which have a rather widespread appeal.[2]

All this is sufficient incentive to probe Berkouwer's position and lay bare the presuppositions from which he operates. Howev-

---

1. For documentation of the shift in the thinking of Ridderbos, see F. W. Buytendach, *Aspekte van die vorm/inhoud problematiek met betrekking tot die organiese skrifinspirasie in die nuwere Gereformeerde theologie in Nederland* (Amsterdam: Ton Bolland, 1972), pp. 237-328. (See especially 284-86, 311-18.)
2. Berkouwer's influence upon Jack Rogers is in evidence ever since Rogers wrote his dissertation, *Scripture in the Westminster Confession* (Grand Rapids: Eerdmans, 1967).

HENDRIK KRABBENDAM, B.A., B.D., Theologische Hogeschool, Kampen, the Netherlands; Th.M., Th.D., Westminster Theological Seminary, is professor of biblical studies and missions at Covenant College, Lookout Mountain, Tennessee. He has written "B. B. Warfield Versus G. C. Berkouwer on Scripture," in *Inerrancy* (1979), ed. Norman Geisler.

er, there is an additional reason to embark upon such a project. Berkouwer's increasingly outspoken opposition to the inerrantist position reflects a shift in his thinking. That shift, which dates back to the late 1940s or early 1950s, is nothing short of dramatic—a reversal of positions. He presents his early views in a 1938 work, *The Problem of Biblical Criticism*, and further develops them in a 1952 lecture series, *Modern Uncertainty and Christian Faith*.[3] His later views are contained in a series called Studies in Dogmatics, culminating in a monograph entitled *Holy Scripture*, originally published in two volumes in 1966 and 1967.[4] In the early stage of his thinking he engaged in a strong apologetic for the absolute authority of Scripture, including its inerrancy; analyzed the presuppositions of the opponents; and rejected their approach as a dead-end street. In the later stage of his thought he capitulated completely to one strand of opposition and promulgates that view with great persuasiveness.

At this point several questions present themselves. How is such a reversal from staunch supporter to strong opponent of biblical inerrancy possible? What is the attractivenes of the particular strand of opposition that Berkouwer eventually adopted? Since reversals like this are present in the thinking of Berkouwer, Ridderbos, and Rogers, what is the likelihood that they will occur in others as well? If such reversal and the consequent rejection of inerrancy cannot be without grave consequences for the individual and the church—this is not just my conviction[5]—how can this be made clear so that further reversals can be prevented? These and similar questions provide the extra impetus to make an inquiry into the presuppositions of Berkouwer's later theology.

To set the stage for this inquiry, Berkouwer's early apologetic for the absolute authority of Scripture will be analyzed first. That will give an early exposure of the presuppositions Berkouwer eventually embraced. Following that, his reversal will be examined, which will deal with the dynamics that prompted the change. Finally, Berkouwer's later theology, with its emphasis on the function of Scripture, will be investigated to demonstrate the

---

3. G. C. Berkouwer, *Het probleem der schriftkritiek* (Kampen: Kok, 1938) and *Modern Uncertainty and Christian Faith* (Grand Rapids: Eerdmans, 1953).
4. G. C. Berkouwer, *De Heilige Schrift*, 2 vols. (Kampen: Kok, 1966-67); *Holy Scripture* (Grand Rapids: Eerdmans, 1975).
5. See Article XIX of The Chicago Statement on Biblical Inerrancy, in *Inerrancy*, ed. Norman Geisler (Grand Rapids: Zondervan, 1979), p. 497.

conditions that make his functional approach possible and necessary.

BERKOUWER'S EARLY APOLOGETIC

HIS POLEMIC STANCE

In 1938, in a sweeping and determined polemic, Berkouwer took to task neo-orthodoxy and liberalism, both classified as modernism;[6] ethical evangelicalism;[7] Roman Catholicism;[8] as well as three individuals who were brought to ecclesiastical trial in the Reformed camp.[9] He charged all of them with vitiating the absolute authority of Scripture.[10] In 1952 he defended that same authority against basically the same foes in order to safeguard "real Christianity" from the dangers of an irremediable uncertainty and for the discharge of its God-given task.[11]

According to Berkouwer, the opponents of the absolute authority of Scripture, which is based on the identification of Scripture and the Word of God, marshal two arguments. The first one, common to all, is scientific. Critical-historical research has once for all driven a wedge between Scripture and the Word of God.[12] The second one, varying from one opponent to another, is religious. The common denominator of this argument is that it runs contrary to the essence of living faith to construe such faith as (cor)related to a mere book. Neo-orthodoxy is committed to the correlation of faith and revelation, both of which transcend the subject-object polarity. For this reason Scripture can never be identified with revelation or function as the ground of faith. It is of a different order. Scripture as a human, fallible book can at best be a witness to revelation and faith.[13] Against this backdrop it is hardly surprising that neo-orthodoxy does not only make room for the critical-historical method, but also calls for it to prevent Scripture from being confused with revelation.

Liberalism emphasizes the relation between the human personality and revelation. Scripture contributes to the religious, ethical, aesthetic, and cultural advancement and enrichment of

---

6. Berkouwer, *Het probleem*, pp. 13-53, 75-84.
7. Ibid., pp. 53-59, 84-89.
8. Ibid., pp. 173-251.
9. Ibid., pp. 258-95.
10. Ibid., pp. 58, 64-65, 247-48, 256.
11. Berkouwer, *Modern Uncertainty*, pp. 11-24, 49-61, 86.
12. Berkouwer, *Het probleem*, pp. 7-13, 19, 40; *Modern Uncertainty*, p. 12.
13. Ibid., pp. 13-39; *Modern Uncertainty*, p. 13.

the human personality, for which it commands respect and admiration. However, it also contains other material that must be sifted out by the scientific method. For that reason it cannot be totally identified with the Word of God.[14]

Ethical evangelicalism stresses the relationship between the moral conscience and revelation. Scripture contains eternal truths that are ethical in nature. Those truths, which may or may not coincide with historical facts constitute the essential Word of God. Only they, therefore, are binding in character. Scripture is not meant to be a book of science and/or history. It does contain errors and does contradict itself in those areas. The nonethical data, therefore, may be helpful but do not demand what would amount to an external submission to Scripture. It would not only lead to a collision with the legitimate results of the scientific and historical methodology, but would also shift the focus away from the essential content of Scripture.[15]

Space does not permit us to deal at length at this point with the Roman Catholic position or with the views of the three individuals who faced ecclesiastical trial in the Reformed camp.[16]

In his final assessment Berkouwer characterized the three approaches that operate with the notion of correlation, whether the correlation of faith and revelation as in neo-orthodoxy, of human personality and revelation as in liberalism, or of moral conscience and revelation as in ethical evangelicalism, as subjectivistic. Only that which is correlative with and serves the purposes of subjective faith, the subjective human personality, or the subjective moral conscience, is accepted as authoritative, whether it is designated as neo-orthodoxy's content of Scripture, liberalism's kernel of Scripture, or ethical evangelicalism's eternal truths of Scripture. The rest, whether it is called the form, the husk, or "the other material," is sacrificed to the acids of the historical-critical method.[17]

Furthermore, he held that they are autonomous in character.

14. Ibid., pp. 39-53.
15. Ibid., pp. 53-58.
16. Ibid., pp. 173-251 and 258-95. It is interesting to note that in Roman Catholicism the critical method is given all the latitude it wishes, as long as it serves, or at least does not violate, the *depositum fidei*, zealously guarded by the church that claims to be its infallible and ultimate judge. Gone is the glory of the Scripture as the deepest foundation of faith, even if it is formally judged to be inerrant. As to the three individuals, the position of one is practically that of neo-orthodoxy, the view of another runs formally parallel to that of ethical evangelicalism, and the approach of the third resembles that of Romanism.
17. Ibid., pp. 34, 44, 247, 277, 385.

All of them refuse to acknowledge the total, absolute, theonomous authority of Scripture, because all of them appeal to a determinant above Scripture. The Bible simply does not have the ultimate, unquestioned say.[18]

Also, Berkouwer warned that the distrust of Scripture, arising from the refusal to identify it as the Word of God and fostered by the sanction given to the critical-historical method, will lead eventually not only to a total rejection of the authority of Scripture, but also to the total secularization of life.[19]

Finally, he expressed his agreement with Bavinck that the opposition to the absolute authority of Scripture is ethical in nature. Scripture, identified as the Word of God, is the servant of Christ and therefore evokes the same enmity in the heart of sinful man as long as he refuses, totally or partially, to yield to it. The solution of all the problems that will be faced in the study and interpretation of Scripture must be preceded by an obedient surrender of heart and thought to the authority of Christ. Thus, for all practical purposes, Berkouwer issued a veiled call to repentance to the opponents of the inerrancy of Scripture.[20]

HIS OWN POSITION

Following his discussion of the several views that have historically weakened or opposed the absolute authority of Holy Scripture, Berkouwer set forth the Reformed doctrine of Scripture, which he admitted occupies a unique, isolated position. At the core of this doctrine lies the conviction that Scripture, as originating in God and produced by God through the agency of the Holy Spirit *(theopneustos)*, has a divine and therefore absolute authority in each part and as a whole.[21] Its trustworthiness, infallibility, and inerrancy is not simply something that must be established in an empirical and a posteriori fashion. Rather, these characteristics are interwoven with the a priori binding and liberating power of the Scripture as the Word of God, which in none of its pronouncements has a higher court of appeal, be it human reason, conscience, or otherwise. This absolute, theonomous authority of Scripture, which is not to be demonstrated but to be acknowledged on the basis of its self-attestation, strikes at the heart of subjectivism and cuts at the root of human autonomy by making every thought captive to the obedience of Christ.

18. Ibid., pp. 19, 47-48, 51, 247, 387, 389.
19. Ibid., pp. 385-87.
20. Ibid., pp. 256-57, 384.
21. Ibid., p. 256.

Consequently Berkouwer, in the footsteps of Kuyper and Bavinck, took an uncompromising stand against the historical-critical and scientific methodology, as it is rooted in human autonomy.[22] He specifically warned against the subtle attempt to justify the critical method by giving it a religious foundation. The views that operate with the notion of correlation claim that the critical method has the "sacred" task effectively to expose and eliminate any material in or aspects of Scripture that will obscure the Word of God, however designated. Such justification is dangerous. Those who heed it may well find themselves removed both from the grace and authority of the written Word of God.[23]

In short, the legitimacy of biblical criticism was contested by Berkouwer on the ground that it violates the simplicity of Holy Scripture and refuses to submit to its theonomous authority acknowledged by Christ Himself in the formula "It is written" (Matt. 4:4, 7, 10). In that regard Berkouwer was unyielding, even as he admitted with Kuyper that the gigantic labor of critical scholars naturally will produce at times results from which Bible believing scholars can profit.

Further, the a priori of a divinely authoritative, self-attesting, trustworthy, infallible, inerrant Scripture is maintained. In this regard Berkouwer was equally unyielding, even as he emphasized that this a priori is not empty or simply to be acknowledged in a formal-theoretical pronouncement concerning the quality of the Bible. It has significance for the full reality of life and must be confessed in unbreakable conjunction with an unconditional submission to the absolute authority of Scripture. The Reformed doctrine of Scripture has never been satisfied with a mere abstract, formal acceptance of the quality of a book. It has always insisted upon a complete and believing acknowledgement of and submission to the authority of all of Scripture in heart, mind, and life—which transcends any and every dualism, whether that of form and contents, husk and kernel, words and Word, or otherwise.[24]

In further defense of the Reformed doctrine of Scripture Berkouwer denied that it precludes a responsible, scientific scholarship. In fact, it supplies the only proper starting point for scholar-

---

22. Berkouwer, *Modern Uncertainty*, p. 22, "Once when Dr. Abraham Kuyper was attacked because of his view of holy Scripture and its authority, he answered: 'This is my prejudice; this is my *a priori;* the Lord has given it to me.' "
23. Ibid., pp. 247-50, 253-58, 384-86.
24. Ibid., pp. 54, 246-47, 255, 297-98, 387-88.

ship (no science is neutral) and the only foundation for a responsible exercise of it. He also denied that the Reformed doctrine of Scripture is undermined by difficulties in the areas of textual criticism and Bible translation. He held that responsible scholarship will do its utmost to establish a text that is as close as possible to the autographa and then will seek to arrive at a translation that as faithfully as possible reflects the established text. He obviously was of the opinion that Reformed scholarship has been remarkably successful in both regards.

In further clarification of the Reformed doctrine of Scripture, Berkouwer finally focused his attention upon the issue of the organic inspiration of Scripture. The term *organic*, in contrast to *mechanic*, was chosen to bring out that the Spirit takes the total man into His service, including his personality, talents, and activity. This operation is influenced no doubt by the man's ethnic background, his historical setting, his cultural milieu, the thought patterns of his day, and the accumulated knowledge of his time.

That, of course, evoked a fundamental question. Was the influence such that outdated, antiquated, impure, false, or errant elements entered into the body of the biblical writings, which the progress of scientific and historical scholarship would expose as such? The so-called biblical cosmology (the issue of the three-decker universe) and biblical historiography (the story of the Fall) are cases in point. The stakes are clearly high. Were errant elements to be present, it would introduce a human factor into Scripture that would compete with, rather than serve, the divine factor. The term *organic* would, then, function as the dynamite that would explode the concept of divine inspiration. The human authors would make their own independent and fallible contributions. This would effectively seal the doom of a trustworthy, infallible, inerrant, and authoritative Scripture.

Of course, the early Berkouwer could not tolerate the foregoing view. But how, then, did he answer the questions? He did so by the distinction between "adaptation" *(aansluiting)* and "accommodation" *(accomodatie)*. The former concept conveys that in His revelation God adapts Himself to man as a father condescends to the level of a child. The language in which the communication is couched is certainly not the most sophisticated from the father's point of view. But that does not make it impure or untrue. In fact, pedagogically it is to be applauded for it produces understanding on its intended level of operation.

The latter concept implies that God adopts a revelatory language that is in itself impure, untrue, false, or errant, but was the only one available at the time of the revelation and therefore simply had to be used in order to get a message across. Berkouwer endorsed only the concept of adaptation with regard to the nature of biblical language. Only so, in his estimation, could the force of the word *organic* be maintained, which does not serve the purposes of an independent human factor in competition with the divine factor, but rather is adjectival to the concept of inspiration. As such it emphasizes that in the divine act of inspiration the Holy Spirit took the human writers in His service and guided them, however imperfect they may have been in themselves, in such a way, however incomprehensible it may have been, that their words at the same time constituted the completely authoritative, utterly trustworthy, and fully infallible Word of God. This process did *not* exclude the sections in which the biblical writers make statements about the universe or give a description of historical events.

The claim has been made that the Bible espouses a Babylonian, geocentric cosmology that is not only primitive, but also incorrect and unacceptable historiographically.

Berkouwer rejected that claim. First, he denied that the Bible espouses any cosmology whatsoever or that the Bible writers reflect a belief in a specific cosmology. Because the Bible is not a textbook of science, why would one even expect a scientifically worked out cosmology? Further, most of the relevant data are found in a poetic context. Because the very nature of poetry implies freedom of expression, what warrant is there to interpret certain phraseologies as a reflection of a belief in a specific cosmology? But even more conclusive, all of the relevant data simply present the phenomena as they are first perceived by all men everywhere throughout all ages. They are described in observation language and not in the exact language of scientific scholarship that results from scientific investigation.

Second, Berkouwer denied that the Bible operates with a concept of history resultant from an incorrect (nonexistent!) biblical cosmology. To be sure, he readily admitted that Scripture has its own historiography. It has its own point of departure, its own direction, and its own goal. As such it must be distinguished from scientific historiography. It does not cover the same material in the same way with the same purpose. But he did not grant that the historiography of Scripture is hamstrung by a defective starting point, hampered by a narrow-minded methodology, or on a collision course with scientific historiography. God Himself selected the component elements of Scripture and produced it through the agency of the Spirit and the instrumentality of human writers in a way that served His purposes and guaranteed the full trustworthiness and authority of Scripture.

All in all, it is both the mystery and miracle of Holy Scripture that there are no two "sides," the human and the divine, in competition with each other. It is also miraculous that the limitation of God's revelation, because of its adaptation to the level of man, does not exclude its purity and infalliblity. Finally it is truly miraculous that the weakness and defectiveness of the human instruments does not preclude Scripture from being simultaneously the Word of man and the Word of God.[25]

HIS APOLOGETIC METHODOLOGY

In summary, Berkouwer's early apologetic methodology could best be characterized as presuppositional and transcendental.

Presuppositional. He rejected the notion that the inductive investigation of all the data must have run its course before the issue of the absolute authority of Scripture could be settled. He was far from opposed to the scientific enterprise, but he held that that enterprise is not independent. The data of Scripture are not at its mercy. That enterprise, rather, must conform itself to those data and may never come up with results that run counter to Scripture. Berkouwer wrote, "The Reformed view of Scripture maintains faith in Scripture as an untouchable a priori, as an unassailable presupposition and concludes on the basis of this a priori to the necessary incorrectness of the results of biblical criticism."[26]

Transcendental. He endeavored to penetrate to the root, to the fundamental conditions that make one's position possible and necessary. He showed that the opponents of biblical inerrancy are motivated by a specific view of the scientific method and by a specific view of the correlation between faith and revelation. The method is critical and historical. It turns the doctrine of inspiration and its concomitant doctrine of infallibility into an impossibility.[27] The correlation is unbreakable and unique. It does not allow for the absolute identification of Scripture as the Word of God. At best the identification is partial or indirect. Liberalism and ethical evangelicalism hold that only part of the content is to be regarded as God's Word. Neo-orthodoxy declares that Scripture

25. Ibid., pp. 10, 296-383; *Modern Uncertainty,* p. 21.
26. Ibid., pp. 219, 220, 248, 255, 257, 261, 275-78.
27. Ibid., pp. 18-19.

is only a witness to God's Word. According to the early Berkouwer, the idea of correlation is subjectivistic, rooted in either autonomous rationalism or autonomous irrationalism, and must ultimately be traced back to enmity in the heart.[28]

It is hard to imagine a more exhaustive, more penetrating, and more conclusive analysis of biblical criticism and defense of biblical inerrancy. Every conceivable attack upon the integrity of Scripture seems to have passed in review and every conceivable reason the inerrancy of Scripture should be espoused seems to have been set forth with inescapable cogency. All the dire consequences of a rejection of the absolute and final authority of Scripture seem to have been spelled out and the only remedy, in the form of a repudiation of a fundamental enmity, seems to have been presented. Berkouwer seemed to have spoken his final word on the subject. But that was not to be the case. A dramatic shift was in the offing. In the late 1940s a new development began to take shape, imperceptibly at first, that eventually would lead to a complete reversal of positions. That reversal, which never has been satisfactorily explained, will now be examined.

BERKOUWER'S REVERSAL

AN UNSATISFACTORY SELF-ASSESSMENT

In 1966-67 Berkouwer's two-volume work on Holy Scripture came off the press in the Netherlands. In 1975 its English translation was published, consisting of two-thirds of the original text. In it the positions are turned. What is attacked in 1938 is basically affirmed in 1966. What is defended in 1938 is basically denied in 1966.

What brought about this reversal?

The early Berkouwer, in the footsteps of Bavinck, would have spoken of a resistance that Scripture evokes in the heart of one who does not (yet totally) wish to submit himself to the Word of God; indeed he spoke of an enmity, the same opposition that Christ arouses.[29] Of course, such a statement can hardly be expected from the later Berkouwer. In reflecting upon his views expressed in the 1938 publication, at the time of his retirement from the Free University, Berkouwer recollects a comment made by one of his fellow ministers. It was a statement to the effect

28. For the charge of irrationalistic autonomy, see Berkouwer, *Modern Uncertainty*, pp. 53-61.
29. Berkouwer, *Het probleem*, pp. 256-57, 384.

that the Reformed view of Scripture is not exhausted by the phrase *It is written*, but that the work of the Spirit also ought to be taken into account. That remark, writes Berkouwer, "had more to it than I realized when I first heard it, though I certainly was ready then to admit its truth."[30]

Berkouwer clearly implies that a more full-orbed insight into the nature and content of the Spirit's activity in the area of biblical authority and biblical faith helped lead to his later views. What that more full-orbed insight was is not explicitly mentioned. However, it appears rather certain from Berkouwer's writings that it pertains to the fact that the testimony of the Holy Spirit as the means of recognizing Scripture as God's Word should not be disassociated from the operation of the Spirit that produces biblical salvation. Reformed theologians have not always been sufficiently careful when they made statements implying that the testimony of the Holy Spirit—totally abstracted from the full saving activity of the Spirit—produces recognition of Scripture as the Word of God. They should at least have added that apart from that full saving activity any recognition of Scripture can at best be merely formal and external and therefore should not be characterized as resulting from a testimony of God's Spirit.[31]

But even if Berkouwer has this in mind, one still must take issue with the implied suggestion that his insight has only expanded. It has dramatically changed! In 1938 he stated as his aim that there would be no tension between the confession of the Spirit and the confession of the infallible Scripture.[32] After his reversal that aim is out of reach. Submission to every word of Scripture is no longer viewed as an evidence of or extension of submission to God and His Christ. The two are not on the same level. The latter is the aim of the divine message of Scripture and is brought about by the Spirit. The former is a subjection to an

---

30. G. C. Berkouwer, *A Half Century of Theology* (Grand Rapids: Eerdmans, 1977), p. 138.

31. See H. Bavinck, *Gereformeerde Dogmatiek* (Kampen: Kok, 1928), 1:552-55, and especially 1:563, "This testimonium Spiritus Sancti is by Calvin and the Reformed theologians too onesidedly related to the authority of Holy Scripture. It seemed that it had no other content than the assurance of Scripture as the Word of God. Thereby this testimonium came to stand by itself; it was disconnected from the life of faith and seemed to point to an extraordinary revelation"; and pp. 564-65, "The . . . object to which the Holy Spirit testifies in the hearts of the believers, is nothing else than . . . the *divinitas* of all those truths, which are revealed in Scripture and given to us by God in Christ."

32. Berkouwer, *Het probleem*, pp. 247-48.

external, relatively human authority that may not be equated with the Word of the Spirit. All in all, Berkouwer's reference to additional study in the work of the Spirit is not sufficient to account for his reversal.

Jack Rogers partially agrees. He accepts Berkouwer's self-analysis when he writes, "A deepening awareness that, for the Reformers, the Holy Spirit convinces us of the authority of Scripture was part of Berkouwer's finding his way back to his own tradition."[33] But Rogers rounds out the picture when he adds that in Berkouwer's later development he has consciously turned away from the methodology of his teacher Valentine Hepp. Hepp had succumbed to the medieval scholastic view that rational proofs were necessary for faith and therefore had to be presented prior to it. In thus shifting the emphasis to apologetics as a prerequisite for systematic theology, he followed in the footsteps of post-Reformation scholasticism, epitomized in Turretin, and adopted the scholastic rationalism of the Hodge/Warfield model in conscious departure from Bavinck and Kuyper. These latter two espoused a methodology in which faith was necessary for, and therefore prior to, understanding. Thus they placed the emphasis upon the systematic presentation of the truths of Scripture prior to apologetics, in the line of Augustine and Calvin. From this Rogers draws the conclusion that for Hepp the philosophical issue of compelling, logical, or evidential proof for the existence of God and the divine character of Scripture was primary, whereas central for Kuyper and Bavinck was the functional issue that God enters into a relationship with His people and that they accept Scripture as authoritative because of its saving message.

Therefore, according to Rogers, Berkouwer temporarily fell victim to a scholastic methodology as a result of the influence of Hepp. That methodology accounted for his 1938 publication and the defense of the divinity of Scripture contained in it. However, for the reason already stated, he returned "to his own tradition." This, then, comes to light in a series of monographs, Studies in Dogmatics, of which his two-volume work on Scripture is one.[34]

That analysis is certainly intriguing. But does it have a basis in fact? It appears not.

33. Jack Rogers, "A Third Alternative: Scripture, Tradition and Interpretation in the Theology of G. C. Berkouwer," in *Scripture, Tradition and Interpretation*, ed. W. Ward Gasque (Grand Rapids: Eerdmans, 1978), p. 73; Jack Rogers and Donald McKim, *The Authority and Interpretation of the Bible* (New York: Harper & Row), p. 427.

34. Rogers, "A Third Alternative," pp. 70-74; Rogers and McKim, *Authority and Interpretation*, pp. 426-28.

For one thing, Berkouwer was not the scholastic thinker in 1938 that he is made out to be. The idea that proof precedes faith has never characterized his theology. In fact, he emphatically states that the Reformed view of Scripture as theonomous is not a matter to be demonstrated, but an unassailable presupposition and an untouchable a priori.[35] How that escaped Rogers is difficult to understand.

For another thing, Berkouwer did not give a defense of the divinity of Scripture in 1938 in the way Rogers formulates it. He maintained that *both* the human and divine factors, in Warfield's terminology, flow "confluently and harmoniously to the production of a common product."[36] Every work of Scripture is God's word *and* man's word. The qualities of divinity *and* humanity are found in every portion of Scripture, with the understanding that the qualities of the one do not exclude the qualities of the other. The words of the human writers are *at the same time* the Word of God. Berkouwer never at any place spoke of a divinity of Scripture abstracted from its human factor. In fact, he emphatically opposed any theological construct that would promote the competition between the human and the divine—anything that would neutralize, endanger, or eliminate either factor, up to and including the humanization or divinization of Scripture.[37] Regrettably, therefore, Roger's formulation is misleading because it suggests that the humanity of Scripture vanished from sight in Berkouwer's earlier thinking. That is definitely not the case!

More important, however, is Rogers's claim that Berkouwer has found his way back to his "own tradition." What is that tradition? At this point the term *functional* emerges, which already was used to describe the theology of Kuyper and Bavinck and is now commonly used to typify the theology of Berkouwer.[38]

AN UNACCEPTABLE CLAIM

In his 1979 book on the authority and interpretation of the Bible, coauthored with Donald McKim, Rogers contrasts two tra-

35. Berkouwer, *Het probleem*, pp. 219-47.
36. *Selected Shorter Writings of Benjamin B. Warfield*, ed. J. Meeter (Nutley, N.J.: Presbyterian & Reformed, 1973), 2:547, 629, 631. See also Berkouwer, *Modern Uncertainty*, p. 22.
37. Berkouwer, *Het probleem*, pp. 381-82.
38. For the use of the term *functional* to describe Berkouwer's theology, see Rogers, "A Third Alternative," pp. 88, 91, n. 110, and G. Lewis, "Categories in Collision?" (section 2) in *Perspectives on Evangelical Theology*, ed. Kenneth Kantzer and Stanley Gundry (Grand Rapids: Baker, 1979), pp. 254-56.

ditions. The one, called "functional" theology, is represented by
Origen, Chrysostom, Augustine, Anselm, Wycliffe, Luther, Calvin,
the Westminster divines, Briggs, Orr, Kuyper, Bavinck, Forsyth,
Barth, and Berkouwer. The second one, called "scholastic" theology,
is represented by Erigena, Abelard, Thomas Aquinas, Me-
lancthon, Zanchius, Beza, Turretin, Owen, Reid, Witherspoon,
Charles Hodge, and Warfield.

The first group is allegedly Platonic-Augustinian, the second
group Aristotelian-Thomistic. When Rogers holds that Berkouwer has found his way back to his own tradition, he means
that Berkouwer has turned away from a scholastic approach to a
functional methodology. That is further supported by Berkouwer's
use of the term *functional*, specifically in connection with his
doctrine of Scripture. He uses *functional* to describe the nature of
the Bible in his analysis of Scripture as God-breathed. Paul's
emphasis in the context of 2 Timothy 3:16 is said to be on "the
great purpose," "the concrete significance," "the usefulness," in
short, "the functional character" of the sacred writings.[39]

But what is the meaning of the term *functional?* Rogers suggests the following ingredient elements.

First, functional theology is committed to the principle of accommodation. In other words, in His self-revelation God humbly
condescended to man's limited and sinful capacities." As creature
the human mind was not on the same level as the Creator. As
sinner the human mind had attained a perverted perspective.[40] It
was God's purpose to bring His message of salvation in Jesus
Christ to man and to effect a life of obedient faith. So that the
message could be savingly grasped, He used weak human instruments with the same language and knowledge as their contemporaries, including lowly forms of speech and modes of thought that
befit children. Rogers and McKim find the principle of accommodation in Clement, Origen, Chrysostom, Augustine, Luther, Calvin, Martyr, Wittich, Kuyper, Bavinck, and Berkouwer.[41] Many of
those men call attention to the so-called incarnational model for
the divine accommodation to human thought and language.

Second, functional theology says the principle of accommodation calls for a sharp distinction to be made between the center
and the periphery, the content and the form of Scripture.[42] The

39. Berkouwer, *Holy Scripture*, pp. 141-42.
40. Rogers and McKim, *The Authority*, pp. 9-10.
41. Ibid., pp. 9-10, 11-12, 18-20, 27-30, 77-79, 98-100, 152-54, 169-71, 390-91, 431-33.
42. Berkouwer, *Holy Scripture*, p. 175, "The problems of the doctrine of accommodation come into clear focus in the general distinction between *essential
content* and *time-related form* as well as in the critical question of the criteria
used to define and legitimize the disassociation of the two factors."

center, or content, is the divine message of the truth in Christ that aims at saving faith and holy conduct. The periphery, or form, is the human supporting garment that consists of the several historical and cultural patterns of thought and modes of expression. Rogers and McKim detect this distinction in Origen, Augustine, Luther, Calvin, the Westminster divines, Barth, and Berkouwer.[43]

Third, functional theology insists that the authority of Scripture is bound up with, and therefore to be sought in, the center of Scripture, as well as with the goal and purpose of Scripture, consisting of the communication of the message of salvation and the promotion of a holy life. For this third element Rogers and McKim point to Augustine, Luther, the Reformed confessions, Orr, Bavinck, and Berkouwer.[44]

Fourth, functional theology contends it is not the purpose of Scripture to provide objective information regarding the periphery, and therefore the Bible is not designed as a textbook of science and history. In this context Rogers and McKim refer to Augustine, the Reformed confessions, and Bavinck.[45]

Fifth, functional theology claims that the divine purpose of Scripture does not allow for "errors," to be defined as "deliberate and deceiving untruths," in its center, but that the nonpurpose of Scripture does not preclude "errors," now defined as "technical inaccuracies, discrepancies or mistakes," in its human periphery. For the first claim Rogers and McKim mention Augustine, the Reformed confessions, and Berkouwer,[46] and for the second claim they cite Luther, Calvin, Briggs, Orr, Barth, and Berkouwer.[47]

Sixth, functional theology states that its principle that faith is prior to and necessary for understanding implies the use of reason in the scholarly and scientific investigation of the human form of Scripture. Such use of reason not only will shed light upon the message but also will lead to the exposure of errors in the sense of technical inaccuracies and discrepancies. To find this principle Rogers and McKim turn to Augustine, Anselm, Wycliffe, Luther, Calvin, the Westminster divines, Kuyper, Bavinck, Barth, and Berkouwer.[48] Rogers and McKim see support for the implication in Luther, Briggs, Kuyper, Bavinck, Forsyth, Barth, and Berkouwer.[49]

43. Rogers and McKim, *Authority and Interpretation*, pp. 12, 28, 30, 77, 79, 99, 205, 421-23, 429.
44. Ibid., pp. 28, 85, 125, 386, 389, 422.
45. Ibid., pp. 26, 125, 390.
46. Ibid., pp. 31, 125, 431.
47. Ibid., pp. 87-88, 109-16, 354-55, 386, 423, 431.
48. Ibid., pp. 23-25, 39-40, 74, 80-82, 88, 100-104, 203, 389, 414, 436.
49. Ibid., pp. 86, 349, 355, 359, 398, 391, 393, 415, 430.

Seventh, functional theology regards human mistakes, inconsistencies, inaccuracies, and discrepancies incapable of frustrating the divine motivation. The central message will reach its goal through and in spite of such shortcomings. Rogers and McKim ascribe this view of Kuyper and Bavinck.[50]

Apart from the fact that the accuracy of Roger's and McKim's vast data ought to be checked, those seven ingredient elements call for at least two additional comments.[51]

First, the notion of "accommodation" is confused, inconclusive, and self-defeating.

It is confused because it speaks of God's condescension to the level of both man's limitation and his sinfulness. The early Berkouwer distinguished between adaptation *(aansluiting)* to man's limitation, which he accepted, and accommodation *(accomodatie)* to human error, which he rejected. Whereas the later Berkouwer at least acknowledges the difference,[52] Rogers and McKim do neither one.

It is inconclusive because none of the views of accommodation referred to by Rogers and McKim include condescension to human sinfulness, whereas the rejection of accommodation by Turretin, Alexander, Hodge, and Warfield only pertains to the condescension to human error in the sense of inaccuracies.[53]

It is self-defeating because the inclusion of the level of human sinfulness forces Rogers and McKim to admit error in the sense of sin, which touches the area of the message or content of Scripture. That, however, according to functional theology is not possible. How much wiser it is, with the early Berkouwer and the Princeton theologians to acknowledge God's fatherly condescension to the level of human weakness or lowliness *(aansluiting)* and not to man's sinfulness or defectiveness *(accomodatie)*. Incidentally, it ought to be noted that the kind of accommodation espoused

50. Ibid., p. 393.
51. Preus and Gerstner come to a totally different conclusion as to the views of Luther and Calvin on the inerrancy of Scripture. See Robert D. Preus, "The View of the Bible Held by the Church: The Early Church through Luther," in *Inerrancy,* ed. Norman Geisler (Grand Rapids: Zondervan, 1979), pp. 372-80; John H. Gerstner, "The View of the Bible Held by the Church: Calvin and the Westminster Divines," in *Inerrancy,* pp. 389-95. Gerstner and Nicole challenge Rogers directly on his interpretation of the Westminster divines, Augustine, Calvin, and Warfield. See Gerstner, "Calvin," pp. 396-400; Roger Nicole in a review article of Rogers and McKim, *Authority and Interpretation,* in *Christian Scholar's Review* 10, no. 2(1981):162-64.
52. Berkouwer, *Holy Scripture,* p. 177.
53. Rogers and McKim, *Authority and Interpretation,* pp. 176, 179, 273, 305, 310, 345, 358-59.

by Rogers and McKim does not follow the incarnational model. Christ, indeed, came in the flesh, even in the likeness of sinful flesh, but sin itself was excluded (John 1:14; Rom. 8:3; Heb. 4:15). All in all, to say that accommodation implies error, however defined, is a non sequitur.[54]

Second, the center-periphery, content-form construct is encumbered with similar problems.

The center-periphery notion is used by liberal theology to reduce Scripture to its kernel of "truth" by removing the husk.

Bavinck uses the same terminology, but the import is radically different. He simply wishes to convey that certain sections of Scripture are more centrally significant than others. That does not mean that one section is more inspired than another, nor, as Rogers suggests, that the center is divine and the periphery human.[55]

Berkouwer speaks about the "centralization" of Scripture, with a reference to Bavinck's terminology, and in the context of a discussion of the distinction between essential content and time-related form. However, Berkouwer's thought does not run parallel to Bavinck's. The essential content comprises the unassailable divine aspect and the time-related form, the relative human aspect in Scripture. The relationship of those two aspects is not comparable to the center-periphery distinction of liberal theology, which is dualistic; nor does it reflect Bavinck's approach, which retains the integrity of all of Scripture. No, Berkouwer construes their relationship as dialectic. Both poles mutually exclude and presuppose each other. On the one hand, content and form may not be identified. Scripture is a human book, bound to its social structures, cultural patterns, historical setting, and modes of thought. It is time-bound. As such it is open to and in need of critical investigation that will expose its relativity. The divinity of Scripture may under no circumstance be sought in its form. That would be tantamount to docetism, which would obscure the humanity of the Bible. On the other hand, content and form may not be separated. There is a continuity between the divine and the human. The Word of God calls the form of the human into being, adopts it, and is heard in the midst of it, in terms of its saving content and by virtue of its scope.

In summary, God's Word disassociates itself from the human Scripture as thoroughly time-bound and associates itself with

54. Gerstner, "Calvin," pp. 388, 394.
55. Bavinck, *Gereformeerde Dogmatiek*, 1:409.

Scripture as human witness. As time-bound, Scripture is relative. As witness, it has universal authority. This is not simply ambiguous, but rather indicative of the dialectic with the simultaneous discontinuity and continuity of the human and the divine.[56] Incidentally, that is what produces in Berkouwer's eyes the mystery of Scripture as the Word of God. The early Berkouwer was faced with a mystery because God did not see fit to disclose the *way* in which He produced an inerrant Bible through fallible men. The later Berkouwer seeks the mystery in the *fact* that God uses a human, errant book to convey a divine, infallible message. The difference is telling.

These different ways in which the center-periphery relationship functions are not distinguished by Rogers and McKim. This hardly inspires confidence in their conclusions.

For one, when they claim that the authority of Scripture is to be found in the center and not in the periphery, this is certainly not applicable to Bavinck. He emphatically declares that Scripture in its totality has authority, not just the Word of God in it or the religious-ethical content.[57] It lays claim to authority over every territory of life, including that of the arts and the sciences. It is untenable, according to Bavinck, to restrict inspiration to the religious-ethical part of Scripture or to separate the religious from other parts of life. In fact, "very much of what is mentioned in Scripture, is also for the other sciences of principial significance." The principles for all of life, including the arts and sciences, are given in Scripture, even if "Scripture never takes up the matter of science as such intentionally."[58] In short, even if Scripture in its primary intention is religious-ethical, Bavinck insists that it is authoritative in everything it asserts. Indeed, why would it not be?

For another, Rogers and McKim claim that the center-periphery distinction implies that Scripture is error-prone in the areas in which it does not function as a rule of faith and practice, but that has not been demonstrated with regard to Luther, Calvin, Kuyper, and Bavinck. Although it must be granted that those older theologians have not systematically dealt with the various aspects of today's inerrancy debate, there is no evidence that they admit to undisputed errors, inaccuracies, and so forth.[59]

---

56. Berkouwer, *Holy Scripture*, pp. 17-19, 32, 170-94; *Modern Uncertainty*, p. 15.
57. Bavinck, *Gereformeerde Dogmatiek*, 1:429.
58. Ibid., 1:414-17; A. Kuyper, *Encyclopaedie der heilige godgeleerdheid* (Amsterdam: Wormser, 1894), 2:467-68, 499.
59. Ibid., 1:410-13; Kuyper, *Encyclopaedie*, 2:492-501.

All in all, Rogers's contention that Berkouwer has found his way back to his old tradition is unacceptable. However, the present discussion does pave the way to the consideration of a third explanation of Berkouwer's reversal.

A PREFERABLE APPRAISAL

According to Hendrikus Berkhof, the seeds of Berkouwer's later development were already present in his 1938 publication. His emphasis on the absolute authority of Scripture was basically indicative of a formal view of Scripture. However, his insistence on the joint consideration of form and content betrayed his uneasiness with the formal approach. The notion of absolute authority, inherent to an objectively present book, was replaced by the authority of the salvation content of Scripture, which produces a personal faith relation as its correlative. The form of Scripture, apart from that faith relation, can no longer be held up as intrinsically authoritative—because that came to be viewed as an intellectualistic, speculative, and formalistic approach.

The tables became truly turned. At first, from the point of view of Scripture as the objectively present written Word of God, all proponents of biblical criticism were called subjectivistic and autonomous. Later, from the point of view of the correlation motive as the final hermeneutical principle, the erstwhile a priori insistence upon Scripture as the written Word of God was said to be indicative of a depersonalizing, externalizing, scholastic, and formalistic objectivism, and to be constitutive of an enslavement to a heteronomous word of man.[60]

With two exceptions this picture of Berkouwer's development, which bears the imprint of Barth's theology unmistakably upon it,[61] must be accepted. The first exception is that the traditional Reformed doctrine of Scripture is not formalistic, even if it must seem that way from the perspective of neo-orthodoxy. The second exception is that Berkouwer did not add an emphasis upon content to neutralize the danger of the form. Content and form in the early Berkouwer as well as in Reformed theology in general are indissolubly connected. That, of course, implies that the later thinking of Berkouwer is not just a further development of a

60. H. Berkhof, "De Methode van Berkouwer's Theologie," in *Ex Auditu Verbi*, ed. R. Schippers (Kampen: Kok, 1965), pp. 44-48. See also Berkouwer, *Het probleem*, pp. 13-17.
61. See G. W. de Jong, *De theologie van Dr. G. C. Berkouwer* (Kampen: Kok, 1971), pp. 32-47.

latent strand. His thinking is, indeed, a complete reversal. But this makes the question even more urgent. Why did Berkouwer give up his allegiance to Scripture as the written Word of God, unassailable in its absolute authority, total trustworthiness, and full inerrancy, which for that very reason he presented as the only light in a dark world?[62] And, equally baffling, why did he come into the grip of a dialectic that holds to the relativity of the human form of Scripture, to be exposed to the critical-historical method? Furthermore, why did he come to a view of the so-called divine content, which we already saw does not merely escape human signification and transcend objective reality, but is by definition discontinuous with them?

Bavinck, in his *Reformed Dogmatics*, will not pass judgment over persons or their intentions as they are involved in the battle against the Bible. However, according to him, one's trust in Scripture increases with one's faith in Christ, whereas there is a connection between sin and error, which often lies beneath the surface, is nearly impossible to point out to someone else, but is at times revealed to the person himself. In any case, "the battle against Scripture is in the first place a manifestation of the enmity of the human heart," even if that enmity is no less present in "dead orthodoxy" as in biblical criticism.[63]

At one time Berkouwer expressed his total agreement with Bavinck's approach. What made him forget his earlier conviction not only that the battle is ethical in nature, but also that biblical criticism would inevitably lead to the secularization of human life? The answer may remain hidden below the surface. It also may be revealed to him. But one thing is sure: neither a reference to a "deeper insight" into the work of the Spirit, nor the claim of a return to the "old tradition," nor the suggestion of a "latent seed" in an earlier publication, is sufficient to account for Berkouwer's reversal.

62. Berkouwer, *Modern Uncertainty*, p. 21, "The Bible may not be called dark, because our hearts are darkened. The Bible is a light, and if we judge the Bible according to the darkness of our hearts, we are mere subjectivists. And as far as I can see, such subjectivism, though called reverence to the Word of God, is an escape from the responsibility of the nearness of the Word. The authority of Scripture has been attacked for more than two centuries. But in all these attacks we recognize a flight from this nearness, in which the grace of God is directed toward us."
63. Bavinck, *Gereformeerde Dogmatiek*, 1:411.

BERKOUWER'S FUNCTIONAL APPROACH

THE HUMAN "FORM"

It must be clear by now that in Berkouwer the distinction between "form" and "function" is prominent. However, further inquiry must be made into the meaning and nature of those terms, as well as the relationship they sustain to each other. What will emerge will be a structure of theologizing not only vastly different from that of Augustine, Calvin, Kuyper, and Bavinck, but also potentially harmful to the total range of biblical teachings.

Berkouwer is tireless in stressing that the form of Scripture is human in every sense of the word. He is obviously of the persuasion that in his earlier thought the full humanity of the Bible did not receive the recognition it deserved. The so-called proper recognition has at least two major implications.

First, room must be made for the historico-critical examination of Scripture. Such examination is rooted in the conviction that there is more to Scripture than just a "divine, extra-special side." It also represents an "honest approach" that takes the human quality of Scripture seriously. Berkouwer takes great pains in emphasizing, contrary to his earlier thinking, that this approach does not necessarily arise from "the assumption that only human reason had the right to judge the truth," and thus it cannot necessarily be accused of "hostility toward God or of refusal to submit to his law."[64] In fact he is persuaded that this critical approach ultimately opens up the "possibility of a deeper and clearer understanding of God's message."[65] (Even if it from one perspective precipitates the problem of a "controversial Bible," which seemed to destroy the ground of certainty.) To resist an honest, historical examination of Scripture is for all practical purposes "to present the divine character in such a manner that the human character could be of little significance," and "to depend on the *divine* as opposed to the *human* word."[66]

Second, the "proper recognition" of the human determines the nature of theology. Because this approach, by definition, is involved with things divine, it may not assume the character of the human form. In other words, it may not be "formal." Again and again the formal approach to Scripture and its teachings is taken

64. Berkouwer, *Holy Scripture*, pp. 13-14.
65. Ibid., pp. 9, 15.
66. Ibid., p. 17.

to task. Berkouwer's view militates against the formalization of Scripture,[67] of the relation between faith and revelation,[68] of the concept of canonicity,[69] of inspiration,[70] of faith,[71] of God's omnipotence,[72] of providence,[73] of inerrancy,[74] and so forth.

The context in which the term *formal* occurs leaves hardly any doubt about the meaning of this designation. A formal approach is objectifying and metaphysical in nature. It presents timeless truths and supernatural doctrines. It speaks in the abstract and in terms of cause and effect. It calls for intellectual assent and mental acceptance. In short, its focus is ontological. It aims at the determination and/or definition of the nature of God and man, truths, and things.

Thus the identification of Scripture and Word of God, which guarantees a basis for absolute certainty, is called a "theoretical objectification,"[75] whereas the "objectification of salvation" is said to destroy the correlation of revelation and faith.[76] Also the "objective distinction" between the elect and the non-elect, or the "static objectification of two closed groups of men," is unacceptable to Berkouwer.[77] Neither are the reliability, perspicuity, and sufficiency of Scripture to be regarded as objective qualities.[78]

With similar reasoning he regards the emphasis upon the divine authorship of Scripture as leading to the metaphysical and theoretical problem concerning how it can be the Word of God and simultaneously the word of man.[79] He also criticizes the view of election that wishes to explain the world as a "metaphysical system."[80]

Further, Berkouwer does not accept a timeless correlation be-

---

67. Ibid., pp. 45, 105-6, 143, 146, 149, 180.
68. Ibid., p. 60.
69. Ibid., pp. 69, 83-84, 87, 89.
70. Ibid., p. 162.
71. Ibid., pp. 308, 345.
72. G. C. Berkouwer, *Divine Election* (Grand Rapids: Eerdmans, 1960), p. 61.
73. G. C. Berkouwer, *The Providence of God* (Grand Rapids: Eerdmans, 1952), p. 67-68.
74. Berkouwer, *Holy Scripture*, pp. 181-82.
75. Ibid., p. 32.
76. G. C. Berkouwer, *Faith and Justification* (Grand Rapids: Eerdmans, 1954), p. 167. The quote in the text is a direct translation from the Dutch edition, G. C. Berkouwer, *Geloof en rechtvaardiging* (Kampen: Kok, 1949), p. 174.
77. G. C. Berkouwer, "Vragen rondom de Belijdenis," *Gereformeerd Theologisch Tijdschrift* 63 (1963):13.
78. Berkouwer, *Holy Scripture*, pp. 248, 268-69, 305.
79. Ibid., pp. 160-63.
80. Berkouwer, *Divine Election*, p. 25.

tween Scripture and faith,[81] neither does he accept Scripture as a source book of supernatural truths.[82] After all, the witness of the apostles is neither "eternalizing" nor "abstract."[83] Also, the Reformation maxim, *"sola Scriptura,"* is not a "lifeless abstraction."[84]

Much of Berkouwer's ammunition is directed against the notion of causality. That notion cannot escape the charge of determinism, and therefore it should be dropped. Berkouwer removes it from his views of Scripture, providence, and election.

As to his view of Scripture, he holds that as long as the relationship between the divine author and the human authors is construed in terms of causality and instrumentality, the doctrine of Scripture will never transcend the formal and metaphysical level. The causal approach should be abandoned and replaced with the perspective of witness. The human Scripture is the prophetic-apostolic witness to the divine Word.[85]

As to his view of providence, Berkouwer does not leave any doubt as to where he stands. If Christianity is to be distinguished from determinism, the notion of causality should be shunned. In his estimation, the Reformed doctrine of providence "does not reason from the idea of causation," does not "involve God . . . as enclosed with a system of causality, a system in which the causal chain extends throughout this world in one unbroken line to God, . . . a causal circle in which God and man alike are involved."[86] Berkouwer specifically opposes the use of causal logic, even if God is called the *first* cause in distinction to men as *second* causes, because it eventually will lead to the conclusion that God is the author of sin.[87] Similar misgivings are expressed in connection with the doctrine of election.[88]

All in all, these various concerns of Berkouwer are indicative of his unalterable opposition to ontological definitions of the nature

---

81. Berkouwer, *Holy Scripture*, p. 16. See also p. 186, "Various statements by Paul regarding womanhood and marriage constitute some of the most discussed illustrations of this particular problem of time-boundness."
82. Ibid., p. 32.
83. Ibid., p. 253.
84. G. C. Berkouwer, *De Heilige Schrift*, 2:355. The particular section in which this quotation is found is not translated in the English edition.
85. Ibid., 2:47-49. This is not found in the English edition either.
86. Berkouwer, *Providence*, pp. 152, 154-55.
87. Ibid., p. 157. See also Lewis B. Smedes, "G. C. Berkouwer," in *Creative Minds in Contemporary Theology*, ed. Philip Hughes (Grand Rapids: Eerdmans, 1966), pp. 71-74; and C. VanTil, *The Sovereignty of Grace* (Nutley, N.J.: Presbyterian & Reformed, 1966), pp. 40-44.
88. Berkouwer, *Divine Election*, pp. 143, 185, 274, 276. See for a critique of Berkouwer's view, F. H. Klooster, "Predestination: A Calvinistic Note," in *Perspectives on Evangelical Theology*, pp. 85-87, 91.

of things, which lead to intellectual knowledge. When Berkouwer
speaks about God's sustaining the world, he refuses to present it
as "a formal or neutral cosmological witness to the fact that God
still holds the world intact," or as an "abstract . . . theory about
the mere continuation of the world's existence."[89] When Berkouwer writes about the sacraments, he does not intend to "construct an 'essence' of the sacrament" that gives a "separate 'gno-
sis.' "[90]

With all the respect that he has for Berkouwer, the foregoing is
"disturbing" to Lewis Smedes. He concludes that constructive
theological statements that will be of assistance to Christian
scholars, for example, in the areas of philosophy or anthropology,
are simply not present in Berkouwer's *oeuvre*—and such statements are not to be expected.[91] Gordon Lewis registers a similar
complaint when he writes, "In the reading of his *Man: The Image
of God* . . . we no more find out what man *is*, than we can learn
about who God *is* in the Bible."[92]

THE DIVINE "FUNCTION"

The question arises concerning what is behind Berkouwer's
later approach, which seems so bound up with his emphasis on
the full humanity of Scripture. Before an attempt will be made to
answer that question, it ought to be noted that Berkouwer is
equally tireless in stressing the divinity of the "function" of
Scripture. The proper recognition of this also has at least two
implications.

First, just as the human form of Scripture is correlative with
the historical-critical method, so the divine function of Scripture
is correlative with faith. Indeed, Berkouwer explains that this
correlation does not imply a mutual, equal interdependence, so
that faith is just as much a determining factor for God's message
as vice versa. Rather, it wishes to convey that the nature of faith
is such that it is directed to, honors, and answers to God's gra-
cious revelation in Christ.[93] However, it ought to be underscored
that both revelation and faith are non-objectifying and nonmeta-
physical. That means revelation is not a set of timeless truths or
supernatural teachings, and faith is not to be viewed in terms of
intellectual assent or mental acceptance.

89. Berkouwer, *Providence*, p. 59.
90. G. C. Berkouwer, *The Sacraments* (Grand Rapids: Eerdmans, 1969), p. 11.
91. Smedes, "G. C. Berkouwer," pp. 94-95.
92. Lewis, "Categories in Collision?" p. 256.
93. Berkouwer, *Justification*, p. 178.

Second, the divine function of Scripture determines the nature of theology positively in terms of its perspective, its focus, and its end.

The perspective of theology is that of faith. Statements to the effect that a Christian doctrine is not a theory but a "pure confession of faith"[94] are to be found throughout Berkouwer's writings. In his estimation, "theology may not travel beyond the borders of faith's perspective."[95] Smedes observes correctly, "Theology is a work of faith, and all of its statements must be such as the believer can recognize as the objects of faith. This is perhaps the single most influential principle of Berkouwer's theology. . . . Only those matters that the believer can and ought to confess as his personal faith . . . are the proper conclusions of theology."[96] This also determines that theology is not in the business of building systems. It would not square with the perspective of faith.

The focus of theology is the content of Scripture. This content is the message of the saving grace of God as it is displayed in Christ, specifically His cross and resurrection, and received by man in faith. This message, and this message only, is the proper subject matter of theology. All the doctrines of Scripture present and promote this message. That is why theology, whether it deals with the doctrine of election, providence, man, sin, Christ, justification, sanctification, perseverance, the church, or the sacraments, both critically exposes any erroneous or objectifying element (view, distinction, deduction, inference, interpretaion, etc.) that obscures the message, and joyfully discloses any element that brings the message into clearer focus. That is why Berkouwer criticizes the notion of an "a priori decree, whereby God's plan in creation and through sin is not yet immediately transparent" as an "abstract sovereignty." "What is revealed in history and through sin is . . . the glory of sovereign love and loving sovereignty."[97] That is why he in his book on Scripture speaks about the reliability, perspicuity, and sufficiency of the *message* of Scripture.[98] That is why he capitalizes in his study of the sacraments on Christ as their "truth."[99]

The end of theology is the response of praise. Throughout his dogmatic studies Berkouwer emphasizes that a living theology

---

94. Berkouwer, *Providence*, p. 39; *Divine Election*, p. 25.
95. Berkouwer, *Justification*, p. 160.
96. Smedes, "G. C. Berkouwer," pp. 65-66.
97. Berkouwer, *Divine Election*, p. 267.
98. Berkouwer, *Holy Scripture*, p. 240-326.
99. Berkouwer, *The Sacraments*, p. 10.

that speaks from the perspective of faith and has a clear view of the message of grace must end up in doxology. That is correctly observed by Smedes.[100]

Still, all this is not met with unqualified approval. Smedes regards it, again, as disturbing that faith and theology appear to fade into identification.[101] Further, Gordon Lewis protests that Berkouwer forces an unacceptable disjunction upon his readers when theology is said to be a matter of personal participation rather than conceptual truths, of functional value rather than supernatural doctrines, of authentic religion rather than intellectual convictions. For Lewis, Scripture contains assertions of truth about ontological realities. Therefore it is erroneous to say that the Bible "knows man only as he functions in relationship to God and knows God only in relationship to changing people."[102]

THE FUNDAMENTAL DIALECTIC

More must be said to clarify the presuppositions of Berkouwer's later thought—to bring into focus what is behind his dual emphasis upon both the human "form" and the divine "content" of Scripture and this viewpoint's implications for theology.

The disjunction, noted by Lewis, is indicative of the dialectic mentioned in the previous section. There is both a total discontinuity and a total continuity between the divine and the human. The discontinuity calls for the critical approach to, and the relativizing of, the form of Scripture and forbids theology to be formal in character. The continuity calls for the correlation of revelation (divine) and faith (human), which are both non-objectifying, and requires theology to focus on the divine content or function of Scripture, also supposed to be non-objectifying. At this point a most serious problem emerges. When theology lapses into the error of objectification, it no longer predicates about the divine and therefore forfeits any truth claim. That is the reason Berkouwer shuns conceptual statements about ontological realities. But when theology "fades into the identification with faith," which should make it simultaneously correlative with revelation, it transcends "formal" human language. But does Berkouwer understand the implications of this? He may be inclined to say yes. Theology leaves, first of all, the error-prone language behind, which is exposed as such by the historical-critical method. Then,

100. Smedes, "G. C. Berkouwer," pp. 66, 69.
101. Ibid., pp. 94-95.
102. Lewis, "Categories in Collision?" p. 256.

it moves beyond the level of ontological language with its ontic realities and abiding truths, further (dis)qualified as static objectifications and timeless abstractions. Finally, it has an uncluttered view of, and can focus upon, the "content" of Scripture. But how does it do so, other than in terms of language? And, what is the nature of that language? Here Berkouwer is faced with the very problem the modern hermeneutical movement, from Barth and Bultmann to Ott, Fuchs, and Ebeling, has never been able to solve.[103]

After everything is said and done, theology does not transcend an objectifying language garment. This puts Berkouwer in a bind! The language that theology uses does not and cannot make meaningful predication about the "content" of Scripture. In fact, even terms like *content* and phrases like *the saving message of God* do not and cannot have any truth claim. Let it be underscored. Revelation is correlative to faith. That is, it comes into meaningful and truthful view only in the act of faith. However, because of its objectifying language garment, theology does not "fade into identification" with non-objectifying faith. For that very reason it does not and cannot make any meaningful predication or any truth claim in any language or terminology.

In Berkouwer's own terminology, "speaking about Scripture [theology?] threatens to be transposed into a whisper"—if that![104] But he has a way to counter the threat. "The preaching of the Gospel is the only way in which we can speak about the Gospel [beyond theology?], not in whispers, but with thankfulness and songs of praise."[105] This is the very way proposed by the "New Hermeneutic," which operates with the same presuppositions and in the same framework.[106] Preaching will transcend the level of theological objectification and bring the "content" of the gospel into view. Where the apologetics of theology failed, there the "apologia" of proclamation is supposed to succeed.[107] But two things ought to be noted. First, preaching is encumbered with the same objectifying language liability as theology. The problem merely shifts. Second, the solution of preaching is proposed by

---

103. This is further analyzed in a paper read at the Conference on Hermeneutics, sponsored by the International Council on Biblical Inerrancy in November 1982.
104. Berkouwer, *Holy Scripture*, p. 168.
105. Ibid., p. 61.
106. E. Fuchs, *Zum hermeneutischen Problem in der Theologie* (Tübingen: J. C. B. Mohr, 1959), pp. 142-43; G. Ebeling, *Word and Faith* (Philadelphia: Fortress, 1963), pp. 328, 331, "The sermon is the EXECUTION of the text."
107. Berkouwer, *Holy Scripture*, p. 37.

theology. Theology has the final word! But since this is already disqualified, its "final" solution is disqualified as well.

However, there is an even more serious problem than the language of Scripture, theology, and preaching. The same discontinuity between the divine and the human that relativizes that language to the point that no meaningful and truthful predication is possible, also has implications for the references to realities made in that language. What is the nature of those realities? They cannot be ontic in character in the sense of being objectively present. Berkouwer made that very clear. Scripture as the Word of God is not such reality, neither is election, nor providence. And this is only a sample.

The full impact of all this is staggering. Not only is the human unable to make any predication about the divine, but also the divine is locked out of the everyday world, life, and affairs of man. *The fundamental discontinuity determines that the two do not coincide at one single point.*

That discontinuity has two aspects. The first one is metaphysical. God *cannot* enter His own created reality. The two are of a different order. The second aspect is ethical. In man's everyday world scientific thought has the final say. Berkouwer insists that a sacrifice of the intellect is not tolerated.[108] Therefore, God *may not* enter His own created reality. It is out of His jurisdiction and control. The notion of causality is preposterous. God may not interfere in direct word (Scripture) or in direct deed (election and providence). The dialectic that produces all this appears to be a veritable declaration of independence. Berkouwer's early assessment that the views that operate with the notion of correlation, including the neo-orthodox version, are autonomous in character and rooted in the hostility of the human heart, consciously or not, could not be more true. Berkouwer's later assessment that they are bound up with honesty—let the human be human!—and not with hostility ought to be rejected.

It may seem in his chapter on the reliability of Scripture that Berkouwer breaks out of the death knell of the dialectic in the area of the resurrection. After all, he makes the statement that "the witness of the apostles is concerned with history," and that this witness and the faith produced by it "are in vain if Christ is not raised." This is said to emphasize that their "testimony" is "backed by the truth."[109] He also quotes Barth to the effect that

108. Ibid., pp. 351-52, 354.
109. Ibid., p. 253.

"we must still accept the resurrection of Jesus, and his subsequent appearances to his disciples, as genuine history in its own particular time."[110] All this gives the distinct impression that both Berkouwer and Barth champion the resurrection as an objectively present reality in full agreement with the Reformed and evangelical faith.

Now, it should be readily admitted that for both thinkers "the witness of the apostles" is reliable by virtue of "the truth of the resurrection." But what is the nature of those two phrases and the relationship they sustain to each other? Berkouwer emphatically states about the word *witness* that "its nature is not eternalizing and abstract.[111] This can mean only one thing. The witness of the apostles (Scripture) cannot and may not be directly identified with the Word of God. It cannot and may not be presented as universally valid truth, in time and for all times ("eternalizing"), whether it is believed or not ("abstract").

Further, Berkouwer and Barth insist upon the truth of the resurrection in a polemic context, in which they express opposition to Bultmann. Both hold that Bultmann's program of demythologizing, with its focus upon existential interpretation, amounts to an intolerable reduction of biblical truth. But when they take Bultmann to task, they do not do so in defense of Reformed and evangelical orthodoxy.[112] It must be pointed out that the word *history* in Barth's statement is a translation, not of the German world *historie*, which means ordinary history, but of the German, *geschichte*.[113] This second term is first of all a predicate of God[114] and denotes the realm that is beyond the disposal of objectifying reason or language.[115] In quoting Barth, Berkouwer takes his side in the debate to safeguard "the *content* (sic!) of the kerygma."[116] In other words, Barth assigns the "resurrection" to the realm of *geschichte*, and Berkouwer makes it a component element of the *content* of Scripture. However, since neither *geschichte* nor *con-*

110. Ibid., p. 258. See G. Lewis, "The Human Authorship of Inspired Scripture," in *Inerrancy*, pp. 239-40, and "Categories in Collision?" p. 255, for a further discussion of this issue.
111. Ibid., p. 253.
112. For the relationship between Barth and Bultmann, see H. Krabbendam, "From Bultmann to Ott," (Ph.D. diss., Westminster Theological Seminary, 1969), pp. 44-71.
113. K. Barth, *Kirchliche Dogmatik* (Zollikon-Zürich: Evangelischer Verlag, 1959), III,2, 537.
114. Ibid., II,1, 291, 394, 556, 562; II,2, 192.
115. C. Trimp, *Om de oeconomie van het welbehagen* (Goes: Oosterbaan, 1961).
116. Berkouwer, *Holy Scripture*, p. 258.

tent are to be equated with objectively present realities, there is, regrettably, no reason to believe that the resurrection of Christ occupies an exceptional place in the theological methodology of Berkouwer or Barth. The nature of "the witness of the apostles" and "the truth of the resurrection," as well as the relationships they sustain to each other, is fully determined and controlled by the dialectic with its two mutually presupposing and excluding poles.

CONCLUSION

The early Berkouwer insisted that Scripture as the written Word of God is inerrant in all that it asserts and authoritative in everything that it addresses.

This is not to say that every assertion is exhaustive in its expression or that it locks in reality. For one thing, in human language God condescends to a finite and lowly level of communication. For another, human language is a set of conventions, consisting of sounds and symbols, to express and communicate thought. But every assertion is truthful and trustworthy as it informs, explains, and directs. As created by God, human language is capable of performing its God-given function.

Neither is the inerrancy assertion to say that every area of life is addressed with equal determination and emphasis. For one thing, the Scriptures teach what man is to believe concerning God and what duty God requires of man. For another, the Bible is not given as a textbook for science or history. Nevertheless, because every territory of life is under God's jurisdiction and every thought of man is to be made captive to the obedience of Christ, whatever area is addressed, it is bound under God by whatever is said in whatever form it is presented. Actually, all of life is religion and should seek submission to what God says in His Word, whether explicitly or implicitly, by example or principle.

Against that backdrop the early Berkouwer charged the opponents of the inerrancy and authority of Scripture with a subjectivist autonomy. This autonomy is characterized by a limitation or perversion of truth, which leads to de-Christianization and secularization and consciously or not is rooted in the hostility of the human heart.

The later Berkouwer is in the grip of the modern dialectic that sets forth the simultaneous and mutual continuity as well as discontinuity of the "divine" and the "human." The continuity requires the correlation of revelation and faith, which are both non-objectifying, and is expressed in the designation of Scripture as witness, in which the human objectifying form points to the divine non-objectifying content. The discontinuity requires that the realm of the non-objectifying divine does not coincide in one single point with the realm of the objectifying human, which includes not only reality as it is daily experienced but also the language of Scripture and theology.

The historical and religious roots of the dialectic, the way it determines the usage of the term *witness*, as well as the manner to escape its deadly grip have been set forth in another context.[117] So, that will not be repeated here. But the following final observations are necessary.

First, there is a vast difference between men like Orr and Berkouwer, who are naïvely lumped together by Rogers as opponents of the inerrancy of Scripture. Orr subscribes to the direct identification of Scripture and the Word of God, except in a certain number of inaccuracies and inconsistencies. He also holds to the direct identification of theology and truth, as long as the former faithfully reflects the Word of God. Berkouwer does neither. That makes his case vastly more serious. For him, Scripture does not predicate direct and original truth and does not have direct and original authority. Theology does not predicate direct and derivative truth and does not have direct and derivative authority. The issue of inaccurate language pales into relative insignificance before the issue of objectifying language, with which all of Scripture and theology are said to be encumbered. At no time do they or can they make any truthful, trustworthy, meaningful, or authoritative predication. The solution of indirect identity is not acceptable. It is a *theological* solution and as such must be disqualified.

Second, there is a vast difference between men like Bavinck and Berkouwer, who are mistakenly lumped together by Rogers as to their positions on the content of Scripture. Bavinck holds that the teachings of Scripture refer to objectively present realities. Berkouwer does not and says the divine activity cannot and may not be equated with space-time events.

Third, there is a vast difference between men like Kuyper and Berkouwer, who are inaccurately lumped together by Rogers as to their views on the influence sphere of Scripture. Kuyper insists that there is not one square inch of created reality that escapes

117. H. Krabbendam, "B. B. Warfield versus G. C. Berkouwer on Scripture," in *Inerrancy*, pp. 434-46.

the authority of Christ as the Son of God and of Scripture as the Word of God. Berkouwer does not agree. He has fallen victim to a (not so?) subtle nature-grace polarity of a particular stripe. It is not simply so that God and Scripture are said to have the area of salvation (grace) as their focus to the virtual exclusion of the rest of created reality (nature). This position, practically espoused by Orr and strongly opposed by Bavinck, curtails the range of authoritative address and regards the presence of technical inaccuracies and other errors as immaterial. No, in Berkouwer's case the relationship between nature and grace is such that neither the divine presence nor the divine Word (grace) can penetrate or interact with the everyday world of man (nature) at any given point.

Fourth, Rogers is naïve when he holds that Berkouwer offers a third alternative that transcends rationalism and subjectivism. Berkouwer's view is a dialectic combination of a subjectivistic irrationalism and an objectivistic rationalism, which is rooted in autonomy and was made possible only after he left behind the sure foundation of the inerrant and authoritative Scripture as the written Word of God. How Berkouwer came to fall into the trap of the dialectic may never be answered. Why Rogers followed Berkouwer may indicate a basic lack of understanding of the constituent elements and the far reaching implications of Berkouwer's later thinking. How any Christian, however, who recognizes that the governing dialectic is rooted in a declaration of independence from God, which removes the world from His jurisdiction and control and inevitably leads to the total secularization of life, could be attracted to Berkouwer's reversed position is a total enigma.

11. Scripture in Liberation Theology: An Eviscerated Authority

Vernon C. Grounds

At the very beginning of this study, let us delimit its scope and purpose. We are not, for one thing, undertaking a history of liberation theology. Its origin and development are matters of absorbing interest, but they lie outside our purview. Anyone desiring such background information is advised to consult J. Andrew Kirk's definitive work.[1]

For a second thing, we are not proposing to set forth in detail the radical reformulation of traditional Christian doctrine made by this theological school. To speak of it as a school is admittedly rather misleading because the liberationists (hereafter so designated for convenience' sake) differ markedly among themselves on key issues. Yet the concerns, emphases, and goals they share justify their inclusion under a common rubric. But suppose we listen, at any rate, to one of this school's foremost spokemen, Gustavo Gutiérrez, as he explains liberation theology's unique nature.

> The theology of liberation offers us not so much a new theme for reflection as a *new way* to do theology. Theology as critical reflec-

1. J. Andrew Kirk, *Liberation Theology: An Evangelical View from the Third World* (Atlanta: John Knox, 1979).

VERNON C. GROUNDS, B.A., Rutgers University; B.D., Faith Theological Seminary; Ph.D., Drew University, is president emeritus and professor of pastoral care and Christian ethics at Denver Conservative Baptist Seminary, Denver, Colorado. He has written *The Reason for Our Hope* (1945), *Evangelicalism and Social Responsibility* (1969), *Revolution and the Christian Faith* (1971), and *Emotional Problems and the Gospel* (1976).

tion on historical praxis is a liberating theology, a theology of the liberating transformation of the history of mankind and also therefore that part of mankind gathered into *ecclesia*—which openly confesses Christ. This is a theology which does not stop with reflecting on the world, but rather tries to be part of the process through which the world is transformed. It is a theology which is open—in the protest against trampled human dignity, in the struggle against the plunder of the vast majority of people, in liberating love, and in the building of a new, just, and fraternal society—to the gift of the kingdom of God.[2]

For another thing, we are not attempting a full-length critique of liberation theology, an evaluation of its strengths and weaknesses, although a thoroughgoing appraisal is obviously imperative. Anyone interested in pursuing that vital matter is referred once more to Kirk's work.

Positively stated, our single purpose is to examine the hermeneutic of this new theological genre, focusing attention on its use of Scripture and thus its untenable beliefs regarding the Bible's nature and authority. Yet a brief overview of liberation theology is in order if we are to enter into fruitful dialogue with its iconoclasts who boldly attack what they regard as ideological obfuscations of biblical truth, obfuscations hallowed by centuries of both Catholic and Protestant tradition, but which throttle and pervert the central message of Christianity. And what is that message as the liberationists discern it? The God of freedom, justice, and love, the God of the Exodus, the God of the prophets and Jesus Christ, is acting in history to liberate the poor, oppressed, marginalized people of the earth.

CONTEMPORARY THEOLOGY OF LIBERATION

Robert McAfee Brown, a sympathetic North American interpreter of *Theology in a New Key*, as he calls it in his book by that name, suggests that there are "six overlapping emphases" that differentiate this new genre from the versions of theology that traditionally have dominated Christendom:

1. A different starting point: the poor
2. a different interlocutor: the nonperson
3. a different set of tools: social sciences
4. a different analysis: the reality of conflict

2. Gustavo Gutiérrez, *A Theology of Liberation: History, Politics and Salvation*, trans. and ed. Sister Caridad Inda and John Eagleson (Maryknoll, New York: Orbis, 1973), p. 15.

5. a different mode of engagement: praxis
6. a different theology: the single "second act"[3]

We will not discuss this helpful inventory of themes *ad seriatum.* Instead, we will venture our own succinct characterization of liberation theology, and it will of course at some points coincide with Brown's.

A LATIN AMERICAN THEOLOGY

This genre emerged initially within Latin American Catholicism but quickly broke through ecclesiastical and geographical limits. It has appealed primarily and powerfully to Third World Christians while creating somewhat of a ferment among Western theologians. Witness, for example, the books by Vanderbilt University professor Peter Hodgson, *Children of Freedom: Black Liberation in Christian Perspective* and *New Birth of Freedom.*

The major makers and shapers of this new mode of theologizing have been and still are, however, Latin Americans: Juan Luis Segundo of Uruguay; Luci Gera of Argentina; Gustavo Gutiérrez, the Peruvian scholar whom we have already mentioned; Hugo Assmann, originally of Brazil but exiled successively from his own country, then from Uruguay, Bolivia, and Chile; Jose Mirando of Mexico; Jose Severino Croatto of Argentina; Jose Miguez Bonino, another Argentine; and Rubem Alves, a Brazilian Protestant. All of these and other theologians like them are products of a continent on which Christianity and oppression have existed cheek-by-jowl since the time of the Iberian conquest. It is the Latin American situation that has therefore motivated a probing reconsideration and a drastic revision of traditional theology.

In effect, consequently, liberationists are protesting against the intolerable conditions in Latin America that Roman Catholicism has tolerated and helped to perpetuate. Gutiérrez quotes the indictment brought against the church in a document drafted by a seminar on the problems of young people that was held under the sponsorship of the Department of Education of CELAM *(Consejo Episcopal Latinoamericano):*

> In Latin America the awareness is spreading—even among Christians—that Christianity has contributed to producing the cultural alienation that is seen today. The Christian religion has

3. Robert McAfee Brown, *Theology in a New Key: Responding to Liberation Themes* (Philadelphia: Westminster, 1978), p. 60.

served, and continues to serve, as an ideology justifying the domination of the powerful. In Latin America Christianity has been a religion at the service of the system. Its rites, temples, and works have contributed to channeling popular dissatisfactions towards another world totally disconnected from this one. This Christianity has checked a popular protest against an unjust and oppressive system[4]

A THEOLOGY "FROM BELOW"

Liberation theology, as Brown points out, is a theology "from below," a theology that voices the needs, frustrations, longings, and hopes of the poor, the oppressed, and the downtrodden, society's nonentities. Gutiérrez forcefully articulates this distinctive.

A good portion of contemporary theology seems to have started off from the challenge laid down by the *nonbeliever.* The nonbeliever calls our religious world into question and demands thoroughgoing purification and renewal. . . . But on a continent like Latin America the challenge does not come first and foremost from the nonbeliever but from the *nonhuman* human being, the human person whom the existing social order does not recongize as such. It comes from the poor, the exploited, people who are legally and systematically stripped of their existence as humans, the people who are scarcely aware of the fact that they are human beings. This nonhuman being calls into question not so much our religious world as our economic, social, political, and cultural world.[5]

Thus if theology is to be authentically Christian it must reflect the significance of the divine enfleshment in a Palestinian peasant, which Jon Sobrino, an El Salvadorian Jesuit, interprets as God's deliberate self-identification with the poor.

It would be anachronistic to look to Jesus for an analysis of classes such as we find in the work of present-day sociology. Yet his general attitude makes it clear that in trying to understand justice Jesus adopts a stance that is rooted in the poor and is meant to benefit them. . . . In that sense the first principle for concretizing moral values is nothing else but the first principle of Christology itself: i.e., incarnation. One must deliberately adopt some partial stance in order to comprehend the totality. To look for some stand that will give us the totality directly is to do the very opposite of incarnation (profound disincarnation).[6]

4. Cited by Gutiérrez, *A Theology of Liberation,* p. 282, n. 35.
5. Cited by Alfredo Fierro, *The Militant Gospel: A Critical Introduction to Political Theologies,* trans. John Drury (Maryknoll, New York: Orbis, 1977), p. 334.
6. Jon Sobrino, *Christology at the Crossroads: A Latin American Approach,* trans. John Drury (Maryknoll, New York: Orbis, 1976), p. 124. Cf. Sobrino's interpretation of the class outlook adopted by Jesus and its bearing on discipleship, pp. 118-31.

Theology, therefore, ought to surge up out of poverty and speak for the poor. That is precisely how the liberationists view themselves—champions of the voiceless poor.

A THEOLOGY OF AND FOR THE OPPRESSED

This new genre of the Christian faith is unapologetically biased. It spurns as impossible, no less than cowardly and immoral, the ideal of a salvation offered to all men equally and indiscriminately, oppressed and oppressors alike. God in Jesus Christ identified Himself with the oppressed and took their side against their oppressors. Theologians who profess allegiance to Jesus Christ ought, then, to follow His example and take sides. So Latin American liberationists are one in spirit with a North American black, James Cone, professor of theology at Union Theological Seminary in New York City:

> Black theology cannot accept a view of God which does not represent Him as being for blacks and thus against whites. Living in a world of white oppressors, black people have no time for a neutral God. . . . there is no use for a God Who loves whites the *same* as blacks. . . . What we need is the divine love experessed in Black Power which is the power of black people to destroy their oppressors, here and now, by any means at their disposal. Unless God is participating in this holy activity, we must reject His love.[7]

But God, as perceived by liberationists, has in fact identified Himself with all downtrodden human beings around the globe, whether black or white. The class-identification of the incarnate Christ disclosed God's bias unmistakably. If Luke 4:18 is taken at its face value, a message of "good news to the poor. . . . release to the captives. . . . liberty to those who are oppressed," then, J. Andrew Kirk rightly asserts, "There is no option; theology must be done from out of a commitment to a living God Who defends the cause of 'the hungry' and who sends 'the rich empty away' (Luke 1:53)."[8] This is the conviction of the liberationists who spurn academic objectivity and detachment.

A THEOLOGY OF PRAXIS

This new genre is a theology that highlights praxis. Indeed, this is perhaps its pivotal distinctive as opposed to traditional

---

7. Cited by Peter C. Hodgson, *New Birth of Freedom: A Theology of Bondage and Liberation* (Philadelphia: Fortress, 1976), p. 318.
8. Kirk, *Liberation Theology*, p. 205.

versions of Christianity. But what exactly is meant by *praxis?* Is it the relatively simple and commonplace insistence that Christians practice the gospel they preach? It is that, no doubt, but it is that insistence understood and implemented at a profound level. Alfredo Fierro in a mosaic of quotations clarifies the meaning of this term, which has been borrowed from Marx but baptized by Christians for their own purposes:

> The statements of theology are pronouncements bound up with the concrete witness and activity of Christians. It is in that witness and activity that they find fulfillment and verification. Every theological statement is a prospective view, a "hermeneutic" or "heuristic" hypothesis that must be lived out experientially by Christians; the actions of Christians will confirm or belie the hypothesis, grounding the hypothesis or invalidating it. . . . Theological propositions are "an anticipation of future practice for each generation of Christians: they are in the nature of a project that can and should be surpassed by a new line of practice". . . . "The criterion of verification of every theological statement is the practice that it makes possible in the future. Its truth is determined by what it produces in praxis insofar as the alteration of existing reality is concerned". . . . As theory, theology precedes and anticipates practice; but praxis in turn constitutes the horizon within which theological theories are formed. Theological theories constitute the discourse that issues out of the exercise of love and Christian hope.[9]

The importance of praxis has been underscored by two European theologians, Jürgen Moltmann and Johannes Baptist Metz, against whom the liberationists sometimes polemicize yet from whom they nevertheless borrow. In Moltmann's opinion, *the new criterion of theology and of faith is to be found in praxis. . . . Truth must be practicable. Unless it contains initiative for the transformation of the world, it becomes a myth of the existing world.*[10]

Metz is of the same opinion: "The so-called fundamental hermeneutic problem of theology is not the problem of how systematic theology stands in relation to historical theology, how dogma stands in relation to history, but what is the relation between theory and practice, between understanding the faith and social practice."[11]

9. Cited by Gutiérrez, *A Theology of Liberation,* p. 244, n. 33.
10. Cited by Theodore Runyan, "Wesley and the Theologies of Liberation," in *Sanctification and Liberation: Liberation Theologies in Light of the Wesleyan Tradition,* ed. Theodore Runyan (Nashville, Abingdon, 1981), pp. 8-9.
11. Cited by Gutiérrez, *A Theology of Liberation,* p. 244, n. 33.

According to the liberationists, however, praxis requires a specific commitment. It is, as we have observed, a biased commitment to the poor and oppressed. It is not commitment to truth as passive cognition; it is commitment to liberating action on behalf of the downtrodden, liberating action that has as its avowed objective the transformation of society. In the often-quoted words of Rubem Alves, "Truth is the name given by an historical community to those historical acts which were, are, and will be effective for the liberation of man. Truth is action."[12]

A SOCIOLOGICALLY ORIENTED THEOLOGY

Liberation theology is sociologically as well as biblically oriented. It thankfully appropriates the data and insights provided by the human sciences. Its revelational sources, consequently, are not just the Scriptures but disciplines such as economics, politics, demography, and any other field of study that contributes to an understanding of the contemporary situation. José Miguez Bonino answers the objection that, because a Christian has God's Word, he does not need illumination from any secular source.

> In what realm of human experience shall we find categories for naming the themes of theology? Religion and metaphysics have traditionally provided the answer. But the world of religion and metaphysics has been growing increasingly dim during the last four centuries. Theology has consequently tried to articulate its knowledge in more decidedly anthropological terms, resorting to psychological or existential analysis. But in the last decades, converging lines of human experience and thought and Biblical research have pointed to the realm of history as the proper quarry for theological building material. Consequently, sciences dealing with historical life—sociology, politics, the sciences of culture— have more and more provided the categories and articulations for theology.[13]

A theology committed to the task of changing oppressive structures and institutions requires an understanding of society's conflicts, maladjustments, and dynamics. Hence, this indispensable material for effective theologizing must be drawn from secular theory and research.

12. Cited by Alfred T. Hennelly, *Theologies in Conflict: The Challenge of Juan Luis Segundo* (Maryknoll, New York: Orbis, 1979), p. 47.
13. José Miguez Bonino, *Doing Theology in a Revolutionary Situation* (Philadelphia: Fortress, 1975), p. 78.

A MARXIST-INFLUENCED THEOLOGY

This new genus of theology is unapologetically Marxist in its approach to the whole problematic of cultural pathology. That there is an affinity between Marxist theory and liberation theology Segundo flatly affirms. He does so despite his awareness that any such affirmation will be seized upon by defenders of an oppressive status quo and cited stridently as indisputable proof that liberationists are covert agents of Moscow!

> The manner of conceiving and proposing the problems of society will never again be the same as it was before Marx. Whether or not everything Marx said is accepted, and no matter how his "essential thought" is explained, it will always remain certain that there is no contemporary social thought that is not to some degree "Marxist," that is, profoundly indebted to Marx. In that sense, liberation theology in Latin America is certainly "Marxist."[14]

Bonino shares Segundo's critical appreciation of Marx and endorses his willingness to employ Marxist categories in order to understand the structures and dynamics of society. Realizing, however, that even a critical utilization of Marx for some very specific purposes is "the source of many misunderstandings," Bonino seeks to dispel the fog of suspicion.

> Our assumption of Marxism has nothing to do with a supposedly abstract or eternal theory or with dogmatic formulae—a view which is not absent in certain Marxist circles—but with a scientific analysis and a number of verifiable hypotheses in relation to conditions obtaining in certain historical moments and places, and which, properly modified, corrected, and supplemented, provide an adequate means to grasp our own historical situation (insofar, moreover, as it is closely related and significantly shaped by the model originally analyzed.)[15]

Bonino does not hesitate to assert that Marxism "has proved and still proves to be, the best instrument available for an effective and rational realization of human possibilities of historical life."[16]

In addition, Marxism holds that all theology, indeed all human systems of thought and interpretations of reality—Christianity included; Marxism, *mirabile dictu*, excluded!—are ideologically

14. Cited by Hennelly, *Theologies in Conflict*, p. 166.
15. Bonino, *Doing Theology*, pp. 95-96.
16. Ibid., p. 97.

contaminated. Admittedly the concept of ideology is very complicated, but, as employed by Marx, it is essentially a collective perceptual grid—a complex of assumptions that are accepted unreflectively and tenaciously, a group mind-set that rationalizes self-interest, justifying the privileged status of the oppressors and the marginalized plight of the oppressed.

Since the liberationists are dedicated, as we shall be observing, to a deideologizing of traditional Christianity and its sanctification of an un-Christian social structure, they find in Marx an ally who, though godless, can be conscripted to serve the cause of the liberating God.

A LIBERATING THEOLOGY

This new mode of theologizing, as its very name implies, singles out liberation as *ex hypothesi* the central theme of Scripture, and therefore the central theme of Christianity. J. Severino Croatto contends, for example, that the Exodus message is *the* message of God's Word:

> The Bible does not discuss "notions" but enunciates and announces
> a message. If the Bible discusses anything, it is to challenge human
> activities. Therefore, whenever we read an account of the liberation
> of the people of Israel, we are being instructed on a call to *us* and
> we are being prompted to embark upon a quest for the "meaning"
> of what God did, and therefore, "said" as Word.[17]

What, though, does the concept *liberation* signify when it is not being bandied about sloganistically but proclaimed and practiced Christianly? According to Gutiérrez, three interpenetrating levels of meaning must be distinguished within this concept. First, "*liberation* expresses the aspirations of oppressed peoples and social classes, emphasizing the conflictual aspect of the economic, social, and political process which puts them at odds with wealthy nations and oppressive classes." Second, "*liberation* can be applied to an understanding of history. Man is seen as assuming conscious responsibility for his own destiny. This understanding provides a dynamic context and broadens the horizons of the desired social changes." Third and foundationally, liberation leads us back to "the Biblical sources which inspire the presence and action of

---

17. J. Severino Croatto, *Exodus: A Hermeneutics of Freedom*, trans. Salvator Attanasso (Maryknoll, New York: Orbis, 1981), pp. 3-4.

man and history. In the Bible, Christ is presented as the One Who brings liberation. Christ the Savior liberates man from sin, which is the ultimate root of all disruption of friendship and of all injustice and oppression." But, Gutiérrez cautions, those three levels must not be viewed as running parallel to one another or occurring in a chronological sequence. They are interdependent, forming "a single complex process, which finds its deepest sense and its full realization in the saving work of Christ."[18]

In taking this approach liberationists are echoing the pronouncement issued by the conference of Roman Catholic bishops at Meddelin, Colombia, in 1968—a pronouncement that identifies sin as the bottommost cause of repressive exploitation and that denounces repressive exploitation as the gross progeny of sin: "It is the same God who, in the fulness of time, sends His Son in the flesh so that He might come to liberate all men from the slavery to which sin has subjected them: hunger, misery, oppression, and ignorance, in a word, that injustice and hatred which has its origin in human sinfulness."[19]

To sum up, then, this new genre of the Christian faith is Latin American in origin, a theology "from below," a theology of the poor and especially nonpersons, a committed theology that takes sides, a theology that stresses praxis, a theology heavily sociological and Marxist in orientation, and a theology that reinterprets all of Scripture from the standpoint of liberation.

A New Approach to the Bible

We are now ready to undertake our inquiry into the distinctive hermeneutic of this theology, which seeks to propound the way that oppressed human beings may experience authentic freedom in a transformed society. Yet before we proceed, a few preliminary remarks are called for.

THE INDISPENSIBILITY OF SCRIPTURE

Sometimes liberationists sound as if they assign virtually no value to Scripture per se. Segundo, in particular, creates that impression. "Our language is so new," he writes, "that to some it seems like a travesty of the Gospel."[20] His language certainly does sound like that. So too does the language of Hugo Assmann. With apparent approval he quotes the cutting remark of a fellow activ-

18. Gutiérrez, *A Theology of Liberation*, p. 37.
19. Cited by Gutiérrez, ibid., p. 110.
20. Cited by Bonino, *Doing Theology*, p. 86.

ist, "The Bible? It doesn't exist. The only Bible that exists is the sociological Bible of what I see happening here and now as a Christian." Assmann quotes the remark elsewhere in a slightly different version: "The Bible? I know of only one Bible; the sociological Bible of facts and events here. Everything else is an abstraction.[21]"

Another preliminary remark seems warranted. In keeping with the liberationist conviction that praxis affords cognitive insight into Christian faith and provides the final norm of Christian doctrine, Segundo renounces any interest in universal truth. Avowedly pragmatic and relativistic, he is concerned not with formulating correct doctrine but with forging ideological weapons that will prove effective in fighting the religious ideologies of an oppressive status quo. How could he be more provocatively blunt? If "it was God's intention to *provide us with information about Himself*" (a supposition that he denies), then we had better admit "that the extant Bible is a complete waste of paper."[22] Or if we imagine that Scripture is, to quote a traditional assumption, our "infallible rule of faith and practice," we are the victims of an illusion. No, Segundo declares, James Cone is entirely right: "We cannot use Jesus' behavior in the first century as a literal guide for our actions in the 20th century. . . . Scripture . . . is not a guide which makes our decisions for us."[23] Thus, however upsetting it may be to those who long for the security of unchanging absolutes, we must recognize, Segundo maintains, that "if God continually presents Himself in a different light, then the talk about Him must be different also." It is necessary, therefore, to challenge orthodoxy's comfortable—but, oh, how stagnant!—doctrine of biblical grounded dogma, which remains fixed and steadfast through the flux of time.

> Faith does not consist in intellectual adherence to a certain body of revealed content as the definitive solution to theoretical or practical problems. Nor does it consist in having confidence in one's own salvation, thanks to the merits of Christ. Instead it entails the freedom to accept an educational process that comes to maturity and abandons its teacher to launch out into the provisional and relative depths of history.[24]

21. Hugo Assmann, *Theology for a Nomad Church*, trans. Paul Burns (Maryknoll, New York: Orbis, 1976), p. 61; cf. Fierro, *The Militant Gospel*, pp. 353-54.
22. Juan Luis Segundo, *The Liberation of Theology*, trans. John Drury (Maryknoll, New York: Orbis, 1976), p. 179.
23. Ibid., p. 31.
24. Ibid., p. 122.

Yet, Segundo protests, this abandonment of "a certain body of revealed content" does not carry the corollary that we can and must dispense with the Bible. Not in the least!

> I hope that it is quite clear that the Bible is not the discourse of the universal God to universal man. Partiality is justified because we must find, and designate as the Word of God, that *part* of divine revelation which *today*, in the light of our concrete historical situation, is most useful for the liberation to which God summons us. Other passages of that same divine revelation will help us tomorrow to complete and correct our present course towards freedom. God will keep coming back to speak to us from the very same Bible.[25]

Segundo, then, for all his radical minimizing of Scripture as the source and norm of truth, stands shoulder to shoulder with radical exegete José Miranda: "I only wish to understand what the Bible says. . . . We want to take the Bible seriously." Let us take seriously, at least provisionally, the insistence of liberationists that they intend to take the Bible seriously.[26]

Let us take seriously, moreover, their burning desire, as expressed by Croatto, "to orchestrate a method for rereading the Bible from the standpoint of our own situation in Latin America. The aim of our method is to enable us to construct a *theology* of liberation and to avoid the opposite danger—the danger of flatly denying the relevance of the Bible, insofar as it is a text from the past, as a message of liberation *for* us."[27]

That the liberationists are sincere in their desire to be committed yet enlightened biblicists Kirk has no doubt whatever. And since he, a Western scholar, is a sympathetic and exceptionally well-informed student of Latin American liberationists, his judgment is weighty and pervasive. Only the Bible, he is convinced, provides the needed leverage that can lift enslaved people out of their bondage; and this is also the liberationist conviction: "The Biblical analysis of liberation from sin. . . . is unique," he argues, "because the Bible is the only source which discerns a fundamen-

25. Ibid., p. 33.
26. José Miranda, *Marx and the Bible: A Critique of the Philosophy of Oppression*, trans. John Eagleson (Maryknoll, New York: Orbis, 1974), p. 35-36. This is perhaps the most impressive piece of sustained exegesis done by any of the liberationists. Whatever our criticisms of Miranda, we are constrained to admire his command of contemporary biblical scholarship, interpretive skill, and moral passion. Equally impressive is his *Being and Messiah: The Message of St. John*, trans. John Eagleson (Maryknoll, New York: Orbis, 1977).
27. Croatto, *Exodus*, p. vi.

tal ontological dimension." Because of this, he argues further, the Bible has authority "for the Christian's contemporary praxis of liberation. . . . and it must be allowed a privileged position in the hermeneutical circle. When we speak of Scripture as the mediator of total and universal liberation, we mean that this text alone points to a liberation which is total, in the sense of producing the new man, free from every alienation; and universal, in the sense of producing the new creation."[28]

Liberationists are also keenly cognizant that their genre of theology demands a new hermeneutic, an interpretive modality that is a radical departure from traditional hermeneutics. If the Christian task, to rephrase Karl Marx's notorious Eleventh Thesis against Feuerbach, is to change rather than simply explain the world, a different approach to Scripture is imperative. Liberationists regard as axiomatic that the world needs changing and that biblical faith ought to be the primary change-agent. So Gutiérrez appropriates as his own the verdict of Edward Schillebeeck: "The church has for centuries devoted her attention to formulating truths and meanwhile did almost nothing to better the world. In other words, the church focused on orthodoxy and left orthopraxis in the hands of nonmembers and nonbelievers." Gutiérrez likewise concurs with Achillebeeckx that, if the world is changed for the better, then to that extent God's kingdom is being established: "The hermeneutics of the Kingdom of God consists especially in making the world a better place. Only in this way will I be able to discover what the Kingdom of God means." That Gutiérrez identifies as "a political hermeneutics of the Gospel."[29]

Gutiérrez gladly aligns himself with another European theologian, Johannes Baptist Metz, against whom, as we have previously observed, some liberationists polemically inveigh and from whom we have already quoted this statement: "The so-called fundamental hermeneutic problem of theology is not the problem of how systematic theology stands in relation to historical theology, how dogma stands in relation to history, but what is the relation between theory and practice, between understanding the faith and social practice.

SUSPICION AND HOPE

Granted that Metz is correct in spotlighting world-transforming praxis as "the fundamental hermeneutical problem of theol-

28. Kirk, *Liberation Theology*, pp. 174-75.
29. Cited by Gutiérrez, *A Theology of Liberation*, pp. 10, 13.

ogy." We can understand, then, why liberationists view suspicion and hope as major components in solving this problem. Suspicion must operate in a dynamic political hermeneutic because the older hermeneutics is strangely silent regarding the oppressive/repressive status quo and remarkably impotent in changing it. Hence liberationists walk in the footsteps of those three iconoclastic critics of Western society, Marx, Freud, and Nietzsche, whom Paul Ricoeur lauds as being "masters of suspicion."[30] As a liberationist suspicious of the ideological captivity of traditional exegesis, Bonino asks: "Why is it, for instance, that the obvious political motifs and undertones in the life of Jesus have remained so hidden to liberal interpreters until very recently?"[31] Segundo joins him in averring that suspicion is an indispensable tool for unmasking ideologies. Hermeneutics in this new context facilitates an identification of the ideological framework of interpretation implicit in a given religious praxis.

Besides suspicion, however, hope must be an operative component in this new approach to Scripture if the Christian faith is to become a society-changing dynamic. Hope? By all means, Beatriz Melano Couch insists. This hermeneutic

> hopes to avoid. . . . the danger of reading into the text only our own conditioning, with the aim of freeing the text, letting the text speak with all its urgency, depth and power. . . . then it hopes to let the text itself rephrase our own questions and rephrase our own conceptions about life and death, our own epistemology, our own knowledge of society, our ethics (and) politics.[32]

But here liberationists take upon themselves a most difficult assignment. Is it possible to reinterpret Christianity into the categories of political theology and still preserve the essence of the historical faith? Alfredo Fierro, who speaks out "theological representations (i.e., ideas, images, and symbols)" puts the issue squarely:

> Is the representational material of tradition still meaningful, or is it now out of date? Which theological representations can be utilized for a political interpretation of the Gospel, and which cannot? Are the most deeply rooted notions of theology such as sin, redemption, grace, and the church susceptible of a political interpre-

30. Anthony C. Thistleton, *The Two Horizons: New Testament Hermeneutics and Philosophical Description* (Grand Rapids: Eerdmans, 1980), p. 113.
31. Cited by Thistleton, ibid., p. 111.
32. Cited by Brown, *Theology in a New Key*, p. 88.

tation? If so, under what conditions and through what sort of transforming hermeneutic process?[33]

Pondering the interaction of biblical studies and political theology, Bonino refuses to sidestep this crucial issue: "Is it legitimate to start Biblical interpretation from a contemporary historical interpretation. . . . How can the freedom of the text be maintained?"[34] This is indeed *the* issue to which, after these preliminary remarks, we now turn our attention: How does liberation theology work out its hermeneutic, and what is the validity of this approach?

THE VALUE OF TRADITIONAL HERMENEUTICS

As a school of scholars who aspire to be responsible as well as radical, liberationists recognize that the tools traditionally employed in a rigorous study of Scripture cannot be laid aside. The time-honored grammatico-historical techniques are still to be honored even though to an exegete like Miranda they are what paper and ink are to a composer—indispensable materials, yet materials that are meaningless in themselves. Thus even Miranda, presumably, would countersign Bultmann's dictum: "The old hermeneutic rules of grammatical interpretation, formal analysis, and explanation of the basis of the conditions of the historical period are indisputably valid."[35]

But liberationists protest against the notion that the *sensus literalis* is unambiguously attainable by linguistic and historical studies. Although not a liberationist himself, Kirk emphatically expresses the liberationist conviction: "There are no absolutely objective and wholly reliable methods for establishing the meaning of any text." Even if one agrees with the 1942 papal encyclical *Divino Afflante* that the *sensus literalis* is the meaning *intended* by a biblical author, he cannot evade the force of Kirk's probing queries: "Is it intrinsically possible to discover what the author intended? Would it not require a degree of insight and knowledge which the modern exegete, so far removed in time, cannot be expected to possess?" Or if one asserts that the *sensus literalis* can best be defined "as what the author said," how does this definition really help? It is simply "a euphemism for what the writer *communicates*."[36]

33. Fierro, *The Militant Gospel*, p. 223.
34. Cited by Thistleton, *The Two Horizons*, p. 110.
35. Cited by Thistleton, ibid., p. 21.
36. Kirk, *Liberation Theology*, p. 181.

THE TWO-SIDED TASK OF HERMENEUTICS

Although liberationists accept a restricted version of the *sensus literalis* principle, they are committed to a hermeneutic that insists there must be a fusing of the two horizons, that of the text and that of the exegete. Hence they likewise insist that no interpretation can be done, or de facto is done, apart from a preunderstanding.

Horizon is a concept that looms large in contemporary biblical and theological studies; it also looms large in recent philosophy. Anthony C. Thistleton discusses it magisterially in his encyclopedic work *The Two Horizons*, which surveys the whole field of hermeneutics from Schleiermacher on down to the present day. The term refers to the perspective from which a human being, with the illuminating viewpoints and inescapable limitations imposed by his unique space-time nexus, writes or interprets. It reminds us that every author stands within his own culture, able to transcend its thought patterns, problems, and values with about as much success as he can step outside his own skin: his culture contaminates his thinking ideologically even if it does not control his mental processes deterministically. What is true of every author is obviously true as well of any exegete who seeks to understand a text that comes out of the past. He brings to it, willy-nilly, presuppositions, perceptions, and even prejudices. In the words of *Christian Believing*, which summarize the conclusions of the Church of England's Communion Report with respect to Scripture: "No one expounds the Bible to himself or to anyone else without bringing to the text his own prior frame of reference, his own pattern of assumptions which derives from sources outside the Bible."[37]

So the two-sided task of exegesis involves, in Hans-Georg Gadamer's phrase "the fusion of horizons,"[38] a principle expounded by Richard Palmer in his *Hermeneutics:* "Explanatory interpretation makes us aware that explanation is contextual, is 'horizontal.' It must be made within a horizon of already granted meanings and intentions. In hermeneutics, this area of assumed understanding is called pre-understanding. . . . This merging of two horizons must be considered a basic element in all explanatory interpretation."[39]

Thus, in order to carry on his work responsibly an exegete

---

37. Cited by Thistleton, *The Two Horizons*, p. 114.
38. Cited by Thistleton, ibid., p. 16.
39. Cited by Thistleton, ibid., p. 307.

must be cognizant of his own horizon, the perspective from which he scrutinizes a document. He must keep in mind Martin Heidegger's observation: "In every case this interpretation is grounded in *something we have in advance*—in a fore-having *(Vorhabe)*. . . . It is grounded in a *fore-conception (Vorgriff)*. . . . Any interpretation is never a presuppositionless apprehending of something presented to us."[40]

The responsible exegete must likewise keep in mind the observations of Bultmann, who appropriates Heidegger's anthropology for his own tradition-breaking interpretation of the New Testament. One observation is made in *Existence and Faith: "Every* theology is dependent *for the clarification of its concepts upon a pre-theological understanding of man that, as a rule, is determined by some philosophical tradition."* A second and similar observation appears in his *Essays Philosophical and Theological:* "A comprehension. . . . is *constantly oriented to a particular formulation of a question, a particular 'objective'.* . . . or, to put it more precisely . . . it is *governed always by a prior understanding of the subject* in accordance with which it investigates the text. The formulation of a question, and an interpretation, is possible at all only on the basis of such a prior understanding."[41]

A responsible exegete must therefore steadily bear in mind the two-sidedness of his task, never forgetting that his own horizon dictates the concerns and questions that he addresses to an author who, if he wrote in the past, did not and could not perceive reality from the same perspective. That unavoidable complication of the hermeneutical task ought never to be ignored because, as F. Wismann warns, "The question is the first groping of the mind in its journeyings that lead towards new horizons. . . . questions lead us on and over the barrier of traditional opinions. Questions seduce us, too, and lead us astray."[42] It is precisely that kind of questioning to which liberation theologians subject Scripture, a tradition-challenging interrogation that may lead to new truth or perhaps to untruth. Questions arise within a context of poverty, injustice, and oppression. Questioned themselves by this context, the liberationists address those questions to the Bible and listen critically to the answers given from the horizon of the ancient text; they then reflect on those answers in the light of their concern for liberation; they return to Scripture with reformulated questions; they listen again to its answers, and thus the process

40. Cited by Thistleton, ibid., p. 105.
41. Cited by Thistleton, ibid., pp. 223, 237.
42. Cited by Thistleton, ibid., p. 309.

continues. Beatriz Melano Couch succinctly depicts this interaction between liberationist question and biblical answer.

> The hermeneutics of the theology of liberation is done in a dialectical relationship between reality as it is described by modern social sciences and then reflection on the Scriptures, going back and forth from the "reading of reality" to the reading of the Scriptures and *vice versa.*[43]

Hypothetically, it would seem, this process must be unending, because new human situations raise new questions that require new answers.

THE HERMENEUTICAL CIRCLE

Liberationists expand the two-horizon hermeneutic in an interpretative practice that, Dow Patrick suggests, might more fittingly be called a hermeneutic spiral instead of a hermeneutic circle[44] or, as Georges Casalis says, the interpretive modality of liberationists might be better described as "a hermeneutical circulation."[45] Segundo is a notable example of this approach. He grounds his hermeneutic in a pre-understanding that for him is the only admissable premise of a Christian theology: "The one key to open up for us the message of God would be . . . a revolutionary commitment in favor of the oppressed." Elsewhere he describes his commitment as "a sensibility of heart toward the poor." It is this assumed premise that for Segundo has the nature of an axiom, which alone enables an exegete to grasp the message of Scripture. Segundo, indeed, is convinced "that a specific Christian contribution, a revolutionary commitment, and a new understanding of the Gospel constitute a hermeneutic circle."[46] In his earlier book, *Massas minorias e la dialectica divinia de la liberacion*, he declares that "a hermeneutic circle always supposes a profound human commitment, that is, a consciously accepted partiality, based certainly not on theological criteria but on human ones." What, however, is that circle or spiral or circulation? Segundo sees it as a four-step process:

> *First,* our manner of experiencing reality, which leads to ideological suspicion; *second,* the application of ideological suspicion to the

43. Cited by Dow Patrick, "A Liberating *Pastoral* for the Rich," in *Sanctification and Liberation*, ed. Theodore Runyan, p. 215.
44. Dow Patrick, *ibid.*
45. Bonino, *Doing Theology*, p. 102.
46. Cited by Hennelly, *Theologies in Conflict*, p. 158.

whole ideological superstructure in general and to theology in particular. *Third*, a new way of experiencing theological reality, which leads us to exegetical suspicion, that is, to the suspicion that current Biblical interpretation does not take into account important data; and, *fourth*, our new hermeneutic, that is, the new way of interpreting the source of our faith, which is Scripture, with the new elements at our disposal.

When these steps are followed, Segundo affirms, there is "continuous change in our interpretation of the Bible, in function of the continuous changes in our present reality, both individual and social."[47] But interpretive change does not imply an abandonment of the Bible as a norm and criterion for theology. Quite the reverse, Alfred T. Hennelly argues, and he is the leading North American authority on Segundo:

> A liberating spirituality would find its constant source of renewal and inspiration in the continual return to Scripture. The hermeneutic circle in this process would free it from all vestiges of fundamentalism and reaction; rather this would establish a life-long process of learning and lead to new and creative solutions to contemporary problems.[48]

A MODIFICATION OF THE *SENSUS PLENIOR* PRINCIPLE

Liberationists also hold, granting their inter se differences, that the hermeneutics they practice cannot be dismissed as a recourse to "arbitrary *inventions*" in order to justify a change-producing practice; their hermeneutic is supposedly one of "engaged *readings*," which motivate, reinforce, and sanction praxis. But how is one to differentiate between Bonino's "engaged readings," which he applauds, as over against the "arbitrary inventions," which he deplores?[49] That is done supposedly by using an interpretive principle that both he and Croatto advocate—a hermeneutical modality akin to the *sensus plenior* of exegetical traditionalism as carried on especially by Roman Catholics. That Scripture demands a *sensus literalis* interpretation has always and necessarily been taken for granted. But is there a deeper meaning underlying the obvious surface significance of a text? Are there, in fact, levels and layers of meaning to be uncovered

47. Cited by Hennelly, ibid., p. 109. Cf. Segundo, *The Liberation of Theology*, p. 9, for the same passage translated with slight variations.
48. Hennelly, ibid., p. 151.
49. Bonino, *Doing Theology*, p. 102.

progressively with the emergence of new challenges and crisis in the ongoing pilgrimage of the church? J. P. Grillmeier pinpoints this problem, which has been a sort of continental divide among biblical scholars:

> Does God only want to say what the author of a book or Scriptural text can be proved historically to have had in mind? . . . Or does the expressive intention of God go further, so that each generation is justified in interpreting Scripture according to its own situation—i.e., *interpreting it and not simply applying it?*[50]

Liberation theology embraces the second of these options ("each generation is justified in interpreting Scripture according to its own situation") and uses as its "main hermeneutical principle"[51] a modified form of the *sensus plenior*. It does not allude specifically to this traditional approach, but in Bonino's case it does allude to "germinal events," and in Croatto's case to "foundational events" that contain a "reservoir of meaning." Croatto contends that even when biblical documents are allowed their "full weight of objective historicity," the meaning of any recorded happening is by no means exhausted in its initial facticity. Some events are dynamically fecund: they have the potential of generating reinterpretations indefinitely in one historical context after another.[52] If an example is asked for, Bonino adduces the "careful and cautious" exegesis of Christ's resurrection done by T. Bonnard, who finds in the New Testament six meanings, each of which is a "present word." Building his argument on Bonnard's exegesis, Bonnino asserts that "the resurrection," instead of being only a past event, "*is* itself (and not merely means or causes) our resurrection, our justification, the defeat of the powers, the power of his death, the general resurrection, the active presence of Christ." Hence, in view of this multi-layered, inexhaustibly rich significance, Bonino raises an entirely pertinent question: "Is it altogether absurd to reread the resurrection today as the death of the monopolies, the liberation from hunger, or a solitary form of ownership?"[53]

Consider now Croatto's modified version of the *sensus plenior*—his appeal to a "reservoir of meaning," a "surplus" of significance that permits successive reinterpretations of the biblical narratives. This approach is nothing radical, Croatto says; it is

50. Cited by Kirk, *Liberation Theology*, . 157.
51. The phrase is from *Kirk*, ibid., p. 157.
52. Croatto, *Exodus*, pp. 3, 8.
53. Bonino, *Doing Theology*, p. 101.

actually the same kind of modality we find in the Bible:

> The primitive church interpreted Jesus from the perspective of the Scriptures, but at the same time it interpreted the Scriptures from the perspective of the Jesus event. In fact the event (Jesus) that generates the word (the New Testament) comes first; but the New Testament, in turn, was possible only as a reading of the Old Testament. These three aspects subsumed in *one* kerygma (the Bible: the Old and New Testaments as interpretation of Christ) form a new pole of hermeneutic circularity that now includes us as its complementary pole. . . . A knowledge of the Scriptures, whether exhaustive or not, can be the basis for a science that explores the redactional or historical meaning of a text. But such an approach does not penetrate its reservoir-of-meaning which surpasses that level. . . . Christians must "read" the events in order to reformulate the traditional message: and they must hearken to the already transmitted Word of God in order to be more open to the salvific events transpiring in the world.[54]

A TROPICAL HERMENEUTIC

The liberationists adopt a hermeneutic that permits biblical events and doctrines to be interpreted with an almost capricious flexibility. Among these Latin American theologians only Rubem Alves, we may presume, has been directly influenced by Paul Lehmann, who was his Princeton mentor. But all of them adhere to the interpretive approach that Lehmann writes about briefly in his major work, *The Transfiguration of Politics.* It is, he asserts, a "hermeneutical option . . . familiar to the early fathers of the Church." It is a nonliteral modality that moves in the tradition of rabbinic Judaism, the Stoic readings of Homer, Origen's notable distinction between the "spiritual" meaning versus the crassly "literal" sense, and the tropical understanding of Scripture that Augustine advocated. Expounding the approach of that greatest of church Fathers, Lehmann quotes the simple dictionary definition: "A trope is a form of figurative speech involving the use of the word in a different sense from that which is proper to it." Hence Lehmann advocates and exemplifies a tropical hermeneutic—nonliteral, figurative, and symbolic.[55] Alves adopts the same hermeneutic in his published Princeton thesis entitled *A Theol-*

---

54. Croatto, *Exodus,* pp. 3, 8.
55. Paul Lehmann, *The Transfiguration of Politics: The Presence and Power of Jesus of Nazarath in and over Human Affairs* (New York: Harper & Row, 1975), p. 231.

ogy of Human Hope.[56] Other liberationists, apparently on their own and entirely apart from Lehmann, also interpret Scripture tropically. Segundo, for example, views biblical events and doctrines as "methodological symbols" by which Christians in the past have "learned how to learn" and by which Christians today can still learn how to learn—that is, learn how to foster their own liberation.[57] Hugo Assmann says flatly that Christianity inhabits a "realm of symbols and myths."[58] Fiero alleges that all political theology, including of course its Latin American liberationist version, works with "useful representations," images and ideas (its ideas in his judgment are first cousins to those of Kant), and "prophetic signposts." Sharply critical of the theoretical fuzziness and shoddy thought-processes of political theology in general and liberation theology in particular, Fierro nevertheless acknowledges that recourse to the complex symbolization of Scripture has pragmatic value. A symbol, he writes, walking in Ricoeur's footsteps,

> is both retrospective and prospective, and that is fully in line with the nature of theological representations. At one end it marks a return to the past, to the pristine sources of life; at the other it suggests an act of yearning and anticipation for the future. Political theology adopts the most ancient archetypes preserved in the historical memory of humanity. These archetypes come to it filtered through the historical memory of the Christian tradition and its notions of salvation, love, conversion, the new person, and so forth. It then turns these archetypes into prophetic signposts of the future, into encompassing horizons that lure us on with their exigencies without ever being fully reachable.[59]

But archetypes turned into "prophetic signposts of the future" are not exactly solid building blocks for either theology or ethics. The future toward which they point may turn out to be a mirage.

A CRITIQUE OF THE LIBERATIONIST HERMENEUTIC

GENERAL THEOLOGICAL STRICTURES

Bear in mind that our announced purpose is not to undertake a full-scale appraisal of the inconoclastic views propounded by li-

56. Rubem Alves, *A Theology of Human Hope* (Washington: Corpus, 1962).
57. Segundo, *The Liberation of Theology*, p. 117.
58. Assmann, *Theology for a Nomad Church*, p. 61.
59. Fierro, *The Militant Gospel*, p. 297.

berationists. So we merely point out that one critic, Dennis P. McCann, discovers "insuperable theoretical difficulties"[60] in this new version of the faith. Another critic, Schubert M. Ogden, reminds its exponents that they cannot ignore the question of Christianity's credibility. He argues that the credibility of any theology cannot be established merely by fervent commitment and sacrificial praxis. If therefore liberationists are concerned that their theology be "concrete and scientific," they must meet "a necessary precondition": they must not merely "assume the truth of their prior commitment as Christians"; they must "ask and answer the question whether even the claims implied in that commitment are really true."

> In fact, unless and until they subject even the constitutive claims of faith itself to the question of truth, their reflection must remain bound so closely to the faith on which it is supposed to reflect that, while it may indeed be a reflection *in* faith, it cannot be a reflection *on* faith, because the only things of which it can really be critical are the expressions of faith in witness.[61]

A third critic, missiologist Peter Wagner, who speaks from within the camp of Protestant traditionalism and who served for long years in Bolivia, has subjected the liberationists to a sustained critique in his book *Latin American Theology: Radical or Evangelical*, which Segundo vigorously attacks.[62]

But our focus is much narrower than those important issues. As we conclude our study, we are seeking to evaluate the hermeneutic that undergirds this new theological paradigm.

SPECIFIC CRITICISMS OF LIBERATIONIST USE OF SCRIPTURE

Liberationists, for one thing, are light years removed from the debates about inerrancy and infallibility that agitate evangelicals. They regard such questions as hangovers from a fundamen-

---

60. The phrase is used by Dennis P. McCann, *Christian Realism and Liberation Theology: Practical Theologies in Creative Conflict* (Maryknoll, New York: Orbis, 1981), p. 232, n. 5.

61. Schubert M. Ogden, "The Concept of a Theology of Liberation: Must a Christian Theology Today Be So Conceived?" in *The Challenge of Liberation Theology*, ed. Brian Mahan and L. Dale Richesin (Maryknoll, New York: Orbis, 1981), p. 134.

62. In his *Liberation of Theology* Segundo describes Wagner's criticisms *in extenso*, terming them "forthrightly honest" though "simplistic and naïve in certain respects," pp. 134-38.

talist obscurantism. An old-fashioned biblicism that still champions the errorlessness of Scripture is of no interest, except possibly as a polemical target, to a theology that either inferentially or explicitly opts for relativism, universalism, and a supernaturalism that is at best one-dimensional, quite completely indifferent to any future other than what transpires in the space-time world of human history.[63]

Second, an evangelical faults liberationists for embracing a radical criticism of biblical sources that makes it difficult, if not impossible, to find a solid kernel of fact within a thick shell of symbol and myth. McCann, to be sure, upraids Gutiérrez because he seems to ignore "the more or less assured results of critical history."

> Not only must the details of these narratives possess a high degree of historical accuracy for Gutiérrez's analogies to be meaningful, but also the paradigmatic relationship between salvation-history and real history must work for liberation theology to hold a genuine promise for historical praxis. But Gutiérrez can make good on neither of these claims and still remain accountable to critical history—unless, of course, he concedes that his theology of history is really the retelling of a religious myth about history.[64]

Hearing a liberationist thus upbraided by a North American disciple of Reinhold Niebuhr, an evangelical might be tempted to rush gallantly to the defense of Gutiérrez. But he ought to resist that temptation because Gutiérrez and his school are by no means believers in the literal truthfulness of the biblical narratives.

63. On relativism, cf. the chapter on "Ideologies and Relativity" in Segundo's *The Liberation of Theology*, pp. 154-81. He concludes by repudiating the notion of unvarying propositions and by averring, "We will never be able to reduce the faith to a specific book or page of the Bible, to a specific Creed, or to a specific dogma. On universalism, cf. Bonino's *Doing Theology in a Revolutionary Situation*, chapter 8, "Church, People, and the Avant-Garde," in which he seeks to clarify and justify the idea that "mankind is destined to become a universal church," pp. 154-73. On the one-dimensionalism of all political theology of which liberation theology is a variant, cf. Fierro's *The Militant Gospel:* "Political theology differs from other Christian theologies insofar as it has a different notion of salvation. It does not picture salvation as liberation from the dominion exercised by cosmic, biological, or demonic forces. Instead it sees salvation as liberation from the dominion exercised by specifically human and social forces. Thus the idea of salvation is no longer construed in terms of the cosmos or the hereafter, but rather in terms of earthly history and the sociopolitical situation," p. 224. Cf. also p. 226, "Liberation theology shifts the stress to the present life, to the here and now of history. Insofar as eternal life is concerned, it maintains a discreet and modest silence. . . . One suspects that it does not believe much in that life, if at all."
64. McCann, *Christian Realism and Liberation Theology*, pp. 204-5.

They do not deny that the events and the characters in Scripture may be historical in a greatly attenuated sense; but they hold that these events and characters include metadimensions. Croata's approach is typical:

> The Hebrews were not content with the unadorned data on Moses and the Exodus—even though the leader of the liberation had *already* been mythologized. So they enlarged his figure with innumerable apocryphal episodes, each more extraordinary than the last. This is not to be viewed as an eagerness to indulge in fabulation but as a hermeneutical expression of a profound understanding of a key personage of their history.[65]

By no exegetical feat, then, can reliable history be extracted from documents that are mythic elaborations, that is, religiously motivated fabrications.

Third, an evangelical is troubled by the inability of liberationists to develop a normative, culture-transcending theology. How can it do so if Scripture is a multilayered complex of symbols resting on a factual and historical foundation that is precariously uncertain? No doubt they, as adherents of a freedom-enhancing relativism and enemies of a freedom-repressing absolutism, may view this as an asset rather than a liability. After all, the tropical approach gives, to take Segundo's words out of context, "liberation theology greater freedom to move in principle, through the Scripture and to work with the faith.[66] But the freedom thus secured appears to be a freedom not just to work with the faith but to rework it to a point where its biblical content is totally absorbed into a nonbiblical ideology.

Are specific illustrations called for? Three will suffice.

ILLUSTRATIONS OF A TROPICAL HERMENEUTIC

First, what does the resurrection of Jesus Christ mean symbolically? The tropical hermeneutic that Alves has appropriated from Lehmann, and that is practiced de facto by other liberationists, permits him to endorse the interpretation of the Easter event proposed by Norman O. Brown.

> The question confronting mankind is the abolition of repression—in traditional Christian language, the resurrection of the body. . . . the resurrection of the body is a social project facing mankind as a

65. Croatto, *Exodus*, p. 26.
66. Segundo, *The Liberation of Theology*, p. 109.

whole, and it will become a practical political problem when the statesmen of the world are called upon to deliver happiness instead of power.[67]

The historicity of the empty tomb is therefore of little consequence. The all-essential significance is its symbolism, its power to motivate a liberating praxis.

As a second illustration of the exegetical freedom indulged in by the liberationists, we turn to their interpretation of the Exodus, a key symbol to which Croatto devotes an entire monograph. The deliverance of enslaved Israel from Egypt is for him the primal event in God's emancipating activity. He calls it "the first kerygmatic 'core' for a theology of liberation."

> If we are to undertake a genuine hermeneutic of the Exodus, from which we should "disentangle" other events which are future to it, then its present *re-interpretation* is essential. For this reason it is not "exhausted." It possesses other connotations, which remain hidden until the "situation" brings them to light. For example: the Exodus was a political (social) happening, but it is also evident that it is an event which inspires every economic and cultural liberation.[68]

Croatto does not simply relate the Exodus to the past as an event that took place back then and there; he sees it rather as an event that continues if and when enslaved peoples now and everywhere respond to its challenge:

> The Exodus is an Event full of meaning (as the Biblical event and Israel's experience show) which even now has not been *concluded*. If our recalling of the Biblical *kerygma* has any relevance, the "memory" of the Exodus becomes, for us—oppressed peoples of the Third World—an inciting Word, the announcement of liberation. It remains for us to prolong the Exodus, for it is not an event for the Hebrews but the manifestation of God's liberating design for all peoples. Within a hermeneutical treatment it is perfectly legitimate to understand ourselves as *from* the Biblical Exodus and above all to understand the latter *from within* our situations of people in economic, political, social, and cultural slavery.[69]

And Croatto, one suspects, would raise no objection to F. Rivera's

---

67. Cited by Fierro, *The Militant Gospel*, p. 297.
68. Cited by Kirk, *Liberation Theology*, p. 101.
69. Cited by Kirk, ibid., p. 102.

suggestion that we ought to perceive in this Old Testament story "an Exodus from security, the bourgeois spirit, and everything created by man to avoid risks."[70]

An evangelical critic finds himself joined here by an unexpected ally, none other than Juan Luis Segundo! He contemptuously dismisses the "naïve explanation" that "maintains that the Exodus event is the key to the interpretation of Scripture as the whole, including the Gospels and the rest of the New Testament." This position is naïve indeed, he fulminates, one "very easy for a scientific Biblical theology to tear apart." It cannot be taken as the "central axis" of the sapiential literature of the Old Testament nor of the New Testament, either, apart from "a terrible process of mutilation."[71] What more need an evangelical say?

So as a third illustration of the exegetical freedom practiced by liberationists, let us observe how Segundo himself handles the Bible concept of flesh attempting to employ Scripture sociologically. After an involuted analysis of the Hebrew and Greek terms, he concludes that, as his interpretation is in turn interpreted by Anthony J. Tambasco, living in the flesh is to live in unfreedom as a member of the masses, controlled by one's environment, allowing one's God relationship to be externally and institutionally dictated. "The Christian," Segundo writes regarding the instruments and agencies that should mediate his God relationship, "allows himself to be led to convert these means into mechanical, deterministic conditions. . . . Living according to the flesh means allowing oneself to be dominated by it."[72] Tambasco charitably comments that Segundo's exegesis of *sarx* "seems to be misdirected."

> It is an attempt to derive from the text what one wants to find. The concern for . . . formulating biblical interpretation to speak to the present situation leads in this instance to reading into the text. Segundo tries to parallel the ambiguity of the masses in his social analysis with ambiguity of the flesh in Paul. In the same way that he drew from social analysis that the masses are in opposition to the minority and at the same time a necessity, so Segundo draws from Paul the insight that the flesh is opposed to freedom, but is not sinful. It is the destiny of all humanity.[73]

---

70. Cited by Kirk, ibid., p. 101.
71. Segundo, *The Liberation of Theology*, p. 112.
72. Cited by Anthony J. Tambasco, *The Bible for Ethics: Juan Luis Segundo and First World-Ethics* (Washington, D.C.: University Press of America, 1981), p. 150.
73. Tambasco, *The Bible for Ethics*, p. 155-56.

Yes, Segundo hopes that through "(t)he work of the Word" all "men may eventually constitute a single body among themselves, a single flesh."[74]

How surprised Paul would be, one imagines, to learn that flesh is a symbol for the unemancipated masses whereas spirit is a symbol for the liberating minority!

THE LACK OF HERMENEUTICAL CRITERIA

An evangelical, furthermore, must challenge the legitimacy of a continuous rereading and reinterpreting of metaevents, mythicized characters, and nonliteral doctrines until at last any relationship with the historical nucleus of the original text has evaporated. There are limits to how far and how freely Scripture can be treated tropically. Certainly too there is no exegetical magic by which new meanings can without limit be conjured out of the Bible under the illuminating creativity of new situations. Kirk is particularly effective in exposing the fallacy of the liberationist hermeneutic at that juncture. The New Testament, he asserts, does claim that in Christ and the apostles a definitive, binding, once-for-all interpretation of the Old Testament has been given. "*Prima facie* our freedom to reinterpret the New Testament is of a wholly different order from that which Christ and His apostles exercised in their interpretation of the Old Testament."[75] In addition, Kirk asserts that, if one concurs with the liberationists in their insistence "that praxis can spontaneously generate new revelation and new unambiguous interpretations of that text," he is in gravest danger of "baptizing all of history in the name of a particular revelation nonetheless esoteric for being contemporary and, as a consequence, easily manipulated in the interests of privilege and oppression."[76] So an evangelical like Kirk, no matter how deeply he emphathizes with the liberationists commitment to social change, must regretfully charge this theology with "using the Bible in an 'inspirational' rather than 'objective' sense— i.e., as a means to further ends over which the Bible has had no decisive say." Because this is the case, the exegesis that it motivates and by which its key principles are allegedly supported is not only "superficial" but likewise "dishonest."[77]

74. Cited by Tambasco, ibid., p. 156.
75. Kirk, *Liberation Theology*, p. 196.
76. Ibid., p. 197.
77. Ibid., p. 189.

In the end, an evangelical must indict the whole hermeneutical procedure of liberation theology because it is without any controlling exegetical criteria. Assmann is stringently forthright. It is "false to state that the whole Biblical framework, with its infinite variety of paradigms and situations, is an adequate basis for establishing a satisfactory complex dialectics of hermeneutical principles." Hence he confesses, "The main problem for us is that of hermeneutical criteria." But it seems impossible, at least thus far, to discover such criteria. "Since the roads leading to the meaning of the historical experiences in the past of Judaeo-Christianity are largely blocked by ideologies (because the criteria governing the means of access themselves need freeing from their ideological domination), where do we go from here?" In his opinion there is no place to go: the search for criteria is futile. They cannot be found: ergo they must be created!

> I suspect there is no other way than through the process of liberating our criteria, including those governing the ethical and political choice that decides our personal commitment. We have to produce essays and criticism that we test constantly against experiments and practice. Gradually we have to bring together interpretation of the present-day reality and a discovery of relevant criteria in the history of Judaeo-Christianity.[78]

A challenging assignment indeed, a task that may prove to be the theological equivalent of squaring the circle.

More than that, in the process of struggling to create hermeneutical criteria, liberationists need to guard, Bonino cautions with some urgency, against the danger of losing their own souls. In his judgment, the problem confronting this revolutionary theology is excruciatingly serious.

> It is not simply a question of some unfortunate or risky formulations of *avant garde* or scandal-loving theologians, but of the very basis of the method of interpretation and the structure of theological reflection used in this theology. It appears as the hopeless prisoner of a hermeneutical circle, the spell of which it cannot break. The text of Scripture and tradition is forced into the Procrustean bed of ideology, and the theologian who has fallen prey of this procedure is forever condemned to listen only to the echo of his own ideology. There is no redemption for this theology, because it has muzzled the Word of God in its transcendance and freedom. . . . It seems to me that our Latin American theology of

78. Assman, *Theology for a Nomad Church*, pp. 104-5.

liberation has not yet become sufficiently aware of the weight of this risk and consequently has not yet developed adequate safeguards against it.[79]

An evangelical devoutly hopes that Bonino's *confrères* will listen responsively to his somber warning.

As he ponders liberation theology, an evangelical joins with Kirk in praising the "great service"[80] it has performed by issuing a prophetic call to a complacent church, drowsily comfortable in its ideological captivity and forgetful of its moral and spiritual obligation to fight for the poor and oppressed. Yet an evangelical is aware at the same time of the great disservice that this new version of Christianity is perpetrating. Perhaps, as Assmann claims, the liberationist is "an opener of new horizons on the use of the name of God."[81] But what if in so doing he closes doors on God's truth and man's salvation—and does that tragic disservice in God's name?

79. Bonino, *Doing Theology*, p. 87.
80. Kirk has high though qualified praise for liberation theology in the last chapter of his incisive study, pp. 204-8.
81. Cited by Patrick, "A Liberating *Pastoral*," p. 223.

12. The Contributions of Charles Hodge, B. B. Warfield, and J. Gresham Machen to the Doctrine of Inspiration

John H. Gerstner

INTRODUCTION

In the history of American theology no nobler chapter on the inspiration of the Bible has been written than that by "Old Princeton." Among the Old Princetonians none has contributed more than the big three of Charles Hodge, B. B. Warfield, and J. Gresham Machen, with Warfield being the unequalled leader. Altogether they have raised a magnificent monument to the Word of God. We trust that the following pages will give some slight evidence of their exceptional defense of inspired Scripture.

Their achievement was essentially a herculean defense of the status quo. Princeton Theological Seminary of the nineteenth and early twentieth centuries (through the 1929 departure of Machen when he felt there was a shaking of the old biblical foundations) has been ridiculed for that in which it gloried—its absolute lack of novelty in bibliology. The modern Princeton faculty seems to find nothing more entertaining than the claim of Old Princeton

JOHN H. GERSTNER, B.A., Westminster College; M.Div., M.Th., Westminster Theological Seminary; Ph.D., Harvard University, is professor-at-large, Ligonier Valley Study Center, Stahlstown, Pennsylvania. He served as professor of church history at Pittsburgh Theological Seminary, Pittsburgh, Pennsylvania, from 1950-1980. He has authored *Theology for Everyman* (1964), *Reasons for Faith* (1970), and *The Theology of the Major Sects* (1971).

(The material on pages 359-72 has been, with certain modifications, reprinted by permission from *God's Inerrant Word* by J. W. Montgomery, published and copyright 1974, Bethany Fellowship, Inc., Minneapolis, Minnesota.)

that no new ideas had originated there. The current mockers, who are usually waiting to hear something new in Jerusalem, seem not to have noticed that the most original stance today is the Old Princeton effort not to be original at all. Fidelity to tradition is the novelty of our times. New Princeton should be eagerly looking for the revival of Old Princeton unless, perchance, it too is determined that no really original idea should appear today. My feeling is that the institutional successors of Hodge-Warfield-Machen are even more rigidly opposed to the entrance of new (old, that is) ideas than the Old Princetonians ever were. They stand as inflexibly for new errors concerning the Bible as the Warfieldians did for old truth—especially for the old truth of the inerrancy of holy Scripture.

If we are to go forward we must start by going backward—all the way to the seventeenth century, which was the zenith of theological dogma concerning the Holy Scriptures. Since that time there has been gradual decline. Our Princetonians were fighting essentially a rearguard action. The enemy of inerrancy has leveled Princeton (where there is not now a sole inerrantist survivor) and many other saints. Now the great counterattack has begun in "The Battle for the Bible." The International Council for Biblical Inerrancy is the spearhead of the drive in which the Evangelical Theological Society and other movements and individuals are actively engaged. Almost all of those sense the need to go back to Warfield if they would then advance forward to meet today's needs. Not all yet realize they must go further back still to get the full benefit of the scholarly faith of our fathers. We hope God will lead His people backward and forward: backward in order to go forward into our time, and forward in order to consolidate the gains of the past. Revisiting Old Princeton is taking one step backward in order to move two steps forward.

CHARLES HODGE (1797-1878)

Charles Hodge's great Lutheran contemporary, Charles Porterfield Krauth, said of him:

> Next to having Dr. Hodge on one's side is the pleasure of having him as an antagonist; for where conscientious men must discuss a subject, who can express the comfort of honorable, magnanimous dealing on both sides—the feeling that in battling with each other they are also battling for each other, in that grand warfare whose

final issue will be what all good men desire, the establishment of truth.[1]

Because our concern is not with Charles Hodge's theology in general or even with his specifically biblical views, but with his contributions to inspiration doctrine, we will not attempt even a summary statement here. An essentially adequate survey may be found in his *Systematic Theology*,[2] as well as in other works cited in this chapter. John Oliver Nelson[3] and John C. Vander Stelt[4] especially present such overviews.

Among the many contributions of Charles Hodge to the doctrine of plenary inspiration we find four items especially worthy of attention: (1) his general defense of the historic, orthodox doctrine; (2) his philosophical defense; (3) evidential defense; and (4) his experiential defense.

HODGE DEFENDED THE HISTORIC, ORTHODOX DOCTRINE GENERALLY

It has been often and thoroughly demonstrated that the historic, orthodox view of inspiration has been plenary, infallible, inerrant, theopneustic, oftentimes even called "dictation" (although not normally considered "mechanical") inspiration, repeatedly sloganized in the words "What the Bible says, God says." This is not to deny the presence of dissent but merely to locate it as the exception to the rule; nor is it to deny that in this century among biblical scholars the exception may have become the rule. Looked at historically, however, the contemporary academic majority is a miniscule historical minority. When it, nevertheless, frequently pretends that because it dominates the present it can rewrite the past, it makes the tail that tried to wag the dog seem a little less ridiculous.[5] To change the metaphor drastically, even the moderns let the cat out of the bag by admitting that the fathers at least

1. Charles Porterfield Krauth, *Infant Baptism and Infant Salvation in the Calvinistic System* (Philadelphia, 1974), p. 9.
2. Charles Hodge, *Systematic Theology*. 3 vols. (Greenwood, S.C.: Attic Press, 1960), 1:151-88.
3. John Oliver Nelson, "The Rise of the Princeton Theology. A Genetic Study of American Presbyterianism until 1850" (Ph.D. diss., Yale University, 1935).
4. John C. Vander Stelt, *Philosophy and Scripture. A Study in Old Princeton and Westminster Theology* (Marlton, N.J.: Mack Publishing, 1978), p. 120.
5. It is one thing for moderns to suppose, as do the writers of *The Myth of God Incarnate*, ed. John Hick (Philadelphia: Westminster, 1977) that the inerrancy doctrine has been decently buried and quite another to deny that it ever lived and reigned supreme. The former, we think, is a mistaken judgment; the latter, bad scholarship.

thought differently from themselves. Kirsopp Lake states this well:

> It is a mistake often made by educated persons who happen to have but little knowledge of historical theology, to suppose that fundamentalism is a new and strange form of thought. It is nothing of the kind; it is the partial and uneducated survival of a theology which was once universally held by all Christians. How many were there, for instance, in Christian churches in the eighteenth century who doubted the infallible inspiration of all Scripture? A few, perhaps, but very few. No, the fundamentalist may be wrong; I think that he is. But it is we who have departed from the tradition, not he, and I am sorry for the fate of anyone who tries to argue with a fundamentalist on the basis of authority. The Bible and the *corpus theologicum* of the Church is on the fundamentalist side.[6]

In my essay "The Church's Doctrine of Inspiration" in *The Foundation of Biblical Authority*, ed. James M. Boice (Grand Rapids: Zondervan, 1978), pp. 21-58, I survey the historical evidence briefly. Focusing on the reason otherwise good scholars draw different conclusions, I cite five non sequiturs that constantly recur when scholars analyze the often impressive data they have amassed. See also "The View of the Bible Held by the Church: The Early Church Through Luther," by Robert D. Preus, and "The View of the Bible Held by the Church: Calvin and the Westminster Divines," by John H. Gerstner, in *Inerrancy*, ed. Norman L. Geisler (Grand Rapids: Zondervan, 1980), pp. 357-410.

The history of the doctrine of inspiration has been repeatedly and thoroughly researched. In addition to extensive studies in encyclopedias and histories of doctrine, innumerable monographs have appeared on the subject in general as well as on details such as "alleged discrepancies": (cf. John Haley, *An Examination of the Alleged Discrepancies of the Bible* [Nashville: Goodpasture, 1951]) and individual theologians (cf. A. D. F. Polman, *The Word of God According to St. Augustine* [Grand Rapids: Eerdmans, 1961]). It is sufficient here to note a few of the more important general historical works. Classical studies include: William Lee, *The Inspiration of Holy Scripture* (New York: Robert Carter and Brothers, 1858); George T. Ladd, *The Doctrine of Sacred Scripture: A Critical, Historical and Dogmatic Inquiry*, 2 vols. (New York: Scribner's, 1883). More recently there are: William Sanday, *Inspiration: Eight Lectures on the Early History and Origin of the Doctrine of Bibli-*

---

6. Kirsopp Lake, *The Religion of Yesterday and Tomorrow* (Boston: Houghton, 1926), p. 61.

cal Inspiration (London: Longmans, 1903); G. D. Barry, The Inspiration and Authority of the Holy Scripture: A Study of the Literature of the First Five Centuries (New York: Macmillan, 1919); Daniel J. Theron, Evidence of Tradition (Grand Rapids: Baker, 1958); Johannes Beumer, Die Inspiration der Heiligen Schrift (Freidburg, Basel, and Vienna: Herder, 1968); Bruce Vawter, Biblical Inspiration (Philadelphia: Westminster; London: Hutchinson, 1972); Robert M. Grant, A Short History of the Interpretation of the Bible, rev. ed. (New York, London: Macmillan, 1972); Daniel Loretz, Das Ende der Inspirations Theologie: Chancen eines Neubeginns, 2 vols. (Stuttgart: Katholisches Bibelwerk, 1974); Jack B. Rogers and Donald K. McKim, The Authority and Interpretation of the Bible (San Francisco: Harper & Row, 1979).

Hodge touches virtually all the bases of the historic, orthodox doctrine. For one thing, he makes revelation more foundational than inspiration, the former providing the content of the divine message whereas the latter secures it certainly. The object of revelation, he taught, was to make men "wiser," but inspiration was necessary to guarantee "infallibility" by keeping the writer free from "error."[7]

Second, Hodge insists that errorless inspiration extends to "all" Scripture. Then writings—not merely the writers—are plenarily inspired. There can be no limitation[8]—no bracketing of the historical, geographical, or scientific.[9] The famous Parthenon[10] statement (the Bible would be the Word of God even if there were some flaw in it just as the Parthenon would be marble even if it had a speck of sandstone it it) finds Hodge napping as far as inerrancy is concerned. He was apparently distracted by the picayune character of some "objections" and was saying that the Bible would still be the Word of God if it had minor error in it (which errors Hodge did not admit). The most famous of the Old Princeton theologians did not even shrink from using the word dictation,[11] though he does not claim to know the exact nature of inspiration.

Third, mirabile dictu, Hodge even locates the inspired Scripture in the autographa. Vander Stelt, citing McAllister and Nelson, claims that Hodge was pressured into stressing autographa the

---

7. Hodge, Systematic Theology, 1:155.
8. Ibid., 1:154, 806.
9. Ibid., 1:162; cf. 1:180.
10. Ibid., 1:170.
11. Vander Stelt, p. 141, cites, "The original texts of Scripture, now lost, were letter-perfect as dictated by Deity and any possible error has somehow crept in since."

last year of his life,[12] though it seems to us that Hodge always assumed *autographa*,[13] because he never defended the inerrancy of transmission.

It is interesting to note that Hodge was guilty of the modern "sin" of deduction or speculation, for errorless inspiration was judged to be the "necessary consequence from the proposition that the sacred writers were the organs of God."[14] This was axiomatic reasoning in the preceding centuries. In our century, however, the most common method for denying inerrancy is denying the relevance of deduction. It was obvious to Hodge, and virtually every other thinker before our era, that if God spoke there could be no error in what He said. Today, that is pejoratively labeled "deductive" reasoning. If we would be truly open and scientific, it is now asserted, we will proceed inductively. That is, we will examine what God actually said and judge from that whether He erred or not (although even spokesmen of our audacious age have not found the courage to state their implications that bluntly).

HODGE DEFENDED THE HISTORIC, ORTHODOX POSITION PHILOSOPHICALLY

That Hodge proceeded theistically along the path of Scottish Common Sense philosophy, as had John Witherspoon and Archibald Alexander before him and B. B. Warfield and J. Gresham Machen after him, is unquestioned.[15] That acknowledged fact does not guarantee, however, that some will not deduce some very erroneous conclusions from it.

For example, Rogers and McKim, page 290, write that under the influence of Scottish realism "the Princeton men were sure that sin had made the emotions unreliable. But they held an almost Pelagian confidence that the mind was essentially undisturbed by sin's influence." In a footnote the authors use me as one of the Princetonians' "later followers," as an illustration (p. 318 n. 165). I feel certain that this is a well-intentioned

---

12. Ibid., p. 141, n. 353.
13. Cf., for example, the discussion of "The Inspiration of the Scriptures extends to the Words," Hodge, *Systematic Theology*, 1:164-65.
14. Ibid., 1:164; cf. 1:183 "necessary implication." It is interesting that Jack Rogers and Donald McKim, *The Authority and Interpretation of the Bible* (San Francisco: Harper & Row, 1979), p. 323, has a section entitled: "From Inductive Science to Deductive Apologetics. Benjamin Breckenridge Warfield (1851-1921)," *Authority and Interpretation*.
15. Vander Stelt, p. 123, n. 203, for example, writes: "Hodge constantly appealed to man's consciousness." Cf. S.E. Ahlstrom, "Scottish Philosophy and American Theology," *Church History* 14 (Sept. 1955): 257-72. Rogers and McKim, p. 289.

(though inexcusable) misinterpretation of Hodge's (and my) position. Because Rogers and McKim do not seem to understand that sin can make an instrument, such as the mind, *malfunction* without destroying the *esse* of the mind itself, they simply do not grasp the "noetic influence" of sin according to Old Princeton (or old Calvinism, for that matter). Therefore, they honestly see the viewpoint as "almost Pelagian" (Why do *they* say "almost"?) We say that this misinterpretation is inexcusable because Hodge and others are constantly pointing out the blinding effects of sin in fallen man. For example, let anyone consult Hodge's treatment of sin in *Systematic Theology*, volume 2, beginning at page 130; or *The Way of Life*, chapter 2; or, his commentary on Romans, especially on 1:20 and following.

Because the fact that Hodge meant to use the realistic approach is granted by all, we will focus here on certain unfortunate inconsistencies he exhibited in employing that epistemology. First, he considered those principles not demonstrable intuitions but mere beliefs; second, he considered the Bible as authenticating them, whereas they are used to demonstrate the Bible; and, third, he was further inconsistent by making the "essence and measure of all faith" to be "cognitive knowledge."

(1) *Hodge considered those principles not demonstrable intuitions but mere beliefs.* According to Scottish Realism, our knowledge of the external world and its causal relationships is a "necessary assumption" and not merely a credible, not to mention gratuitous, assumption.[16] For Hodge, "truths" about that world are received by "faith," which is a "degree less than knowledge and stronger than probability."[17] A necessary assumption, unlike a belief, would have to be true if anything is known, whereas a belief would be desirable truth but not necessary. One may risk building on a belief, but he would not have to do so. A foundation that is optional is no secure foundation. So Hodge is off to a shaky start though he soon forgets it and proceeds as if there were no questions. As a matter of fact, he does this so constantly that we may wonder if he does not, after all, truly agree with Common Sense Philosophy and only occasionally doubt it. This "failure of nerve" runs throughout Hodge in other matters also and may be

16. Cf. especially J. McCosh's most important work *The Intuitions of the Mind.* In his *Realistic Philosophy*, 2 vols. (New York: Macmillan, 1887), 2:240, he writes of Thomas Reid that he met Hume "by calling in great mental principles, which reveal and guarantee truth, which can never be set aside, and which have foundations deep as the universe."

17. Hodge, *Systematic Theology*, 3:62.

the reason that Emil Brunner sensed a gentler form of thought in him than in the later, more rigid (more consistent?) Warfield.

(2) *Hodge considered the Bible as authenticating Common Sense principles, whereas they were supposed to authenticate the Bible.* According to Hodge, "everything that can be legitimately learned from that source [nature] will be found recognized and authenticated in the Scriptures."[18] Scripture assumes all primary truths—whether principles of reason or facts of consciousness—and thereby authenticates them. The only way Hodge could be justified in such a remark is by insisting on the necessity of these assumptions for all, including biblical thinkers (which we have shown that he does not consistently do); or, by assuming initially that the Bible is the Word of God and therefore whatever it assumes it thereby authenticates. However, this "presuppositional" approach was opposed, not approved, by Hodge and Old Princeton until Van Til. Nevertheless, we must admit that there is a certain circularity of reasoning in Hodge (not utterly unlike that which presuppositionalists practice and defend). But if Hodge practices it, he certainly does not defend it. This subject merits far more space than is available here.

(3) *Hodge is further inconsistent by making the "essence and measure of all faith" to be "cognitive knowledge."*[19] This is a return to his Scottish Realistic base, as we noted it above.

Will the Real(istic) Charles Hodge please stand up? Is the Thomas Aquinas of Old Princeton not Thomistic at all? or even Neo-Thomist? but a crypto-presuppositionalist? We fear that he was not so distinguished as a philosopher as he was as a theologian. The presuppositionalists, such as Van Til, Clark, and Dooyeweerd, have been saying all along that Hodge was a great theologian but not so great an apologist. They are right but not for the right reason. They think his deficiency was in not being a consistent presuppositionalist, whereas it was because he was not always a consistent realist. His realism was not to be eschewed but rather his inconsistency. Curing inconsistent realism by presuppositionalism is to jump from the fire into the furnace.

HODGE DEFENDED THE HISTORIC, ORTHODOX POSITION EVIDENTIALLY

Hodge goes into a fairly full discussion of the three functions

---

18. Ibid., 1:11, cf. Vander Stelt, p. 123; Rogers and McKim, p. 294.
19. Hodge, *Systematic Theology*, 3:84-88.

of reason at the beginning of his *Systematic Theology.*[20] He speaks of the *usus organicus,* by which he refers to the basic function of rational perception. Even revelation, which conveys truths, requires reason for its apprehension. "About this there can be no dispute," said Hodge, not dreaming of what the next century would bring forth. Second, he considers the *usus contradictionis* by which reason judges whether what it has learned is sense or nonsense. If it is a contradiction, or nonsense, it is rejected. If it is conceivable and makes sense, the task still remains for reason to determine whether the conceivable thing actually occurred. It is the *usus verificationis* which determines that. One could say that for Hodge the first two uses were the source of his Common Sense Realism and the third was the source of his Christianity.[21] Verification, for Hodge, is essential; we cannot believe "without evidence."[22] Faith in the Bible is "rationally arrived at,"[23] and nothing can reach the heart except through the head.[24]

What, then, is the verification of Christianity—the evidence that it is the truth of God and that the Bible is the Word of God? There are at least four points of importance to notice: (1) the Bible has internal verifications; (2) the Bible has external verifications; (3) "seeing" the evidence for the truth is not the same thing as understanding that truth; (4) reason cannot in any case change the heart to accept the truth.

First, the Bible has internal evidence virtually verifying itself. It shines "in its own light,"[25] though Hodge does speak of its truthfulness being a "premise."[26] Although he is somewhat ambiguous, it seems reasonable to conclude that this internal evidence is not the Bible's mere assertion of its own inspiration. For Hodge, Scripture seems to be *axiopistic.* This kind of "internal" evidence we may consider "external"/internal evidence because it is not considered true simply *because* it is in the Bible although it *is* in the Bible.

What will be foundational for Warfield's case for inspiration seems secondary to Hodge's—namely, miracles. Yet there can be no doubt that Hodge, too, sees them as establishing what John Locke called "the credit of the proposer" of doctrine.[27] He once

20. Ibid., 1:49.
21. Vander Stelt, p. 135.
22. Hodge, *The Way of Life* (Philadelphia, 1841), p. 16.
23. Hodge, "Ground of Faith," *Essays and Reviews* (New York: Robert Carter and Brothers, 1857), p. 192.
24. Hodge, *Systematic Theology,* passim.
25. Hodge, *Princeton Review,* 12 (1840).
26. Cf. W. M. Coleman, *An Examination of the A Priori Principles Assumed by Dr. Charles Hodge in His Treatise on Systematic Theology* (Washington, 1874).
27. John Locke, *Essay Concerning Human Understanding* 4. 18.

again vacillates in his argument, which makes one wonder whether the miracles prove Christ (he said that Christianity is "unprovable"[28] and only believers can fully appreciate it)[29] or Christ's miracles.

Hodge emerges into the light with his third point that seeing evidence for truth is not synonymous with understanding that truth. Hodge "does not require us to believe without evidence; but he does require us to believe what we cannot understand . . ."[30] As Jonathan Edwards would say, there can be a demonstration of a truth that is incomprehensible. However, this in Edwards or Hodge is anathema to Van Til, who constantly denies any possibility of denotation without connotation.

Hodge's fourth point, and probably most important, is that reason cannot change the heart.[31] This is probably what he meant by asserting that Christianity is "unprovable"—rational demonstration is not rational persuasion.[32] Hodge was not a rationalist but an advocate of Christian rationality. This distinction the orthodox almost always make and the unorthodox almost always fail to comprehend, invariably confusing and misrepresenting it as Machen will later point out.

Notwithstanding, Hodge can write what Tom Paine would have been proud of: "The human mind is so constituted that it cannot refuse its assent to evidence, when clearly perceived [can a rationalist say more?]. . . . Confidence in his [God's] word cannot be withheld, and especially when all he says finds its confirmation in our own experience, and commends itself to our conscience and judgment."[33] (If this is so, would a rationalist not agree?)

If reason enlightens the mind but cannot change the heart, what does? The answer to that leads to Hodge's fourth contribution.

HODGE DEFENDED THE HISTORIC, ORTHODOX, DOCTRINE EXPERIENTIALLY

However zig-zag his route, Hodge arrives at his evidential goal and then falters again. We noted above that the evidence seemed compelling, yet now it appears to be not quite compelling. One is inclined to ask, Will Hodge not make up his mind? To this the

28. Hodge, *Systematic Theology*, 2:604.
29. Hodge, *Way of Life*, p. 125.
30. Ibid., pp. 66-67.
31. Ibid., p. 223.
32. Cf. *Westminster Confession of Faith*, chap. 1, line 5.
33. Hodge, *The Way of Life*, p. 16.

reply seems to be, Hodge cannot make up his mind; the Holy Spirit must do it for him (and all the other elect).

In his *Systematic Theology* Hodge discusses the *Testimonium Spiritus Sancti* rather extensively.[34] Before turning to this final statement, which idea appeared in print in 1870, let us review his position as stated in 1841, *The Way of Life*. Although the internal testimony of the Spirit is not mentioned in those terms, it is still clear from the beginning that that is what Hodge has in mind. When he starts out observing that the Bible demands faith in itself as the Word of God he concludes that "faith cannot be more extensive than the exhibition of evidence."[35] Therefore, the Bible must carry its evidence in itself: "*Section II. The internal evidence of their Divine origin is the proper ground of faith in the Scriptures.*"[36] From where does this evidence come? Not from mere argument or miracle.[37] It must come from "spiritual apprehension," which is a "gift." It is a demonstration of the Spirit and power. This amounts to what Calvin calls the internal testimony of the Spirit—*Testimonium Spiritus Sancti.*

For Hodge this is the "proper ground" of faith, but precisely here Hodge is unconsciously departing from the Reformed tradition, in which the internal testimony is not the "ground" but the "persuasion" of the ground. For example, the Westminster Confession of Faith, after listing the various perfections of Scripture as "arguments whereby it doth abundantly evidence itself to be the Word of God," observes: "Yet, notwithstanding, our full persuasion and assurance of the infallible truth, and divine authority thereof, is from the inward work of the Holy Spirit, bearing witness by and with the Word in our hearts."[38] The ground is the evidence (in and out of Scripture), but the assurance comes from the Holy Spirit. The Spirit's witness persuades of the evidence; it does not provide the evidence. Hodge unfortunately confuses these in his *The Way of Life*.

How does Hodge present the internal testimony in his magnum opus, *Systematic Theology*? Better than in *The Way of Life* but yet not without some remaining confusion. Here he uses the term *testimony* for every kind of evidence, including what is usually meant by evidence (internal *and* external).[39] Unregenerate men can grasp the external evidence but "the spiritual form of testi-

34. Hodge, *Systematic Theology*, 3:69.
35. Ibid., 3:13.
36. Ibid., 3:20.
37. Ibid., 3:23.
38. Ibid., 1:5.
39. Ibid., 3:69.

mony is confined to the regenerate."[40] The continuing confusion is seen in these words: "When, therefore, a Christian is asked, Why he believes the Scriptures and the doctrines therein contained, his simple answer is, On the testimony or authority of God."[41] Hodge then proceeds to enumerate again external and internal evidence, showing that his final statement is still unclarified in his mind. (We can only assume that he means this: we believe the authority of Scripture on its being God's Word; we believe it is God's Word on the basis of evidence.)

What is crystal clear is that Hodge recognized the absolute necessity of supernatural, divine illumination for anyone who was ever "persuaded" savingly that the Bible is the Word of God. Hodge may have overstated his case, attributing more to the internal testimony than the Spirit thereby afforded; but, there can be no doubt whatever that he recognized and stressed the absolute necessity of that witness for saving faith in the inerrant Word of God. When we come to Warfield we will notice the same staunch advocacy but with 20/20 vision.

CONCLUSION

Considering that Hodge's teaching and writing career spanned the second and third quarters of the nineteenth century, when the Enlightenment spirit was casting its dark shadows over the American religious scene, his defense of the infallibility of Scripture was impressive. Lacking the profundity of an earlier Edwards and the precision of a later Warfield, Hodge may well have been the ablest proponent of the historic, orthodox doctrine between those two giants. He took the torch from Edwards and though it was burning less brightly when he handed it on to Warfield it was still shining. When Charles Hodge died in 1878 there was no doubt that Old Princeton was still the national and world champion of an inerrant Scripture. The approach was that of a still-popular Realism, which was now articulated with a more "American" emphasis on common sense and practicality. Though somewhat garbled, his evidentialism met and survived the onslaughts of Kantianism, Darwinism, and Romanticism, just as his Reformed theology had successfully battled Taylorism, Finneyism, Arminianism, and Romanism. All in all, Hodge takes his

---

40. Ibid.
41. Ibid., 3:70.

place among the scholarly heroes of the faith who fought for and under the banner: "What the Bible says, God says!"

BENJAMIN BRECKENRIDGE WARFIELD (1851-1921)

As with Hodge, so with Warfield: we are concerned less with his general doctrine of inspiration than with his contributions to and defense of that doctrine. These contributions surpass not only those of Hodge and Machen but those of the entire Old Princeton School, which was founded on the doctrine of inspiration.

W. A. Hoffecker, in his work *Piety and the Princeton Theologians*,[42] has shown the unity of Princeton Seminary's theology from its founding father, Archibald Alexander, continued in its most famous systematic theologian, Charles Hodge, and climaxed in its most distinguished Reformed scholar, Benjamin Breckenridge Warfield. Hoffecker discusses both the thought and piety of these men in their backgrounds, their formal writings and their devotional literature. Carefully, fairly, and critically considering these three faces of the three men, Hoffecker comes to this general conclusion that although the historical context had changed greatly over the century the Princeton theology remained virtually unchanged.

Among the contributions of these Princetonians, Warfield's major one was clearly the doctrine of the inspiration of the Bible. His was not only the major contribution of the whole "Old Princeton" to that major theme, but it may well be the greatest contribution to the theme ever made by any Christian scholar before or since. As John R. Mackay wrote in a bibliographical article shortly after the death of Warfield in 1921:

> Looking over this series of articles, one makes bold to say that not in the whole range of Christian literature will one find the exegetical facts, upon which the doctrine of the plenary Inspiration of the Scriptures rest, brought out so fully and established after so severely scientific a manner as they are brought to light in the foregoing articles on Inspiration by Professor Warfield. I submit that his work on Inspiration on this account marks in this department of theology an epoch.[43]

---

42. W. A. Hoffecher, *Piety and the Princeton Theologians* (Grand Rapids: Baker, 1981).

43. John R. Mackay, "B. B. Warfield—A Bibliography," *The Expositor*, Eighth Series, 24 (July 1922):37.

WARFIELD'S CONTRIBUTION CONTESTED

Notwithstanding, some of his contemporaries and many modern scholars think that Warfield's magnificent effort failed and may even have damaged the cause of true biblical inspiration. Tom Torrance, writing in 1954 on the occasion of the publication of *The Inspiration and Authority of the Bible*, faults the writer, whose greatness he acknowledges, for a certain scholastic rationalism that Torrance does not really prove.[44] Emil Brunner, as a guest lecturer at Princeton Seminary in 1937, defended his own view of inspiration by appealing to Charles Hodge against Warfield, who, Brunner maintained, had driven the historic Princeton doctrine to an extreme in verbal inerrancy.[45] Cornelius Van Til regards the entire Princeton School's case for inspiration harmed by an underlying doctrine of the autonomy of man derived from Bishop Butler—justifying his own Introduction to Presbyterian and Reformed Publishing Company's new 1948 edition of Warfield's *Works* by his agreement with Warfield's position on the absolute necessity of biblical revelation.[46] The author of the ablest recent doctoral dissertation on Warfield's theory of revelation. J. J. Markarian, after very carefully stating and weighing the Princetonian's case, concludes that it fails of its purpose because "in his zeal to deal with historical criticism he was driven into the extreme position of suspending the truth of the Christian faith upon the ability of the scholar to beat back the attacks against Jesus' historicity."[47]

Jack Rogers's *Scripture in the Westminster Confession*, although not a major study on Warfield, does take deliberate aim at his interpretation of the Westminster Confession's doctrine of inspiration because Warfield's errant view on inerrancy (as Rogers thinks) has led even modern Princeton (which is normally allergic

---

44. *Scottish Journal of Theology* 7, no. 1 (March 1954):104ff. Torrance writes: "Here we are given an account of inspiration that is eminently sober and scholarly, and which is grounded upon an exposition of the Biblical teaching itself. Thus presented, it is a view which must be reckoned with, and not one to be set aside under an opprobrious label like 'American fundamentalism'— which is only too often done by Liberal reactionaries." After the criticism I mentioned, Torrance concludes that Warfield's work is one "of great scholarship and power which has much that is essential to offer us today."
45. Cf. below my discussion of Sandeen (who mistakenly made the same point).
46. B. B. Warfield, *The Inspiration and Authority of the Bible*, ed. Samuel G. Craig (Philadelphia: Presbyterian and Reformed, 1948), pp. 3-68.
47. J. J. Markarian, "The Calvinistic Concept of the Biblical Revelation in the Theology of Benjamin Breckenridge Warfield" (Ph.D. diss., Drew University, 1963). p. 75.

to Warfield) to sin. In Rogers's opinion, Warfield's error is in projecting his own view of biblical inerrancy to the Westminster divines who (with the possible exception of George Gillespie) did not share it.[48]

Probably the most severe modern critic of the Old Princeton doctrine of Scripture is Ernest R. Sandeen, who in his 1970 book *The Roots of Fundamentalism: British and American Millenarianism 1800-1930*[49] sees this doctrine as reaching its peak in Warfield. Of particular interest to us is chapter 5: "Biblical Literalism: Millennialism and the Princeton Theology." Here Sandeen represents nineteenth-century fundamentalism as centering its case for biblical authority on Christian religious experience. When criticisms against inerrancy increased, however, the movement turned to Princeton Seminary for help and especially to Warfield—"probably the most intellectually gifted professor ever to teach on that faculty."[50] Because of the influence and typicality of this critique we will set it forth more fully and critically.

First, Sandeen attempts to drive a wedge between the Westminster Confession of Faith and the Princeton theology, saying that the Confession "insists that only the witness of the Holy Spirit can convince any man that this [the inspiration of the Bible] is so, whereas Hodge prefers to argue that the Scriptures are the Word of God because they are inspired."[51] This reveals, on Sandeen's part, an inability to understand the positions involved. The Confession's statement about the Bible, "Our full persuasion and assurance of the infallible truth, and divine authority thereof, is from the inward work of the Holy Spirit, bearing witness by and with the Word in our hearts," follows a recital of proofs whereby the Bible "doth abundantly evidence itself to be the Word of God."[52] In other words, the proof or evidence that the Bible is the Word of God is one thing; the persuasion of acceptance of this evidence is another. The Confession recognizes the necessity of evidence prior to persuasion and so states; Hodge

---

48. Jack Rogers, *Scripture in the Westminster Confession* (Grand Rapids: Eerdmans, 1967), passim. Cf. also Rogers's essay "Van Til and Warfield on Scripture in the Westminster Confession of Faith," in E. R. Geehan, ed., *Jerusalem and Athens* (Nutley, N.J.: Presbyterian and Reformed, 1971), where Rogers finds Van Til as well as Warfield wrong and the Westminster Confession of Faith correct in teaching that "The Bible offers not proofs, but a person to persuade us" (p. 165).
49. Ernest R. Sandeen, *The Roots of Fundamentalism* (Chicago: U. of Chicago, 1970).
50. Ibid., p. 115.
51. Ibid., p. 119.
52. Westminster Confession of Faith, chap. 1, line 5.

recognizes the necessity of evidence prior to persuasion and so states. Sandeen fixes on the persuasion element in the Confession and the evidence element in Hodge and, of course, notes a difference. But let him compare the evidence element in both and let him compare the persuasion element in both and he will note an essential agreement. This is the author who a few pages later accuses Warfield of an "inability to understand history"!

Having manufactured (unintentionally, we assume) a nonexistent difference between the Confession and Princeton (Hodge), Sandeen next proceeds to manufacture (unintentionally, we again assume) a nonexistent difference between Hodge and Warfield. On page 119 Sandeen quotes these words from Hodge: "If the sacred writers assert that they are the organs of God . . . then, *if we believe their divine mission*, we must believe what they teach as to the nature of the influence under which they spoke and wrote" (italics added). On page 120 Sandeen writes: "For Charles Hodge's depending upon previously acquired biblical reverence, Benjamin Breckenridge Warfield substituted the externally verified credibility of the apostles as teachers of doctrine. . . . Thus he shifted the ground on which Charles Hodge had established the proof of the doctrine of inspiration and made Princeton's dependence upon external authority complete." One does not have to read anything in Hodge that Sandeen has quoted to recognize that Sandeen's "shift of ground" is pure fiction. We underlined the words in Hodge "if we believe their [the apostles'] divine mission" because they are quite equivalent to Warfield's "externally verified credibility of the apostles as teachers of doctrine." One can see throughout Hodge's many writings that he, no less than Warfield, accepted the Bible with the noted "reverence" for the same reason that Warfield did—namely, that they were sanctioned by verified messengers of God.

Sandeen is not yet finished: he must manufacture (unintentionally, we still assume) a difference between Princeton's founder Archibald Alexander and both Hodge and Warfield. How? He quotes Alexander: "In the narration of well-known facts, the writer [of Scripture] did not need a continual suggestion of every idea but only to be so superintended as to be preserved from error."[53] This is taken to mean that Alexander did not hold verbal inspiration (while, in fact, Sandeen's interpretation shows that Sandeen does not understand verbal inspiration). Practically equivalent statements can be found in all verbal inspirationists, as, for example, in Warfield himself:

53. Cited in Sandeen, *Roots*, pp. 123-24.

This mode of revelation differs from prophecy, properly so called, precisely by the employment in it, as is not done in prophecy, of the total personality of the organ of revelation, as a factor. It has been common to speak of the mode of the Spirit's action in this form of revelation, therefore, as an assistance, a superintending, a direction, a control, the meaning being that the affect aimed at—the discovery and enunciation of Divine truth—is attained through the action of the human powers—historical research, logical reasoning, ethical thought, religious aspiration—acting not by themselves, however, but under the prevailing assistance, superintendency, direction, control of the Divine Spirit.[54]

The second Princetonian position identified by Sandeen is inerrancy, which he claims to have been an innovation—though he offers no proof of it. In this context he charges that Princeton, by championing inerrancy, "in a sense seemed to risk the *whole Christian faith* upon one proved error."[55] This is so dreadful a misrepresentation that while one is wondering how anyone who knows anything about the Princeton theologians could write it, Sandeen immediately goes on to mention that Warfield most certainly did distinguish between the Christian religion and the inerrancy of the Bible; but then Sandeen has the audacity to call that a "compromise" by which Warfield was able to have his cake and eat it too. That Sandeen really meant this slanderous and utterly unsubstantiated remark is seen in the still more slanderous statement about the whole school several pages later (p. 130): they manifested a "continuing tendency to treat every opponent of the Princeton theology as an atheist or non-Christian."

The third alleged distinctive of the Princeton theology—and the especial responsibility, according to Sandeen, of A. A. Hodge and Warfield—was appeal to the autographa. To this point we will return later.

So we see that though it is generally recognized by all that Warfield is one of the greatest champions of biblical inspiration, at the same time many (if not most) modern scholars seem to think that his effort in this regard was one of the greatest of failures. To put it in other words, the absolute errancy in Warfield is seen in his doctrine of the inerrancy of Scripture. Warfield would like that juxtaposition and would readily admit that if the Bible is not totally inerrant his greatest work is virtually totally errant. And to those who, like Kuyper and Van Til, agree that his

54. Warfield, "The Biblical Idea of Revelation," in *The Inspiration and Authority of the Bible*, p. 95.
55. Sandeen, *Roots*, p. 126 (italics added).

doctrine of inerrancy is true but his method of proving it is not, he would say the reverse: Kuyper and Van Til's doctrine is true but their method of proving it is not.

So as we now consider Warfield's case for inerrancy the reader is invited to judge whether the doctrine of inerrancy is or is not true and whether Warfield's case for it is or is not true. This chapter will consider not Warfield's doctrine of inerrancy but Warfield's *case* for inerrancy. It will include the doctrine, of course, but will deal with more than the doctrine itself. We move right to the point by considering Warfield's treatment of supernatural revelation. Under this head we deal with (1) supernatural revelation *to* men (revelation proper) and (2) supernatural revelation *through* men (inspiration).

WARFIELD ON SUPERNATURAL REVELATION

Supernatural revelation to men (revelation proper). Supernatural Cause (Miracle) as Evidence of Supernatural Revelation. Warfield believed, as Francis Bacon did, that miracles were not necessary to prove God; natural revelation did that. Nature efficiently yielded her theistic proof. God has revealed himself through the creation and preservation of the universe (Ps. 19:1-2).

But *supernatural* revelation was from God as Judge and Savior to man as sinner.[56] Each of these revelations "is incomplete without the other."[57] For Warfield, God could not address Himself to man as a sinner unless He had first identified Himself by addressing man as man. Man, knowing his Creator to exist, could well understand God's speaking to man the sinner in the role of Judge and Savior.

So miracle, or supernatural causality, is the crux of Warfield's case for special, supernatural, divine revelation. This was not only the Old Princeton position but the Old Christian tradition from the second-century apologists to the present.

However, since the eighteenth-century Enlightenment, many theologians—such as Friedrich Schleiermacher—have apologized *for* rather than *with* miracles. Instead of believing that God was especially revealing Himself as indicated by the presence of miracles, they have argued for revelation in spite of the alleged miracles. For example, instead of miracles proving the revelation of Christ, the revelation of Christ was used as the proof of miracles.

---

56. Warfield, "The Biblical Idea of Revelation," in *The Inspiration and Authority of the Bible*, p. 74.
57. Ibid., p. 75.

Revelation was taken on faith and miracles were deduced from that revelation, rather than the miracles serving as facts from which the revelation was inferred. Consequently, although miracles were no more foundational to Warfield's case for divine revelation than for Alexander's and Hodge's, they received greater emphasis in Warfield.

Jack Rogers, in his previously cited work *Scripture in the Westminster Confession* maintains that the Westminster divines believed the Bible to point to the Person of Christ rather than to proofs. Warfield (and he interpreted the Westminster divines as of the same mind as himself) argued that the Bible offered *proofs of a Person*, the divine Christ. Rogers sees Scripture in the Westminster theologians merely as a direct witness to Christ who needs no proof, whereas Warfield viewed their Scripture citations as proof that the confessional witness to Christ as divine was actually true. Faith rested on this evidence, according to Warfield, although it contained its own evidence, or, rather, needed none, according to Rogers.

"Counterfeit Miracles." If Warfield was concerned with anything more than miracles it was "counterfeit miracles." Those were closer home! In his defense of true miracles and their significance Warfield was opposing the rationalistic ideology of the Enlightenment, which had spread everywhere by the turn of the century; his attack on counterfeit miracles was in opposition to the charismatic tendency that was only beginning to take shape then and has reached massive proportions in our time. Although Pentecostalism began in earnest at the turn of the century and has only poured over the banks of Warfield's as well as the other "mainline" denominations in the form of Neo-pentecostalism since 1960, producing a flood of literature in its train, Warfield's *Counterfeit Miracles* remains the ablest critique yet of the fundamental principles at stake.

In Warfield's thinking, counterfeit miracles were of two basic kinds: internal and external.

Counterfeit Internal "Miracles." For Warfield, it was a perversion of the internal witness of the Holy Spirit to the Christian heart (precious as it was to him) when that experience was used as proof of the supernatural revelation of Scripture. This it was never intended to be. One must not employ the *testimonium internum Spiritus sancti* as a demonstration when, in fact, it is a confirmation. The internal testimony seals to the heart what external miracles provide for the mind. To make the internal experience a substitute for external miracle at once eliminates the role of the true miracle and changes the nature of the internal experience.

Counterfeit External "Miracles." Unfortunately, when Warfield's classic book *Counterfeit Miracles* was republished the title was changed to *Miracles Yesterday and Today*. People who get their cue to books by titles alone would be totally misled by the new title if they did not know Warfield. His original title, admittedly rather flamboyant for a classical scholar, tells the story. In Warfield's judgment, the "yesterday" miracles of the biblical period, and only those of the biblical period, are genuine. All post-apostolic, "today" miracles are spurious. All nonbiblical "miracles" are "counterfeit miracles." The contents of the volume make this plain: "The Cessation of the Charismata"; "Patristic and Mediaeval Marvels"; "Roman Catholic Miracles"; "Irvingite Gifts"; "Faith-Healing"; "Mind-Cure."

Supernatural revelation through men (inspiration). Reason for Inspiration. Warfield now has a supernatural revelation of God to men. It has been clearly revealed to its recipients, to whom it has also been miraculously demonstrated to be from God. But if this revelation is to come not only to individuals but to mankind in general, it must be *communicated* through these individuals. Here an obvious danger arises. How is mankind to know that those who have indeed encountered God have accurately relayed and interpreted the revelation? I learned once of a gift some people gave me that was never relayed to me. Even though it was given, it has never yet reached me. But even if it reached me by the person who was to deliver it, how would I know it was the gift that was originally sent? Only those who sent it could ultimately assure me. Warfield teaches that the God who gave His revelation to individuals saw to it that they delivered it to mankind of His actually speaking through those individuals Himself. This is what Warfield called inspiration, and it is this doctrine to which he has given definitive statement and defense.

The Definition of Inspiration. Early in his career Warfield defined the doctrine that he devoted much of his life to developing and defending and from which he never departed. Although known as a Princetonian and identified in the distinguished succession of Alexander, Hodge, Vos, Green, Wilson, and Machen, Warfield began his career at Western Theological Seminary in 1880. His inaugural address there defined inspiration as the "extraordinary influence (or, passively, the result of it) exerted by the Holy Ghost on the writers of our Sacred Books, by which their words were rendered also the words of God, and therefore, perfectly infallible." Anyone familiar with Warfield knows that reflected in all his work is this classical Christian position that "what Scripture says, God says."

The Proof of Inspiration. How does Warfield prove the Bible to be inspired as defined? Because (he will attempt to show) the Bible says so. When it is further asked, Do we not have to assume the Bible is inspired if we would believe it when it says it is inspired? Warfield answers: No, we need not and we do not. Rather, we believe the writers of the Bible, because they have been shown, independently of an assumed inspired Bible, to be the accredited messengers of the God who cannot lie or err. The miracles that attested them established their "credit as proposers" (Locke), as has been shown above. God, who cannot lie, would not accredit messengers who, in His name, could and might lie. His accrediting of them is not quite tantamount to His inspiring them because it is conceivable that He could have revealed Himself to them and then left them to communicate or not communicate that experience in their own fallible terms. But if He did that, He would never, after accrediting them, have permitted them to say otherwise. And if He did inspire their inscripturation of the message, He would never have allowed them to deny this. So, in brief, Warfield's proof of inspiration is in *three non-circular stages:* (1) the Bible teaches its own inspiration, (2) God accredited its writers as His messengers independently of an inspired Bible, and (3) God would never have permitted them to err or lie in so teaching.

To show that the Bible does, in fact, teach its own inspiration, Warfield enlists his best exegetical efforts. His texts range all over the Bible, Old Testament and New. He deals with minutiae and general principles. He enters into criticism, to exegesis, and to sermonizing. Without doubt, in the total corpus of Warfieldean literature the majority of it concerns the "inspiration and authority of Scripture."

For two reasons (besides space) we need not enter here into a full exposition of Warfield on inspiration. First, many have already written on this subject. To mention a few: There is the important older article by T. M. Lindsay "The Doctrine of Scripture in the Reformers and the Princeton School."[58] F. L. Patton's oration following the death of Warfield is significant.[59] W. M. Counts produced an important master's thesis in 1959 at the Dal-

58. *The Expositor,* 1895.
59. F. L. Patton, "Benjamin Breckenridge Warfield," *The Princeton Theological Review* 19 (1921): 369-91.

las Theological Seminary on Warfield's doctrine of inspiration. In 1961, C. N. Kraus did a formidable doctoral dissertation at Duke titled "The Principle of Authority in the Theology of B. B. Warfield, W. A. Brown, and G. B. Smith." Trites wrote a useful Th.M. thesis at Princeton on "B. B. Warfield's View of the Authority of Scripture" (1962). W. Behannon's Th.D. dissertation dealt with "Benjamin B. Warfield's Concept of Religious Authority."[60] Livingston's Yale thesis, to which we have referred, bears on Warfield's view of inspiration, though its concentration is on his apologetic. Daniel Fuller's article "Benjamin Breckenridge Warfield's View of Faith and History"[61] is important, and his recent joint article with Clark Pinnock ("On Revelation and Biblical Authority")[62] debates the issues. We have already mentioned Rogers's fine critical comments on the Warfield doctrine. Probably the best extensive—though essentially critical—study is the work of J. J. Markarian, "The Calvinistic Concept of the Biblical Revelation in the Theology of Benjamin Breckenridge Warfield."[63]

Second, and more to the point, it is not essential to our purpose to present a full exposition of Warfield's doctrine of inspiration. We are trying to set forth his *case* for inspiration, and this is much more comprehensive than his *doctrine* of inspiration. Hence we need consider his doctrine of inspiration only sufficiently to explain it clearly and see its place in his "case."

There are, in Warfield's opinion, three major biblical texts on inspiration and to those he gave special attention.[64] They are: John 10:35, 2 Timothy 3:16, and 2 Peter 1:20-21, the greatest being 2 Timothy 3:16. His treatment of that single *locus classicus* gives us his perspective. He insists that the crucial word *theopneustia* in 2 Timothy 3:16 does not mean "*in*spired of God." The Greek term, he says, refers not to in-spiring, but only to "spiring" or spiration. God breathed out the Scriptures, and they are the outflowing of His power. "Scriptures are," Warfield concludes, "a divine product, without any indication of how God has operated in producing them."[65]

The Method of Inspiration. Warfield has relatively little to say

---

60. Th.D. dissertation, Southwestern Baptist Theological Seminary, 1963.
61. *Bulletin of the Evangelical Theological Society* 11, no. 2 (Spring 1968): 75-83.
62. *Journal of the Evangelical Theological Society* 16, no. 2 (Spring 1973): 67ff.
63. Markarian. (See note 49 above).
64. Of course, Warfield surveyed all relevant passages. In this connection, his "Biblical Idea of Revelation" (in *The Inspiration and Authority of the Bible*) is characteristic.
65. Warfield, "The Biblical Idea of Inspiration," in *The Inspiration and Authority of the Bible*, p. 133.

about the method of inspiration, because he believed the Bible itself had very little to say on the subject. The great theopneustic passage, as he interpreted it, reveals only the *that* of inspiration, not the *how.* According to him the same is true of most other biblical passages relevant to this theme.

However, Warfield found some intimations in the Bible of its method of inspiration. There is the great Petrine statement (2 Pet. 1:20, 21): "No prophecy ever came by impulse of man, but men moved by the Holy Spirit spoke from God." The crucial verb here is *pherō*, "move or bear along." Admittedly, the writers are described as passive in one sense, but at the same time Warfield insists that "reception itself is a kind of activity." The point, he reminds us, is that there is "no ground for imagining that God is unable to frame his own message in the language of the organs of his revelation without its thereby ceasing to be, because expressed in a fashion natural to these organs, therefore purely His message."[66] *Concursus* is Warfield's view; he sees Scripture in a true sense human but still divine.[67] The main idea that seems most to have impressed Warfield was, whatever the method of inspiration, it assured as end product the pure and unalloyed, infallible and authoritative Word of God.

In his zeal for the divine purity of the sacred text, Warfield at times overstated himself—and even overstated John Calvin. He rightly maintains that Calvin never meant to teach "dictation" but only "that the result of inspiration is as if it were by dictation"; but then Warfield adds "free from all human admixture."[68] Both Calvin and Warfield deny any *sinful* or *errant* admixture but neither really goes so far as to deny "all *human* admixture." The whole *concursus* concept is against such a notion. One can only remark that while talking about inerrancy, Warfield on this occasion spoke errantly! By this slip he seems to give some substance to the oft-heard charge that the orthodox doctrine of inspiration is docetic. This is most unfortunate, for Warfield did not mean that; and, as we have seen above, he labors the point that docetism and mechanical inspiration are not taught by the church either explicitly or implicitly.

The Extent of Inspiration. For Warfield, the extent of inspiration is the canon, the whole canon, and nothing but the canon. We have noted that in his view the end result of inspiration is that

66. Ibid., p. 93.
67. Ibid., p. 95. Warfield developed this theme in his essay "The Divine and Human in the Bible," *Presbyterian Journal,* 3 May 1894.
68. Warfield, *Calvin and Calvinism* (New York: Oxford, 1931), p. 64.

"what the Bible says, God says." The crucial question then becomes, What is the Bible? or—more specifically—What is the extent of the Bible? i.e., What is the canon?

Among his many writings on the canon and aspects of it are:

"Lectures and Abstracts on the New Testament Text, Language and Canon" (unpublished manuscript, 1878)

Syllabus on the Canon of the New Testament in the Second Century (Pittsburgh, 1881)

"The Canonicity of Second Peter," *Southern Presbyterian Review* (1882)

"The Christian Canon," *The Philadelphian* (June 1887)

The Formation of the Canon of the New Testament (Philadelphia: American Sunday School Union, 1892)

In all these studies, Warfield assumes the individual scholar's ability and responsibility to ascertain the canon. Always the practitioner of the Protestant principle of the right of private judgment, he consciously rejects the viewpoint of the traditionalists. The canon, he insists, is a collection of inspired books. The statement of a Roman Catholic scholar that he believed the Bible to be the inspired Word of God because his church told him so, and had the church said that Aesop's *Fables* were inspired he would have believed that, would be no more blasphemous than nonsensical to Warfield.

But if Warfield opposed ecclesiastical authority as the criterion of canon, he was even more opposed to subjectivism. He was understandably cool to the sentiment Coleridge expressed in his well-known adage "That is inspired which inspires me," and he would equally have rejected Karl Barth's later characterization of inspired Scriptures as "das mich findet." In his "Introductory Note" to Beattie's *Apologetics*, Warfield designates rationalism and mysticism as the two great enemies of apologetics. In 1917 he took up the question of "Mysticism and Christianity."[69] In this essay he shows that mysticism tends to degenerate into pantheism. Mysticism is based on feeling and is necessarily inarticulate. It must use the language that is at hand. We hear of "Christian mysticism," but all true Christianity rests on external authority, whereas all mysticism is purely internal[70] and is therefore the antithesis of Christianity. "The history of mysticism only too

---

69. Warfield, *The Biblical Review* 2 (1917):169-91 (reprinted in *Studies in Theology,* pp. 649-66).
70. Ibid., p. 659.

clearly shows that he who begins by seeking God within himself may end up by confusing himself with God." As G. K. Chesterton says bluntly: "Jones worships Jones." "Christ" in this view "enters the heart not to produce something new but to arouse what was dormant."[71]

Between the authoritarian Roman claim on the one hand and the mystical or subjectivistic claim on the other, Warfield saw *apostolicity* as the genuine criterion of canon. To be sure, Christ Himself authenticated the Old Testament, but the authentication of the gospel records about Christ and the rest of the New Testament literature depended squarely on apostolic authorship or sanction. In "The Formation of the Canon of the New Testament,"[72] Warfield carefully distinguishes the gradual recognition of the New Testament canon from the immediately recognized principle of canonicity. The apostles from the beginning imposed the Old Testament and their own and others' writings as the law of the church. This was recognized in the New Testament itself and in the post-apostolic age. "The principle of canonicity was not apostolic authorship," insists Warfield, *"but imposition by the apostles as 'law.'"* For example, Paul in 1 Timothy 5:18 imposed a text from the non-apostle Luke. Of course, there was considerable confusion in the early churches about the application of this criterion, but Warfield warns that "we must not mistake the historical evidences of the slow circulation and authentication of these books over the widely-extended church, for evidence of slowness of 'canonization' of the books."[73]

CONCLUSION

Warfield's case for biblical inerrancy has been stated and tried—and we, unlike Markarian, have not found it wanting. Not Warfield's case was wanting, but, we fear, Markarian's understanding of it. Like other uninspired humans, Warfield erred on occasion but not at the point of maintaining the inerrancy of Holy Scripture. His parting words to all who would demonstrate errors in the Bible remain a permanent challenge:

> Let (1) it be proved that each alleged statement occurred certainly in the original autographa of the sacred book in which it is said to be found. (2) Let it be proved that the interpretation which occa-

71. Ibid., p. 664.
72. Originally published by the American Sunday School Union in 1892, and reprinted in Warfield's *Inspiration and Authority of the Bible*, p. 411.
73. Ibid., p. 416.

sions the apparent discrepancy is the one which the passage was evidently intended to bear. It is not sufficient to show a difficulty, which may spring out of our defective knowledge of the circumstances. The true meaning must be definitely and certainly ascertained, and then shown to be irreconcilable with other known truth. (3) Let it be proved that the true sense of some part of the original autographa is directly and necessarily inconsistent with some certainly known fact of history, or truth of science, or some other statement of Scripture certainly ascertained and interpreted. We believe that it can be shown that this has never yet been successfully done in the case of one single alleged instance of error in the Word of God.[74]

J. GRESHAM MACHEN (1881-1937)

The last of the Princeton big three was also the least. Although J. Gresham Machen possessed the same scholarly equipment, the careful articulation and definition, the polemic commitment to orthodoxy, he achieved neither the scholarship nor the influence of his predecessors. This was probably not because of any lack of native ability, but rather was the result of the immense time and energy consumed in ecclesiastical struggles and separations that overwhelmingly dominated the prime time of his relatively short life (about fifteen years shorter than Warfield's and a quarter century less than Hodge's). In a sense Hodge laid the foundation, Warfield perfected the building, and Machen spent most of his time moving it from one location to another. Whatever one thinks of the ecclesiastical move, it left little opportunity to improve the building or even to prevent deterioration. We will see that though "Das" (Mädchen) continued the able defense of the positions of the old Princetonians before him, he lost some ground in each area. Machen himself acknowledged his profound dependence on Charles Hodge and Warfield (as well as A. A. Hodge, Caspar Wistar Hodge, and Geerhardus Vos, not to mention F. L. Patton).[75]

MACHEN DEFENDED THE HISTORIC ORTHODOX DOCTRINE

One way or another, Machen is acknowledged as a classic defender of orthodoxy. H. L. Mencken remarked: "If the Bible is true, then it is true from cover to cover . . . Dr. Machen's position

---

74. A. A. Hodge and B. B. Warfield, "Inspiration," p. 242 (cited by Sandeen, *Roots*, p. 129).
75. J. Gresham Machen, *The Christian View of Man* (New York: Macmillan, 1937), Preface.

is completely impregnable."[76] Allyn Russell, as we noted, regards Machen as the last of this line of scholarly "fundamentalists," which is another way of recognizing that he was a learned defender of the church's historic stance. Cullen Story admired Machen as an "apologist and a courageous one at that. And for this very reason I am drawn to him, but only partway. . . ."[77] Story's drawing back ("partway") no less than his admiration are evidences of Machen's historic orthodoxy. The reason for Dr. Story's hesitation is Machen's claim "that faith gives assent to propositions about what is there in the Bible," which, according to Story, "is hardly a viable position."[78] What Story claims is not "viable" is precisely what the historic, orthodox position has maintained as absolutely certain: "What the Bible says, God says." The validity of that statement we will discuss later. George Marsden also proves Machen orthodox by faulting him for virtually the same reason, his too great objectivity (facts "stay put").[79] We noted that subjectivism was invading orthodoxy in Warfield's day in the form of Abraham Kuyper. That cloud, which was then the size of a man's fist, became an evangelical storm in Machen's time. Today it is the Reformed hurricane, Cornelius!

The Bible for the Princeton-Westminster professor was plenarily, infallibly, inerrantly, nonmechanically inspired in the autorapha, of course (not the transmission),[80] and free from all error. It is "in all its parts the very Word of God, completely true in what it says regarding matters of fact and completely authoritative in its commands."[81] The grand conclusion of *The Virgin Birth of Christ* is not merely that the virgin birth is true, but that the Bible is true. In the tradition of Charles Hodge, Machen sees theology as an inductive science gathering together and depending upon data, external and internal.[82]

76. Cited by T. E. W. Engelder, *Scripture Cannot Be Broken* (St. Louis: Concordia, 1945), p. 76.
77. Cullen Story, "J. Gresham Machen: Apologist and Exegete," *The Princeton Seminary Bulletin*, no. 2 (New Series, 1979), p. 103.
78. Ibid., p. 96.
79. George Marsden, "J. Gresham Machen, History, and Truth," *Westminster Theological Journal* (Fall 1979), p. 163.
80. Machen, *Christian Faith in the Modern World* (New York: Macmillan, 1936), p. 39. "Only the autographs of the Biblical books, in other words—the books as they came from the pen of the sacred writers, and not any one of the copies of those autographs which we now possess—were produced with that supernatural impulsion and guidance of the Holy Spirit which we call inspiration."
81. Ibid., p. 37. This is an essential doctrine for the ministry, though not for the congregation (*What Is Faith?* [Grand Rapids: Eerdmans, 1962], p. 151) as indeed the General Assembly has rightly affirmed (1910).
82. Machen, *The Virgin Birth of Christ* (New York: Harper & Brothers, 1930), p. 383.

MACHEN DEFENDED THE HISTORIC, ORTHODOX POSITION PHILOSOPHICALLY

J. Gresham Machen was not only in the tradition of Warfield and Old Princeton but in that of Origen, Augustine, Athanasius, Aquinas, Luther, Calvin, Reformed and Lutheran orthodoxy as well—in a word, he was part of the ecclesiastical consensus of the ages. This includes a starting point in human consciousness with reliance on logical analysis, deduction, and "common sense." Machen advocated traditional theistic proofs and insisted that special, supernatural revelation and natural revelation—just as faith—had to rely on facts. Although soundly opposed, apparently, to presuppositional subjectivism, his own case for Christianity was not altogether logic-tight.

The "starting point" for Machen was clearly personal consciousness, which must necessarily be trusted. Once started on his intellectual odyssey with personal consciousness, like Hodge, Patton, and Warfield before him, Machen traveled the route of Thomas Reid and Scottish Realism. Denying troublesome "ideas," he had confidence that he apprehended reality directly, although he was unable to understand how that could be. The Scottish Realists such as James McCosh, former president of Princeton University, did this by "intuitions," which do not seem to play any great role in Machen's thought. In fact, Machen does not have much to say about the "Common Sense" philosophy in general. That he seems to go along with it is clear enough. That he read O. M. Jones's *Empiricism and Institutionism in Reid's Common Sense Philosophy* (Ph.D. diss., Princeton University, 1927), which was dedicated to him, seems likely. That Machen was far from a naïve Realist is also clear. "I am not altogether unaware of the difficulties that beset what may be called the common-sense view of truth; epistemology presents many interesting problems and some puzzling antinomies which puzzle the human mind; they indicate the limitations of our intellect, but they do not prove that the intellect is not reliable as far as it goes."[83]

Such knowledge was viewed as only "probable"; but nevertheless it was seen as essential for faith. Machen followed the classic pattern: first there is this *notitia* (cognitive knowledge), then *assensus* (feeling), which leads in turn to *fiducia* (faith).[84] Faith must be "reasonable,"[85] though reason does not produce faith. Liberalism's root error (today, it would be "evangelicalism's" root

83. Machen, *What Is Faith?* p. 27.
84. Ibid., p. 48.
85. Ibid., p. 65.

error) was the failure to distinguish between reason's being "insufficient" and its being "unnecessary."[86]

"The primacy of the intellect" was therefore a central, indispensable principle. Christian experience is no substitute.[87] The primacy of facts is a kind of correlative of the primacy of reason, for it is facts with which reason must deal and only reason can deal. Experience—even Christian experience—cannot jump the rational gun. "Christian experience is rightly used when it helps to convince us that the events narrated in the New Testament actually did occur; but it can never enable us to be Christians, whether the events occurred or not."[88] Even liberals must ultimately genuflect before the shrine of logic. Though Liberalism tries to get started without reason, "it tends more and more to eliminate from itself *illogical* remnants of Christian belief."[89]

What does rational investigation of nature discover? God. He is discovered by human nature. God may be known by the natural voice in the rational soul[90] even as He is revealed in external nature.[91] Machen nowhere fully develops the theistic proofs of which he approves. We will cite therefore one comprehensive statement in which he outlines his theism:

> And without that belief no type of religion can rightly appeal to Jesus to-day. Jesus was a theist, and rational theism is at the basis of Christianity. Jesus did not, indeed, support His theism by argument; He did not provide in advance answers to the Kantian attack upon the theistic proofs. But that means not that He was indifferent to the belief which is the logical result of those proofs, but that the belief stood so firm, both to Him and to His hearers, that in His teaching it is always presupposed. So to-day it is not necessary for all Christians to analyze the logical basis of their belief in God; the human mind has a wonderful faculty for the condensation of perfectly valid arguments, and what seems like an instinctive belief may turn out to be the result of many logical steps. Or, rather, it may be that the belief in a personal God is the result of a primitive revelation, and that the theistic proofs are only the logical confirmation of what was originally arrived at by a different means. At

---

86. Ibid., p. 26.
87. Ibid., p. 51.
88. Machen, *Christianity and Liberalism* (New York: Macmillan, 1923), p. 72.
89. Ibid., p. 173 (italics added); cf. Machen, *Christian Faith in the Modern World*, pp. 62-63.
90. Machen, *Christian Faith in the Modern World*, p. 17. Cf. pp. 24-28, 32.
91. Ibid., pp. 17-19.

any rate, the logical confirmation at the belief in God is a vital concern to the Christian.[92]

Sharing an emphasis that we noted in Warfield, and resisting the neo-orthodox tendency to reverse the order, Machen insists that "theism" is the "logical prius" of faith. Faith must know that God exists; it must be reasonable. To reverse that order is to throw the entire apologetics out of joint. In other words, the older order of apologetics is correct in arguing: first, there is a God; second, it is likely that He should reveal Himself; third, He has actually revealed Himself in Christ.[93] Nevertheless, strangely, Machen does speak of moving intellectually from the Bible to creation,[94] apparently exhibiting some of the vacillation we noticed in Charles Hodge.

MACHEN DEFENDED THE HISTORIC ORTHODOX POSITION EVIDENTIALLY

Machen relates the following incident:

Some years ago I attended a conference of Christian students. Various methods of Christian testimony were being discussed, and particularly the question was being discussed whether it is necessary to engage in a reasoned defense of the Christian faith. In the course of the discussion, a gentleman who had had considerable experience in work among students arose and said that according to his experience you never win a man to Christ until you quit arguing with him. Well, do you know, my friends, when he said that I was not impressed one tiny little bit. Of course a man never was won to Christ *merely* by argument. . . .[95]

So seriously did Machen take apologetics that he delayed his very ordination until he felt he had a satisfactory answer to Kant's critiques. Later, when Princeton's famous apologist William Benton Green retired and Machen could not persuade Clarence Edward Macartney to accept the vacated chair, Machen himself, under the urgent pleading of the Princeton Board, reluctantly gave up his beloved New Testament position to fill the apologetics chair. That move was supported by Francis L. Patton and many others.

Machen's apologetic is in four steps. First, there must be accu-

---

92. Machen, *Christianity and Liberalism*, pp. 57-58.
93. Cf. Machen, *What Is Faith?* p. 65.
94. Machen, *Christian Faith in the Modern World*, p. 68.
95. Ibid., pp. 62-63.

rately ascertained "facts, facts, facts," and these require an adequate explanation. We have seen that this is fundamental to his whole approach and basic to the motivation for his meticulous scholarship. Second, this is especially true of the biblical, historical facts. The Bible presents not merely good views but good news. Walking across Harvard Yard once with my adviser professor, the celebrated historian Arthur Darby Nock, I was teased about "my nails growing through my palms" (because I rested my faith on history rather than doing as he did—totally separating the two). Machen would have complimented me for seeing that Christianity is a historical religion. If Christ were not born of a virgin in historical time and resurrected bodily three days after death, then my "faith" would have been in vain![96]

Third, miraculous facts especially must have adequate explanation. Since the days of Schleiermacher some theologians have been apologizing *for* rather than *with* miracles. They use Christ to vindicate the claims of miracles rather than the miracles to vindicate the claims of Christ. Machen would have none (or almost none) of this. We say "almost" because in the fullest description of miracles we can find, Machen, like Hodge but unlike Warfield, seems to be close to apologizing for miracles. After a standard, traditional definition—"a supernatural event is one that takes place by the immediate, as distinguished from the mediate, power of God"—the ensuing development reveals a number of tell-tale clues: first, "certainly it is a mistake to *isolate miracles from the rest* of the New Testament"; second, "no doubt the existing evidence for such an event [isolated], strong as the evidence is, *might be insufficient*"; third, "acceptance of a complex of miracles is made *vastly easier* when an adequate reason can be detected for the complex as a whole"; "the *truly penitent man* glories in the supernatural, for *he knows* that nothing natural would meet *his* needs"; "yet an *acceptance of the presuppositions* of miracles does not render unnecessary the plain testimony . . . and that testimony is exceedingly strong."[97]

Machen concentrated on two miracles especially: the virgin birth and, most important of all, the bodily resurrection of Christ. His magnum opus, *The Virgin Birth of Christ*,[98] proved far more than the supernaturalness of Jesus. It proved the supernatural infallibility of the Bible. About the same time that an "unrecon-

96. Cf. especially "History and Faith," but this conviction is expressed everywhere in Machen's writings.
97. Machen, *Christianity and Liberalism*, pp. 99-107 (italics added).
98. Machen, *Christian Faith in the Modern World*, pp. 214-16.

structed liberal," Julius Seelye Bixler, was telling me that if anything would ever convince him of the resurrection of Christ it was the faith of the early church, Machen was writing that it was exactly that which convinced him.[99]

Thus Machen established the case for Christianity rationally—the miraculous facts compelling assent to the truth claims of Christ and the Bible, and such convincing rational evidence being an essential foundation for genuine, saving faith.

Machen has been dubbed Mr. Valiant-for-Truth by fellow conservatives, the liberal translation being "fighting fundamentalist." All are agreed, Machen included, that he was *doctor polemicus*.

Nevertheless, his apologetics was very largely restricted to one crucial issue, naturalistic liberalism. His crucial volume in that battle was *Christianity and Liberalism*, which led to Wieman's and Meland's in their *American Philosophies of Religion* (Chicago: Willett, Clark, 1936) selecting him as the representative, par excellence, of "traditional supernaturalism" alongside recognized contemporary exponents of "neo-supernaturalism." Machen himself would have said that the "neo" in "neo-supernaturalism" should have been spelled without the letter *e*. For him, the miracles are the main thing; they are the thing for which the narratives exist. How absurd, then, to say that the narratives have grown up out of utterly trivial events upon which a supernaturalistic interpretation was wrongly put! And how wrong to say that "they are simply myths—that is, they are popular expressions, in a narrative form, of certain religious ideas."[100] He adds later that the two-source theory of the synoptic gospels tried to account for this alleged supernaturalizing tendency; but it has been shown that the supernatural runs through those sources also.[101] "We never ought to have tried to reject the miracles in the Gospels at all."[102]

Many later nonconservative scholars have agreed with Machen. Thus Henry Joel Cadbury wrote his *The Peril of Modernizing Jesus*—that is, the peril of reducing this purportedly supernatural figure to a twentieth-century social reformer. Incidentally, Cadbury used Machen's *The Origin of Paul's Religion* as a textbook in one of his Harvard courses. When asked why such a liberal-radical scholar used such a conservative book, he replied that it contained the best presentation and critique of the various cur-

99. Cf. Machen, *What Is Christianity?* chap. 4.
100. Machen, *Christian Faith in the Modern World*, p. 196.
101. Ibid., p. 198.
102. Ibid., p. 200.

rent theories attempting to account for the origin of Paul's religion. The questioner then asked if Cadbury accepted Machen's conclusion that the origin was in the supernatural Christ. I was the questioner and can attest to the accuracy of this report. No, responded Cadbury, for though Machen has refuted thoroughly all current theories, that does not prove that an adequate naturalistic explanation may not yet be found.

The contemporary scholar Gunther Bornkamm is another who agrees with Machen that the ideas of Paul compare very favorably with those of James. Cullen Story, New Testament professor at Princeton, concludes a survey of Machen's work in the area with this remark: "In brief, it can be said that the apologetic which Machen presented with consummate skill over fifty years ago, points to the live issues in Pauline scholarship today."[103]

However, Lefferts Loetscher of Princeton, with James Barr (*Fundamentalism* [Philadelphia: Westminster, 1978]) concurring, rises to the defense of embattled liberalism. Machen is guilty, they charge, not only of a lack of charity (the usual response to his intellectual indictments), but to a lack of logic. Specifically, he has committed the syllogistic sin of the "undistributed middle":

> The argument of Dr. Machen's book was partly vitiated by the fallacy of the "undistributed middle." This book, as well as many of his public utterances and other writings, described "liberalism" in terms of the most radical, naturalistic implications, and then, by implication at least, included in this classification all those who differed from traditional orthodoxy even on subordinate points.[104]

James Barr comments that Loetscher need not have been surprised by this, for it is nothing peculiar to Machen; on the contrary, the "same procedure is entirely normal in conservative evangelical and fundamentalist circles."[105]

Barr does not here substantiate, but merely assumes, his statement about the common negative characteristic of conservative apologists. Assuming it to be true, he traces it not to the twentieth-century liberalism of Adolf Harnack, but to eighteenth-century Deism, apparently unaware that John Orr has demonstrated, in his *English Deism, Its Roots and Its Fruits* (Grand Rapids, Eerdmans, 1934), that twentieth-century liberalism, specifically

---

103. Story, "Machen: Apologist and Exegete," p. 94.
104. Lefferts Loetscher, *The Broadening Church* (Philadelphia: U. of Pennsylvania, 1957), p. 116.
105. James Barr, *Fundamentalism* (Philadelphia: Westminster, 1978), p. 165.

that of its famous American champion Harry Emerson Fosdick, who was Machen's major target, was the direct fruit of anti-supernaturalistic Deism. We return to Loetscher and his charge, which charge would make Machen guilty of slander. But it is not Machen who is guilty of slander or of the "undistributed middle." Throughout his works, as we have seen, he defines liberalism as naturalism, and Loetscher has not given one instance in which Machen applies the term to a person who is not essentially naturalistic.

In my own *Theology of the Major Sects* (Grand Rapids: Baker, 1978) I discuss liberalism as a sect only after carefully defining it, as Machen did. I constantly warned students in class to be careful of the use of the term and, if using it in Machen's sense, carefully so to indicate.

MACHEN DEFENDED THE HISTORIC, ORTHODOX DOCTRINE EXPERIENTIALLY

When it came to the bottom line, how sinful man came to be *persuaded* of what he *understood*, Machen stood in Princeton midstream: it was by regeneration and illumination of the Holy Spirit. Midstream, to be sure, but moving toward shore and shallower, murkier water, rather than out to greater, clearer depth.

The noetic influence of sin Machen recognized. Exactly *how* sin affected the mind he nowhere clearly explains. In fact, there seems to be an unresolved inconsistency in his thinking. Unregenerate man can[106] and must[107] know. Nevertheless, sin is said to "blind."[108] If sin blinds the unconverted, how can they know? We may surmise what Machen had in mind, but that is the point—it would have to be our surmise. He probably is thinking of the traditional distinction between merely rational knowledge and saving or experiential knowledge. Machen obviously believed that unconverted persons could understand or grasp the meaning of biblical doctrines. Regeneration brought a persuasion or conviction that the things they understood were indeed the sublime, transforming Word of God.

The same inconsistency—we prefer to say "unresolvedness"—affects Machen's view of the relation of the Spirit to biblical knowledge. Men "see clearly,"[109] and there is no opposition be-

---

106. Cf. Machen, "The Relation of Religion to Science and Philosophy," *Princeton Theological Review*, 1926.
107. Machen, *What Is Faith?* p. 51.
108. Ibid., pp. 13,51; cf. *Christian Faith in the Modern World*, p. 21.
109. Machen, "Relation of Religion to Science and Philosophy."

tween science and spiritual knowledge.[110] On the other hand, it is the Holy Spirit who, by regenerating, makes the human reason "intellectually trustworthy."[111] Listen to this desperate prayer of our apologist of Christian rationality:

> O, that God would open men's eyes that they might see, that they might detect the grand sweep and power of His testimony to Himself in His Word! Oh, that He would take away the blindness of men's minds! Has He taken away the blindness of *your* minds, my friends? Do you know the risen Christ today as your Saviour and your Lord? If you do not yet know Him, will you not bow before Him at this hour, and say, 'My Lord and my God'![112]

The last sentence above, incidentally, shows how unclarity and inconsistency can make well-intentioned men to sin grievously. For surely it is simply wicked to ask or urge a person who does not "know" God to call Him "my God."

SUMMATION

Having briefly surveyed the field we have indicated (if we have not had space sufficient to prove) that the Old Princeton School in general, Charles Hodge, B. B. Warfield, and J. Gresham Machen especially (and Warfield most particularly), represent the ablest defense of the classical doctrine of biblical inerrancy in the nineteenth and twentieth centuries. Modern Princeton attacks what the Old Princeton defended. The new Old Princeton, Westminster, although continuing to advocate, propagate, and defend absolute inerrancy with a thoroughness unsurpassed by Old Princeton itself, does so in a way that Hodge-Warfield-Machen would consider an undermining of it.[113]

---

110. Machen, *What Is Faith?* pp. 134-35.
111. Ibid., p. 135.
112. Machen, *Christian Faith in the Modern World*, p. 216.
113. We do not have space here to show that the presuppositionalism dominant at Westminster Theological Seminary is apologetically antithetical to the Old Princeton. However, Vander Stelt relates a personal conversation with Cornelius Van Til (July 12, 1973) which tells everything. "Cornelius Van Til asked Machen in 1934 whether he wanted him to stay at Westminster Theological Seminary 'in spite of the differences that existed between them.' Machen replied: 'I know we disagree, but I want you to stay.'" Vander Stelt, *Philosophy and Scripture*, p. 220, n. 153.

13. The Arian Connection: Presuppositions of Errancy

Harold O. J. Brown

INTRODUCTION

When one examines the many arguments on both sides of the dispute concerning the infallibility or inerrancy of the Bible,[1] he is struck by two so-called sociological aspects of the controversy. First, so much of the discussion is dominated by the presuppositions, expressed and implied, of those taking part; second, so many of those involved on both sides of the debate are not primarily biblical scholars but are involved in other aspects of religious studies, such as systematic theology, church history, comparative religion, and so forth. We may even go so far as to acknowledge that much of the "thunder on the right" in this controversy has come from philosophers and theologians who see the logical implications of errancy but are not themselves specialists on the controverted points. For example, Harold Lindsell, still the editor of *Christianity Today* when he ignited "The Battle for the Bible," was a missions scholar in academic life.

Although most evangelicals who are specialists in biblical languages and in Old and New Testament studies are committed to the doctrine of inerrancy, they have not been in the forefront of

---

1. In this discussion the terms *infallible* and *inerrant*, as applied to the Bible, will be treated synonymously. The tendency of some writers to use *infallible* to mean subjectively reliable but objectively not inerrant seems to me to be objectionable because it goes against the older and more common usage and suggests a false dichotomy.

384 / Challenges to Inerrancy

the effort to defend it. Nor has the attempt to tone down commitment to inerrancy among evangelicals come to any substantial degree from Bible scholars who believe they have encountered undeniable errors or irreconcilable contradictions in the text of Scripture itself. Why then—if we may put it thus—are there so many philosophers among the Bible scholars? For the same reason, one may reply, that there are so many philosophers among the theologians: the questions that the Bible raises are not merely literary, historical, and doctrinal; they touch the very foundations of all knowledge.

There have been many doctrinal controversies during the long course of the history of Christianity, but there are only a few that stand out as crucial. Had they turned out differently, Christianity as we now know it would have disappeared. We may mention two to begin: the crisis of Gnosticism in the second century and the Arian controversy in the fourth. Gnosticism and Arianism were very different, but they had some things in common: both were interested in an intellectual understanding rather than in the experiential réality of salvation by faith; each was potentially capable of destroying Christianity. The defeat of Gnosticism firmly established the doctrine of creation as an essential part of the Christian faith. The defeat of Arianism established the doctrine of the Trinity. Without creation, Christianity would not be itself; without the doctrine of the Trinity, it would not be Christianity.

Arianism, as is well known, existed in a number of variations: originally, the Arians rejected the doctrine that has come to be known as the *homoousion*, the consubstantiality of the Son with the Father. A more moderate group was willing to accept the *homoousia* of the Son, as affirmed at the Council of Nicaea in A.D. 325, but would not extend the concept of consubstantiality to the Holy Spirit; these so-called semi-Arians were rejected by the orthodox with some appearance of harshness, particularly because they appeared to have conceded the main point with the doctrine of the consubstantiality of the Son. But in retrospect it is apparent that if the Holy Spirit is not consubstantial with the Father and the Son, the doctrine of the Trinity must collapse and we are left either with patripassianism or ditheism.

Have there been other controversies as fraught with danger as the Gnostic and Arian controversies? The controversy over justification by faith split the church, but both products of the split, Protestantism and Roman Catholicism, are conceded to be Christian. The controversy over inerrancy may appear to be smaller than that over justification in the sixteenth century, especially insofar as both sides are in wide agreement concerning the trust-worthiness and normative authority of the Scripture. Yet I suggest that, like the Arian controversy, this one has the potential not merely to alter the church somewhat or to split it, but to destroy it.

PROBLEMS FOR INERRANTISTS

THE MATTER OF THE AUTOGRAPHS

Inasmuch as it is undeniable that the text of Scripture as we now have it has passed through a long transmission process, it is evident that our present Old and New Testament texts contain at least some discrepancies, problems, and uncertainties. All of the statements affirming the doctrine of inerrancy apply it only to "the original writings," the autographs. Those original writings, however, are no longer available and hence cannot be inspected for possible errors. If an error could conclusively be demonstrated in any present edition of a Bible text, the inerrantist could always make the unverifiable claim that the error was not in the original. This claim is essentially a matter of a definition or a presupposition; hence, it is natural that debate concerning it will deal with presuppositions or with what we may call a priori matters. Inerrantists, as is well known, claim that our best Bible texts correspond very closely to the original. Such a claim is a matter of practical necessity if the doctrine of inerrancy is to have any functional value. Although existing texts are not the inerrant autographs, we can consider them, "for all practical purposes," to be inerrant and entirely reliable. Indeed, the celebrated Francis Pieper (1852-1931), for many decades the dean of conservative Lutheran theologians in the United States, went so far as to say that an accurate *translation* is for all practical purposes inerrant.

The precedent statement, however, is not very different, in its immediate practical impact, from what a noninerrantist evangelical such as Jack Rogers appears willing to say: although the Bible is not absolutely inerrant, for all practical purposes (literally, for "faith and life") one may trust it and rely upon it as though it were. Inasmuch as the practical or functional value of inerrancy does not and cannot depend on inerrant autographs (if for no other reason than because we do not possess them) but must depend only on copies that are "for all practical purposes" free of error and are altogether reliable, what is the actual difference between the strict inerrantist such as Harold Lindsell and the moderate errantist such as Jack Rogers? If Lindsell, for example, does not claim that any present edition of Scripture is inerrant but treats all accurate translations of Scripture as God's inerrant Word, and if Rogers, although he repudiates the doctrine of inerrancy, also treats Scripture as our perfect rule, what is the difference? It would be difficult to point to any doctrine that Lindsell claims to be biblical that Rogers would dispute on the grounds that, although the Bible teaches it, at a given point it is in error.

Lindsell does claim to find a doctrine in Scripture—biblical inerrancy—that Rogers disputes. But Rogers does *not* think Scripture erroneously teaches it, but rather he contends that it is not actually there. If Rogers were to see inerrancy there, for example in 2 Timothy 3:16 as Lindsell does, his view of Scripture as not absolutely inerrant would not permit him simply to disregard it on the grounds that it might be one of the few errors in his noninerrant Bible. Just as the inerrantist in a sense postulates something that he can no longer find, i.e., inerrant autographs, the errantist is likewise in a sense postulating something he does not claim to be able to produce but knows, on the basis of his understanding of Scripture, must be there: insignificant but real errors in the Bible. It would be a mistake to exaggerate the difference, as though the evangelical critiques of inerrancy were saying, "The Bible is full of errors." Indeed, very few of them would claim to be able to produce a specific, demonstrable error; what they claim instead is that one need not hold to inerrancy as a theory for the Bible to achieve its wonderful task of revealing God and His salvation to man.

Is this not another example of the sort of issue that separated the orthodox, homoousian party from the moderate Arian homoiousians in the fourth century: nothing more than an iota? Indeed, the inerrancy controversy is similar to the Arian controversy in that the difference between the positions appears to be small but in reality is of tremendous significance. To have abandoned the Nicene definition of the Son as *homoousios to patri*, of one substance with the Father, for *homoiousios to patri*, of similar substance with the Father, would have undermined the basic structure of trinitarian faith with its fundamental confession that the Son *is* God, identical in nature to the Father although distinct in His personhood from Him. In addition, to abandon the term *homoousios* would have been to confess that the whole church, for decades, had been fundamentally mistaken as to the true nature of Jesus the Messiah. The parallel with the inerrancy controversy is this: to abandon the definition "inerrant autographs, virtually inerrant copies" would also be a step of tremendous magnitude; it would undermine the basic structure of biblical authority with its principle that the Scripture *is* the Word of God. In addition, to abandon the definition would be to confess that the whole church has been mistaken about inerrancy for seventeen and more centuries. It is important to see precisely where the conflict lies in order to understand the crucial significance of the inerrancy debate and of its ultimate outcome for conservative Protestantism, indeed, for Christianity as a whole.

The affirmation that the Scripture is inerrant in the original writings is not an affirmation about our present texts, which we acknowledge to be only "virtually" inerrant, in other words not inerrant in the strict sense of the word. But inerrancy in anything other than the strict sense of the word is not inerrancy, any more than "virtual virginity" is virginity. To admit this may seem unwise on the part of one committed to the doctrine of inerrancy and committed to defending it. Is it not admitting that our conflict with the errantists is a matter of form and appearance rather than of substance? I hold that it is preferable to acknowledge this problem, in order to lay bare the very significant difference that does still divide the camps, rather than to ignore it in the hope that those outside our camp will not notice that we do have this singular "mental reservation" when we speak of biblical inerrancy.

It is precisely to show why the doctrine of inerrancy is of cardinal importance even though we acknowledge that we do not have inerrant autographs that we must frankly acknowledge the apparent practical similarity between our views and those of the opposing party. To see the similarity and not to realize that it is only apparent would be very dangerous; for this reason we must point it out, even though initially it might appear to make our position excessively pedantic and a trifle ridiculous to those whose attention it has not yet caught. No one would mistake the poisonous rattlesnake for a harmless variety, because the rattler proclaims his deadly difference. Unfortunately the even more poisonous coral snake closely resembles harmless snakes and is frequently mistaken for them with grave consequences.

Why do we, on the one hand, insist that it is necessary, or even merely important, to make an unverifiable claim for a set of autographs we no longer possess? Why is it also so important, on the other hand, for the anti-inerrantists—a small minority among conservative evangelicals, but of course the overwhelming majority among other Protestants—to persuade themselves and others that we must not claim inerrancy for those inaccessible autographs. This is especially so because we are claiming no more (virtual inerrancy) for the extant texts than they themselves generally concede. The answer to this pair of questions has three aspects, and they will lead us to the first of three theses.

ASPECTS OF THE INERRANCY OF THE AUTOGRAPHS

The claim that the autographs are inerrant cannot be verified objectively. But neither can it be disproved. Even if our present versions were full of demonstrable errors, inerrantists could always claim that the originals were entirely free of such errors. And even if no error or discrepancy at all could be found in the present versions, errantists would be able to assert, quite correctly, that that does not prove that the autographs in their day were inerrant. It is at least conceivable, although rather implausible, that the autographs could have contained errors that were removed by later copyists. This is, after all, what happens when new editions of old works are published. Inasmuch as inerrancy is unverifiable a posteriori, on the basis of evidence gathered from the existing, non-autographic texts, it must be defended a priori, on the basis of things we already know or to which we are committed by faith.[2] But inasmuch as it is also impossible to disprove the claim of inerrancy a posteriori, it is also necessary for those who attack it to do so on the basis of a priori assumptions.

We can point to three of these assumptions: (1) that the divine origin of Scripture, which both inerrantists and errantists confess, has no necessary implications for the inerrancy of the text: in other words, the text can be divinely inspired without necessarily being inerrant; (2) that the human share in the composition of Scripture has necessary implications for the errancy of the text: in other words, the text cannot be human unless it does contain at least some errors: (3) that the suggestion that humanity or humanness, as applied to Scripture, implies the necessity of some error does not mean that the concept of humanity or humanness, as applied to Jesus Christ, necessarily implies error or sin. The inerrantist position is consistent with an orthodox (Chalcedonian) understanding of the relationship between the human and the divine natures in Christ, who is "in all things like us, without sin."

2. There is so much evidence for the consistency and accuracy of the existent texts of Scripture that the evidence creates the presumption that they must go back to divinely inspired, faultless originals. But this is at best a probability, not a proof.

The errantist position would be consistent with the opposite contention—although no evangelicals among the errantists wish to make it. We are speaking of the suggestion that Jesus, as human, must have been capable of mistakes and perhaps even of sin, inasmuch as all men are sinners.

Although it would not demonstrate that the autographs also contained errors, if it were possible to point to undeniable, substantial errors in the present Hebrew and Greek texts of Scripture, it would certainly suggest the presumption that the originals had errors. The fact that it is still possible today to claim the autographs were inerrant is an indication that no one has yet succeeded in showing there is even one substantial, undeniable error or contradiction in our present copies. If such an error could be found, it would wreak havoc within the ranks of the inerrantists.

THESIS I: INERRANCY IS A DOXOLOGICAL STATEMENT

From the foregoing, it should be apparent that the statement "The Scriptures are without error in the original writings" is essentially a confession of faith in the nature and character of God and consequently in the nature of Scripture as God's Word. We contend, therefore, that the doctrine of inerrancy is essentially a theological doctrine, pertaining to the character of God, and only secondarily a bibliological one, pertaining to the nature of the Bible. It is doxological in the sense that it is an expression of praise to the God whom we know as the author of Scripture. To affirm inerrancy is to pay a particular kind of honor to certain aspects of God's nature and character; to deny it, or even simply to refuse to affirm it, is to say either that those aspects are less important than Christians have traditionally thought them to be or that they are not displayed in Scripture.

THESIS II: ERRANCY IS AN ANTHROPOLOGICAL STATEMENT

The converse of the first thesis immediately suggest itself: errancy is a statement about man. Acknowledging that there is a human element in Scripture—as contenders on both sides of the inerrancy debate do—those who reject inerrancy must in effect say, "To err is human"; if human, then Scripture must be errant, or at least it cannot be inerrant. This has far-reaching implications, for it suggests that error and perhaps even sin are necessary attributes of humanity, and that nothing—and no one—human can be free of all error. There is a tremendous difference between saying, "All that is human is finite," and, "All that is human contains error." Clearly, it is possible for humans, within a limited frame of reference, to produce something that is free of error. The familiar "twelve times" multiplication table from 1 to 144 offers an example. Of course, the multiplication table is much simpler and smaller than the Bible, and it is hard to imagine a purely human project the size of the Bible with no errors. To say that the Bible, if human, must contain error of some kind does not necessarily suggest that it must contain moral error, for the Bible is a book, not a moral agent.

On the other hand, to state as an axiom *errare humanum est*, and mean by it "to be human is to err," and then to apply that to Scripture because, although it is God's Word, it is spoken by the mouth of man, is to maintain that the power of God does not preserve that which is both divine and human from the defects of humanity. Applied to the Lord Jesus Christ Himself, this would necessarily suggest not only that He must have been limited in knowledge and thus naturally have made mistakes, but also that He must have sinned. Even if we do not go so far as to say that the necessity of being human, and hence of making mistakes, also implies that the human being will also be involved in at least some sin, it is evident that the proposition "to err is human" has Christological as well as anthropological implications.

THESIS III: ERRANCY HAS CHRISTOLOGICAL IMPLICATIONS

The doctrine of errancy clearly implies that God cannot so interact with what is human in a way that He preserves it from all error without destroying its essential humanness. The Christological parallel would be the suggestion that God cannot assume a human nature in Christ without totally overwhelming His essential humanness—in other words, that the doctrine of the incarnation produces a monophysite Christology: if Jesus is God, then His human nature has been absorbed and He is no longer fully man. One of the reasons errantists want to preserve the idea of errors in Scripture is because they want to preserve the Bible as a human book, and they fear that to lose the errors would be to lose the humanity.

The parallel in Christology, as we have noted, would be the suggestion that to be human, Christ must have erred, quite possibly even sinned. This is not to suggest that evangelicals who think Scripture must contain error in order to be human as well as divine will also hold that Jesus, in order to be human, may or must have made errors and perhaps even committed sins. To the best of my knowledge, no evangelical has made such an allegation. But it is worth noting that the same theological procedure that makes one feel obliged to posit errors in no-longer-existent autographs logically ought also to lead one to posit errors or even sin in the God-man, Jesus Christ.

TWO CAVEATS FOR INERRANTISTS

Those who reject the doctrine of inerrancy while holding firmly to the rest of an orthodox, evangelical faith are a minority among conservative Protestants, but they could readily find a welcome among the hosts of liberals who long ago abandoned the idea that the Bible has more than a relative authority. Most non-inerrantists are reluctant to accept the welcome nonevangelicals would offer them because they do not want to be drawn into a situation of compromising additional doctrines, ones that they acknowledge to be vital. Because the inerrancy controversy is potentially capable of being as dangerous to the church in our day as the Arian controversy was in the fourth century, conservative Protestants who do hold to inerrancy should beware of making it worse than it already is. One way of making it worse and creating a position with which many inerrantists would not be happy is to create the impression that we think that biblical inerrancy is the central doctrine of Christianity. The moment we give the impression that we hold this cardinal doctrine to be central, we will necessarily estrange those who correctly recognize that the Bible first of all proclaims Christ, not itself. Even though it proclaims Him inerrantly, its first concern is that He be proclaimed, not that its own inerrancy be acknowledged. We must beware, then, of appearing to suggest that our primary zeal is for the doctrine of Scripture.

There is another false claim that inerrantists might be tempted to make and should beware of doing so. It is the claim that Christians and the church have always recognized the importance of confessing the inerrancy of Scripture. A parallel to this is offered by the way in which the Reformers tried to counter the Roman Catholics' claim that it is the church that establishes the authority of the Bible. The Reformers said, in effect, that the church was established in accordance with the teachings of Holy Scripture. Historically such a claim cannot be true, for the church was in existence and had taken on a well-defined structure before the canon of the New Testament was acknowledged in more or less its present extent at the end of the second century. The Bible was trusted and venerated as befits an inerrant guide long before it was explicitly defined as such. The errantists would have us believe that this explicit definition came very late indeed and was the result of superimposing human philosophical categories onto the dynamic thought world of Scripture. The proper way to counteract that error is not to exaggerate in the other direction and to claim, in effect, that the bibliology of the early church was already as clear and explicit as that of John Quenstedt or the Westminster divines in the seventeenth century.

Presuppositions of Biblical Errancy: Two Anathemas

An anathema is stronger than a caveat; if we reserve the caveats for upholders of inerrancy while preparing anathemas for errancy, this is not solely because inerrancy is "our" position and errancy "theirs." It is also because the damage that an exaggerated presentation of inerrancy can do, though not insignificant, is less than the harm that will be caused by the triumph of errancy. Those who maintain this latter view, consciously or unconsciously seem to have made two important presuppositions, both of which are unsound and so dangerous that they really do deserve to be warded off with the heaviest weapon in the ecclesiastical armory, the anathema. One presupposition is that a prompt surrender of inerrancy is necessary; the second is that we can safely surrender it and still protect the gospel and the substance of the Christian faith, because inerrancy was never a part of the ancient and historic Christian faith.

THE PREMATURE SURRENDER

The cause of biblical inerrancy was vigorously defended by the overwhelming majority of committed Christians during the nineteenth and early twentieth centuries, at a time when the majority of the scholarly world took it as axiomatic that the Bible contains certifiable errors. To hold to the doctrine of inerrancy seemed to outsiders to be an obscurantist position that ignored all substantial evidence. By the second half of the twentieth century, however, it had become apparent that inerrancy could be plausibly and forcefully defended on respectable scholarly grounds without resorting to blind dogmatism and obscurantism. Precisely because most of the opponents of inerrancy among evangelicals do not come from the biblical discipline, it seems possible that many if not all may be making the same sort of well-intentioned but dangerous error that characterized the neo-orthodoxy of Karl Barth: accepting the presumption that the Scripture *does*, indeed *must*, contain at least some errors, even if they have not been precisely located. Yet the opponents make an effort to uphold the Bible's authority despite the presence of supposedly insignificant errors. Too hasty a surrender is sometimes based on the false assumption that the inerrancy position is untenable in the light of modern knowledge about the Bible. In order to save the evangelical faith and the Christian tradition from the disastrous consequences of being tied to a false and indefensible doctrine, they claim that inerrancy is neither an integral part of biblical faith nor a constant part of traditional Christian beliefs.

When we observe this procedure, we note that a commendable motive is combined with questionable means to produce a bad end. The commendable motive is the desire to protect the substance of the Christian faith from being discredited because it is attached to discreditable, indefensible traditions. This is indeed a perfectly correct desire; difficulties arise, however, if the "tradition" is in fact an integral part of the "faith once delivered to the saints" (Jude 3), so that abandoning it damages the faith. The means are questionable if something that is both taught in Scripture and has been held to be fundamental by Christians through many centuries is suddenly declared to be an unwarranted accretion. We cannot deny that Christianity has accumulated unwarranted accretions through the centuries or that some traditional, time-honored ways of understanding particular Bible texts may be unwarranted. Nevertheless, our desire to protect the Bible and the faith from being discredited does not authorize us to prune away elements that are actual part of the substance of our faith simply because we fear they are or might become discredited. If they are part of the substance of the faith and are demonstrated to be discreditable, then instead of trying to save the faith by changing it substantially, we ought honestly to face the possibility that Christianity itself is substantially discredited. To protect the faith by altering it to meet objections is an unworthy means to protect the faith "once delivered"; furthermore, if a doctrine or tenet such as inerrancy in fact is part of the substance of the faith, then to "protect" the faith by amputating it will be a grievous mutilation. If, in addition, the perceived danger that the doctrine will surely be discredited is unduly pessimistic, then one is in the awkward situation of having used a questionable means to avoid a nonexistent danger and has thereby damaged what one was trying to protect.

394 / Challenges to Inerrancy

To return to our fourth-century parallel: the Arian movement was motivated at least in part by the desire to avoid a Sabellian, modalistic interpretation of the doctrine of God, one that would have said Jesus is not merely of the same nature as God the Father, while being a distinct Person, but rather that He *is* God the Father in another manifestation or mode. In order to avoid this dreadful confusion between Christ and the Father, the Arians insisted that the Son is different from the Father in nature as well as in personhood and is in fact a created being. The remedy was as bad as the disease. Our contemporary evangelical errantists, in the commendable effort to prevent the doctrine of the authority of Scripture from being damaged by the claims that the Bible contains errors, say that its authority is quite a different thing from inerrancy and independent of it. In so doing, although they conceive that they are preventing presumptive errors in Scripture from undermining its authority, they themselves undermine that authority in the minds of most other Christians by contending that nothing is lost if Scripture contains errors.

THE "NONANTIQUITY" OF INERRANCY

The hasty surrender of the doctrine of inerrancy, done lest the doctrine be proved indefensible and drag all the authority of the Bible down with it, would be responsible only if it could be shown that biblical inerrancy is not a part of the historic Christian faith. Unfortunately for that project, it is apparent that the inerrancy of Holy Scripture, if not explicitly taught, has been assumed and taken for granted ever since the earliest days of the church. Even before all Christians had agreed on exactly which writings make up Holy Scripture, they acknowledged that all that is Holy Scripture must be altogether free of error and utterly trustworthy. In order to cut the essential doctrine of the authority of the Bible free of entanglement with the controverted doctrine of inerrancy, a number of projects have been undertaken to show that inerrancy is a late concept of philosophical rather than biblical origin. The most impressive of these is by Jack Rogers and Donald McKim,[3] but a number of others have also attempted to show the same thing, many of them noted in an incisive review of Rogers and McKim.[4] However, it ought to be apparent that by the

---

3. Jack Rogers and Donald McKim, *The Authority and Inspiration of the Bible: An Historical Approach* (New York: Harper & Row, 1979).
4. John D. Woodbridge, "Biblical Authority: Towards an Evaluation of the Rogers and McKim Proposal," *Trinity Journal*, NS vol. 1, no. 2 (Fall 1980): 164-236.

end of the third Christian century, the text of the canonical New Testament had been universally acknowledged as the rule of faith for the church, superseding the earlier creedal statements as the ultimate authority.[5]

It is difficult to contend that that which was acknowledged as the final authority for the Christian faith can err without appearing to suggest, with Paul, that "we are found false witnesses" (1 Corinthians 15:15). There seems never to have been a time when that which was accepted as Holy Scripture was regarded as less than inerrant. The second-century heretic Marcion rejected the Hebrew Scriptures and accepted only a portion of the New Testament because he thought the rejected portions were contradicted in what he did accept. With respect to what he actually did accept, however, he held it to be absolutely reliable. The young catholic church, in rejecting Marcion and reaffirming the authority of the parts of Scripture that he had rejected, naturally maintained that the whole of Scripture *is* harmonious and free of contradictions as well as errors. The fact that theologians in the early church so frequently resorted to a rather fanciful allegorical exegesis certainly reflects their conviction that every passage of Scripture speaks with divine authority and hence must be of great importance to us. If the literal meaning appears objectionable or trivial, a more satisfactory meaning must be found by allegorizing. If those early theologians had been able to assume that the Scripture contains at least some errors, that allegorizing would not have been necessary.

Against this background, and remembering the anathemas of Nicaea, we may say, "But if anyone say that there was a time when the Scripture was not held to be inerrant, let him be—if not anathama—at least taken with some very substantial grains of salt." The Arian controversy could not have raged on as it did had the orthodox been able to interpret verses such as Proverbs 8:22, with its possible suggestion that the Logos had a beginning, as an error[6] that one need not take too seriously. Because it was there, they had to deal with it and seek a plausible way to explain it.

---

5. "The old canon of Greek Christendom has disappeared; Scripture has taken its place." Reinhold Seeberg, *Lehrbuch der Dogmengeschichte*, 2d ed. (Leipzig: Deichert, 1908), 1:522-23, speaking of the close of the third century.
6. "The Lord possessed me at the beginning of his way, before his works of old." Wisdom (Hebrew, *ḥokmāh*, Greek, *Sophia*), which is speaking, was equated by many, especially Arians, with the Logos, the Word of God (i.e., the Son). Proverbs 8:22 was read as saying that He is a created being. This text presented the orthodox with a challenge that would not have existed had it been possible to admit error or contradiction into canonical Scripture.

THE IMPACT OF HUMANITY

Another commendable motive of the anti-inerrancy movement is the desire to protect as a part of human history[7] the humanity of Scripture and what we might call its genesis. An explanation of the method or process by which a particular document or idea came to be formulated will not necessarily tell us if what it communicates is objectively true. Here too we may have a parallel to Arianism, for in claiming that Christ is of a different nature from the Father, Arius arrived at a Christ who was neither God nor man.[8] By seeing the Bible as errant, one lowers it beneath the level of the truly divine, but by attributing to it the power infallibly to convey saving truth (Rom. 1:16), one raises it above the human.

A basic defect of the errantist position is this: inasmuch as it continues to treat the Scripture as divinely authoritative, it continues to confront believers with the necessity of accepting a tangible, real, divine intervention into the affairs of men. This makes errancy just as objectionable to the adherent of a closed, this-worldly view as inerrancy. The tension between the divine and the human is not removed; it is only apparently lessened by saying, "God intervened, but not totally effectively." The tension exists the moment that it is said that God intervenes at all. This formula does not relieve the tension any more than that of the Arians did; it creates a kind of tertium quid—not a Scripture that is both divine and human, but a Scripture that is supernatural yet not fully divine, human yet not natural.

ERRANCY NOT DAMAGING?

Inasmuch as the opponents of inerrancy among conservative Protestants genuinely and sincerely seek, like their predecessors the neo-orthodox in Europe, to preserve the substance of the Christian faith, it is apparent that they assume that inerrancy is not an essential of biblical faith and that the substance of the Christian faith will not be damaged if it is removed. The whole enterprise of the errantists, protecting the faith by ridding it of a nonessential accretion is honorable only if we may presuppose that inerrancy is a nonessential. For this reason, the errantist ought to be carefully examined concerning the reasons he believes

---

7. I have virtuously resisted the temptation to use a German expression here and speak of the *historisches Gewordensein* of Scripture.
8. Adolf von Harnack, *Lehrbuch der Dogmengeschichte*, 4th ed. (Tubingen: Mohr, 1909), 2:221-22.

his presupposition to be sound. If we acknowledge that inerrancy is a nonessential, then we forfeit much of the reason for defending it. For purposes of this inquiry, we shall assume that the Bible itself does not conclusively tell us if it is to be regarded as inerrant.

Inerrantists usually maintain that the Bible does teach that it is inerrant, but the errantist evangelical would not be able to maintain his position if he agreed unless he repudiated Scripture, which he is not willing to do. Here we are not examining the biblical evidence for errancy but rather the presuppositions that permit a Bible-believing evangelical to interpret the biblical evidence in a way that makes inerrancy unnecessary.

THE CLARITY OF SCRIPTURE

Theoretically, Protestants believe in the *claritas Scripturae*, the clarity or perspicuity of Scripture. Scripture is to be interpreted by Scripture and does not need the aid of an authorized teaching body or of church tradition to be understood. On the basis of this assumption, noninerrantists would be justified in rejecting inerrancy if they believed their exegesis showed that the Scripture makes no such claim for itself, no matter what else Christian tradition might say or have said. And this is precisely what they must do and in fact do do: ignore the unequivocal testimony of the church through the ages and allege that the self-attestation of the Scripture has been misunderstood. This is not per se impossible; one might argue that Romans 3:28 concerning justification by faith, apart from the works of the law, was generally misinterpreted in the church until Luther. But in order to assert this, Luther was forced to assume an adversary relationship with the Pope and Roman Catholicism and eventually to establish a new church. This is precisely what the errantist evangelicals do not want to do, but the logic of their position will inevitably drive them to it.

We should note that during all the centuries prior to Luther, there was a strong tradition of justification by faith, even if it was not dominant in Christendom. There has been no such background tradition of errancy during most of the centuries of Christian history.

In the effort to understand and to appreciate why the errantist position does appeal to at least some evangelicals even though it really does not satisfy the major objections of the liberals and their successors, we must acknowledge one of the inconveniences if not weaknesses of our contrasting inerrantist position. There simply are no passages of Scripture that plainly and unequivocally teach inerrancy. Not even the passages that we normally cite as proof texts (e.g., Matt. 5:17; John 10:35; 2 Tim. 3:16; and 2 Peter 1:21) actually state in so many words that the Bible is inerrant. In addition, we must presuppose verbal inspiration accompanied by inerrancy in order to prove inerrancy from a proof text—for otherwise it might always be possible that the proof text itself contained an error. In fact, the reason Jesus' words in John 10:35, "The Scripture cannot be broken," can be cited in defense of inerrancy is because they show that He presupposes an inerrant Scripture, with the inerrancy extending to the very words. His argument here depends on the assumption that the word "gods" in "Ye are gods" is precisely what God intended when superintending the composition of the text. If there were a chance that "gods" might be an interpolation or interpretation or error, the argument of Jesus would be untenable. But in order to use this report of Jesus' dialogue to support inerrancy, we must presuppose that it is an infallibly trustworthy account of what He said on that occasion, for the possibility of even a small inaccuracy would make the passage useless as evidence that Jesus believed in inerrancy.

Of course, Scripture does not say in so many words, "Jesus Christ is God." We are persuaded that the doctrine of the deity of Christ underlies all the factual statements that make no sense unless He is divine, but we must acknowledge that a term such as *homoousios* does not occur in Scripture. As with this term, we are persuaded that it is proper to use another nonscriptural term, *inerrancy*, because it truly fits the meaning of scriptural assertions. If we are willing to confess that Jesus Christ is true God and true man in the absence of an absolutely explicit proof text, to speak of the inerrancy of Scripture in a similar situation is certainly not excessive.

The majority of conservative Protestants agree with the great Reformers Luther and Calvin that trusting the Scripture as the Word of God is part of the response of faith. It is produced by the internal testimony of the Holy Spirit, not by an examination of the evidence alone. How are we to demonstrate that the Holy Spirit witnesses to Christians so that they acknowledge that through Scripture itself God teaches all Scripture is *theopneustos*, God-breathed? Whereas it certainly seems plain to us that the quality of *theopneusty* necessarily implies that Scripture is inerrant, it does not seem so plain to others. How can we claim, against them, that the witness of the Holy Spirit authenticates theopneusty and therefore inerrancy? We must inquire of God's people.

The internal testimony of the Holy Spirit is by definition an internal phenomenon; we do not say it is subjective in the sense of arising within the believer's own subjectivity: we believe that God, who is objectively real and not part of the individual's subjectivity, works upon the consciousness of the believer to show him it is God's voice he hears in Scripture. However, the individual's reception of this testimony and his response to it are necessarily subjective and cannot be evaluated on any other basis, except perhaps as a comparison with his objective behavior in response thereto.

Consider, for example, the optical phenomenon called a mirage, which gives a traveler in the desert the illusion that he sees a lake. Objective stimuli that can be identified and described produce the illusion. Subjectively, a traveler may be deceived and genuinely think that he sees a lake, or he may be able to interpret as an illusion the stimuli that appear to reveal a lake and know that it is only caused by low-frequency infra-red radiation from the hot surface of the sand, not by a body of water. The outside observer can know that an objective phenomenon, the radiation, is there to be perceived, but he cannot know whether the traveler understands it as a real lake or only an illusion unless the traveler discloses this to him, either in words or by some revealing action, such as running towards the image with an empty water bottle.

When we read in 2 Timothy 3:16 *pasa graphe theopneustos*, we can see the words, but we cannot know the interpretations of those words to which the Holy Spirit has led and still leads the church unless we listen to the church's testimony and observe her actions. We can say that the overwhelming body of testimony from Christians through the ages, combined with their actions, clearly indicates they have understood theopneusty to mean inerrancy. Against this background, then, it seems appropriate to pronounce our second anathema: "If there be those who assert that the doctrine of the inerrancy of Scripture is not a vital part of Christian faith, then let them be, if not anathema in the traditional sense of the word, at least recognized as eccentrics."

IMPLICATIONS

There seem to be therefore three distinct if hidden presuppositions of the errantist position; these presuppositions will determine the long-range impact that errancy will have on the church. For this reason we may speak of them as implications as well as presuppositions. They are (1) anthropological, (2) Christological, (3) ecclesiological and pneumatological.

ANTHROPOLOGICAL

If we assume that in order to be human, the Scripture must contain errors, we are inverting the proverb *errare humanum est* ("to err is human") and making it say *non errare inhumanum est* ("not to err is inhuman"). This suggests that man cannot have been created good, as is taught in Genesis 1:31, or that he fell of necessity, inasmuch as, being human, he was not capable of not falling. This changes the problem of sin from a moral problem into an ontological one: man does not sin because he wills to, but because he is finite. This position ultimately removes the guilt of sin from man, the creature, and attaches it to God, the Creator, who is viewed as making man in such a way that he had to sin. It also has implications for man's future state, for it implies that in order to be perfect he must become something other than human.

CHRISTOLOGICAL

If our definition of the nature of humanness involves error, then this has implication for the Nicene-Chalcedonian orthodoxy that confesses that the Son of God "was made man" (Nicaea) "in all things like us, without sin" (Chalcedon). Either the phrase "without sin" must fall, in which case Jesus too would need to be saved and could not save others (this would lead to a concept of salvation by imitating Jesus in obedience, not by faith in His finished work), or, on the other hand, the expressions "man" and "in all things like us" must fall and Jesus will be seen in a monophysite sense, as fully divine but not human. This monophysite tendency has always been implicit in popular religion, and it is a recurrent danger for modern evangelicalism, which does not stress theological sophistication or even theological clarity. Monophysitism removes Jesus too far from man to be able to function as our "one mediator" (1 Timothy 2:5) and leads to the interposition of other mediators, for example dead saints or living gurus.

ECCLESIOLOGICAL AND PNEUMATOLOGICAL

To the extent that the errantists ask us to accept their position, they are asking us to break with almost two thousand years of ecclesiastical tradition. To do so suggests that the church has lived happily in a major error for centuries. (In the case of justification by faith, the majority of the church was befuddled prior to the Reformation, but the testimony to this evangelical doctrine never entirely vanished.) This clearly suggests that the Holy Spirit, who had been promised to "lead you into all truth" (John 16:13), has done a consistently poor job. In order to avoid implying that the entire church has been in the dark about Scripture for most of its history, the errantists tell us that the greatest theologians—Augustine, Luther, and Calvin, to name three of great stature—really did accept an errantist position, although that fact has only recently been recognized. Even if this assertion were defensible it would have serious ecclesiological implications, for it would imply that the faith of the common people in inerrancy through the centuries was naïve and inadequate; the greatest leaders, it is true, would have always known the errantist truth but would have manifestly failed or neglected to communicate it to their people. This is rather akin to a gnostic view of knowledge.

CONCLUSION

Admittedly, the lurid tableau of implications far exceeds anything that errantist evangelicals desire or would accept. It may even appear as excessive rhetorical bombast to point to the long-range, ultimate implications of a position that is still being hotly opposed even in its mildest form. Yet there is a case to be made for seeing in full clarity both where the idea of inerrancy must be derived from and where it shows every indication of ultimately leading. So, with an awareness that the picture is somewhat sweepingly drawn, I nevertheless make these observations because I believe they are fundamentally correct and must be made.

Index of Subjects

Index of Persons

Alexander, Archibald, 359, 362
Alves, Rubem, on liberation theology, 319, 337
Aquinas, Thomas, 175, 248-49
Assmann, Hugo
  on tropical hermeneutics, 338
  view of Scripture, 326-27
Augustine, on miracles, 37

Bacon, Francis, 14
Barclay, William, and authority of Scripture, 105
Barr, James, 39, 42, 45, 93, 99, 105, 109-10, 379
Barth, Karl, 175, 186
  on authority of Scripture, 124, 129-31
  and doctrine of Scripture, 135
  and inerrancy, 125-26, 133-34
  on inspiration, 125
  and neo-orthodoxy, 122-36
  on resurrection, 313
  on revelation, 123-24
  and Word of God, 122-24
Bavinck, H., 289, 294, 296-97, 299-301
  and authority of Scripture, 302
  view of Scripture, 304, 315-16
Berkhof, Hendrikus, 303
Berkouwer, G. C., 171
  apologetics (early), 293-94
  on authorship of Scripture, 306

  on centralization of Scripture, 301
  and cultural relativism, 40
  on faith (later), 307, 308-10
  and formal approach to Scripture, 305-6
  functional theology of, 285-316
  on inerrancy (early), 289-90, 314
  and inspiration (early), 291-93
  and language, 310-12
  on resurrection, 312-14
  theological reversal of, 294-304
  view of Scripture (early), 287-89, 303, 310-12, 315-16
  view of Scripture (later), 294-96, 307, 309, 310-11
Blake, William, 56-57
Boehme, Jakob, 55
Bonhoeffer, Dietrich, 177
Bonino, Jose Miguez, on liberation theology, 319, 323-24
Bornkamm, Gunther, 180, 379
Brunner, Emil, 180, 186-87
  and inerrancy, 42-43, 137
  and neo-orthodoxy, 136-44
  on revelation, 136, 141
Buber, Martin, 178, 180, 184, 186, 195
Bultmann, Rudolf, 41, 136, 175-76
  on incarnation, 180, 190
  on inerrancy, 189-90

Index of Scripture

413

The inerrancy debate is more than an academic squabble. In fact, its implications are potentially devastating to the church. Thinking Christians must clearly understand and evaluate the theological contexts of the assumptions on which some scholars base their denial of the inerrancy of Scripture.

Challenges to Inerrancy: A Theological Response is an attempt to answer some of the most influential modern presuppositions that lead to the denial of an inerrant Bible. Twelve leading scholars uncover the roots of the controversy in theological schools of thought from the eighteenth century to the present.

The case for biblical inerrancy as developed in the classic Princeton tradition is considered. An epilogue suggests ways that this study can warn and challenge thinkers in the Christian church today.

Gordon Lewis (A.B., Gordon College; M.Div., Faith Theological Seminary; M.A., Ph.D., Syracuse University) is professor of systematic theology and philosophy at Denver Conservative Baptist Seminary.

Bruce Demarest (B.S., Wheaton College; M.S., Adelphi University; M.A., Trinity Evangelical Divinity School; Ph.D., University of Manchester, England) is professor of systematic theology at Denver Conservative Baptist Seminary.

THEOLOGY   ISBN 0-8024-0237-2